THE
GERMAN
COOKBOOK

THE

GERMAN

COOKBOOK

ALFONS SCHUHBECK

Introduction

Introduction

Food has always played a central role in my life. My family had a big garden. My mother would get everything she needed from there including fruits, vegetables and herbs. The most important lesson I learned from her was that a good cook makes the most of what is in season – as that is when the ingredients taste best. The most anticipated meals of my childhood were when my mother prepared the first fresh mushrooms for her dumplings.

I began my cooking career in 1980 at the age of seventeen. On my first day working as a chef, in Waging am See in Upper Bavaria, I served blood and liver sausage with apple sauerkraut; it set the tone for my style of cooking, turning classic home-cooked dishes into something more elevated. Three years later, I received my first Michelin star. Then came more accolades, including Gault & Millau's Chef of the Year in 1989. I even cooked modern German cuisine at The White House in Washington, DC.

I decided to write *The German Cookbook* because I had seen nothing comparable, or as comprehensive, on German food in nearly forty years of professional experience. There was something missing, a gap that I feel is now filled by this book.

To make this book possible, I went through the huge collection of recipes I had built up over the previous decade. In the process, I also benefited from my countless travels throughout Germany and lively conversations with fellow Germans and culinary colleagues. I was always interested in the different methods and ingredients found in other regions of Germany.

Deciding on which recipes to include in the book was difficult, because German cooking has so many wonderful, yet very different, recipes. Naturally, I included recipes that are iconic and famous around the world, but also regional ones that are relatively unknown, such as *Lübecker Schwalbennester* (Lübeck-style 'swallows' nests'; p. 193) and *Verschleiertes Bauernmädchen* ('veiled peasant girls'; p. 336), which are deeply rooted in German culinary history. It was important to show a very interesting and comprehensive cross section. I have adapted some recipes – such as *Franzbrötchen* (cinnamon rolls; p. 380) and *Grünkohl und Pinkel* (kale with sausages; p. 318), which were found mostly in modern, often Bavarian, versions – to take them back to their culinary roots.

History and Culture

Germany is a young country: It did not become a nation until 1871. Prior to that there were several German countries, and although they shared much in language and culture, they were distinct in many ways, one of which was food. Germany is the largest country in the European Union in both population and area, and yet, to outsiders, it is not widely known for its food. The past fifty years have seen huge changes in food styles and habits, inspiration in and curiosity about foods from other countries, and a rebirth of interest in local food traditions and ingredients. In a country of such size and diversity – there are sixteen *Bundesländer* or states – there is a great deal of variety.

Under Prussian rule, kings renounced the splendour of court and culinary refinement to give their citizens a model of thrift and modesty. In 1713, when King Frederick William I came to the throne, he fired nearly all fifty of his kitchen staff, leaving just a few cooks to manage on their own. Then Frederick II 'the Great' made his priority military strength, not refined food. When Germany developed into a nation, through the power of Prussia, Prussian Protestant sentiment dominated. The principle that food should solely nourish people and not necessarily give them enjoyment, persisted in the minds of many people until the end of World War II.

Historically, the development of German cooking has taken a different path from that of France and other European countries. In the 1950s, more variety came to German dining. Later, the opening of countless Italian restaurants in the 1960s made the cuisine of Italy, Germany's favourite vacation destination, available year-round. And in the mid-1970s, there was a new wave of creative German chefs, encouraged by French role models and celebrated by the media. The exchange of food products and goods became cheaper and easier, and knowledge of neighbouring countries' cultures grew on both sides of the border. Gourmets wrote about French, Italian and Austrian table manners, also urging German chefs and their patrons to turn towards haute cuisine. Since then, German home cooking has generally become lighter, subtler and more refined. German restaurants now hold the second place in world rankings for Michelin stars, and there are many Michelin three-star restaurants here.

The list of German foods that have a long history in America and elsewhere is lengthy. Although many are equally traceable to other European countries, the German names they are known by reveal the route they took to the United States: Pretzels, Sauerkraut, Bratwurst, Liverwurst and Black Forest Cake, to name the most popular. American beer was also influenced by the huge and growing presence of German immigration in the nineteenth century.

The hamburger and hot dog also have German roots. Although the precise origins of the modern-day hamburger are not known, it clearly has its roots in something called the 'Hamburg steak', made popular by nineteenth-century German immigrants to New York City. It is from these minced beef patties (raw, partially or wholly cooked) that American hamburgers developed.

Frankfurters, as the name suggests, originated in Frankfurt, and *Wiener* is a name derived from Vienna – *Wieners* are a mixed beef and pork version of Frankfurt's pork-only original.

There is a huge variety of *Wurst* (sausages) in Germany, with over fifteen hundred types. German sausage has high meat content and little forcemeat, with grains added to bulk sausages and aid in cooking. There have been strict rules in place in German sausage making since the Middle Ages, meaning that the fillings of German sausages are of a very high quality. Pork is the most popular meat in Germany and is by far the most commonly used in sausages, with *Bratwurst* (spiced pork sausage), as a perfect example. *Wiener* (Viennese sausages) can be either pork, beef or a mixture, and are smoked. *Blutwurst* (blood sausage) is also very popular – the blood usually from a pig or goose. *Currywurst* (steamed then fried sausage with curry-ketchup; p. 36) has influences from other food cultures, and this very popular street food is said to have been invented in 1949 in Berlin, when Herta Heuwer started selling grilled bratwurst with ketchup mixed with curry powder. She got the powder from British soldiers. It is estimated that 800 million currywurst are eaten in Germany every year.

German Breads

Throughout Germany there is an amazing selection of bread, the quality and variety of which is unparalleled. Germans are proud of their bread and rightly so. Lye bread – bread dipped in a lye solution before it is baked – and its unconventional shape of crossing strings of dough, have an interesting symbolism: Early Christians prayed by folding their arms over their chests as a sign of inner composure. The Bavarian word for pretzel, *Breze* or *Brez'n*, derives from the Latin *brachium,* which means 'arm'. It is said the best pretzels today are found in Baden-Württemberg and Bavaria (p. 50). By contrast, lye bread is not very popular in northern Germany. But probably the best-known, and most popular, export of the German bakery trade is *Sauerteig* (sourdough), which is made with a 'starter' of baker's yeast and bacteria.

The majority of breads in Germany are sourdough – using naturally occurring rather than industrially produced yeasts to rise. There are over two hundred types of bread produced in the country – the greatest number in the world – the most popular of which is *Roggenmischbrot* (mixed rye and wheat bread). German breads tend to be whole grain and almost every type of grain is used – wheat, barley, corn, millet, spelt and oats – as well as potato. The most famous German variety of pumpernickel, a dense rye bread, is from the Westphalia region – it is mentioned in a 1450 Westphalian document – where it is made in long-lidded pans and baked at low temperatures, in heavily steamed ovens over long periods.

The typical German *Graubrot* is a mixed rye bread. Johann Wolfgang von Goethe made a distinction between the French and the Germans where bread was concerned: Germans ate black bread, whereas French preferred white. By and large, this holds true today. There are still many German baked goods that are not commonly found in other countries. Flavour and ingredient combinations include poppy, caraway and potato *Brötchen* (rolls) – called *Semmel* in the south and *Schrippen* in Berlin, *Salzstangerl* (salt rolls) – also known as *Seelen* in Swabian.

German Meals

Like that of many other northern and central European countries, German food, while often delicious in its traditional form was heavy and geared towards fuelling laborious physical work. As the need for such fuel has dwindled, and health consciousness has grown in recent years, the emphasis has fallen on lighter versions.

Frühstück (breakfast) in Germany traditionally consists of coffee, tea or hot chocolate; fruit juice; and bread or bread rolls with hams, sausages, cheese, honey and jam. Lighter, healthier breakfasts have gained a lot of ground in recent decades and muesli served with yogurt or milk is much more common now. Commercial breakfast cereals are also popular among younger generations.

Snacking is a part of German eating habits – it is typical to eat a second breakfast halfway through the morning, and is known by several names: *grosse Pause, zweites Frühstück,* or *Pausenbrot*. It was usually a sandwich in the past, but today it is just as likely to be fruit, yogurt or a muesli bar. The *Zwischenmahlzeit* (in-between meal), is another example – again its most usual form is a sandwich, but it is meant to keep one going between meals.

Traditionally, the main meal of the day in Germany was *Mittagessen* (lunch) – although in most places, lunch now takes second place to *Abendessen* (dinner). Lunch was, and often still is, a carb-heavy meal of potato salad with meatballs (p. 210), sausage or dumplings (pp. 268–269), or schnitzel (pp. 186–187, 214, 218) with buttered vegetables.

Kaffee und Kuchen (coffee and cake) is a widespread and popular tradition in Germany, which takes place in the mid to late afternoon. Home baking thrives and popular cakes to eat with coffee include the famous *Schwarzwälder Kirschtorte* (Black Forest cake; p. 398), *Zwetschenkuchen* or *Apfelkuchen* and *Käsekuchen* (cheesecake made with quark; p. 396). German coffee is rich and dark-roasted and usually served with cream or condensed milk.

Abendessen was once a light supper because lunch was the main meal, but these days it tends to be the main meal in many German households. The traditional offerings were usually breads, cold meat, sausage, cheese, pickles and salads or a selection of vegetables, along with beer or wine.

German Regions and Their Specialities

The most important thing I have learned about the cuisine of my country is to always look beyond the borders of my own area. There is so much variety to discover in German cuisine – dishes vary dramatically from region to region. What is considered daily fare on the coastline is almost completely unheard of by the time you get to the foothills of the Alps.

Take eel for instance, Berliners eat theirs 'green', with herb sauce and cucumber salad (p. 141); natives of Hamburg enjoy eel soup with dried fruits (p. 100); while on the Mosel River, eel is cooked in a Riesling sauce and served with boiled potatoes. To make a salad dressing, northern Germans mix cream with salt, lemon juice and sugar, while Swabians mix vinegar with oil and mustard (pp. 52–71). Rhinelanders marinate their chicken in beer; those of the Palatinate region use dry white wine; and those of Baden prefer lemon juice and pepper (pp. 160–168).

The differences between the German regions are largely the result of culinary influences from neighbouring countries. Many influences came from France, by way of Alsace – a region that often changed hands between Germany and France – crossing over the Rhine into Baden-Württemberg and Rhineland-Palatinate. As a result, the area between Heidelberg, Freiburg and Lake Constance is often considered to have the best cuisine in Germany. Bavarian cuisine, which was less significant until the end of World War II, has been enriched by the influence of Austria and Bohemia (now Czech Republic). By contrast, the northern German states acquired the Scandinavian custom of seasoning pickles and spicy dishes with sugar, in addition to adopting the extravagantly hearty English breakfast.

From 1949 to 1990, Germany was divided. The territories of Mecklenburg-Vorpommern, Brandenburg, Sachsen-Anhalt, Sachsen and Thüringen, as well as East Berlin, were part of East Germany, also known as the German Democratic Republic (GDR) – or Deutsche Demokratische Republik (DDR). During that time, East Germany was more exposed to and influenced by the cultures of Russia, Poland and Bulgaria. People from those countries were often in East Germany and East Germans vacationed in the USSR.

The dish that is most established on German menus through this influence is *Soljanka* (p. 105), a thick, spicy and sour Russian soup. There are three main types – meat, fish and mushroom – but all have pickled cucumber, and often cabbage, mushrooms, potatoes, *Smetana* (sour cream) and dill. Many brands and foods of the former GDR have since disappeared, but a phenomenon of the food culture in the former East Germany that has been much discussed in German media is 'Ostalgie', a portmanteau of the German words for 'nostalgia' and 'east'. For many people who lived in the GDR, there remains a longing for everyday eastern products.

There are dishes that are enthusiastically embraced throughout Germany, such as Rhenish-style *Sauerbraten*, a marinated pot roast that originally used horsemeat (p. 204), but now uses beef. Others include Baden-Baden–style roe venison, stuffed with pears and lingonberries (p. 248); Black Forest cake, made with kirsch (p. 398); and Bavarian snacks complete with typical white sausages (p. 34), sweet mustard, warm meatloaf (p. 29) and freshly baked soft pretzels (p. 50). Berlin-style liver with fried apple slices and onion rings (p. 194) can be found in homes and on menus in Munich, while ready-to-use bunches of assorted herbs for Frankfurt-style *grüne Soße* (thick herb vinaigrette; p. 116) can be found at vegetable stalls in Stuttgart. *Leipziger Allerlei* – five kinds of young vegetables of different colors coated in crayfish butter and garnished with crayfish – is considered a delicacy all over Germany (p. 321). *Königsberger Klopse* (anchovy-flavoured meatballs in a light caper sauce; p. 216) are popular among Germans, even though their place of origin, Königsberg is now Kaliningrad, Russia.

Baden-Württemberg is in the far southwest of Germany, east of the upper Rhine, which forms the border with France. The capital and largest city is Stuttgart. Baden-Württemberg has the greatest number of Michelin stars of any German region, perhaps unsurprisingly given its proximity to Alsace. The cooking of this area of Germany shares much with that of eastern France.

Baden-Württemberg is known for both asparagus and wine. The asparagus season runs from mid-April to the feast of St. John the Baptist on June 24, and even has its own name: *Spargelzeit*. Snails are eaten in the region in *Schneckensuppe* (snail soup; p. 101) and tripe is also popular. Made from flour, water, salt and eggs, *Spätzle* noodles (p. 288) are a characteristic dish. They are usually served as a side dish, but can also stuffed with cheese, meat or spinach as *Maultaschen*. Black Forest ham is a favourite regional speciality.

Bavaria is Germany's most southeastern state and borders Austria to the south and the Czech Republic to the east. Munich is the state capital and Germany's third largest city after Berlin and Hamburg. Northern and southern Bavaria are culturally distinct in themselves, with dialects and accents easily distinguishable to Germans. Beer is strongly associated with the region – half of Germany's breweries are found here and many of the beers are world-famous: Schneider, Löwenbräu, Hacker, Tucher and Paulaner to name but a few. Hamburg is home to Oktoberfest, a folk and beer festival that has been running since 1810 – it now attracts six million visitors annually and runs for two weeks until the first weekend in October. Bavarian food shares much with Austria, and *Schnitzel* is an obvious example. It is made with veal or pork and served in a variety of ways, including the familiar breaded variety with lemon (p. 214), or the *Jäger Art* with mushrooms and peppers (p. 218). *Weißwurst* (white sausage; p. 34) is a Bavarian specialty and traditionally served with *Weißbiere* (white wheat beer).

Berlin, the capital of Germany, is the most ethnically diverse city in the country, with a population of 3.4 million. A state in itself, Berlin is surrounded on all sides by the state of Brandenburg, in the northeast of Germany. Under communism, although all of Brandenburg was in East Germany, Berlin was divided into East and West. West Berlin remained the capital of West Germany, and East Berlin the capital of the GDR. The home-grown cuisine of Berlin is most famously represented by *Currywurst* (p. 36) served at street stalls with French fries or bread rolls. *Eisbein mit Sauerkraut* (pork knuckle on sauerkraut; p. 231) is a typical Berlin specialty – the pork is cooked until the crackling is very crispy. The significant Turkish influence has popularised döner kebabs.

Brandenburg, in the northeast of Germany, borders Poland to the east, and the capital of Brandenburg is Potsdam, which borders Berlin to its east. Brandenburg is famous for its vegetables, particularly turnips, mushrooms, sauerkraut and pickles. Freshwater fish, eel and carp also feature heavily in the cuisine.

Hamburg is a city with its own statehood and is properly called 'The Free and Hanseatic City of Hamburg'. It is situated in a harbour on the Jutland Peninsula between Continental Europe to the south and Scandinavia to the north. It is on the River Elbe where it meets the Alster and Bille rivers, and as such the city has always been rich in fish. Herring is popular here, in dishes such as *Matjes* (soused herring; p. 133) and *Brathering* (fried herring marinated in vinegar; p. 130). Carp is served for Christmas dinner in Hamburg, and a popular street snack is *Fischbrötchen* (raw or fried fish served in a bread roll; p. 26). Another notable dish is *Schwarzsauer* (blood soup made with black pudding).

Hesse is in west central Germany, its capital is Wiesbaden and the largest city is Frankfurt, Germany's financial centre. Its location means that an amalgam of dishes typical to both the north and south can be found there. Sour flavors predominate – in dry wines, ciders, and the local *Handkäse* (strong, sour milk cheese). *Grüne Soße* (a sauce of green herbs, eggs, oil and vinegar; p. 141) is usually served here with potatoes, eggs or meat.

Rhineland–Palatinate in southwest Germany borders Belgium, Luxembourg and Alsace, France. The state capital and largest city is Mainz. The area has a tendency towards hotter, spicier foods. Marjoram is also used extensively. *Saumagen* (pig stomach) is a traditional dish in which sausage meat, pork, potatoes, herbs and spices are boiled together in a pig's stomach. The cooked stomach is cooled and cut into slices, then served with bread, mashed potatoes and often a brown sauce (p. 236).

Saxony in the east of Germany borders Poland and the Czech Republic. Its cuisine shares much with that of Eastern Europe. Trout and carp are popular here. *Knödel* (dumplings; p. 268–272) are a typical side dish in the region. There are a huge variety of sauces produced here. This is an area particularly steeped in the *Kaffee und Kuchen* culture (which originated here under King Hedrick the Fat), still part of grand coffeehouses in Leipzig, its largest city, and Dresden, its capital.

Thuringia is a small, landlocked state in east central Germany; its capital is Erfurt. Thuringia is known for its *Thüringer Klöße* (potato dumplings; p. 268). Many vegetables are grown there and it is heavily forested, so mushrooms are used extensively in the diet – as is game: red and roe deer, wild boar, rabbit, duck and sheep. Sausages typical of the area are *Mettwurst* (spreadable, cured sausage), *Feldkieker* (cured, air-dried sausage dried up to eight months), *Leberwurst* (steamed pork and liver sausage) and *Rotwurst* (steamed blood sausage).

The German Cookbook is a diverse collection of recipes from all of the German regions, with a variety that managed to surprise even me. The book offers a journey of discovery, especially for non-German admirers of both restaurant dining and home cooking. This ambitious over-view of German cooking and baking provides an opportunity for the curious to discover new favourites, for traditionalists who want tried and tested dishes, and for anyone who wants to create simple and delicious German dishes at home. Explore, choose, cook and above all, eat to your heart's content, as you explore the cuisine of my homeland.

Dairy free

Gluten free

Contains nuts

One pot

Vegetarian

Less than 30 minutes

Less than 5 ingredients

Beef

Chicken

Pork

Lamb

Game

Fish or seafood

N.B. Dairy and Gluten free recipes exclude serving suggestions

Herb, Egg and Cucumber Dip

All regions

	Preparation time:	10 minutes
	Cooking time:	10 minutes
	Serves:	4

1	egg	1
¼ cup/2 oz	low-fat Quark	500 g
2 tbsp	mild olive oil	2 tbsp
3 tbsp	vegetable stock	3 tbsp
1 tsp	Dijon mustard	1 tsp
2–3 tbsp	finely chopped basil, chervil, parsley and dill	2–3 tbsp
*	salt	*
1	pinch chopped garlic	1
¼	cucumber	¼
5	radishes, trimmed	5
*	farmhouse bread, to serve	*
*	boiled potatoes, to serve	*

Hard-boil the egg (about 10 minutes) then refresh in iced water, peel and finely chop. Mix the Quark with the oil and stock until smooth. Add the mustard and herbs and mix, then season with the salt and garlic.

Trim and peel the cucumber, and halve lengthwise. Remove the seeds with a teaspoon. Coarsely grate the cucumber halves. Trim, wash and finely dice the radishes.

Mix the egg, cucumber and radish into the Quark mixture. Adjust the seasoning if needed. Serve the dip with farmhouse bread, or with boiled potatoes.

Radishes with Open-Faced Chive Sandwiches

Bavaria

	Preparation time:	20 minutes
	Serves:	4

1–2	long white or red radishes	1–2
*	salt	*
1	bunch chives	1
4	slices farmhouse bread	4
2–3 tbsp	butter	2–3 tbsp

Trim and wash the radishes. For the accordion-cut radish, push a white radish onto the prongs of the radish slicer (or apple peeler) shaft. Position the shaft in the machine, attach the blade to the end of the shaft, and turn the handle.

For the Munich-style cut radish, cut off the root tips and slice the radishes very thinly with a vegetable slicer or mandoline. Arrange the radishes in a fan on a plate, season with salt and let stand for 10 minutes before serving.

For the open-faced chive sandwiches, wash, shake dry and finely chop the chives. Spread the bread thickly with butter. Scatter the bread with chives and sprinkle with salt.

Serve the chive sandwiches with the radish slices.

Pork and Apple Spread

Bavaria

Preparation time:		15 minutes
Cooking time:		15 minutes
Makes:		about 200 g/7 oz

1 lb 2 oz	rindless pork belly	500 g
2	onions	2
1	apple (e.g. Cox's Orange Pippin)	1
1 tsp	dried marjoram	1 tsp
1	pinch of ground cumin	1
*	salt	*
*	freshly ground pepper	*

Cut the pork into ½ cm (¼ inch) dice. Cook gently in a frying pan over medium heat for 10–15 minutes until the fat melts and turns light golden. Remove the rendered fat a little at a time, filter through a sieve. Let the strained fat cool and set aside the resulting lard in a cool place.

Fry the meat pieces in the rest of the fat until crispy. Take them out of the pan and let cool to room temperature.

Peel and dice the onions. Peel, core, and dice the apple. Fry the onions in 2 tbsp of leftover fat, over a medium heat, until golden. Add the diced apple and cook briefly.

Add the marjoram and a pinch of cumin, let cool, then mix into the cold lard. Add the fried meat and season with salt and pepper. Fill sterilised jars with the lard, leaving 1 cm (½ inch) space at the top, let cool, cover and seal, then store in a cool place. This spread will keep for about 6 months if stored in a cool place, such as a pantry.

Mashed Potato and Sour Cream Dip (Kartoffelkäs)

Bavaria

Preparation time:		15 minutes
Cooking time:		25 minutes
Serves:		4

14 oz	standard white potatoes	400 g
3¾ tsp	cumin seeds	3¾ tsp
1	onion	1
2 tbsp	butter	2 tbsp
1 tbsp	coriander seeds	1 tbsp
1 tbsp	peppercorns	1 tbsp
¾ cup/7 oz	sour cream	200 g
4 tbsp	Beurre Noisette (p.112)	4 tbsp
*	salt	*
1	pinch dried marjoram	1
1	pinch freshly grated nutmeg	1
2 tbsp	finely chopped chives	2 tbsp
*	brown bread, to serve	*

Wash the potatoes and put in a pan with salted water and 1½ tsp cumin seeds. Boil for 20–25 minutes until soft, and then drain. Peel the potatoes while they're still as hot as possible, then press through a ricer into a bowl.

Peel and finely chop the onion. Melt the butter in a frying pan and lightly brown the onion over a low heat. Put the coriander seeds, peppercorns, and remaining cumin seeds into a spice grinder and grind to a fine powder.

Add the onion, sour cream, and Beurre Noisette (p.112) to the mashed potato in the bowl and mix well. Season the spread with salt, marjoram, nutmeg and the ground spices. Finally, stir the chives into the spread. The spread tastes best on brown bread.

Cheese Dip (Kochkäse)

Hesse and Bavaria

Preparation time:		2 minutes
Cooking time:		6 minutes
Serves:		4

2¼ sticks/9 oz	butter	250 g
1 cup/9 oz	cottage cheese	250 g
1 scant cup/7 oz	cream cheese	200 g
¾ cup/7 fl oz	single (light) cream	200 g
1 cup/9 oz	low-fat Quark	250 g
1–2 tsp	cumin seeds	1–2 tsp
1 tsp	baking soda	1 tsp
*	salt	*
*	bread, to serve (optional)	*

Combine the butter, cheese and cream in a bowl and melt over a bain-marie for about 6 minutes, then whisk until smooth.

Mix in the Quark, cumin seeds and baking soda, and season with salt. Serve with bread.

Cheese with Onion Marinade (Handkäs mit Musik)

Hesse, Frankfurt and Palatinate

Preparation time:		10 minutes
Marinating time:		1 hour
Serves:		4

2	onions	2
2 tbsp	white wine vinegar	2 tbsp
2 tbsp	cider	2 tbsp
*	salt	*
*	freshly ground pepper	*
1 tsp	cumin seeds	1 tsp
2 tbsp	oil	2 tbsp
14 oz	Harzer (sour milk) cheese	400 g
4	thick slices brown bread	4
*	butter, to serve	*

Peel and finely chop the onions.

Mix 150 ml (⅔ cup/5 fl oz) water with the vinegar and cider. Season with salt, pepper and cumin seeds. Stir in the oil. Mix the onions with the marinade. Marinate for 1 hour.

Slice the cheese and drizzle with the marinade. Serve the cheese with thick slices of bread and butter.

Cream Cheese Dip (Spundekäs)

Rhine Hesse

Preparation time:		5 minutes
Chilling time:		2 hours
Serves:		4

1 scant cup/7 oz	cream cheese	200 g
1⅓ cups/11 oz	high-fat Quark	300 g
1	onion	1
1	large clove garlic	1
1 tbsp	paprika	1 tbsp
*	salt	*
*	freshly ground pepper	*
*	small salted pretzels, optional	*

Mix the cream cheese with the Quark. Peel the onion and garlic and chop as finely as possible.

Mix the onion, garlic, and paprika into the cheese mixture and season with salt and pepper. Refrigerate the dip for 2 hours before serving. It can be accompanied with small salted pretzels.

Bavarian Cheese Dip (Obatzda)

Bavaria

Preparation time:		10 minutes
Serves:		4

½	bunch chives	½
7 oz	ripe Camembert cheese	200 g
1 cup/9 oz	cream cheese	250 g
3–4 tbsp	milk	3–4 tbsp
⅔ tbsp	Beurre Noisette (p. 112)	⅔ tbsp
1	shot pear brandy or wheat beer	1
*	salt	*
*	freshly ground pepper	*
1	pinch hot paprika	1
1	pinch ground cumin	1
1	pinch freshly grated nutmeg	1
*	red onion rings, optional	*
*	farmhouse bread, to serve	*
*	Bavarian Soft Pretzels (p. 50)	*
*	radishes, to serve	*

Wash, shake dry, and finely chop the chives. Cut the cheese into small dice. Mix the cream cheese with the milk, then mix in the chives and cheese.

Melt the Beurre Noisette (p. 112) and add to the cheese mixture with the brandy or beer and mix well. Season with salt, pepper, and one pinch each of paprika, cumin, and nutmeg. The spread should be very creamy and turn a light pink colour. Add more paprika if needed.

Serve the dip on a plate, preferably at room temperature. Optionally, it can be covered with red onion rings. Serve with fresh farmhouse bread, Bavarian Soft Pretzels and radishes.

Deep-Fried Camembert

All regions

Preparation time:		10 minutes
Cooking time:		5 minutes
Serves:		4

2	eggs	2
*	salt	*
*	freshly ground pepper	*
4	Camembert cheese wheels	4
1½ cups/4½ oz	dry breadcrumbs	125 g
4 cups/34 fl oz	oil, for deep-frying	1 litre
*	a few lettuce leaves, to serve	*
*	jarred lingonberries, to serve	*
*	bread or toast, to serve	*

Whisk the eggs well in a bowl and season with salt
and pepper.

Coat the Camembert wheels in the beaten egg and
dredge in the breadcrumbs. Repeat.

Heat the oil in a pan to 180°C/350°F. The oil is hot
enough when bubbles form around a bamboo skewer
dipped into it. Deep-fry the cheese wheels for 3–4 minutes.
Use a skimmer or slotted spoon to remove from the oil
and drain well on paper towels.

Arrange the cheese wheels on plates with lettuce
leaves and lingonberries. Accompany with bread or toast
spread with butter.

Cheese and Mustard Sandwich (Halve Hahn)

Rhineland

Preparation time:		5 minutes
Serves:		4

1	onion	1
4	gherkins (dill pickles), optional	4
4	rye buns	4
4 tbsp	butter	4 tbsp
4	slices Gouda cheese	4
4 tbsp	medium-strength mustard	4 tbsp
¼–½ tsp	sweet paprika	¼–½ tsp

Peel the onion and cut into thin rings. Slice the gherkins
(optional).

Halve the buns across the middle. Spread the 4 bottom
halves of the buns with butter and cover each with a slice
of cheese. Spread with mustard. Cover with onion rings
and gherkins, and sprinkle with paprika. Cover with the top
halves, or leave as open-faced sandwiches.

Herring Spread (Heringshäckerle)

Silesia and Saxony

Preparation time:		5 minutes
Cooking time:		10 minutes
Serves:		4

8	pickled herring (matjes) fillets	8
3 tbsp	capers	3 tbsp
1–2	sour apples	1–2
1	skin-on potato, boiled	1
1	bunch chives	1
2 tbsp	olive oil	2 tbsp
1 tbsp	crème fraîche	1 tbsp
1–2 tbsp	chopped chervil	1–2 tbsp
1 tsp	mustard	1 tsp
*	salt	*
*	freshly ground pepper	*
*	a few lettuce leaves, to serve	*

Finely chop the herring fillets. Put into a bowl and put the bowl inside a larger bowl filled with ice. Finely chop the capers.

Peel, halve, and core the apples and peel the potato. Cut the apples and potato into small dice. Fry the diced potato in 1 tbsp olive oil until golden and crispy, then let cool.

Wash, shake dry, and finely chop the chives. Mix together the apple and potato dice, crème fraîche, chervil, mustard, remaining oil, capers and herring. Season with salt and pepper.

Divide the mixture between four plates, and garnish with a few lettuce leaves.

Pickled Herring and Onion Rolls (Fischbrötchen)

Northern Germany

Preparation time:		5 minutes
Serves:		4

1	onion	1
1–2	gherkins (dill pickles)	1–2
4	buns	4
4	pickled herring double fillets	4

Peel the onion and cut into thin rings. Slice the gherkins.

Halve the buns across the middle. Cover the herring fillets with sliced gherkins, fold in half, and put on the bottom halves of the buns. Cover with onion rings and the top halves of the buns.

Seasoned Raw Ground Pork Sandwich (Mettbrötchen)

Northern Germany

Preparation time:		10 minutes
Serves:		4

14 oz	pork neck	400 g
3½ oz	pork belly	100 g
1	onion	1
*	salt	*
*	freshly ground pepper	*
½ tsp	paprika	½ tsp
1	pinch ground allspice	1
4	buns	4
1	large Pickled Cucumber (p. 29)	1
*	onion rings (optional)	*

Coarsely mince the pork in a mincer (or have your butcher do it).

Peel and finely chop the onion, and add to the minced pork. Season with a level teaspoon of salt, pepper, the paprika, and allspice, and mix thoroughly.

Halve the buns across the middle and spread the bottom halves with the pork mixture. Slice the Pickled Cucumber (p. 29) and add, together with a couple of onion rings, if you like. Cover with the top halves of the buns.

Fish Burger

All regions

Preparation time:		15 minutes
Cooking time:		10 minutes
Serves:		4

1 lb 2 oz	skinless salmon fillet	500 g
2 oz	white bread	50 g
½	bunch spring onions (scallions)	½
1 tbsp	hot mustard	1 tbsp
1	egg	1
50 g	dry breadcrumbs	2 oz
*	freshly grated nutmeg	*
*	salt	*
*	freshly ground pepper	*
4 tbsp	oil	4 tbsp
4	sesame buns	4
1 tbsp	butter	1 tbsp
1–2	sprigs thyme	1–2
*	Remoulade to serve (p. 114)	*

Wash the fish and pat dry. Cut the fillet and the white bread into small dice. Trim, wash and finely slice the spring onions. Mix the diced fish and bread with the mustard, egg, half of the breadcrumbs, the nutmeg, salt, and pepper.

Wet your hands and shape the mixture into 4 patties. Coat in the remaining breadcrumbs. Heat the oil in a frying pan and slowly fry the fish patties on both sides over a medium heat.

Halve the buns across the middle. Melt the butter in a frying pan or skillet with the thyme and lightly toast the buns on their cut sides. Cover each of the bottom halves of the buns with tomato,1 tablespoon Remoulade (p.114), the fish patties and and pickled cucumber slices. Cover with the top halves of the buns. Accompany with more Remoulade.

Homemade Liverwurst

All regions

Preparation time:		30 minutes
Cooking time:		4 hours
Makes:		about 200 ml (¾ cup/7 fl oz)

11 oz	calve or poultry liver(s)	300 g
⅓ tbsp	pickling salt	⅓ tbsp
2	onions	2
1	bay leaf	1
3	cloves	3
1 lb 11 oz	50–70% fat pork belly	750 g
¼	apple	¼
½ tsp	garlic powder	½ tsp
2 tsp	sugar	2 tsp
2 tbsp	dried marjoram	2 tbsp
½ tsp	freshly ground pepper	½ tsp
½ tsp	ground fennel seeds	½ tsp
½ tsp	ground allspice	½ tsp
1 tsp	ground coriander seeds	1 tsp
*	freshly grated nutmeg	*
*	salt	*

Wash the liver(s) and cut into cubes. Blend together with the pickling salt to a paste until bubbles appear in the mixture. Set aside in a cool place.

Peel the first onion. Attach the bay leaf to the onion by studding with the cloves. Bring salted water to a boil in a pan and add the onion and pork belly. They should be well covered by the water. Simmer gently for 2 hours 30 minutes until the meat is tender, skimming regularly.

Peel and dice the second onion. Peel, core, and dice the apple. Combine the diced onion and apple in a frying pan or skillet with 100 ml (⅓ cup/3½ fl oz) hot pork cooking liquid, and heat until it comes to a boil. Let cool, then purée with a stick (immersion) blender.

Preheat the oven to 80°C/175°F/Gas Mark 4. Fill a deep baking tray with 2 cm (1 inch) hot water, put 2 sheets of paper towel in the tray, and put on the lowest shelf of the oven.

Take the pork belly out of the pan, chop into small pieces, and pass through a mincer twice, using the fine plate. Mix the hot minced meat with the apple and onion purée and cold liver paste. Add 100 ml (⅓ cup/3½ fl oz) of the hot pork cooking liquid. Season with garlic powder, sugar, marjoram, pepper, fennel, allspice and coriander seeds, nutmeg, and about 10 g (¼ oz) salt.

Fill sterilised jars with the mixture leaving a space of 1.5 cm (¾ inch) under the rim. Close the jars tightly with their lids, put the jars inside the water bath in the oven, spaced apart, and cook the liverwurst for up to 1 ½ hours.

Take the jars out of the oven and let cool. The liverwurst will keep at a cool room temperature for several months.

Steak Tartare

All regions

Preparation time:		15 minutes
Serves:		4

1 lb 2 oz	beef fillet (tenderloin)	500 g
1	Pickled Cucumber (p. 29)	1
1–2 tsp	pickled capers	1–2 tsp
3	anchovy fillets	3
½	onion	½
1 tbsp	oil	1 tbsp
2 tbsp	olive oil	2 tbsp
1 tbsp	sweet chilli sauce	1 tbsp
1 tbsp	ketchup	1 tbsp
1	pinch sweet paprika	1
2 tbsp	finely chopped chives	2 tbsp
1	very fresh egg, optional	1
1	dash lemon juice	1
*	salt	*
*	freshly ground pepper	*
*	sugar	*
*	bread, toast or rösti, to serve	*

Trim the meat of any fat or tendons, and pass through a mincer. Finely chop the Pickled Cucumber (p. 29), capers, and anchovies. Peel and finely chop the onion. Heat the oil in a frying pan or skillet. Sauté the onion over moderate heat until translucent, then let cool.

Mix the minced meat with the finely chopped onion, Pickled Cucumber, capers, and anchovies, the olive oil, sweet chilli sauce, ketchup, paprika, and chives. You can add a very fresh egg at this point if you wish. Season well with lemon juice, salt, pepper, and add a pinch of sugar.

Shape the steak tartare into 4 neat discs and arrange on plates. If you like, you can sprinkle with finely chopped Pickled Cucumber and onion. Serve with bread, toast, or rösti.

Leberkäse Sandwiches

Southern Germany

Preparation time:		3 minutes
Serves:		4

4	sesame buns	4
1 oz	spreadable butter	30 g
8	slices Leberkäse Aufschnitt	8
	(similar to bologna sausage)	
*	mustard (optional)	*
1	large Pickled Cucumber (p.29)	1

Halve the buns across the middle and spread the bottom halves with butter. Cover with the sausage slices. Add mustard if you like. Slice the Pickled Cucumber (p. 29) and add to the sandwiches. Cover the buns with their tops. This can also be served warm by heating the Leberkäse Aufschnitt in a frying pan until warm.

Pickled Cucumbers (Essiggurken)

All regions

Preparation time:		20 minutes
Salting:		overnight
Steeping time:		4–6 weeks
Makes:		enough for 1 Mason jar
	(1 litre/4 cups/34 fl oz capacity)	

2 lbs 4 oz	ripe yellow pickling cucumber	1 kg
*	salt	*
1	white onion	1
50	mustard seeds	50
15	peppercorns	15
1	bay leaf	1
1	dill flower head	1
1½ cups/13 fl oz	white wine vinegar	375 ml
½ cup/3½ oz	sugar	100 g

Peel the cucumbers. Halve them lengthwise and remove the seeds with a teaspoon. Sprinkle the cucumber halves with salt, cover with a cloth, and let stand for a few hours, preferably overnight.

Thoroughly pat dry the cucumbers, then cut into slices the thickness of a finger. Peel the onion and slice into very thin rings. Layer the mustard seeds, peppercorns, and bay leaf, alternating with the cucumber slices, in a large Mason jar. Put the dill flower head at the top.

Briefly boil the vinegar with the sugar, then let cool. Pour the mixture into the jar, cover, and steep for 24 hours.

Drain the pickling liquid into a pan, bring to a boil, and pour the boiling liquid back into the jar. Repeat the operation after 14 days. Then close the jar tightly and store in a cool place away from light. The pickles will be ready to eat after 4–6 weeks, depending on how vinegary you like your pickles.

White Asparagus Wrapped in Ham

All regions

	Preparation time:	10 minutes
	Cooking time:	8 minutes
	Serves:	4

8	white asparagus spears	8
*	salt	*
*	sugar	*
8	thin slices cooked ham	8
*	Remoulade, to serve (p. 112)	*

Peel the asparagus spears and cut off the woody ends. Boil in water with a generous pinch of salt and sugar, for about 8 minutes, until tender but still firm to the bite. Plunge into iced water, let drain, and pat dry thoroughly with kitchen towels.

Roll each spear inside a ham slice, leaving the tip exposed.

Arrange the rolls on a serving dish and serve accompanied with Remoulade (p. 112).

Pickled Pumpkin

All regions

	Preparation time:	15 minutes
	Steeping time:	1 week
	Makes:	enough for 1 Mason jar
		(1 litre/4 cups/34 fl oz capacity)

2 lbs 4 oz	fresh pumpkin flesh	1 kg
1	small piece ginger	1
1¾ cups/14 fl oz	white wine vinegar	400 ml
3 cups/1 lb 5 oz	sugar	600 g
*	salt	*
4	cloves	4
10	peppercorns	10
1 tbsp	mustard seeds	1 tbsp

Cut the pumpkin into 2 cm (¾ inch) dice and put into a Mason jar. Peel and finely chop the ginger.

Combine 200 ml (¾ cup/6¾ fl oz) water with the vinegar, sugar, a generous pinch of salt, ginger, cloves, peppercorns, and mustard seeds, in a pan and boil for 5 minutes.

Pour the pickling liquid into the jar over the pumpkin cubes. They should be completely covered. Close the jar tightly and let steep in the refrigerator for at least 1 week.

Snacks & Light Meals

Scrapple (Panhas)

Westphalia and Rhineland

Preparation time:		30 minutes
Cooking time:		3 hours
Cooling time:		12 hours
Makes:		about 1.5 kg (3¼ lbs)

9 oz	pork belly	250 g
9 oz	ham hock, de-boned	250 g
1⅔ tbsp	salt	1⅔ tbsp
12½ oz	blood sausage	350 g
1 tsp	finely grated nutmeg	1 tsp
1 tsp	ground allspice	1 tsp
1 tsp	dried marjoram	1 tsp
2 cups/9 oz	buckwheat flour	250 g
1 tsp	freshly ground pepper	1 tsp
1 tbsp	oil	1 tbsp
*	pumpernickel, to serve	*
*	Pan-fried Potatoes (p. 263)	*
*	mashed potatoes, optional	*

Put the pork belly, ham hock, and 600 ml (2½ cups/20¼ fl oz) water into a large pan. Add 1 tsp salt. Cover with the lid, leaving a small gap, and simmer until the meat is tender, about 3 hours.

Take out the meat, let cool slightly, and cut into 3–4cm (1–1½ inch) chunks. Remove the casing from the blood sausages. Cut in half lengthwise and cut into slices. Grind the meat and sausage in a meat grinder using a coarse plate, 5 mm (¼ inch) or slightly smaller, then mix with the cooking liquid in the pan. Add the rest of the salt and the spices and stir constantly until the liquid is just below the boil. Mix in the flour gradually to form a thick paste. Season again if necessary. The paste needs to be well seasoned as it is still absorbing flavour.

Stuff artificial sausage casings or fill plastic containers with the paste, let cool, then close the sausages or cover the containers and refrigerate overnight.

Cut the panhas into 1–1.5 cm (½–¾ inch) discs and fry lightly on both sides in a frying pan or skillet with oil. Accompany with pumpernickel, Pan-fried Potatoes (p. 263), or mashed potatoes.

Pigs in Blankets

All regions

Preparation time:		10 minutes
Cooking time:		20 minutes
Serves:		4

9 oz	frozen puff pastry, defrosted	250 g
*	plain (all-purpose) flour, to dust	*
4	frankfurters (hot dogs)	4
1	egg yolk	1
1 tbsp	single (light) cream	1 tbsp
*	ketchup, to serve, optional	*

Preheat the oven to 220°C/425°F/Gas Mark 7. Roll out the pastry on a floured work counter to a 30 × 15 cm (12 × 6 inch) rectangle. Halve the pastry to form two 15 cm (6 inch) squares. Halve the squares diagonally.

Lay each sausage over the long side of a pastry triangle and roll it up inside the pastry. With the tip of the triangle underneath, lay the rolls on a baking sheet lined with baking paper. Mix the egg yolk with the cream and brush the pastry with the mixture.

Place the baking sheet on the lowest shelf of the oven and bake for 15–20 minutes, until golden. Can be served with ketchup.

Snacks & Light Meals

Pork in Aspic (Tellersülze)

Southern Germany

Preparation time:		30 minutes
Cooking time:		2 hours 30 minutes
Cooling time:		5 hours
Serves:		4

12 cups/100 fl oz	chicken stock	3 litres
½ cup/3½ fl oz	white wine vinegar	100 ml
1	onion	1
1	bay leaf	1
1	clove	1
*	sugar	*
3 lbs 4 oz	cured ham hock, with rind	1.5 kg
1	carrot	1
3½ oz	celeriac	100 g
3	juniper berries	3
½ tsp	peppercorns	½ tsp
2	allspice berries	2
10	sheets gelatin	10
*	freshly grated nutmeg	*
*	salt	*
*	freshly ground pepper	*
1	Pickled Cucumber (p. 29)	1
1	boiled egg	1
1	Pan-Fried Potatoes, (p. 263)	1

Combine the stock with 80 ml (generous ⅓ cup/2¾ fl oz) vinegar in a large pan. Peel and halve the onion. Attach the bay leaf to the cut side of one onion half by studding with the clove. Put into the stock. Stir 1 tsp sugar into the stock and bring to a boil. Put the ham hock into the stock and cook gently on moderate heat for 2 hours 30 minutes until the meat is tender and easily separated from the bone.

Trim and peel the carrot and celeriac, and add to the pan with the remaining onion half after cooking for 30 minutes. After 30 more minutes, put the juniper berries, peppercorns, and allspice berries in a spice bag or muslin cloth tied with string, then close and add to the stock.

When it's cooked, take the ham hock out of the stock, remove the rind, and separate the meat from the bone. Cut the meat into slices against the grain. Use paper towels to remove the fat from the stock, and filter the stock through a sieve lined with a paper towel. Cut the vegetables into small pieces and set aside.

Soften the gelatin sheets in cold water. Bring 1 litre (4¼ cups/34 fl oz) stock to a boil in a pan. Drain the gelatin well and melt in the stock. Season with the remaining vinegar, a pinch of sugar, nutmeg, salt, and pepper and let cool to room temperature.

Slice the Pickled Cucumber (p.29) Slice the egg across the middle. Arrange the meat, vegetables, egg, and pickles in deep plates. Pour the aspic over the contents of the plates and refrigerate for a few hours to set. Serve with Pan-Fried Potatoes (p. 263).

Goose Legs in Aspic (Gänseweißsauer)

Mecklenburg-Western Pomerania and Berlin

Preparation time:		20 minutes
Cooking time:		2 hours
Cooling time:		5–6 hours
Serves:		4

4	goose legs	4
1	onion	1
2	bay leaves	2
1	clove	1
10	peppercorns	10
1	leek	1
2	carrots	2
*	parsley, to serve	*
5	sheets gelatin	5
⅓ cup/2½ fl oz	red wine vinegar	75 ml
*	salt	*
*	sugar	*

Wash the goose legs. Peel and slice the onion. Put the legs, onion, bay leaves, clove, and peppercorns into a pan and cover with water. Bring to a boil, then simmer gently for 1 hour 30 minutes–2 hours.

Cut the roots and green leaves off the leek, cut the white part in half lengthwise, and wash well. Peel and thinly slice the carrots lengthwise. Then cut the carrot slices and individual leek layers into large, uniform diamond shapes.

Refresh the goose legs briefly under cold running water. Remove the skin, and carefully remove the meat from the bones. Boil the carrot and leek diamonds in the goose broth until tender but firm to the bite.

Arrange the meat and vegetables on four soup bowls and garnish with bay leaves, peppercorns, and parsley. Soften the gelatin sheets in cold water.

Remove the fat from the goose broth. Drain the gelatin well and melt in the warm broth. Transfer to a bowl placed in iced water and stir until it cools. Before the aspic begins to set, season with vinegar, salt, and sugar, and pour it over the contents of the soup plates. Set the aspic in the refrigerator for 5–6 hours.

Bratwurst Cooked in Vinegar (Saure Zipfel)

Franconia and Bavaria

Preparation time:		10 minutes
Cooking time:		15 minutes
Serves:		4

2	onions	2
1	small carrot	1
3½ oz	celeriac	100 g
1 tbsp	oil	1 tbsp
2 tsp	icing (confectioners') sugar	2 tsp
4 tbsp	red wine vinegar	4 tbsp
4 cups/34 fl oz	chicken stock	1 litre
1 tsp	juniper berries	1 tsp
1 tsp	allspice berries	1 tsp
1 tsp	mustard seed	1 tsp
1 tbsp	peppercorns	1 tbsp
1	small bay leaf	1
1 tbsp	sugar	1 tbsp
*	salt	*
1 lb 2 oz	Franconian bratwurst sausages	500 g
1–2	parsley stems	1–2
*	freshly grated nutmeg	*
*	farmhouse bread, to serve	*
*	Bavarian Soft Pretzels (p. 50)	*

Peel the onions and trim and peel the carrot and celeriac. Cut them all into ½ cm (¼ inch) dice.

Heat the oil in a pan and sauté over a moderate heat until translucent. Sprinkle with the icing sugar and cook briefly. Deglaze the pan with the vinegar, then add the stock.

Put the juniper and allspice berries, mustard seeds, and peppercorns in a spice bag, seal it and add it to the stock with the bay leaf. Season the stock with sugar and salt.

Add the bratwurst and parsley to the pan and let steep for 10–15 minutes over a low heat. Season the broth with nutmeg. Remove the spice bag and bay leaf.

Arrange the sausages in deep plates and pour the hot broth over them. Arrange the vegetables on top. Serve with farmhouse bread or Bavarian Soft Pretzels (p.50).

Bavarian Breakfast Sausages (Weißwürste)

Bavaria

Preparation time:		20 minutes
Serves:		4

*	salt	*
8	white pork and veal sausages	8
2–3	strips lemon zest	2–3
2–3	parsley stems	2–3
*	Bavarian Soft Pretzels (p. 50)	*
*	sweet mustard, to serve	*

Put enough water in a pan to amply cover the sausages. Heat the water to 75–80°C/165–175°F and add salt.

Put the sausages into the pan and add the zest and parsley.

Steep the sausages for about 15 minutes (do not boil as they will burst). When the sausages float to the surface, they're ready to eat. Serve with Bavarian-Soft Pretzels (p. 50) and sweet mustard.

Open-Faced Ham and Fried Egg Sandwich

Saxony and Berlin

4	slices farmhouse bread	4
1–2 tbsp	butter	1–2 tbsp
*	salt	*
4	eggs	4
4	lettuce leaves	4
3–4 tbsp	Yoghurt Dressing (p. 54)	3–4 tbsp
8	slices cooked ham	8
1 tbsp	chopped chives	1 tbsp
*	freshly ground pepper	*

Preparation time:	10 minutes
Cooking time:	5 minutes
Serves:	4

Lightly toast the slices of bread on both sides in a dry frying pan or skillet. Keep warm.

Melt the butter in a non-stick skillet and add a little salt. Crack the eggs and slide them gently into the pan to avoid bursting the yolks. Cook over a low heat to almost poach them in the butter rather than hard fry them.

Wash the lettuce leaves and pat them dry thoroughly. Put the toasted slices of bread on warmed plates. Dress the lettuce with the Yoghurt Dressing (p. 54) and lay one leaf on each slice of bread. Place 2 ham slices and 1 egg on each, sunny-side up. Season with pepper and sprinkle with chives.

Dortmund-Style Sandwich

Northern Germany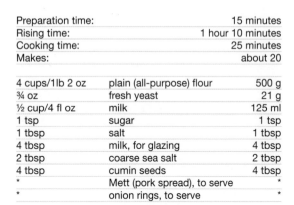

Preparation time:	15 minutes
Rising time:	1 hour 10 minutes
Cooking time:	25 minutes
Makes:	about 20

4 cups/1lb 2 oz	plain (all-purpose) flour	500 g
¾ oz	fresh yeast	21 g
½ cup/4 fl oz	milk	125 ml
1 tsp	sugar	1 tsp
1 tbsp	salt	1 tbsp
4 tbsp	milk, for glazing	4 tbsp
2 tbsp	coarse sea salt	2 tbsp
4 tbsp	cumin seeds	4 tbsp
*	Mett (pork spread), to serve	*
*	onion rings, to serve	*

Sift the flour into a bowl and make a well in the centre. Dissolve the yeast completely in 125 ml (½ cup/4 fl oz) lukewarm water and pour into the well. Mix with some of the flour, cover the bowl, and let stand in a warm place for 10 minutes.

Add the milk, sugar, and salt, and use a hand mixer with a dough hook to knead everything into a smooth dough. Cover the bowl with clingfilm (plastic wrap) and let rise in a warm place for 30 minutes.

Dust the work counter with flour and shape the dough into 5 or 6 thick rolls, then slice into 20 discs altogether. Lightly dust your hands with flour, then press down into the centre of each disc to make a hole, leaving a ring that's not much bigger than the size of the original disc.

Space the rings apart over a baking sheet lined with baking paper, cover with a dish towel, and let rise for 30 minutes.

Preheat the oven to 220°C/425°F/Gas Mark 7. Brush the rings with milk, sprinkle with sea salt and cumin seeds, place on the second shelf of the oven, and bake for 20–25 minutes.

Let cool, halve the buns through the middle, and fill with Mett and onion rings.

Omelette with Prawns (Shrimp)

Northern Germany

Preparation time:		5 minutes
Cooking time:		5 minutes
Serves:		1

7 oz	brined shrimp	200 g
¼	bunch dill	¼
*	lime juice	*
*	unwaxed lime zest, grated	*
2 tbsp	olive oil	2 tbsp
*	sweet paprika	*
3	eggs	3
1 tsp	butter	1 tsp
*	salt	*
*	freshly ground pepper	*
*	freshly grated nutmeg	*

Let the shrimp drain a little. Wash, shake dry, and coarsely chop the dill. Put the shrimp and dill in a bowl and mix in a little lime juice, grated lime zest, and oil. Season with a pinch of paprika.

Whisk the eggs in a bowl. Heat the butter in a non-stick frying pan or skillet. Pour the beaten eggs into the pan and let set over moderate heat.

Season the omelette with salt, pepper, and nutmeg. Slide the omelette onto a plate, cover with the shrimp, and fold.

Meat and Barley Groats (Stippgrütze)

Westphalia

Preparation time:		30 minutes
Cooking time:		4 hours
Serves:		4

1	bay leaf	1
2	onions	2
3	cloves	3
12 oz	pig head meat	350 g
3½ oz	stewing (beef chuck or round)	100 g
5 oz	pig heart	150 g
2 cups/18 fl oz	chicken stock	500 ml
¼ cup/2 oz	pearl barley	50 g
*	salt	*
½ tsp	ground allspice	½ tsp
¼ tsp	freshly grated nutmeg	¼ tsp
1 tbsp	Worcestershire sauce	1 tbsp
*	rye bread, to serve	*
*	gherkins (dill pickles), to serve	*

Attach the bay leaf to the first onion by studding with the cloves. Put the pig head meat, beef, pig heart, studded onion, and stock in a pan. Cover with the lid, leaving a small gap, and simmer until the meat is tender with the liquid just at a boil, for about 3 hours.

Remove the onion. Take out the meat, let cool slightly, and cut into coarse chunks. Measure out 150 ml (⅔ cup /5 fl oz) cooking liquid and set aside.

Peel and finely chop the other onion, put into the stock in the pan with the pearl barley, and simmer with the liquid just at a boil, about 45 minutes, stirring often until soft.

Meanwhile, finely mince the meat chunks in a mincer. Stir the minced meat into the soft barley, season with salt and simmer for 45 more minutes with the liquid just at a boil, stirring often. Top up the stock if you need to. Season with salt, the spices, and the Worcestershire sauce.

Stuff 8–10 cm (3½–4 inch) sausage casings or fill plastic containers with the meat and barley mixture, let cool, then close the sausages or cover the containers and refrigerate overnight. Before serving, cut the Stippgrütze into thick slices and fry in a dry frying pan or skillet. It can be mashed into a spread and served with rye bread and dill pickles.

Nuremberg Sausages with Sauerkraut in a Bun

Bavaria

Preparation time:		15 minutes
Cooking time:		35 minutes
Serves:		4

½	small onion	½
1 tbsp	Beurre Noisette (p.110)	1 tbsp
1¼ cups/7 oz	sauerkraut	200 g
3 tbsp	dry white wine	3 tbsp
1 cup/8 fl oz	vegetable stock	250 ml
5	peppercorns	5
2	juniper berries, lightly crushed	2
¼ tsp	coriander seeds	¼ tsp
¼ tsp	cumin seeds	¼ tsp
½	bay leaf	½
1 tbsp	apple purée	1 tbsp
2 tbsp	single (light) cream	2 tbsp
1 tbsp	cold butter	1 tbsp
*	salt	*
1–2 tbsp	oil	1–2 tbsp
12	Nuremberg sausages	12
4	crusty buns	4

Peel and finely chop the onion. Heat the Beurre Noisette (p. 110) in a pan and lightly fry the onion over a moderate heat. Put the sauerkraut into a sieve and wash under cold running water, then squeeze out the water, add to the onions, and cook briefly. Add the wine and stock.

Put the peppercorns, juniper berries, coriander seeds, cumin seeds and bay leaf in a spice bag, close, and add to the sauerkraut. Make a lid from baking paper and cover the pan. Infuse the sauerkraut over a moderate heat, about 35 minutes.

Remove the spice bag, stir the apple purée, cream, and cold butter into the sauerkraut, and season with salt if needed.

Heat the oil in a frying pan or skillet over medium heat. Fry the sausages on both sides.

Halve the buns across the middle and toast them a little in a dry skillet. Put a little sauerkraut cream and 3 sausages on the bottom half of each bun. Finally, cover with the top halves of the buns.

Currywurst

Berlin

Preparation time:		15 minutes
Cooking time:		45 minutes
Serves		4

4	red or white bratwurst sausages	4
1 tbsp	oil	1 tbsp
1	onion	1
1 tbsp	brown sugar	1 tbsp
1 tbsp	mild curry powder	1 tbsp
1	cinnamon stick	1
1	dried red chilli pepper	1
2¼ tbsp	pineapple juice	2¼ tbsp
½ cup/3½ fl oz	vegetable stock	100 ml
2 tbsp	tomato purée (paste)	2 tbsp
1¾ cups/14 fl oz	canned chopped tomatoes	400 ml
1 tbsp	white wine vinegar	1 tbsp
5 tbsp	olive oil	5 tbsp
*	French fries, to serve	*

Score the sausages across several times with a sharp knife. Heat the oil in a frying pan or skillet and fry the sausages slowly on all sides over a medium heat.

To make the ketchup, peel and finely chop the onion, and sauté in a dry pan over a medium heat. Add the brown sugar and caramelise the onion.

Add the spices, cook briefly, and add the pineapple juice. Stir in the stock, tomato purée (paste), chopped tomatoes and vinegar, then cook for 30–45 minutes. Strain through a sieve, then blend in the olive oil with a stick (immersion) blender.

Serve the sausages with the ketchup. They can be accompanied with French fries.

Eggs with Mustard Sauce

Berlin and Northern Germany

Preparation time:		5 minutes
Cooking time:		15 minutes
Serves:		4

3 oz	waxy potatoes	80 g
1¼ cups/10½ fl oz	vegetable stock	300 ml
⅓ cup/3 fl oz	single (light) cream	80 ml
1⅓ tbsp	cold butter	1⅓ tbsp
2 tbsp	Dijon mustard	2 tbsp
*	salt	*
*	freshly ground pepper	*
*	sugar	*
8	eggs	8
*	chives or watercress, to serve	*
*	Boiled Potatoes (p. 260), to serve	*

Peel and wash the potatoes, and cut into 1 cm dice. Simmer in the stock until soft, about 15 minutes.

Add the cream, butter, and mustard, and blend with a stick (immersion) blender. Season with salt, pepper, and a pinch of sugar. The sauce should be a little runny.

Medium-boil the eggs, 6–7 minutes, then refresh in iced water, peel, halve lengthwise, and arrange over the sauce. The sauce can be reheated if necessary. Scatter watercress or finely chopped chives over the sauce.

This can be accompanied with Boiled Potatoes (p. 260) or potatoes boiled in their skins.

Devilled Eggs

All regions

Preparation time:		10–15 minutes
Serves:		4

Basic recipe:		
4	hard-boiled eggs	4
scant ½ cup/ 3 oz	cream cheese	80 g
*	salt	*

For the devilled eggs with roe:		
1	basic recipe (see above)	1
2	butterhead lettuce leaves	2
6–8	cherry tomatoes	6–8
4 tsp	trout roe	4 tsp

For the devilled eggs with curry:		
1	basic recipe (see above)	1
½ tsp	mild curry powder	½ tsp
1 tbsp	hot vegetable stock	1 tbsp
*	basil and parsley, to serve	*

For the devilled eggs with herbs:		
1	basic recipe (see above)	1
1	handful baby spinach	1
1	bunch parsley	1
*	salt	*
1	pinch chopped garlic	1
1 tbsp	grated Parmesan cheese	1 tbsp
1 tsp	toasted sliced almonds	1 tsp
1 tbsp	Beurre Noisette (p.112)	1 tbsp
2 tbsp	olive oil	2 tbsp
*	freshly grated nutmeg	*
1 tbsp	Parmesan shavings	1 tbsp

For the basic recipe: Peel and halve the eggs lengthwise and remove the yolks. Press the yolks through a sieve or finely chop. Mix with the soft cheese, to a smooth paste, and season with salt. Fill a piping bag with the paste, attach a star tip, and fill the egg halves.

For the devilled eggs with roe: Trim, wash and pat dry the lettuce leaves. Cut the leaves into strips and spread them over four plates. Wash the tomatoes and cut into 8. Arrange over the lettuce strips. Arrange the devilled eggs on top and garnish each one with ½ tsp of trout roe.

For the devilled eggs with curry: Stir the curry powder into the hot stock. Add this to the basic recipe and mix to a smooth paste. Fill a piping bag with the mixture, attach a star tip, and pipe into the egg halves. Garnish with herbs.

For the devilled eggs with herbs: Wash the spinach and parsley. Blanch both in boiling salted water for 2 minutes, drain in a sieve, plunge into iced water, and let drain. Squeeze any water out, then finely chop and put into a blender. Add the garlic, Parmesan, almonds, Beurre Noisette (p. 112), and olive oil, add a pinch of nutmeg, and blend to a paste. Mix the herb paste into the basic recipe. Season with salt. Fill a piping bag with the mixture, attach a star tip, and fill the egg halves. Garnish with Parmesan shavings.

Snacks & Light Meals

Pickled Eggs

Berlin and Rhineland

Preparation time:		10 minutes
Cooking time:		10 minutes
Steeping time:		2 days
Serves:		4–6

6	eggs	6
*	salt	*
1	bay leaf	1
1 tsp	mustard seeds	1 tsp
½ tsp	peppercorns	½ tsp
*	vinegar	*
*	hot mustard	*
*	oil	*
*	freshly ground pepper	*

Hard-boil the eggs, about 10 minutes. Refresh in iced water and lightly crack the shell all over. Put the eggs into a mason jar.

Boil 750 ml (3¼ cups/25 fl oz) water with 80 g (3 oz) salt, bay leaf and the spices for a few minutes, let cool, and pour over the eggs. Store in a cool place and steep for at least 1–2 days.

When it's time to eat, peel and halve the eggs lengthwise and carefully remove the yolks. In the well left by the yolk, season with a little vinegar, hot mustard, and few drops of oil. Sprinkle with pepper and replace the yolks. Eat in one mouthful.

Quark, Herbs and Flaxseed Oil Sauce

Berlin, Brandenburg and Saxony

Preparation time:		5 minutes
Cooking time:		2 minutes
Serves:		4

2¼ cups.1 lb 2 oz	low-fat Quark	500 g
2 tbsp	flaxseed oil	2 tbsp
*	salt	*
*	sweet paprika	*
½ cup/3½ fl oz	vegetable stock	100 ml
1–2 tbsp	Spice Mix (p. 428)	1–2 tbsp
2 tbsp	parsley and chives, chopped	2 tbsp
*	Boiled Potatoes, (p. 260), to serve	*

Mix the Quark with the oil and a little salt and paprika in a bowl.

Heat the stock in a small saucepan, add the Spice Mix (p. 428), and infuse for 1–2 minutes.

Add the stock and spice mixture to the Quark while blending with a stick (immersion blender) to a glossy sauce. Mix in the herbs and season again.

Serve with Boiled Potatoes (p. 260) or baked potatoes.

Buckwheat Pancakes with Ham

Lower Saxony

Preparation time:		10 minutes
Resting time:		30 minutes
Cooking time:		20 minutes
Serves:		4

1 cup/8 fl oz	cold coffee	250 ml
½ cup/4 fl oz	cold milk	125 ml
2 cups/9 oz	buckwheat flour	250 g
2	eggs	2
*	salt	*
4 tbsp	Beurre Noisette (p. 112)	4 tbsp
16	thin slices Westphalian ham	16
*	green salad, to serve	*

Mix the coffee and milk with 125 ml (½ cup/4 fl oz) cold water in a bowl. Add the flour and mix to a smooth batter. Mix in one egg at a time, season with salt, cover, and rest for 30 minutes.

Heat the Beurre Noisette (p. 112) in a 24 cm (9 inch) diameter frying pan or skillet. Put 2 slices of ham side-by-side in the pan, pour ⅛ of the batter over them, and cook until the underside turns golden brown.

Turn the pancake over and cook briefly on the other side. Cook the other seven pancakes in the same way. Serve the pancakes with a green salad.

Green Spelt Patties

All regions

Preparation time:		10 minutes
Cooking time:		30 minutes
Serves:		4

1	onion	1
1½ cup/13 fl oz	vegetable stock	375 ml
1 scant cup/3½ oz	green spelt flakes	100 g
1	clove garlic	1
½ cup/2 oz	extra-fine rolled oats	50 g
2⅔ oz	Emmental cheese	75 g
1	egg	1
1–2 tbsp	parsley and dill, chopped	1–2 tbsp
*	salt	*
*	freshly ground pepper	*
*	freshly grated nutmeg	*
*	oil, for frying	*
*	Mayonnaise, (p.114), to serve	*

Peel and finely chop the onion. Combine the onions with the stock and green spelt flakes in a pan and simmer for 15–20 minutes, stirring constantly, until a thick paste forms. Peel and finely chop the garlic, then mix it into the spelt paste. Transfer to a bowl and let cool completely.

Add the oats, cheese, egg, and herbs to the green spelt paste, and season with salt, pepper, and nutmeg. Wet your hands and shape the paste into small patties.

Heat oil in a large frying pan or skillet and fry the patties over a medium heat for about 4 minutes, until golden brown. Turn them over and fry for 4 more minutes on the other side. Drain on paper towels.

Mini Snail Ragout Pies

Baden-Württemberg

	For the pie casings:	
1 lb 2 oz	puff pastry	
*	plain (all-purpose) flour, to dust	*
1	egg yolk	1
1 tbsp	cream	1 tbsp

	For the ragout:	
2	shallots	2
1 tbsp	oil	1 tbsp
3 tbsp	Baden white wine	50 ml
1 cup/8 fl oz	chicken stock	250 ml
⅓ cup/3 fl oz	single (light) cream	80 ml
1 tsp	cornflour	1 tsp
2 oz	button mushrooms	50 g
1	bay leaf	1
2	cloves garlic	2
2 tbsp	parsley, tarragon, basil, finely chopped	2 tbsp
1	pinch unwaxed lemon zest	1
*	a few drops lemon juice	*
6 oz	Weinberg snails (jarred, drained)	180 g
*	salt	*
*	freshly ground pepper	*

Preparation time:	30 minutes
Cooking time:	15 minutes
Serves:	4

For the pie casings: Preheat the oven to 210°C/410°F/Gas Mark 7. Roll out the pastry over a floured work counter to a thickness of about 3 mm (⅛ inch). Use a serrated cookie cutter about 8 cm (3 inches) in diameter to cut out 12 discs.

Line a baking sheet with baking paper. Lay 4 discs on the baking sheet and brush with cold water.

Use a 5-cm- (2-inch-) diameter cookie cutter to cut out the centres of the other 8 discs. Set aside. Take 4 of the pastry rings and lay one on each of the pastry discs. Lightly brush with water and place the other 4 rings on top of the others, so that there are 2 rings stacked on each pastry circle. Prick the pastry in the centres to prevent them from rising too much. Lay the set-aside discs next to the pie casings and prick with a fork. They will be the lids.

Beat the egg yolk with the cream and brush the surfaces of the pastry discs and the lids with the mixture. Bake for 10–15 minutes, until golden.

For the ragout: Peel and finely chop the shallots. Heat the oil in a pan and sauté the shallots over moderate heat until translucent. Add the wine and reduce almost completely. Add the stock and cream. Dissolve the cornflour in a little cold water and mix it into the sauce gradually to bind and lightly thicken it.

Wash clean, wipe dry, and quarter the mushrooms. Add to the sauce. Season with the bay leaf, garlic, herbs, lemon zest and lemon juice. Add the snails and heat in the sauce. Season the sauce with salt and pepper. Remove the aromatics that are still whole.

Lightly warm the pie casings in the oven and fill with ragout. Cover with the pastry lids and serve.

Bacon Pancake

Rhineland

½ cup/2 oz	plain (all-purpose) flour	50 g
½ cup/4 fl oz	milk	125 ml
1	egg	1
*	salt	*
*	freshly grated nutmeg	*
1–2 tsp	oil	1–2 tsp
5	slices bacon	5
1–2 tbsp	finely chopped chives	1–2 tbsp
*	sour cream, optional	*

Preparation time:	5 minutes
Cooking time:	10 minutes
Serves:	1

Turn on the grill (broiler). Mix the flour with the milk until smooth. Separate the egg and stir the yolk into the batter. Season with a little salt and nutmeg.

Beat the egg white to soft peaks with a pinch of salt, and fold into the batter.

Heat the oil in a large, ovenproof frying pan or skillet and fry the bacon. Cover the bacon with the batter, and cook until the underside of the pancake turns light golden.

Put the pan on the lowest shelf of the oven and cook until the top of the pancake turns golden. Slide the pancake onto a plate, sprinkle with chives, and serve.

Leek Pie

For the basic pastry:		
1 scant cup/7 oz	softened butter	200 g
2	egg yolks	2
2 tbsp	milk	2 tbsp
1	pinch sugar	1
1 tsp	salt	1 tsp
3 scant cups/12 oz	plain (all-purpose) flour	350 g
*	butter, for greasing	*
*	flour, for dusting	*

For the filling:		
3	onions	3
2	leeks	2
1 tbsp	oil	1 tbsp
*	salt	*
*	freshly ground pepper	*
*	ground cumin	*
¾ cup/7 fl oz	milk	200 ml
¾ cup/7 fl oz	single (light) cream	200 ml
4	eggs	4
*	paprika	*
*	freshly grated nutmeg	*

Preparation time:	30 minutes
Resting time:	1 hour
Cooking time:	1 hour
Serves:	4

For the basic pastry: Combine the butter with the egg yolks, milk, a pinch of sugar, and 1 tsp salt in a bowl and mix well. Gradually add the flour, and use a stand or hand mixer with a dough hook to knead everything into a smooth dough. Shape the pastry into a flat brick, cover with clingfilm (plastic wrap), and rest in the refrigerator for at least an hour.

Preheat the oven to 180°C/350°F/Gas Mark 4. Grease a baking pan with butter. Knead the pastry briefly with your hands and roll out over a floured work counter into a thin sheet the size of the baking pan. Line the baking pan with the dough and prick all over the bottom with a fork. Place the baking pan on the middle shelf of the oven and bake for 8–10 minutes until light golden.

For the filling: Peel and finely chop the onions. Trim and halve the leeks lengthwise, then wash and cut across into thin strips. Heat the oil in a frying pan or skillet and sauté the onions and leeks over moderate heat. Season with salt, pepper, and a pinch of cumin, and let cool. Spread the onion and leek mixture over the pastry.

Whisk the milk with the cream and egg. Season with salt, pepper, and a pinch of paprika and nutmeg. Cover the onion and leeks with the milk and egg mixture, place the baking pan on the middle shelf of the oven, and bake until the pastry turns golden, about 50 minutes.

Münsterländer Pie

Preparation time:	30 minutes
Cooking time:	50 minutes
Serves:	4

5 oz	spinach	150 g
3 oz	bread	80 g
⅓ cup/3 fl oz	milk	80 ml
4 tbsp	single (light) cream	4 tbsp
½	small onion	½
1 tbsp	oil	1 tbsp
2	eggs	2
2 tsp	hot mustard	2 tsp
*	salt	*
*	freshly ground pepper	*
*	freshly grated nutmeg	*
½	grated zest of unwaxed lemon	½
1	clove garlic	1
9 oz	minced (ground) veal	250 g
9 oz	minced (ground) pork	250 g
2 tsp	dried marjoram	2 tsp
2 tbsp	finely chopped parsley	2 tbsp
*	butter, for greasing	*
1 lb 2 oz	puff pastry	500 g
*	flour, for dusting	*
1	egg yolk	1
*	mustard, to serve, optional	*

Choose the best spinach leaves, then wash, spin dry, and remove the larger stems. Blanch the spinach in boiling salted water, drain in a sieve, plunge into iced water, and let drain. Squeeze the leaves with your hands to remove as much water as possible, and cut into small pieces.

Cut the bread into cubes and mix with the milk and 3 tbsp cream. Peel and finely chop the onion. Heat the oil in a frying pan or skillet and sauté the onion over a moderate heat until translucent. Beat the egg with mustard, salt, pepper, nutmeg, and lemon zest. Peel and finely chop the garlic.

Mix both kinds of minced meat with the soaked bread, beaten egg, spinach, onion, marjoram, garlic, and parsley.

Grease a 26-cm- (10¼-inch-) diameter springform pan with butter. Preheat the oven to 200°C/400°F/Gas Mark 6.

Dust a work counter with flour and roll out half the pastry into a 35 cm (14 inch) diameter disc and line the springform pan. Fill the pie shell with the minced (ground) meat mixture, smooth the surface, and fold the overhanging pastry into the middle.

Mix the egg yolk with the rest of the cream and brush the edges of the pastry with the mixture. Roll out the remaining half of the pastry into a 26-cm- (10¼-inch-) diameter disc and cover the pie filling with it. Brush the surface with the egg and cream mixture. You can use the back of a knife or a fork to make patterns over the pastry if you like.

Put the pie on the middle shelf of the oven and bake until golden, about 50 minutes. Cut into portions and serve.

Crumbed Milzwurst

Bavaria

Preparation time:		5 minutes
Cooking time:		10 minutes
Serves:		4

2 tbsp	plain (all-purpose) flour	2 tbsp
1 cup/2 oz	breadcrumbs	50 g
4 × 4¼ oz	thick slices Milzwurst	4 × 125 g
1	egg	1
*	oil, for frying	*
*	Potato Salad (p. 62)	*

Put the flour and breadcrumbs separately into deep plates. Beat the egg in a deep plate. Dip the sausage slices in floor, then beaten egg and then dredge in the breadcrumbs.

Put plenty of oil in a large frying pan or skillet and place over medium heat. Fry the crumbed sausage slices on both sides until golden. Drain on paper towels. Serve with Mustard and Potato Salad (p. 62).

Flatbread with Onion and Bacon (Flammkuchen)

Palatinate and Baden

Preparation time:		30 minutes
Rising time:		30 minutes
Cooking time:		20 minutes
Serves:		4

For the dough:		
2 cups/9 oz	plain (all-purpose) flour	250 g
⅓ oz	fresh yeast	10 g
2 tbsp	olive oil	2 tbsp
1 level tsp	salt	1 level tsp
*	olive oil, for greasing	*
*	plain (all-purpose) flour, to dust	*

For the topping:		
3	onions	3
2 tbsp	oil	2 tbsp
⅓ cup/3½ fl oz	vegetable stock	100 ml
2	tomatoes	2
1¼ cups/11 oz	sour cream	300 g
*	salt	*
*	paprika	*
1 tsp	dried savoury	1 tsp
1 tsp	cumin seeds	1 tsp
1 tsp	coriander seeds	1 tsp
1 tsp	peppercorns	1 tsp
7 oz	bacon rashers	200 g

For the dough: Sift the flour into a bowl and make a well in the centre. Lightly warm 5 tbsp water and dissolve the yeast. Pour into the well and mix with a little of the flour. Add the olive oil, salt, and 7 tbsp water, and knead into a smooth dough. Cover the dough with clingfilm (plastic wrap) and let rise in a warm place for 30 minutes.

For the topping: Peel and cut the onions into strips. Heat 1 tbsp oil in a frying pan or skillet and sauté the onions. Deglaze with the stock and reduce completely. Cut a cross in the base of the tomatoes, blanch, plunge into iced water, peel, quarter, and seed. Cut the tomato quarters into 1 cm (½ inch) dice. Season the sour cream with salt, paprika, and savoury.

Preheat the oven to 210°C/410°F/Gas Mark 6. Grease a baking sheet with olive oil. Roll out the dough over a floured work counter into a rectangle the size of the baking sheet. Line the baking sheet with the dough. Combine the cumin seeds, coriander seeds and peppercorns in a spice grinder and season the dough with them. Spread the sour cream evenly over the dough, leaving a 1 cm (½ inch) uncovered space around the edge. Cover the sour cream with the onions and tomatoes, place the baking sheet on the lowest shelf of the oven, and bake until the dough turns golden, about 20 minutes.

Meanwhile, cut the bacon into 2 cm (1 inch) wide strips. Heat the remaining oil in a skillet and fry the bacon until crispy. Drain on paper towels then add to the cooked flammkuchen.

Potato, Vegetable and Ham Omelette

All regions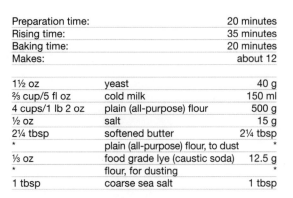

Preparation time:		15 minutes
Cooking time:		35 minutes
Serves:		4

14 oz	waxy potatoes	400 g
1	onion	1
3½ oz	cooked ham	100 g
½ cup/3 oz	Romano (flat) beans	80 g
1	carrot	1
3½ cups/5 oz	broccoli florets	150 g
⅔ cup/3½ oz	cherry tomatoes	100 g
1 tbsp	oil	1 tbsp
*	salt	*
*	freshly ground pepper	*
*	paprika	*
*	dried savory	*
1 tbsp	finely chopped parsley	1 tbsp
½	clove garlic, finely chopped	½
5	eggs	5
⅔ cup/5 fl oz	milk	150 ml
*	freshly grated nutmeg	*
¾ cup/3 oz	grated alpine cheese	80 g

Peel and wash the potatoes, and cut into 5 mm (¼ inch) thick rounds. Boil for 15–20 minutes in plenty of salted water, then drain in a colander until they are no longer steaming.

Peel and finely chop the onion. Finely dice the ham. Trim and wash the beans, then cut diagonally into 1.5 cm (¾ inch) lengths. Trim, wash and slice the carrot. Trim and wash the broccoli, and cut into small florets. Blanch the beans, carrot, and broccoli separately in boiling salted water until tender but al dente. Take them out of the pan with a skimmer oe slotted spoon, plunge into iced water, and let drain. Wash and halve the cherry tomatoes.

Preheat the oven to 180°C/350°F/Gas Mark 4. Heat the oil in an ovenproof frying pan or skillet. Fry the potatoes and onion over medium heat until golden. Add the ham, beans, carrot, broccoli, and tomatoes. Season with salt, pepper, and pinch of paprika and savory. Add the parsley and garlic.

Use a (stick) immersion blender to beat the eggs with the milk in a measuring jug. Season the mixture with a little nutmeg, salt, pepper, and paprika, and pour it over the contents of the pan. Leave the pan on the stove for 30 seconds or so, then transfer to the oven. Put the pan on the middle shelf and continue to cook the omelette for about 20 minutes.

After 15 minutes, scatter the grated cheese over the omelette. To serve, transfer the omelette to a serving dish and cut into portions.

Bavarian Soft Pretzels

Bavaria

Preparation time:		20 minutes
Rising time:		35 minutes
Baking time:		20 minutes
Makes:		about 12

1½ oz	yeast	40 g
⅔ cup/5 fl oz	cold milk	150 ml
4 cups/1 lb 2 oz	plain (all-purpose) flour	500 g
½ oz	salt	15 g
2¼ tbsp	softened butter	2¼ tbsp
*	plain (all-purpose) flour, to dust	*
⅓ oz	food grade lye (caustic soda)	12.5 g
*	flour, for dusting	*
1 tbsp	coarse sea salt	1 tbsp

Dissolve the yeast in a little cold milk. Sift the flour into a bowl. Add the salt, butter, 130 ml (½ cup/4 ½ fl oz) cold water, the remaining milk, and the dissolved yeast, and use a hand or stand mixer with a dough hook to knead everything into a smooth dough. Cover and let rise, about 15 minutes.

Cut the dough into 12 equal pieces, dust with a little flour, and shape into balls. Cover and rest at room temperature for 10 minutes.

Preheat the oven to 180°C/350°F/Gas Mark 4 and spray the interior of the oven with water. Very carefully, heeding the instructions given by the chemist (pharmacist), mix the lye with 300 ml (1⅓ cups/10½ fl oz) cold water and let stand for 10 minutes until completely dissolved. Pour the solution into a casserole dish or another deep, flat dish.

Dust the work counter lightly with flour and shape the dough balls into ropes of about 30 cm (12 inches) in length, tapering at the ends. Twist into a pretzel shape by twisting the ends of the ropes together, then bringing the twisted ends back to the middle section of the rope, and lay, spaced apart, on a baking sheet lined with baking paper.

Brush the pretzels with the lye (always wear disposable gloves for this) and let rise for 10 more minutes. Sprinkle with sea salt and bake for 15–20 minutes. They can be enjoyed hot or cold.

Salads

Green Salad with Vinaigrette

All regions

Preparation time:		15 minutes
Serves:		4

1 head	lettuce (chicory or romaine)	1 head
⅓ cup/3 fl oz	vegetable stock	80 ml
2 tbsp	white wine vinegar	2 tbsp
1 tsp	mustard	1 tsp
*	salt	*
*	freshly ground black pepper	*
*	sugar	*
3 tbsp	oil	3 tbsp

Remove the outer leaves from the head of lettuce and discard. Separate, wash and dry the remaining leaves. Tear or cut the leaves into bite-sized pieces.

Combine the stock, vinegar, mustard, salt, pepper and a pinch of sugar in a measuring jug using a stick (immersion) blender, adding the oil in a fine stream.

Dress the leaves with the vinaigrette and serve.

Lamb's Lettuce (Corn Salad) with Bacon and Croutons

Baden-Württemberg

Preparation time:		20 minutes
Cooking time:		15 minutes
Serves:		4

⅓ cup/3 fl oz	vegetable stock	80 ml
1 tbsp	cider vinegar	1 tbsp
1 tbsp	olive oil	1 tbsp
*	salt	*
*	freshly ground black pepper	*
*	sugar	*
1 tbsp	oil, for frying	1 tbsp
5 oz	bacon rashers	150 g
2	shallots	2
2	slices white bread	2
1–2 tbsp	butter	1–2 tbsp
12 oz	lamb's lettuce (corn salad)	350 g

Mix the stock with the vinegar and oil in a measuring jug and season with salt, pepper and a pinch of sugar.

Heat the oil in a large frying pan or skillet and fry the bacon over a medium heat for 10 minutes, until crispy. Drain on paper towels. Fry the shallots gently in the oil for about 10 minutes until translucent.

Cut the bread into 5–10 mm (¼–½ inch) cubes for croutons. Melt the butter in a frying pan or skillet and toast the cubes for 5 minutes, turning occasionally, until golden all over.

Shortly before serving, pour the dressing over the lamb's lettuce (corn salad), serve on plates and crumble over the bacon, shallots and croutons.

Tomato and Onion Salad

All regions

Preparation time:		10 minutes
Serves:		4

8	tomatoes	8
1	red onion	1
*	salt	*
*	freshly ground black pepper	*
4 tbsp	red wine vinegar	4 tbsp
8 tbsp	olive oil	8 tbsp

Cut the tomatoes into thin slices. Arrange the tomato slices, slightly overlapping, on a large, flat plate. Finely chop the onion, scatter over the tomato slices and season with salt and pepper.

Combine the vinegar and oil in a measuring jug, season with salt and pepper, then mix using a stick (immersion) blender. Drizzle the dressing over the tomato salad and serve.

Green Bean Salad

All regions

Preparation time:		15 minutes
Cooking time:		15 minutes
Serves:		4

1⅔ cups/7 oz	Romano (flat) beans	200 g
1⅔ cups/7 oz	green beans	200 g
⅓ cup/3 fl oz	vegetable stock	80 ml
1 tbsp	red wine vinegar	1 tbsp
2 tbsp	oil	2 tbsp
*	salt	*
*	freshly ground black pepper	*
*	sugar	*
½	onion	½
1–2	sprigs savory	1–2

Cook the different beans separately in boiling salted water until tender. Take them out of the pan with a slotted spoon or skimmer, plunge into iced water, then drain and place in a bowl.

Mix the stock with the vinegar and oil and season with salt, pepper and a pinch of sugar.

Finely chop the onion and mix with the savory sprigs and stir into the dressing. Dress the beans. Remove the savory before serving.

Dandelion Salad

Saarland

Preparation time:		5 minutes
Cooking time:		5 minutes
Serves:		4

2 tsp	lemon juice	2 tsp
2 tsp	oil	2 tsp
*	salt	*
*	freshly ground black pepper	*
*	sugar	*
5½ cups/7 oz	tender dandelion leaves	200 g
3½ oz	white bread	100 g
1 tbsp	butter	1 tbsp
½	bunch chives	½

Thoroughly mix the lemon juice with the oil, a pinch each of salt, pepper, and sugar, and dress the dandelion leaves with it.

Chop the bread into small dice. Melt the butter in a frying pan or skillet and toast the croutons until golden. Drain on paper towels.

Scatter the croutons and chives over the salad and serve.

Cucumber Salad with Yoghurt Dressing

All regions

Preparation time:		10 minutes
Serves:		4

⅔ cup/5 oz	plain yoghurt	150 g
2 tbsp	vegetable stock	2 tbsp
1 tbsp	vinegar or lemon juice	1 tbsp
*	salt	*
*	sugar	*
1–2 tbsp	oil	1–2 tbsp
1 tbsp	finely chopped dill	1 tbsp
1	large cucumber	1

Mix the yoghurt with the stock and vinegar or lemon juice and season with salt and a pinch of sugar, then mix in the oil and dill.

Trim, peel and thinly slice the cucumber.

Shortly before serving, mix the dressing with the cucumber slices and let stand for a few minutes.

Salads

Coleslaw with Radish

Southern Germany

Preparation time:		15 minutes
Steeping time:		15 minutes
Serves:		4

1 lb 2 oz–1lb 5oz	white cabbage	500–600 g
1 tsp	salt	1 tsp
1 tsp	sugar	1 tsp
5	radishes	5
1	carrot	1
2 tbsp	white wine vinegar	2 tbsp
2 tbsp	oil	2 tbsp
1 tbsp	parsley, finely chopped	1 tbsp
¼–½ tsp	ground cumin	¼–½ tsp

Finely slice the cabbage, then sprinkle with the salt and sugar, lightly toss and let stand for 10–15 minutes.

Slice the radishes and carrot, then mix with the vinegar and oil, stir in the parsley and season with cumin. Let stand for 10–15 minutes, then adjust the seasoning if needed.

Carrot and Apple Slaw

All regions

Preparation time:		10 minutes
Steeping time:		10 minutes
Serves:		4

9 oz	sour apples	250 g
4 cups/1 lb 2 oz	grated carrots	500 g
½ cup/4 fl oz	orange juice	125 ml
1–2 tsp	lemon juice	1–2 tsp
1–2 tbsp	oil	1–2 tbsp
*	salt	*
*	freshly ground black pepper	*
1	pinch of sugar	1

Peel, quarter and core the apples. Coarsely grate and combine with the grated carrots in a bowl.

Mix the orange juice with the lemon juice and oil. Season with salt, pepper and the sugar.

Pour the dressing over the carrot and apple mixture and toss. Let stand for at least 10 minutes, then adjust the seasoning, if needed.

Salads

Red Coleslaw

Preparation time:		10 minutes
Steeping time:		10 minutes
Serves:		4

1 lb 5 oz	red cabbage	600 g
2 tbsp	lingonberry juice	2 tbsp
½ cup/3½ fl oz	fresh orange juice	100 ml
5 tbsp	red wine vinegar	5 tbsp
*	salt	*
*	freshly ground black pepper	*
1 tsp	sugar	1 tsp
4 tbsp	oil	4 tbsp

Finely slice the red cabbage. Put into a bowl and mix with the lingonberry and orange juices.

Mix the vinegar with a little salt, pepper, the sugar and the oil. Coat the cabbage well with the dressing. Let stand for at least 10 minutes, then adjust the seasoning with salt and pepper, if needed.

Bavarian Coleslaw

Preparation time:		20 minutes
Steeping time:		10 minutes
Serves:		4

1 lb 2 oz	young white cabbage	500 g
1 tbsp	icing (confectioners') sugar	1 tbsp
5 tbsp	red wine vinegar	5 tbsp
½ cup/4 fl oz	vegetable stock	125 ml
3 tbsp	oil	3 tbsp
*	salt	*
*	freshly ground black pepper	*
*	ground cumin	*
*	sugar	*
2 oz	smoked bacon rashers	50 g

Finely slice the cabbage. Put into a metal bowl and lightly season with salt.

Put the icing sugar into a frying pan or skillet over medium heat and lightly caramelise. Deglaze the pan with the vinegar and reduce by half. Add the stock and bring to a boil. Pour the hot liquid over the cabbage and mix well. Stir in 2 tbsp of oil and season with salt, pepper, a pinch of cumin and a little sugar. Let stand for 10 minutes.

Heat the remaining oil in a frying pan or skillet and fry the bacon over a low heat for 5 minutes until crispy. Drain the bacon on paper towels and crumble over the coleslaw.

Potato Salad

Northern Germany

Preparation time:		30 minutes
Cooking time:		25 minutes
Serves:		4

2 lbs 4 oz	waxy potatoes	1 kg
4	eggs	4
5 oz	cooked ham	150 g
3	large gherkins (dill pickles)	3
⅔ cup/3½ oz	fresh or frozen peas	100 g
4	spring onions (scallions)	4
1 cup/8 fl oz	hot meat stock	250 ml
6 tbsp	white wine vinegar	6 tbsp
*	salt	*
*	freshly ground black pepper	*
1	egg yolk	1
½ cup/ 4 fl oz	oil	125 ml
*	sweet paprika, to season	*
1–2 tbsp	chopped chives, watercress	1–2 tbsp

Wash the potatoes and boil for 20–25 minutes until tender in plenty of salted water in a large pan. Let them steam, then peel while still hot and cut into thin slices. Hard boil the eggs for 8–10 minutes, then refresh in iced water, let cool and peel.

Finely dice the ham, gherkins (dill pickles) and eggs. Blanch the peas for a few minutes in boiling salted water, then plunge into iced water. Clean and finely slice the spring onions (scallions).

Whisk the stock with 4 tbsp vinegar and season with salt and pepper. Pour the mixture over the combined salad ingredients. Mix well with salad servers and let stand for about 10 minutes.

Whisk the egg yolk constantly while adding the oil in a fine stream (this can be done more quickly in a blender or using a stick (immersion) blender). Season the resulting mayonnaise with salt, paprika and the remaining vinegar and add it to the potato salad. If necessary, add a little stock or gherkin (dill pickle) pickling liquid. Sprinkle with herbs and serve.

Potato Salad with Chicken Stock and Vinegar Dressing

Southern Germany

Preparation time:		30 minutes
Cooking time:		25 minutes
Serves:		4

For the salad:		
2 lbs 4 oz	potatoes	1 kg
½ tbsp	cumin seeds	½ tbsp
1	small onion	1
1 tbsp	oil	1 tbsp
2 tbsp	Beurre Noisette (p. 112)	2 tbsp
*	freshly ground black pepper	*
1–2 tbsp	finely chopped chives	1–2 tbsp

For the dressing:		
1¾ cups/14 fl oz	chicken stock	400 ml
3 tbsp	red wine vinegar	3 tbsp
1 tbsp	hot mustard	1 tbsp
*	salt	*
*	sugar	*

Wash the potatoes and boil until tender in plenty of salted water with the cumin in a large pan. Drain and, while still as hot as possible, cut each into 4–5 thick slices then put in a bowl.

For the dressing: Heat the stock, add the vinegar and mustard and season with salt and sugar. Add a handful of potato slices and blend with a stick (immersion) blender. Gradually mix this dressing into the rest of the potato slices to bind completely.

Peel and finely chop the onion. Heat the oil in a frying pan or skillet and sauté the onion over a low heat until translucent. Gently mix the onion and Beurre Noisette (p. 112) into the potato salad. It can be seasoned with pepper. Finally, mix in the chives.

Potato and Kale Salad

All regions

Preparation time:		25 minutes
Cooking time:		25 minutes
Serves:		4

2 lbs 4 oz	potatoes	1 kg
½ tbsp	cumin seeds	½ tbsp
1	small onion	1
2 tbsp	oil	2 tbsp
1¾ cups/14 fl oz	chicken or vegetable stock	400 ml
3 tbsp	red wine vinegar	3 tbsp
2 tbsp	oil	2 tbsp
*	salt	*
*	sugar	*
1 tbsp	hot mustard	1 tbsp
3 tbsp	Beurre Noisette (p. 112)	3 tbsp
5½ cups/14 oz	kale	400 g

Wash the potatoes and boil until tender in plenty of salted water with the cumin in a large pan. Drain and let steam briefly. Peel while still as hot as possible and cut into thin slices.

Peel and finely chop the onion. Heat 1 tbsp oil in a frying pan or skillet and sauté the onion over a low heat until translucent. Add the onion to the potatoes. Heat the stock, mix with the vinegar and oil and season with salt and a pinch of sugar. Add the mustard. Transfer the mixture to a bowl. Mix in a handful of potato slices. Then gradually mix in the remaining potato slices until the liquid is fully mixed in. Finally, mix in the Beurre Noisette (p. 112).

Wash the kale, pluck the leaves from the stems and blanch in boiling salted water for 3–4 minutes. Drain the blanching water, plunge in iced water and let drain. Squeeze the leaves well to remove as much water as possible and cut into small pieces. Mix into the potato salad. Adjust the seasoning if needed.

Asparagus Salad

All regions

Preparation time:		15 minutes
Cooking time:		10 minutes
Serves:		4

For the salad:		
2 cups/9 oz	white asparagus spears	250 g
2 cups/9 oz	green asparagus spears	250 g
2	carrots	2
1	bunch spring onions (scallions)	1
¾ cup/7 fl oz	vegetable stock	200 ml
2	tomatoes	2

For the dressing:		
2 tbsp	tarragon vinegar	2 tbsp
1 tsp	Dijon mustard	1 tsp
*	sugar	*
*	salt	*
2 tbsp	olive oil	2 tbsp
2 tbsp	rapeseed oil	2 tbsp
1 tbsp	finely chopped chives	1 tbsp
1 tbsp	finely chopped parsley	1 tbsp
a few	small basil leaves	a few

For the salad: Peel the white asparagus spears. Wash the green asparagus spears and peel only the bottom third. Remove any woody ends from the spears. Halve the spears lengthwise and cut diagonally into lengths of about 5 cm (2 inches). Trim, wash and quarter the carrots lengthwise. Trim and wash the spring onions. Cut both carrots and spring onions diagonally into lengths of about 5 cm (2 inches).

Combine the asparagus and carrots with the stock in a pan, cover with a lid and simmer for about 10 minutes. After 5 minutes, add the spring onions and cook together. Drain the vegetables in a colander and reserve the stock.

Measure out 120 ml (½ cup/4 fl oz) stock and set aside.

Cut a cross in the base of the tomatoes, blanch in boiling water for 3 minutes then plunge into iced water and peel. Quarter, de-seed and finely dice the tomatoes.

For the dressing: Use a stick (immersion) blender to blend the set-aside stock with the vinegar, mustard, a pinch each of sugar and salt. Gradually mix in the two oils. Mix the lukewarm vegetables with the dressing and diced tomatoes. Mix in the chives, parsley and basil.

Beef Salad

Preparation time:		20 minutes
Cooking time:		10 minutes
Serves:		4

1 tsp	icing (confectioners) sugar	1 tsp
4–5 tbsp	cider vinegar	4–5 tbsp
¾ cup/7 fl oz	beef stock	200 ml
2–3 tbsp	oil	2–3 tbsp
*	salt	*
*	freshly ground black pepper	*
*	sugar	*
2	shallots	2
¾ cup/3½ oz	Romano (flat) beans	100 g
½ cup/2 oz	canned haricot beans	50 g
1	small red apple	1
*	dried savory	*
1 lb 2 oz	cooked beef brisket (p.74)	500 g

Lightly caramelise the icing sugar in a small pan over a medium heat. Deglaze the pan with the vinegar and stock and let it cool to lukewarm. Combine the liquid from the pan with the oil in a measuring jug and blend with a stick (immersion) blender. Season the dressing with salt, pepper and a pinch of sugar.

Peel and finely chop the shallots and blanch in boiling salted water for 1–2 minutes. Drain, plunge into iced water and drain again. Then mix the shallots into the dressing.

Trim and wash the Romano beans, then cut diagonally into 1.5-cm (¾-inch) lengths. Cook in heavily salted boiling water until tender but firm to the bite. Then drain off the blanching water in a colander, plunge into iced water and drain. Drain the haricot beans in a sieve, wash under cold running water and let drain. Wash, quarter and core the apple, then cut into 5–10 mm (¼–½ inch) dice.

Mix the beans and apple in a bowl with a quarter of the dressing. Season with a pinch of savory and adjust the seasoning with salt, pepper and sugar.

Take the cooked beef brisket used to make the Clear Beef Broth (p.74) out of the cooking liquid, trim off the fat if necessary and cut across the grain into thin slices. Serve the beef slices with the bean and apple salad on warmed plates and drizzle with the rest of the dressing.

Potato Salad with Sour Cream

Preparation time:		40 minutes
Cooking time:		10 minutes
Serves:		4

For the salad:		
2 lbs 4 oz	waxy potatoes	1 kg
*	salt	*
1	small onion	1
1	cucumber	1
6	radishes	6

For the dressing:		
1¼ cups/10½ fl oz	chicken broth	300 ml*
2 tbsp	white wine vinegar	2 tbsp
1-2 tsp	hot mustard	1-2 tsp*
*	sugar	*
2 tbsp	Beurre Noisette (p.112)	2 tbsp
⅓ cup/3½ oz	sour cream	100 g
2 tbsp	finely chopped chives	2 tbsp

For the salad: Boil the potatoes in their skins in salted water until tender. Drain and let steam briefly. Peel while still as hot as possible, slice, and put into a bowl.

Peel and mince the onion. Cook in a frying pan or skillet with 100 ml (⅓ cup/3½ fl oz) water until soft and the liquid evaporates completely. Peel the cucumbers, trim and wash the radishes, and cut into thin rounds.

For the dressing: Heat the broth, put into a mixing beaker, and stir in the vinegar and mustard. Season with salt and a pinch of sugar, add a handful of potato slices, and blend with a stick (immersion) blender.

Gradually mix this dressing into the rest of the potato slices to bind, until the liquid is evenly distributed. Stir in the sour cream until smooth. Mix the Beurre Noisette, (p. 112) onion, cucumbers, radishes and chives into the salad.

Bean Salad with Crayfish

Westphalia

Preparation time:		25 minutes
Cooking time:		20 minutes
Serves:		4

1⅓ cups/7 oz	yellow wax beans	200 g
1⅓ cups/7 oz	green beans	200 g
1	onion	1
4 tbsp	oil	4 tbsp
*	salt	*
*	freshly ground black pepper	*
1 tsp	finely chopped savory	1 tsp
1–2 tbsp	red wine vinegar	1–2 tbsp
20	crayfish tails, boiled	20
*	crayfish tail cooking liquid	*

Cut off the stems and tips of the beans, de-stringing if necessary and cut into large, uniform pieces. Boil the beans in salted water for about 7 minutes. Drain in a colander and immediately plunge into iced water to preserve their colour.

Peel and finely chop the onion. Heat 1 tbsp oil in a frying pan or skillet and sauté the onion until translucent. Season with salt and pepper.

Combine the savory leaves with the onion in a bowl. Add the vinegar and remaining oil, mix well and season with salt and pepper. Pour the dressing over the beans and mix well. Let stand for at least 15 minutes.

Reheat the crayfish tails in a little of the reserved cooking liquid. Divide the bean salad between four plates and arrange the crayfish tails on top.

Herring and Beetroot (Beet) Salad

Northern Germany

Preparation time:		15 minutes
Cooking time:		1 hour
Serves:		4

7 oz	beetroot (beets)	200 g
*	cumin seeds	*
1	apple	1
1	small onion	1
1	Pickled Cucumber (p. 29)	1
8	pickled herring fillets	8
¾ cup/7 oz	sour cream	200 g
1 tbsp	creamed horseradish	1 tbsp
1	pinch lemon zest	1
1 tbsp	cucumber pickling liquid	1 tbsp
*	salt	*
*	freshly ground pepper	*
*	sugar	*

It is quicker to use pre-cooked vacuum-packed beetroot (beets), but if you're using fresh, wash if necessary and cut off the leaves carefully, without damaging the root. Boil in salted water with a pinch of cumin seeds until tender, about 1 hour. Let cool a little, then peel, quarter and dice.

Peel, quarter and core the apple and cut into 5-mm (¼-inch) thick slices or dice. Peel and finely chop the onion. Dice the Pickled Cucumber (p. 29). Drain the herring fillets and cut into 15–20 mm (½–¾ inch) lengths.

Mix the sour cream with the horseradish, lemon zest and pickling liquid and season with salt, pepper and a pinch of sugar.

Mix the beetroot (beets), apple, onion, pickle and herring with the sour cream. Adjust the seasoning if needed, then serve.

Prawn (Shrimp) Salad

Northern Germany

Preparation time:		15 minutes
Cooking time:		10 minutes
Serves:		4

1	egg	1
1 × 1 oz	Pickled Cucumber (p. 29)	1 × 30 g
1	onion	1
⅓ cup/3 fl oz	vegetable stock	80 ml
3½ oz	bacon rashers	100 g
1 tbsp	oil	1 tbsp
1¾ cups/14 oz	sour cream	400 g
¾ cup/9 oz	cooked prawns (shrimp)	250 g
1–2 tbsp	finely chopped chives	1–2 tbsp
1 tsp	hot mustard	1 tsp
*	salt	*
*	freshly ground black pepper	*
*	pumpernickel bread or toast	*

Hard-boil the egg for about 10 minutes, then refresh in iced water, peel and finely chop. Peel and finely chop the Pickled Cucumber (p. 29). Peel and finely chop the onion and cook in the stock until soft and the liquid has completely evaporated.

Finely dice the bacon. Heat the oil in a frying pan or skillet and fry the bacon, then drain it on paper towels.

Mix the sour cream with the shrimp, chopped egg, diced Pickled Cucumber (p. 29), onions, bacon, chives and mustard. Season with plenty of salt and pepper. The shrimp salad can be served with a few slices of pumpernickel or toast.

Egg Salad

All regions

Preparation time:		20 minutes
Cooking time:		15 minutes
Serves:		4

For the dressing:		
1	fresh egg yolk	1
½–1 tsp	hot mustard	½–1 tsp
1 tbsp	white wine vinegar	1 tbsp
1	pinch of finely chopped garlic	1
*	salt	*
*	sugar	*
⅓ cup/2½ fl oz	oil	75 ml
¼ cup/2 fl oz	vegetable stock	50 ml
¼ cup/2 fl oz	single (light) cream	50 ml

For the salad:		
6	eggs	6
1 tbsp	oil	1 tbsp
4 slices	bacon	4 slices
2 trays	garden cress	2 punnets
1	handful mixed sprouts	1

For the dressing: Combine the egg yolk, mustard, vinegar and garlic with a pinch of salt and sugar in a blender. Blend on a low speed while adding the oil in a thin stream until thick and smooth. Mix in the stock and cream and season the dressing.

For the salad: Hard-boil the eggs for 10 minutes then plunge into iced water, then peel and quarter. Heat the oil in a frying pan or skillet and slowly fry the bacon on both sides over a medium heat until crispy. Drain on paper towels and cut into strips.

Cut the cress tips, wash and pat dry. Put the sprouts into a sieve, wash and drain. Put the dressing into a deep plate. Mix the cress with the sprouts and arrange in the middle of the plate. Arrange the egg quarters around the salad and scatter the bacon over the top.

Ox Cheek Salad

Southern Germany

Preparation time:		15 minutes
Serves:		4
2	small shallots, peeled	2
⅓ cup/3 fl oz	vegetable stock	80 ml
1–2 tbsp	mild white wine vinegar	1–2 tbsp
½ tsp	Dijon mustard	½ tsp
1	pinch of sugar	1
4 tbsp	light vegetable oil	4 tbsp
14 oz	salted, cooked and pressed ox cheeks	400 g
6	radishes	6
4–6	gherkins (dill pickles)	4–6
2 tbsp	finely chopped chives	2 tbsp

Peel and finely chop the shallots. Mix the stock with the vinegar and mustard in a bowl, season with a pinch of sugar and mix in the oil thoroughly. Add the shallots.

Cut the ox cheek into thin slices and then into 2–3 cm (1–1½ inch) wide strips. Mix with half of the shallot dressing and let stand for a while.

Trim, wash and thinly slice the radishes. Thinly slice the pickles.

Mix the ox cheek with the radishes, pickles and chives and adjust the seasoning if needed.

Bavarian Sausage Salad

Bavaria

Preparation time:		10 minutes
Steeping time:		20 minutes
Serves:		4
1 lb 2 oz	cooked pork sausage	500 g
2	red onions	2
4	gherkins (dill pickles)	4
2 tbsp	sunflower or rapeseed oil	2 tbsp
⅔ cup/5 fl oz	white wine vinegar	150 ml
1	pinch of sugar	1
*	salt	*
*	freshly ground black pepper	*
3 tbsp	chopped chives, to serve	3 tbsp
*	Bavarian Soft Pretzels (p. 50)	*

Remove the skins from the sausages and cut into thin slices. The sausages can also be cut into strips. Peel the onions and cut into thin rings. Thinly slice the gherkins (dill pickles). Mix the sausage, onions and gherkins (dill pickles) together in a bowl.

Mix the oil with 300 ml (1⅓ cups/10½ fl oz) of water, the vinegar and a pinch of sugar. Season well with salt and pepper. Pour the dressing over the sausage mixture, mix well and refrigerate for about 20 minutes. Sprinkle with the chives before serving. Accompany with Bavarian Soft Pretzels (p. 50).

Sausage Salad

All regions

Preparation time:		10 minutes
Serves:		4

14 oz	cooked pork sausage	400 g
9 oz	gherkins (dill pickles)	250 g
¾ cup/7 oz	mayonnaise or salad cream	200 g
1–2 tsp	Dijon mustard	1–2 tsp
3 tbsp	gherkin pickling liquid	3 tbsp
*	salt	*
*	freshly ground black pepper	*
*	sugar	*
2 tbsp	finely chopped chives	2 tbsp

Remove the skins from the sausages and cut into long and thin strips. Do the same with the gherkins (dill pickles).

Mix the mayonnaise with the mustard and pickling liquid from the gherkins (dill pickles) jar until smooth and season with salt, pepper and a pinch of sugar. Mix in the sausage and gherkin (dill pickle) strips and chives.

Baden-Style Sausage Salad

Baden-Württemberg

Preparation time:		10 minutes
Steeping time:		10 minutes
Serves:		4

12 oz	veal lyoner or pork sausage	350 g
5 oz	Allgäuer Bergkäse cheese	150 g
1	large red onion	1
1	Pickled Cucumber (p. 29)	1
2 tbsp	cucumber pickling liquid	2 tbsp
3 tbsp	white wine vinegar	3 tbsp
2 tbsp	oil	2 tbsp
*	salt	*
*	freshly ground black pepper	*
*	sugar	*
*	farmhouse bread, to serve	*

Remove the skins from the sausages and cut into about 3 mm (⅛ inch) slices and then into about 5-mm (¼-inch)–wide strips. Do the same with the cheese. Peel the onion and cut into thin rings. Finely dice the Pickled Cucumber (p. 29).

For the dressing: Mix the pickling liquid with 150 ml (⅔ cup/5 fl oz) water, the vinegar and oil and season well with salt, pepper and sugar. Add the sausage, cheese, onion and Pickled Cucumber (p. 29) and coat with the dressing. Let stand for 10 minutes and adjust the seasoning if needed. Serve with farmhouse bread.

Clear Beef Broth

All regions

Preparation time:		10 minutes
Cooking time:		2 hours 30 minutes
Serves:		4

2 lbs 8 oz	beef brisket	1.2 kg
1–2 tbsp	oil, for frying	1–2 tbsp
2	onions	2
1	carrot	1
5 oz	celeriac	150 g
3½ oz	leeks	100 g
1	bay leaf	1
3	juniper berries	3
½ tsp	peppercorns	½ tsp
1 strip	unwaxed lemon zest	1 strip
5	parsley stems	5
1	small lovage leaf	1
2	garlic slices	2
*	salt	*

Sear the brisket all over in a frying pan or skillet over a medium heat. Transfer to a large pan and add 3 litres (12½ cups/100 fl oz) water, covering the meat completely. Simmer the meat for about 3 hours until soft, skimming regularly.

Meanwhile, peel the onions and add the skins to the pan. Trim and peel the carrot and celeriac and cut, together with the onions, into chunks about 1.5 cm (¾ inch). Trim and halve the leeks lengthwise, then wash and cut across into 1.5-cm (¾-inch) lengths. After 2¼–2½ hours of cooking, add the onions, carrot, celeriac, bay leaf, juniper berries and peppercorns to the meat. Add the leeks 15 minutes before the meat finishes cooking.

Take out the meat (cut into thin slices for later use in Beef Salad, p. 65) and carefully filter the broth through a fine sieve into a clean pan. Add the lemon zest, parsley stems, lovage and garlic and infuse for a few minutes, remove, and season the broth with salt. The carrots and celeriac chunks can be added as a garnish.

Clear Chicken Broth

All regions

Preparation time:		15 minutes
Cooking time:		1 hour 30 minutes
Serves:		4

1 × 2¼–2½ lbs	stewing chicken	1 × 1–1.2-kg
*	salt	*
1	carrot	1
1	leek	1
3½ oz	celeriac	100 g
1	onion	1
1	garlic clove	1
½	bunch parsley	½
1	sprig thyme	1
1 tsp	peppercorns	1 tsp
1	bay leaf	1
*	freshly ground pepper	*
*	freshly grated nutmeg	*

Thoroughly rinse the chicken inside and out in cold water. Remove the parson's nose (tail). Put the chicken into a large pan with around 3 litres (12½ cups/100 fl oz) water and bring to a boil, skimming regularly. Add 1 tablespoon salt and simmer for 1 hour.

Wash and cut the carrot, leek and celeriac into small dice. Peel the onion and garlic. Quarter the onion and leave the garlic whole. Add the vegetables, parsley and thyme to the pan. Add the peppercorns and bay leaf. Simmer for 30–40 more minutes.

Take out the chicken and carefully filter the broth through a fine sieve into a clean pan. Season the broth with salt, pepper and nutmeg. Remove the skin from the chicken, then debone and cut the meat into small pieces. The meat can be used as a garnish.

Soup Garnish: Soup Pearls (Backerbsen)

Southern Germany

Preparation time:		20 minutes
Cooking time:		5 minutes
Serves:		4

½ cups/4 fl oz	milk	125 ml
2 tbsp/1 oz	butter	25 g
⅔ cup/2¾ oz	plain (all-purpose) flour	75 g
2	eggs	2
*	oil, for deep-frying	*
*	salt	*

To make this, you will need a spätzle maker; see p. 438 in the glossary.

Combine the milk with the butter and a pinch of salt in a pan and bring to a boil over a medium heat. Add the flour and stir constantly with a wooden spoon until the mixture clumps and a white layer forms on the bottom of the pan.

Remove the pan from the heat and transfer the paste to a bowl. Mix in the first egg until smooth. Add the second egg and mix to a smooth dough.

Heat plenty of oil in a pan to 170°C/350°F. Use the spätzle maker (p. 438) to make and carefully drop the pearls into the hot oil and deep-fry until golden brown, about 3 minutes. Take them out of the pan with a slotted spoon or skimmer and drain on paper towels.

Soup Garnish: Veal Dumplings

Southern Germany

Preparation time:		20 minutes
Cooking time:		10 minutes
Serves:		4

5 oz	finely minced (ground) veal	150 g
3 tbsp	single (light) cream	3 tbsp
1 pinch	unwaxed lemon zest	1 pinch
*	freshly grated nutmeg	*
½–1 tbsp	finely chopped parsley	½–1 tbsp
*	salt	*

Combine the minced veal with the cream in a bowl and mix until smooth. Season with lemon zest, nutmeg and parsley.

Bring salted water to a boil in a pan and remove from the heat. Use two wet teaspoons to form small dumplings from the mixture and drop into the water at 90°C/200°F. Place the pan over low heat and simmer for about 10 minutes.

Keep the dumplings warm in the salted water until it's time to serve, then take them out of the water and add to the hot broth.

Soup Garnish: Butter Dumplings

Bavaria

Preparation time:		35 minutes
Cooking time:		12 hours
Serves:		4

3 oz	bread, crusts removed	90 g
4½ tbsp/2¼ oz	soft butter	60 g
1	egg yolk	1
1	egg	1
2 tbsp	semolina	2 tbsp
1 tsp	plain (all-purpose) flour	1 tsp
*	salt	*
*	freshly grated nutmeg	*
1	bay leaf	1
2	garlic slices	2
3	parsley stems	3

The day before cooking, blitz the bread in a blender, spread the crumbs over a flat plate and let dry overnight. The following day, beat the butter until fluffy. Gradually add in the egg yolk and the whole egg. Mix the semolina with the flour and breadcrumbs and stir into the butter mixture. Season with salt and nutmeg. Let stand for 10 minutes.

Bring salted water to a boil in a pan with the bay leaf. Add the garlic and parsley stems. Use two wet teaspoons to shape the mixture into small dumplings and drop them into the water. Simmer the dumplings for about 15 minutes, until they float to the surface. Serve the dumplings in a clear broth.

Soup Garnish: Cheese Diamonds

Bavaria

Preparation time:		15 minutes
Cooking time:		15 minutes
Serves:		4

½ cup/2 oz	plain (all-purpose) flour	50 g
*	baking powder	*
3½ oz	Emmental or Bergkäse cheese	100 g
2 oz	soft butter	50 g
4	egg yolks	4
*	freshly ground black pepper	*
*	freshly grated nutmeg	*
¼ cup/2 fl oz	single (light) cream	50 ml
4	egg whites	4
*	salt	*

Preheat the oven to 180°C/350°F/Gas Mark 4 and line a baking tray, about 20 × 30 cm (8 × 12 inches), with baking paper. Mix the flour with a pinch of baking powder and sift. Cut the cheese into small dice.

Beat the butter until fluffy and add in the egg yolks one at a time. Season the mixture with pepper and a pinch of nutmeg and beat until light and fluffy. Gradually add in the cream. Beat the egg whites, with a pinch of salt, into soft peaks. Fold the beaten egg whites and flour into the butter mixture.

Spread the batter in the baking tray in a 5–10 mm (¼–½ inch) thick layer and cover evenly with the cheese dice. Put the tray on the middle shelf of the oven and bake until golden, about 15 minutes. Let cool a little, then cut into 15–20 mm (¾–1 inch) diamond shapes.

Soups, Stews & Sauces

Soup Garnish: Pancake Strips

Southern Germany

Preparation time:		35 minutes
Cooking time:		15 minutes
Serves:		4

2	eggs	2
⅔ cup/2¾ oz	plain (all-purpose) flour	70 g
¾ cup/6 fl oz	milk	170 ml
3–4 tbsp	melted butter, lukewarm	3–4 tbsp
1 tbsp	finely chopped parsley	1 tbsp
*	salt	*
*	freshly ground black pepper	*
*	freshly grated nutmeg	*
*	butter, for frying	*

Beat the eggs in a bowl, add the flour and mix thoroughly. Gradually stir in the milk and work into a smooth batter. Stir in the melted butter and finely chopped parsley and season the batter with salt, pepper and a pinch of nutmeg. Cover the batter and rest for 30 minutes.

Melt some butter in a frying pan or skillet over a low heat. Use a small ladle to pour in some batter and spread thinly by tilting the pan. Turn the pancake over when the underside is golden. Cook the other side the same way and take the pancake out of the pan. Do the same with the remaining batter and stack the finished pancakes to prevent them drying out. Immediately before serving, roll them up and cut into thin strips no wider than 5 mm (¼ inch) and serve in a clear broth.

Soup Garnish: Farina Dumplings

Southern Germany

Preparation time:		1 hour 25 minutes
Cooking time:		15 minutes
Serves:		4

4 tbsp/2 oz	soft butter	50 g
1	egg, at room temperature	1
⅔ cup/3 oz	farina	80 g
*	salt	*
*	freshly grated nutmeg	*

Beat the butter until light and fluffy, add the egg and mix until smooth. Stir in the farina and season with salt and nutmeg. Rest the mixture for at least 1 hour at room temperature, to swell.

Bring salted water to a boil in a pan. Use two wet teaspoons to shape the mixture into uniform dumplings. Dip the spoons in hot water between making each dumpling.

Simmer the dumplings in the salted water for about 15 minutes. Take them out of the water with a slotted spoon or skimmer and serve in deep plates in clear broth.

Soup Garnish: Liver Dumplings

Rhineland-Palatinate and Bavaria

Preparation time:		20 minutes
Cooking time:		8 minutes
Serves:		4

½	onion	½
1 tbsp	oil	1 tbsp
9 oz	bread, crusts removed	250 g
1	egg	1
1	egg yolk	1
1 tsp	hot mustard	1 tsp
11 oz	minced (ground) calves' liver	300 g
*	dried marjoram	*
*	salt	*
*	freshly ground black pepper	*
*	freshly grated nutmeg	*
1	pinch grated lemon zest	1
1 tbsp	finely chopped parsley	1 tbsp
1	bay leaf	1
1	strip lemon zest	1

Peel and finely chop the onion. Heat the oil in a frying pan or skillet and sauté the onion over a moderate heat until translucent. Cut the bread into 5–10-mm (¼–½-inch) cubes.

Mix the whole egg, egg yolk and mustard with the minced liver. Add the bread, onion, a pinch of marjoram, salt, pepper, nutmeg, grated lemon zest and parsley and mix well. Wet your hands and shape the mixture into 8 dumplings.

Bring plenty of salted water to a boil in a pan. Add the bay leaf and the lemon zest strip. Simmer the dumplings in the salted water for 8 minutes. Take them out of the pan with a slotted spoon or skimmer and drain on paper towels. Serve the dumplings in a clear broth.

Soup Garnish: Liver Spätzle

Bavaria

Preparation time:		20 minutes
Cooking time:		5 minutes
Serves:		4

¼	onion	¼
1 tsp	oil	1 tsp
1½ oz	soft butter	40 g
1	egg, separated	1
¼ cup/1¼ oz	white breadcrumbs	30 g
2 tbsp	corn flour	2 tbsp
3½ oz	calves' liver	100 g
1 tbsp	finely chopped parsley	1 tbsp
*	salt	*
*	freshly ground black pepper	*
½ tsp	grated lemon zest	½ tsp
1	pinch dried marjoram	1

To make this, you will need a spätzle maker; see p. 438 in the glossary.

Peel and finely chop the onion. Heat the oil in a frying pan or skillet and sauté the onion over a moderate heat until translucent.

Beat the butter until fluffy and add in the egg yolk. Add the egg white, breadcrumbs and flour and mix well. Add the onion, finely chop the liver, then add with the parsley. Season the dumpling dough with salt, pepper, lemon zest and a pinch of marjoram.

Bring plenty of salted water to a boil in a pan. Briefly immerse a spätzle maker in the boiling water, fill with the dough and slide the box from side to side, dropping the dumplings into the water. When the dumplings float to the surface, cook briefly and then remove with a slotted spoon or skimmer.

Hearty Chicken Soup

All regions

Preparation time:		20 minutes
Cooking time:		1 hour
Serves:		4

1	onion	1
3 lbs 5 oz	chicken legs	1.5 kg
2	celery stalks	2
1	carrot	1
1	parsnip	1
1	thin leek	1
1–2 tbsp	dried mushrooms	1–2 tbsp
2 oz	fresh mushrooms	50 g
1	bay leaf	1
1 tsp	peppercorns	1 tsp
4	allspice berries	4
*	salt	*
*	freshly grated nutmeg	*
4 tsp	medium sherry	4 tsp
*	finely chopped chives	*

Peel the onion and set both it and its skin aside. Wash and pat dry the chicken legs.

Bring 2.5 litres (10 cups/85 fl oz) water to a boil in a large pan, add the chicken legs and onion skins and simmer for 1 hour, skimming regularly.

Meanwhile, trim, wash and slice the celery stalks. Trim and peel the carrot and parsnip and halve lengthwise. Quarter the onion. Trim, halve lengthwise and wash the leek. Add the prepared vegetables, mushrooms, bay leaf, peppercorns and allspice to the meat after about 30 minutes of cooking.

Take the chicken legs out of the pot and remove the skin. Remove the flesh from the bones and cut into small pieces. Filter the broth through a fine sieve or sieve lined with a paper towel into a clean pan. Season the broth with salt. Take the carrot, parsnip and celery out of the sieve and cut into small pieces. Discard the mushrooms, onion, leek and spices.

To serve, grate a little nutmeg into warmed soup plates and add the vegetable and chicken pieces. Pour the hot broth into the plates and add 1 tsp sherry to each plate. The soup can also be garnished with finely chopped chives.

German Wedding Soup with Royale

Northern Germany and Westphalia

Preparation time:		45 minutes
Cooking time:		3 hours 15 minutes
Serves:		4

For the broth:		
1 lb 12 oz	beef, silverside or brisket	800 g
1 tsp	oil, for frying	1 tsp
*	salt	*
1	tomato	1
3	onions	3
4 oz	celeriac	120 g
1	carrot	1
1	parsnip	1
½	leek	½
1	bay leaf	1
1 tsp	peppercorns	1 tsp
3	juniper berries	3
1–2	parsley stems	1–2
2	lovage leaves	2
1	strip unwaxed lemon zest	1
9 oz	white asparagus	250 g
⅔ cup/3½ oz	frozen peas	100 g

For the royale:		
2	egg yolks	2
2	eggs	2
¾ cup/6 fl oz	milk	175 ml
*	grated nutmeg	*
*	butter, for greasing	*

For the dumplings:		
3½ oz	white bread, crust removed	100 g
2	eggs	2
3½ oz	beef bone marrow	100 g
*	freshly ground black pepper	*
*	freshly grated nutmeg	*

For the broth: Sear the meat in oil over a medium heat. Bring 3 litres (12½ cups/100 fl oz) water to a boil and add the meat and season. Cover and simmer for 3 hours, skimming regularly. Meanwhile, quarter and deseed the tomatoes and quarter the onions. Peel the rest of the vegetables, add after 2 hours. Add the leek and aromatics after a further 30 minutes. Finally, add the herbs and zest.

For the royale: Mix the eggs with the milk, salt and nutmeg. Brush a 20 × 15-cm (8 × 6 inch) ovenproof dish with butter. Fill with the mixture and cover with foil. Fill a roasting pan with 2 cm (1 inch) of hot water and heat to 80°C/175°F on the stove. Put the dish inside the pan. Leave to set, about 45 minutes. Remove from the dish.

For the dumplings: Cube the bread. Combine the eggs, marrow and bread in a bowl and season with salt, pepper and nutmeg. Mix thoroughly then mince. Chill for 30 minutes, then shape into small dumplings.

Roughly chop the asparagus. Remove the meat and vegetables from the broth. Dice everything except the tomato. Sieve the broth, season and return the meat and vegetables to the pan. Reheat with the asparagus for 15 minutes. After 5 minutes, add the dumplings and after 10 minutes add the peas. Cut the custard into discs and add to the soup.

Soups, Stews & Sauces

Clear Oxtail Soup

Preparation time:	20 minutes
Cooking time:	4 hours
Serves:	4

2 tbsp	oil	2 tbsp
2 lbs 3 oz	oxtail, cut and ready to cook	1 kg
1 lb 2 oz	beef shin (shank), ready to cook	500 g
3 tbsp	madeira	3 tbsp
12 cups/100 fl oz	vegetable or beef stock	3 litres
1	onion	1
½	carrot	½
3 oz	celeriac	80 g
¼	leek	¼
1	tomato	1
5	juniper berries	5
½ tsp	yellow mustard seeds	½ tsp
5	allspice berries	5
1 tsp	peppercorns	1 tsp
1 tsp	dried thyme	1 tsp
1	bay leaf	1
1	clove	1
*	salt	*
1	pinch of freshly grated nutmeg	1
1 dash	sherry	1 dash
1 tbsp	finely chopped chives	1 tbsp

Heat the oil in a large casserole (Dutch oven) and brown the oxtail and beef shin (shank) on all sides over a medium heat. Deglaze with the madeira and add the stock, covering the meat and bones well. Let simmer for about 4 hours until the meat is soft, skimming off the scum and fat regularly.

Meanwhile, peel the onion, carrot and celeriac and trim and wash the leek. Cut all the vegetables into pieces. Wash and halve the tomato. Fill a spice bag with the herbs and spices, close the bag, then add to the stock together with the vegetables 1 hour before the meat finishes cooking.

Take out the cooked oxtail and let cool a little. Remove the meat from the bones. Remove the beef, carefully filter the stock through a sieve lined with a paper towel into a clean pan and then return the beef to the stock to keep warm.

Heat a sufficient amount of stock and season with salt, a pinch of nutmeg and the sherry. Cut the beef into thin slices and arrange with the oxtail meat in warmed, soup plates. Sprinkle with finely chopped chives and pour the stock over everything.

Herb Soup

Preparation time:	15 minutes
Cooking time:	25 minutes
Serves:	4

For the herb pesto:		
⅔ cup/2 oz	baby spinach	50 g
⅔ cup/2 oz	parsley leaves	50 g
*	salt	*
¾ cup/3½ oz	basil, dill, mint, wild garlic	100 g
⅓ cup/3–3½ fl oz	cold vegetable stock	80–100 ml
1	garlic clove	1
1 tsp	grated lemon zest	1 tsp
a few drops	lemon juice	a few drops

For the soup:		
1	onion	1
2½ oz	potato	70 g
4 cups/34 fl oz	chicken stock	1 litre
¾ cup/7 fl oz	single (light) cream	200 ml
1	slice white bread	1
1–2 tsp	Beurre Noisette (p. 112)	1–2 tsp
*	salt	*
1 oz	cold butter	30 g
*	freshly grated nutmeg	*
*	fresh herbs, to serve, optional	*

For the herb pesto: Sort and wash the spinach and parsley leaves. Blanch in boiling salted water for 3 minutes. Drain in a sieve, plunge into iced water and drain again. Squeeze the leaves well with your hands, then finely chop. Wash, shake dry and finely chop the assorted herb leaves.

Combine the spinach, parsley and fresh herbs in a measuring jug. Add the vegetable stock, garlic and lemon zest and juice then finely purée with a stick (immersion) blender.

For the soup: Peel the onion and potato and cut into small dice. Put the onion and potato dice into a pan, add the stock and simmer for 25 minutes. Add the cream and blend with a stick (immersion) blender.

Cut the bread into 1-cm (½-inch) cubes and toast all over a medium heat until golden in a frying pan or skillet with the Beurre Noisette (p. 112). Season with salt.

Shortly before serving, add the herb pesto and butter to the soup and blend using a stick (immersion) blender. Season the soup with salt and a little nutmeg, pour into warmed soup plates and sprinkle with croutons. The soup can be served garnished with fresh herbs.

Wild Garlic Soup

Southern Germany

Preparation time:		10 minutes
Cooking time:		30 minutes
Serves:		4

1⅓ cups/3½ oz	baby spinach	100 g
1⅓ cups/3½ oz	wild garlic leaves	100 g
1	onion	1
2½ oz	potato	70g
1 oz	cold butter	30 g
4 cups/34 fl oz	chicken stock	1 litre
¾ cup/7 fl oz	single (light) cream	200 ml
1	strip lemon zest	1
1	garlic clove	1
*	salt	*
*	freshly ground black pepper	*
*	freshly grated nutmeg	*

Sort and wash the spinach leaves. Blanch in boiling salted water for 3 minutes. Drain in a sieve, plunge into iced water and drain again. Squeeze the leaves well with your hands, then finely chop.

Wash and shake dry the wild garlic, then remove the stems and finely chop. Peel the onion and potato and cut into small dice.

Melt 1 tablespoon butter in a pan and sauté the onion and potato dice over a low heat until translucent. Add the stock and simmer for 25 minutes. Add the cream and blend with a stick (immersion) blender. Add the lemon zest, let it infuse for a few minutes, then remove.

Peel and slice the garlic. Shortly before serving, add the spinach, wild garlic, sliced garlic and the remaining butter to the soup and blend using a stick (immersion) blender. Season with salt, pepper and a little nutmeg. Serve immediately in warmed soup plates.

Chervil Soup

All regions

Preparation time:		10 minutes
Cooking time:		30 minutes
Serves:		4

1⅓ cups/3½ oz	baby spinach	100 g
1⅓ cups/3½ oz	chervil leaves	100 g
1	onion	1
2½ oz	potato	70g
1 oz	cold butter	30 g
4 cups/34 fl oz	chicken stock	1 litre
¾ cup/7 fl oz	single (light) cream	200g
1	strip lemon zest	1
1	garlic clove	1
*	salt	*
*	freshly grated nutmeg	*

Sort and wash the spinach leaves. Blanch in boiling salted water for 3 minutes. Drain in a colander, plunge into iced water and drain again. Squeeze the leaves well with your hands, then finely chop. Wash, shake dry and finely chop the chervil. Peel the onion and potato and cut into small dice.

Melt 1 tablespoon butter in a pan and sauté the onion and potato dice over a low heat until translucent. Add the stock and simmer for 25 minutes. Add the cream and blend with a stick (immersion) blender. Add the lemon zest, let it infuse for a few minutes, then remove.

Peel and slice the garlic. Shortly before serving, add the spinach, chervil, sliced garlic and the remaining butter to the soup and blend using a stick (immersion) blender. Season with salt and a little nutmeg. Serve immediately in warmed soup plates.

Sorrel Soup

East Prussia and
Northeastern Germany

Preparation time:		15 minutes
Cooking time:		10 minutes
Serves:		4

2⅔ cups/7 oz	baby spinach	200 g
2	shallots	2
1	garlic clove	1
2 oz	butter	60 g
2 cups/18 fl oz	vegetable or veal stock	500 ml
½ cup/4 fl oz	single (light) cream	125 ml
*	salt	*
*	freshly ground black pepper	*
*	freshly grated nutmeg	*
1⅓ cups/3½ oz	sorrel	100 g

Sort, wash and thoroughly drain the spinach leaves, remove the stems and cut the leaves into thin strips. Peel and finely chop the shallots and garlic.

Sauté the shallots and garlic in the melted butter until translucent. Add the spinach and let wilt. Add the stock and cream and simmer for a few minutes.

Blend with a stick (immersion) blender until frothy. Bring the soup back to a simmer and season well with salt, pepper and nutmeg.

Wash and thoroughly drain the sorrel leaves, remove the stems and cut the leaves into thin strips. Mix into the hot soup and serve immediately in warmed soup plates.

Nettle and Watercress Soup

All regions

Preparation time:		10 minutes
Cooking time:		30 minutes
Serves:		4

1⅓ cups/3½ oz	baby spinach	100 g
½ cup/1½ oz	stinging nettle leaves	40 g
¾ cup/2 oz	watercress leaves	60 g
1	onion	1
2 oz	potatoes	60 g
4 cups/34 fl oz	vegetable stock	1 litre
¾ cup/7 fl oz	single (light) cream	200 ml
1 strip	unwaxed lemon zest	1 strip
1	garlic clove	1
1 tbsp	cold butter	1 tbsp
*	salt	*
*	freshly ground black pepper	*
*	freshly grated nutmeg	*

Sort, wash and thoroughly drain the spinach leaves. Blanch the spinach and nettle leaves separately in boiling salted water, then plunge into iced water, squeeze well and finely chop.

Wash, drain and finely chop the watercress leaves. Peel the onion and potatoes, cut into small dice and simmer in the stock for 20–30 minutes, until tender. Add the cream and blend with a stick (immersion) blender. Add the lemon zest and let it infuse for a few minutes, then remove.

Peel and finely chop the garlic. Shortly before serving, add the spinach, nettles, watercress, garlic and butter and blend with a stick (immersion) blender. Let stand for 3 minutes, then season with salt, pepper and nutmeg. Serve immediately in warmed soup plates.

Soups, Stews & Sauces

Beer Soup

North Rhine-Westphalia

Preparation time:		10 minutes
Cooking time:		5 minutes
Serves:		4

4 slices	farmhouse bread	4 slices
1½ tbsp/¾ oz	butter	20 g
¼ cup/1¼ oz	plain (all-purpose) flour	30 g
3	egg yolks	3
3 cups/25 fl oz	milk	700 ml
1 cup/8 fl oz	German lager	250 ml
½ cup/3½ fl oz	single (light) cream	100 ml
*	salt	*
*	freshly ground black pepper	*
2 tbsp	finely chopped chives	2 tbsp

Cut the bread into cubes and toast in a frying pan or skillet with the butter over a medium heat. Set aside.

Mix the flour with the egg yolk until smooth. A little milk may be added.

Slowly bring the milk to a boil and stir in the flour mixture with a whisk. Add the lager and cream, bring to a simmer.

Season the soup with salt and pepper. Pour the soup into warmed soup plates. Arrange the croutons in the centre and sprinkle with chives.

Riesling Soup

Rhineland-Palatinate

Preparation time:		10 minutes
Cooking time:		2 minutes
Serves:		4

3 cups/25 fl oz	German riesling white wine	750 ml
½ cup/4 fl oz	vegetable stock	125 ml
1	strip unwaxed lemon zest	1
½	cinnamon stick	½
½ cup/3½ oz	sugar	100 g
4	egg yolks	4
½ cup/3½ fl oz	single (light) cream	100 ml
*	salt	*
*	freshly ground white pepper	*
*	freshly grated nutmeg	*
3 tbsp/1½ oz	cold butter	40 g
*	a few sprigs chervil	*
4	slices toasted bread, to serve	4

Combine the wine, stock, lemon zest, cinnamon stick and sugar in a pan and bring to a boil. Filter through a sieve back into the pan.

Beat the egg yolks well with the cream and add the mixture in a thin stream to the soup while stirring constantly. Remove from the heat immediately. Season with salt, pepper and nutmeg.

Finally, blend in the cold butter with a stick (immersion) blender. Pour into warmed soup plates and sprinkle with chervil leaves. Serve with toasted bread.

Bread Soup

Bavaria

Preparation time:		15 minutes
Cooking time:		5 minutes
Serves:		4

7 oz	stale rye bread	200 g
2	shallots	2
3 tbsp/1½ oz	butter	40 g
1 tbsp	flour	1 tbsp
5 cups/40 fl oz	meat stock	1.2 litres
*	salt	*
*	freshly ground black pepper	*
1–2 tbsp	red wine vinegar	1–2 tbsp
2 tbsp	double (heavy) cream	2 tbsp
1 tbsp	finely chopped parsley	1 tbsp

Cut the bread into cubes. Peel and finely chop the shallots. Heat the butter in a pan, add the flour and toast until golden. Add the shallots and cook briefly.

Add the stock, bring to a boil and add the bread. Season well with salt, pepper and vinegar then simmer for a few minutes over a medium heat.

Blend the soup with a stick (immersion) blender. Adjust the seasoning with salt, pepper and vinegar, if needed, and fold in the cream. Sprinkle with parsley and serve.

Pearl Barley Soup

All regions

Soaking time:		1 hour
Preparation time:		15 minutes
Cooking time:		45 minutes
Serves:		4

¾ cup/5 oz	pearl barley	150 g
1	shallot	1
1	carrot	1
3½ oz	celeriac	100 g
1	thin leek	1
1 oz	smoked bacon rashers	30 g
2 oz	butter	50 g
3 cups/25 fl oz	meat stock	750 ml
*	salt	*
*	freshly ground black pepper	*
11 oz	boiled beef	300 g
1 tbsp	finely chopped parsley	1 tbsp

Soak the barley in cold water for about 1 hour, then pour into a sieve, rinse thoroughly and drain.

Peel the shallot, carrot and celeriac. Cut off the root and green leaves from the leek, halve lengthwise and wash thoroughly. Cut the vegetables and bacon into small dice.

Melt the butter in a pan and fry the bacon until crisp. Add the vegetables and sauté. Mix in the barley, add the stock and season with salt and pepper. Bring to a boil and simmer for 25–30 minutes.

Cut the beef into strips and heat briefly in the soup. Pour into warmed soup plates and sprinkle with parsley before serving.

Weimar-Style Onion Soup

Thuringia

Preparation time:		15 minutes
Cooking time:		10 minutes
Serves:		4

4	onions	4
1	small leek	1
4 cups/34 fl oz	meat stock	1 litre
2 tbsp	butter	2 tbsp
1 tsp	tomato purée (paste)	1 tsp
½ cup/3½ fl oz	beer	100 ml
½ tbsp	dried marjoram	½ tbsp
½ tsp	ground cumin	½ tsp
*	salt	*
*	freshly ground black pepper	*
*	sugar	*
1	large slice rye bread	1
1 cup/3½ oz	grated Emmental cheese	100 g
1	egg yolk	1
1 tsp	mustard	1 tsp
*	finely chopped chives	*

Peel the onions. Cut into thin rings or strips, according to preference. Trim, wash and cut the leek into thin rings. Heat the stock.

Melt the butter in a pan and sauté the onions over a medium heat. Add the leek rings and sauté briefly. Add the tomato purée (paste), stir and cook briefly.

Add the hot stock and the beer. Simmer the soup briefly, then season with the marjoram, cumin, salt, pepper and a pinch of sugar. Keep the soup warm.

Turn on the oven grill (broiler). Toast the bread and cut into four pieces. Mix the cheese with the egg yolk and mustard. Spread the mixture over the bread, place on the middle shelf inside the oven and grill until golden. Take the toast out of the oven and season with pepper.

Pour the soup into deep plates, arrange the toast on top and serve. Sprinkle with chopped chives if you like.

Merzig-Style Cider Soup

Saarland

Preparation time:		10 minutes
Cooking time:		30 minutes
Serves:		4

5	onions	5
4 oz	celeriac	120 g
2	apples	2
5	garlic cloves	5
4 tbsp/2 oz	cold butter	50 g
1⅔ cups/14 fl oz	chicken stock	400 ml
1⅔ cups/14 fl oz	cider	400 ml
1⅔ cups/14 fl oz	single (light) cream	400 ml
*	salt	*
*	freshly ground black pepper	*
*	freshly grated nutmeg	*
1 tbsp	finely chopped parsley	1 tbsp

Peel and finely chop the onions. Peel the celeriac and cut into 5-mm (¼-inch) dice. Wash, quarter and core the apples, then cut into 5–10-mm (¼–½-inch) dice. Peel and finely chop the garlic.

Gently sauté the onions, celeriac, apples and garlic in 2 tablespoons butter over a medium heat. Add the stock and cider and simmer for 20–30 minutes until the vegetables are soft. Add the cream, bring to a simmer and blend with a stick (immersion) blender. Add the remaining butter and continue until blended. Season with salt, pepper and nutmeg.

Pour the soup in warmed soup plates and sprinkle with parsley before serving.

Mushroom Soup

All regions

4 cups/34 fl oz	vegetable or chicken stock	1 litre
4 tbsp	dried mushrooms	4 tbsp
¾ cup/7 fl oz	single (light) cream	200 ml
2 tbsp	plain (all-purpose) flour	2 tbsp
2 tbsp	cold butter	2 tbsp
14 oz	button mushrooms	400 g
½	onion	½
1	garlic clove	1
1 tsp	oil, for frying	1 tsp
1 tbsp	finely chopped parsley	1 tbsp
*	salt	*
*	freshly ground black pepper	*
1 tsp	Beurre Noisette (p. 112)	1 tsp
1 pinch	grated unwaxed lemon zest	1 pinch

Preparation time: 15 minutes
Cooking time: 20 minutes
Serves: 4

Heat the stock, add the dried mushrooms and simmer for 20 minutes. Drain the mushrooms in a sieve and reserve the broth. Let the mushrooms cool a little then finely chop.

Add the cream to the broth and bring to a simmer. Dissolve the flour completely in a little cold water, add to the soup and simmer for 2 minutes. Add the butter and mix in with a stick (immersion) blender.

Clean the fresh mushrooms, if necessary, wipe dry and cut into pieces. Peel and finely chop the onion and garlic.

Heat a frying pan or skillet over a medium heat, add the oil and sauté the onions and garlic. Add the mushrooms and fry for about 3 minutes, then add the parsley, season with salt and pepper and finally add the Beurre Noisette (p. 112) and lemon zest.

Divide the mushrooms between four warmed soup plates, blend the soup again and pour over the mushrooms.

Potato Soup with Prawns (Shrimp)

Northern Germany

9 oz	floury potatoes	250 g
2	shallots	2
1 oz	smoked back bacon	25 g
3 cups/25 fl oz	beef stock	750 ml
½ cup/4 fl oz	single (light) cream	125 ml
1	thin leek	1
1	carrot	1
1 small piece	celeriac	1 small piece
1	sprig tarragon	1
*	salt	*
*	freshly ground black pepper	*
scant 1 cup/11 oz	prawns (shrimp)	300 g
*	lemon juice	*
½	bunch chives	½

Preparation time: 15 minutes
Cooking time: 30 minutes
Serves: 4

Peel and dice the potatoes. Peel and finely chop the shallots. Cut the bacon into small cubes. Render the bacon in a pan. Add the shallots and sauté until translucent. Mix in the potatoes, sauté briefly, then add the stock and cream. Simmer for about 20 minutes.

Cut off the root and green leaves from the leek. Halve the leek lengthwise and wash thoroughly. Peel the carrot and celeriac. Finely dice the carrot, celeriac and leek.

Filter the soup through a sieve and return to the pan. Add the diced vegetables to the pan with the tarragon and simmer for 10–12 more minutes. Season with salt and pepper.

Drizzle the prawns (shrimp) with lemon juice. Wash, shake dry and finely chop the chives. Arrange the prawns in four deep plates and pour the hot potato soup over them. Sprinkle with finely chopped chives before serving.

Potato Soup

All regions

Preparation time:		10 minutes
Cooking time:		30 minutes
Serves:		4

2 oz	celeriac	50 g
1	small carrot	1
2 × 11 oz	potatoes	2 × 300 g
½	onion	½
3 cups/25 fl oz	vegetable stock	750 ml
1	bay leaf	1
⅔ cup/5 fl oz	single (light) cream	150 ml
1½ tbsp/¾ oz	cold butter	20 g
2	garlic slices	2
*	salt	*
*	freshly ground black pepper	*
*	dried marjoram	*
*	ground cumin	*
*	freshly grated nutmeg	*
*	grated unwaxed lemon zest	*
2	thin spring onions (scallions)	2

Trim and peel the celeriac and carrot. Peel the potatoes and the onion half. Cut the vegetables into 5–10-mm (¼–½-inch) dice.

Bring the stock to a simmer in a pan. Add the diced vegetables and bay leaf to the pan and simmer for about 30 minutes until tender.

Discard the bay leaf, take out one-third of the vegetables at the most and set them aside as garnish for the soup. Add the cream, butter and garlic to the soup and blend with a stick (immersion) blender. Season with salt, pepper, a pinch each of marjoram, cumin, nutmeg and lemon zest.

Trim, wash and cut the spring onions (scallions) into thin rings. Add them to the soup and simmer briefly. Pour the potato soup into warmed soup plates and serve with the vegetable garnish.

Sauerkraut Soup

All regions

Preparation time:		10 minutes
Cooking time:		40 minutes
Serves:		4

1	onion	1
1	garlic clove	1
2 tbsp	lard	2 tbsp
2 cups/11 oz	sauerkraut	300 g
1	bay leaf	1
½ tsp	cumin seeds	½ tsp
2 tsp	sugar	2 tsp
*	freshly ground black pepper	*
4 cups/34 fl oz	meat stock	1 litre
scant ½ cup/9 oz	sour cream	125 g
1 bunch	bunch chives	1 bunch
*	Liver Dumplings (p. 79)	*
*	Meatballs (p. 210), optional	*
*	salt	*

Peel and finely chop the onion and garlic. Heat the lard in a pan and sauté the onion and garlic. Cut the sauerkraut into very small pieces and add to the pan with the bay leaf, cumin seeds, sugar and a pinch of pepper. Mix well and cook for a few minutes. Add the stock, cover with a lid and simmer for 30–40 minutes.

Add the sour cream and blend with a stick (immersion) blender. Wash, shake dry and finely chop the chives. Adjust the seasoning with salt if necessary and pour the soup into warmed soup plates. Sprinkle with chives before serving. The soup can be garnished with a few Liver Dumplings (p. 79) or Meatballs (p. 210).

Rhineland-Style Potato Soup

Rhineland

Preparation time:		10 minutes
Cooking time:		30 minutes
Serves:		4

1 lb	potatoes	450 g
2 oz	celeriac	60 g
1	carrot	1
1	bay leaf	1
5 cups/40 fl oz	vegetable stock	1.2 litres
½ cup/4 fl oz	single (light) cream	125 ml
1 oz	cold butter	30 g
*	salt	*
*	freshly ground black pepper	*
1	pinch of freshly grated nutmeg	1
1	pinch of cayenne pepper	1
4 oz	smoked bacon	120 g
*	oil, for frying	*
1 tbsp	finely chopped parsley	1 tbsp

Peel and dice the potatoes, celeriac and carrot into 1-cm (½-inch) dice. Combine with the bay leaf and stock in a pan and simmer for about 30 minutes until tender. Discard the bay leaf. Add the cream and butter and blend with a stick (immersion) blender. Season with salt, pepper, a little grated nutmeg and a pinch of cayenne pepper.

Cut the bacon into small cubes and fry with oil in a frying pan or skillet over a medium heat until the fat is crispy. Drain in a sieve.

Pour the soup into warmed soup plates and sprinkle with bacon cubes and parsley before serving.

Asparagus Soup

All regions

Preparation time:		10 minutes
Cooking time:		30 minutes
Serves:		4

9 oz	white asparagus	250 g
9 oz	green asparagus	250 g
3⅓ cups/27 fl oz	vegetable stock	800 ml
¾ cup/7 fl oz	single (light) cream	200 ml
1 strip	unwaxed lemon zest	1 strip
4 tsp	cold butter	4 tsp
*	salt	*
*	freshly grated nutmeg	*
*	lemon juice	*

Wash the asparagus spears. Peel the white spears and peel only the bottom third of the green ones. Cut the woody ends off both.

Bring the stock to a boil in a pan, add the asparagus peels and simmer for about 20 minutes.

Filter the stock through a sieve back into the pan. Press the peels well in the sieve with a ladle to collect all of the liquid, then discard.

Cut the asparagus spears on the diagonal into 3–4 cm (1–1½ inch) lengths, add to the stock and simmer for 5–10 minutes until tender but firm to the bite. Filter the stock again through a sieve back into the pan. Set aside the asparagus pieces and keep warm.

Add the cream to the stock and heat to a simmer. Remove the soup from the heat. Add the lemon zest and let it infuse for a few minutes, then remove and discard.

Add the cold butter and blend with a stick (immersion) blender. Season the soup with salt, nutmeg and lemon juice. Blend again until frothy, then pour into soup plates and garnish with the asparagus pieces before serving.

Soups, Stews & Sauces

Carrot Soup

Preparation time:		15 minutes
Cooking time:		20 minutes
Serves:		4

9 oz	carrots	250 g
1	large onion	1
1	tomato	1
2 tsp	icing (confectioners') sugar	2 tsp
3⅓ cups/27 fl oz	vegetable stock	800 ml
1	red apple	1
2	garlic slices	2
1 tsp	allspice berries	1 tsp
1 tsp	peppercorns	1 tsp
¾ cup/7 fl oz	single (light) cream	200 ml
4 tbsp	cold butter	4 tbsp

Peel and finely dice the carrots and onion. Wash and finely dice the tomato, removing the stem.

Lightly caramelise 1 teaspoon of the icing (confectioners') sugar in a pan, add the vegetables and cook briefly. Add the stock and simmer the vegetables for about 20 minutes.

Wash, quarter and core the apple. Cut the flesh into thin wedges. Peel and finely chop 2 apple wedges and add to the stock together with the garlic. Grind the allspice and peppercorns in a spice grinder and season the soup. Add the cream and 3 tablespoons butter to the soup and blend with a stick (immersion) blender until smooth.

Put the remaining icing sugar into a frying pan or skillet over a medium heat and lightly caramelise. Add the unpeeled apple wedges and remaining butter and lightly fry the apple wedges on both sides.

Blend the soup again until frothy, pour into warmed soup plates and garnish with the apple wedges before serving.

Pumpkin Soup

All regions

Preparation time:		10 minutes
Cooking time:		20 minutes
Serves:		4

1 lb 5 oz	Musquée de Provence pumpkin	600 g
3 cups/25 fl oz	chicken stock	750 ml
⅔ cup/5 oz	single (light) cream	150 ml
1	garlic clove	1
1½ oz	cold butter	40 g
*	salt	*
*	freshly ground black pepper	*

Peel the pumpkin, remove the seeds with a spoon and cut the flesh into 1-cm (½-inch) dice.

Combine the diced pumpkin with the stock, in a pan, and simmer for about 20 minutes until tender. Add the cream and blend the soup with a stick (immersion) blender.

Add the garlic, let it infuse for a few minutes, then remove and discard. Mix in the butter and season the soup with salt and pepper.

Pea Soup

All regions

Preparation time:		10 minutes
Cooking time:		15 minutes
Serves:		4

2 cups/11 oz	frozen peas	300 g
1	onion	1
2 tbsp	oil, for frying	2 tbsp
3½ tbsp	white wine	50 ml
3⅓ cups/27 fl oz	vegetable stock	800 ml
¾ cup/7 fl oz	single (light) cream	200 ml
*	salt	*
*	sugar	*
*	freshly grated nutmeg	*
3½ oz	bacon	100 g
4 tbsp	mint leaves, to garnish	4 tbsp

Thaw the peas. Peel and finely chop the onion. Heat 1 tablespoon oil in a pan and sauté the onion over a medium heat until translucent. Add the wine and reduce almost completely.

Add the stock and simmer for 15 minutes. Add the peas and bring the stock to a simmer for 3–5 minutes. Mix in the cream and blend the soup with a stick (immersion) blender. Briefly bring the soup back to a simmer and season with salt, a pinch of sugar and a pinch of nutmeg.

Cut the bacon into 1-cm (½-inch) wide strips. Heat the remaining oil in a frying pan or skillet and fry the bacon until crispy. Drain on paper towels.

Blend the soup again until frothy, then pour into warmed soup plates. Scatter the bacon over the top, garnish with mint leaves and serve.

Pea Soup with Smoked Eel

Northern Germany

Preparation time:		15 minutes
Cooking time:		30 minutes
Serves:		4

11 oz	smoked eel	300 g
3 cups/25 fl oz	vegetable stock	750 ml
2	shallots	2
1 oz	butter	30 g
2 cups/11 oz	young green peas	300 g
*	salt	*
*	freshly ground black pepper	*
*	sugar	*
5 oz	crème fraîche	150 g
1	piece horseradish root	1
1 tbsp	finely chopped parsley	1 tbsp

Remove the skin and bones from the eel. Bring the stock to a boil and remove from the heat. Put the eel skin in the stock and simmer for 15 minutes, then remove and discard.

Peel and finely chop the shallots and sauté in the melted butter in a pan until translucent. Add the peas, season with salt, pepper and pinch of sugar and stir briefly to mix in well. Add the stock and simmer for about 15 minutes.

Blend the soup with a stick (immersion) blender until smooth, press through a sieve and mix in the crème fraîche. The soup needs no further cooking.

Cut the eel flesh into small pieces and arrange on four warmed soup plates. Briefly blend the soup again until frothy, then pour over the eel. Grate a little horseradish over the soup and sprinkle with parsley before serving.

Tomato Soup

Preparation time:		10 minutes
Cooking time:		20 minutes
Serves:		4

1	small onion	1
⅓ cup/3 fl oz	olive oil	80 ml
2 cups/17 fl oz	vegetable stock	500 ml
1	garlic clove	1
2¾ cups/1 lb 7 oz	tinned chopped tomatoes	650 g
*	a few basil stems	*
*	salt	*
*	freshly ground black pepper	*
*	sugar	*
*	cayenne pepper	*
1 tbsp	finely chopped basil	1 tbsp

Peel and finely chop the onion. Heat 1 tablespoon olive oil in a pan and sauté the onion over a medium heat until translucent. Add the stock and simmer for about 5 minutes, until cooked.

Peel and slice the garlic. Add the chopped tomatoes to the stock and bring to a simmer. Add the garlic slices and blend the soup with a stick (immersion) blender, gradually adding the remaining olive oil.

Add the basil stems, let them infuse for a few minutes, then remove and discard. Season the tomato soup with salt, pepper, and a pinch each of sugar and cayenne pepper. Pour into warmed soup plates and sprinkle with basil before serving.

Savoy Cabbage Soup

Preparation time:		10 minutes
Cooking time:		10 minutes
Serves:		4

1 lb 2 oz	savoy cabbage	500 g
3 cups/25 fl oz	strong vegetable stock	750 ml
¾ cup/7 fl oz	single (light) cream	200 ml
2 tbsp	creamed horseradish	2 tbsp
*	salt	*
*	freshly grated nutmeg	*
2 tbsp	finely chopped parsley	2 tbsp
1	handful parsley leaves	1

Trim, wash and divide the cabbage into individual leaves. Cut off the ribs and, if necessary, cut the leaves into smaller pieces. Boil in salted water, about 8 minutes, until tender. Drain off the water in a sieve, plunge into iced water and drain again.

Bring the stock to a simmer in a pan and add the cabbage, cream and creamed horseradish. Season with salt and nutmeg, then blend the soup with a stick (immersion) blender.

Mix in the finely chopped parsley. The soup needs no further cooking. Adjust the seasoning with salt and nutmeg if needed.

Pour the soup into warmed soup plates or bowls. Garnish each with a few parsley leaves before serving.

Cheese and Leek Soup

All regions

Preparation time:		10 minutes
Cooking time:		20 minutes
Serves:		4

1	large leek	1
2 tsp	icing (confectioners') sugar	2 tsp
½ cup/4 fl oz	sparkling wine	125 ml
3 cups/25 fl oz	vegetable stock	750 ml
½	small bay leaf	½
½ cup/3½ fl oz	single (light) cream	100 ml
2 tbsp	plain (all-purpose) flour	2 tbsp
1 strip	unwaxed lemon zest	1 strip
1	sprig thyme	1
1	garlic clove	1
5 oz	Edam cheese	150 g
4 tsp	cold butter	4 tsp
*	salt	*
*	freshly ground black pepper	*
*	white bread, to serve	*

Trim, wash and cut the leek into rings. Lightly caramelise the icing (confectioners') sugar in a pan, add the leek and sauté for a few minutes. Deglaze with the wine and simmer until reduced by two-thirds. Add the stock and bay leaf and simmer for 10 minutes.

Add the cream and bring back to a simmer. Dissolve the flour completely in a little cold water, stir into the soup. Add the lemon zest, thyme and garlic then simmer for 2 more minutes. Take out and discard the spices then filter the soup through a sieve.

Cut the cheese into small pieces, add to the soup and blend with a stick (immersion) blender. The soup needs no further cooking. Blend in the butter, season with salt and pepper, then mix in the leek. Pour into warmed soup plates and serve immediately. Accompany with white bread.

Allgäu-Style Cheese Soup

Allgäu and Swabia

Preparation time:		10 minutes
Cooking time:		5 minutes
Serves:		4

2 tsp	icing (confectioners') sugar	2 tsp
½ cup/3½ fl oz	sweet white wine	100 ml
3 cups/25 fl oz	vegetable stock	750 ml
½ cup/3½ fl oz	single (light) cream	100 ml
2 tbsp	plain (all-purpose) flour	2 tbsp
5 oz	Emmental cheese	150 g
1½ tbsp/¾ oz	cold butter	20 g
*	salt	*
*	freshly ground black pepper	*
*	freshly grated nutmeg	*
1 tbsp	mixed parsley, chives, dill	1 tbsp
*	white bread, to serve	*

Lightly caramelise the icing (confectioners') sugar in a pan over a low heat. Deglaze with the wine and simmer until reduced by two-thirds. Add the stock, followed by the cream and bring to a simmer.

Dissolve the flour completely in a little cold water and stir into the soup.

Cut the cheese into small pieces and blend into the soup with a stick (immersion) blender until smooth. The soup needs no further cooking. Blend in the butter and season with salt, pepper and nutmeg.

Pour the soup into warmed soup plates and sprinkle with the herbs. Accompany with white bread.

Fish Soup

Preparation time:		30 minutes
Cooking time:		20 minutes
Serves:		4

11 oz	waxy potatoes	300 g
2 cups/17 fl oz	vegetable stock	500 ml
1	bay leaf	1
1	onion	1
½	carrot	½
1	celery stalk	1
¼	fennel bulb	¼
1 tsp	icing (confectioners') sugar	1 tsp
4 tbsp	vermouth	4 tbsp
⅔ cup/5½ fl oz	white wine	160 ml
5 cups/40 fl oz	fish stock or vegetable stock	1.2 litres
½ tsp	fennel seeds	½ tsp
3½ oz	green asparagus	100 g
1	handful of spinach leaves	1
2	tomatoes	2
12	mussels	12
1 lb 2 oz	fish fillets (e.g. cod, pollack)	500 g
10	large prawns (shrimp)	10
*	salt	*
*	basil, celery leaves, dill	*

Peel and halve the potatoes lengthwise. Bring the vegetable stock to a boil with the bay leaf and cook the potatoes until tender.

Meanwhile, peel the onion and carrot. Trim, wash and roughly chop the celery and fennel. Brown the vegetables in a pan over a medium heat without oil. Sprinkle with the sugar and lightly caramelise. Add the vermouth and wine and let simmer for a short time. Add the fish stock and fennel seeds then continue to simmer for about 15 minutes.

Wash the asparagus spears, peel only the bottom third and cut off the woody ends then cut them on the diagonal into 2 or 3 pieces. Blanch the spinach in boiling salted water until tender but firm to the bite, then drain in a sieve, plunge into iced water and drain again.

Cut a cross in the base of the tomatoes, blanch for 3 minutes, plunge into iced water, peel, quarter, seed and dice. Thoroughly brush the mussels under cold running water and discard any open ones. Cook with the wine in a covered pan for about 1 minute, until they open.

Wash and pat dry the fish fillets and prawns (shrimp). Make a shallow cut along the back of the prawns (shrimp) and remove the dark vein. Cut the fish and prawns (shrimp) into 3-cm (1-inch) pieces. Bring salted water to a boil in a pan, remove from the heat and poach the fish and prawn pieces for 2 minutes. Use a slotted spoon or skimmer to take the pieces out of the pan, add to the soup with the blanched asparagus and diced tomato and simmer for 1–2 minutes.

Pour the fish soup into warmed deep plates and add the mussels, wine and potatoes. It can be served garnished with basil and celery leaves or dill tips.

Hamburg-Style Eel Soup

Preparation time:		15 minutes
Cooking time:		30 minutes
Serves:		4

7 oz	assorted pitted dried fruit	200 g
1 lb 2 oz	fresh eel	500 g
5 oz	celeriac	150 g
2	carrots	2
1	leek, trimmed	1
*	bunch of parsley, tarragon, chervil	*
2 tbsp	oil	2 tbsp
½ cup/4 fl oz	dry white wine	125 ml
3 cups/25 fl oz	meat stock	750 ml
1 cup/5 oz	frozen peas	150 g
*	salt	*
*	vinegar	*
*	sugar	*

Cut the dried fruit into bite-size pieces. Put into a pan, cover with water and bring to a boil. Cover with a lid and let swell for about 10 minutes over a low heat.

Cut the eel into lengths of about 4 cm (1½ inches). Trim and peel the celeriac and carrots and cut into small dice. Cut off the root and green leaves from the leek. Halve lengthwise, thoroughly wash and slice the leek. Wash and shake the herbs dry, then pluck the leaves and finely chop.

Heat the oil in a pan and sauté the vegetables. Add the wine and stock. Let simmer for about 10 minutes. Add the dried fruit, eel, peas and herbs then simmer for 15 more minutes.

Season the soup with salt, vinegar and a pinch of sugar for a sweet and sour flavour.

Büsum-Style Soup

Schleswig-Holstein
and Northern Germany

Preparation time:		5 minutes
Cooking time:		5 minutes
Serves:		4

3 cups/25 fl oz	vegetable or chicken stock	750 ml
1 cup/8 fl oz	fish stock	250 ml
¾ cup/7 fl oz	single (light) cream	200 ml
2 tbsp	plain (all-purpose) flour	2 tbsp
1 oz	crayfish butter	30 g
*	salt	*
*	lemon juice	*
¾ cup/9 oz	North Sea prawns (shrimp)	250 g
1 tbsp	finely chopped chervil	1 tbsp

Combine the two stocks with the cream in a pan and bring
to a simmer. Dissolve the flour completely in a little cold
water and gradually mix it into the lightly simmering stock
until it takes on a creamy consistency. Add the crayfish
butter and mix it in with a stick (immersion) blender.
Season with salt and a dash of lemon juice.

Arrange the prawns (shrimp) in warmed soup plates
and pour the soup over them. Sprinkle with chervil and
serve.

Baden-Style Snail Soup

Baden-Württemberg

Preparation time:		15 minutes
Cooking time:		5 minutes
Serves:		4

3½ oz	butter	100 g
*	salt	*
*	freshly ground black pepper	*
*	cayenne pepper	*
1	garlic clove	1
3 tbsp	parsley	3 tbsp
1 tbsp	chives	1 tbsp
2–3	tarragon leaves	2–3
1 tbsp	chervil	1 tbsp
2	onions	2
2 tbsp	oil	2 tbsp
24	snails	24
½ cup/4 fl oz	Baden white wine	125 ml
2 cups/17 fl oz	veal stock	500 ml
½ cup/3½ fl oz	single (light) cream	100 ml
2 tbsp	double (heavy) cream	2 tbsp
*	crispy toasted bread, to serve	*

Beat the butter until fluffy and season with salt, pepper
and cayenne pepper. Peel and crush the garlic in a garlic
crusher and mix into the butter with 2 tablespoons of
parsley and the other herbs. Set aside in the refrigerator.

Peel and finely chop the onions and sauté in the hot
oil until translucent. Wash, pat dry then coarsely chop the
snails and add to the onions. Cook briefly, then add the
wine, stock and cream and bring to a boil. Let simmer for
about 5 minutes.

Cut the cold herb butter into small pieces and stir into
the soup. Bring the soup back to a boil and fold in the
whipped cream. Sprinkle with the remaining parsley and
serve with crispy toasted bread.

German Goulash

All regions

Preparation time:		25 minutes
Cooking time:		2 hours 30 minutes
Serves:		4

For the soup:		
1 lb 8½ oz	beef shin (shank or chuck)	700 g
14 oz	onions	400 g
1–2 tbsp	oil	1–2 tbsp
1 tbsp	tomato purée (paste)	1 tbsp
3 cups/25 fl oz	chicken stock	750 ml
½	yellow bell pepper	½
½	red bell pepper	½
½	courgette (zucchini)	½
14 oz	potatoes	400 g
*	salt	*
*	hot paprika	*
1	bay leaf	1
2 tbsp	finely chopped parsley	2 tbsp

For the goulash seasoning:		
2	garlic cloves	2
2 strips	unwaxed lemon zest	2 strips
½ tsp	cumin seeds	½ tsp
½ tbsp	dried marjoram	½ tbsp
½–1 tbsp	sweet paprika	½–1 tbsp
1–2 tbsp	chicken stock	1–2 tbsp
*	salt	*
*	freshly ground black pepper	*

For the soup: Trim the fat and large tendons from the beef and cut the meat into 1-cm (½-inch) cubes. Peel, halve and finely chop the onions. Heat the oil in a large, shallow pan, brown the meat well on all sides then remove from the pan.

Add the onions to the pan and sauté until translucent. Stir in the tomato purée (paste) and cook for a few minutes. Return the meat to the pan and add the stock. Cover with a lid and simmer for about 2 hours 30 minutes.

Meanwhile, trim, seed and wash the bell peppers then cut into 5–10 mm (¼–½ inch) squares. Trim and wash the courgette (zucchini) then cut into pieces the same size as the bell peppers. Peel and cut the potatoes into 1-cm (½-inch) dice.

After 2 hours of cooking, add the bell peppers, courgette (zucchini) and potatoes to the soup. Season with salt and paprika, add the bay leaf and continue to cook for 30 more minutes.

For the goulash seasoning: Peel and slice the garlic, then finely chop together with the lemon zest, cumin seeds and marjoram. Dissolve the paprika completely in a little cold stock or water. Season the soup with a little of the seasoning and dissolved paprika then simmer for 5 more minutes (don't add the entire seasoning mixture, just use it to adjust the flavour).

Take out the bay leaf and discard. Season the soup with salt and pepper, pour into warmed soup bowls and sprinkle with parsley.

Bean, Pear and Bacon Stew (Birnen, Bohnen, Speck)

Schleswig-Holstein, Lower Saxony, Mecklenburg-West Pomerania and Hamburg

---

Preparation time:		15 minutes
Cooking time:		40 minutes
Serves:		4

1	onion	1
1 tbsp	oil	1 tbsp
5 cups/40 fl oz	meat stock	1.2 litres
11 oz	smoked back bacon	300 g
2	pears (Williams or Bartlett)	2
1 lb 2 oz	green beans	500 g
1 lb 2 oz	potatoes	500 g
1 tbsp	savory	1 tbsp
2 tsp	plain (all-purpose) flour	2 tsp
*	salt	*
*	freshly ground black pepper	*

Peel and dice the onion. Sauté the onion in oil in a pan until translucent. Add the stock and bacon. Cook for 20 minutes.

Peel, halve and core the pears. Poach in a little water for 3 minutes, then drain. (Small cooking pears are usual in this recipe and are cooked with the beans; however, as these are not readily available, Williams or Bartlett pears are used here instead, but these should never be cooked for long, or they will disintegrate.)

Trim, wash and cut the beans into 2–3 cm (¾–1 inch) lengths. Peel and cut the potatoes into chunks.

Take the bacon out of the stock and cut into slices. Add the beans, savory and potatoes and cook for 15–20 minutes.

Dissolve the flour completely in a little cold water and use it to thicken the stock. Season with salt and pepper. Heat the bacon and pears in the stock. Arrange the beans, pears, bacon and potatoes on warmed deep plates and pour over the desired amount of stock.

Vegetable Stew

All regions

Preparation time:		20 minutes
Cooking time:		20 minutes
Serves:		4

1	potato	1
1	carrot	1
1	onion	1
3½ oz	young white cabbage	100 g
½	small fennel bulb	½
1	celery stalk	1
3 oz	small white mushrooms	80 g
2 oz	courgette (zucchini)	50 g
½ bunch	spring onions (scallions)	½ bunch
3 oz	flat green beans	80 g
3½ cups/27 fl oz	vegetable stock	800 ml
1	small bay leaf	1
1	garlic clove	1
1	sprig thyme (or savory)	1
1	strip unwaxed lemon zest	1
*	salt	*
1 tbsp	finely chopped parsley	1 tbsp

Peel and cut the potato into 10-mm (½-inch) dice. Trim, wash and slice the carrot on the diagonal. Peel the onion and cut into 15-mm (¾-inch) pieces. Trim and wash the cabbage and cut the leaves into 15-mm (¾-inch) pieces. Trim, wash and halve the fennel lengthwise, then cut crosswise into 15-mm (¾-inch) pieces. Trim, wash and cut the celery on the diagonal into 5-mm (¼-inch) thick slices.

Wash, wipe dry and quarter the mushrooms. Wash and halve the courgette (zucchini) lengthwise, then slice. Trim, wash and cut the spring onions (scallions) on the diagonal into 5-mm (¼-inch) thick rings.

Trim, wash and cut the beans on the diagonal into 15-mm (¾-inch) lengths. Cook in boiling salted water for 4–5 minutes until tender. Drain off the water in a sieve, plunge into iced water and drain again.

Combine the potato, carrot, onion, cabbage, fennel and celery with the stock in a pan. Add the bay leaf and simmer the vegetables for 10–15 minutes until tender. Peel and halve the garlic clove.

Shortly before the end of the cooking time, add the mushrooms, courgette (zucchini), spring onions (scallions), beans, thyme, garlic and lemon zest to the pan. Infuse with the spices for a few minutes, then remove and discard. Season the stew with salt. Serve the stew in warmed soup plates sprinkled with parsley.

Meat and Vegetable Stew (Pichelsteiner)

Bavaria

Preparation time:		15 minutes
Cooking time:		1 hour 30 minutes
Serves:		4

7 oz	veal braising steak	200 g
7 oz	beef braising steak	200 g
1–2 tbsp	oil	1–2 tbsp
6¼ cups/50 fl oz	vegetable or beef stock	1.5 litres
2	waxy potatoes	2
2	onions	2
1	carrot	1
1	parsnip	1
5 oz	celeriac	150 g
7 oz	white cabbage	200 g
½	leek	½
¾ cup/3½ oz	flat green beans	100 g
1 cup/4¼ oz	canned haricot beans	120 g
½ tsp	allspice berries	½ tsp
½ tsp	peppercorns	½ tsp
¼ tsp	cumin seeds	¼ tsp
1	bay leaf	1
1	garlic clove, sliced	1
3	parsley stems	3
*	salt	*
*	freshly grated nutmeg	*

Cut the meat into 15-mm (¾-inch) cubes. Heat the oil in a frying pan or skillet and brown the meat on all sides in batches. Put the browned meat into a pan with the stock and steep in the liquid just below boiling for about 1 hour, without bringing to a simmer.

Peel the potatoes. Peel the onions. Trim and peel the carrot, parsnip root and celeriac. Cut everything into small dice. Trim and wash the cabbage, remove the ribs and cut the leaves into diamond shapes. Add the potatoes, onions, carrot, parsnip, celeriac and cabbage to the meat and cook together for about 20 minutes.

Trim, wash and cut the leek into thin rings. Trim, wash and cut the green beans on the diagonal into 1.5-cm (¾-inch) lengths. Bring salted water to a boil in a pan and cook the beans until tender but firm to the bite. Drain off the blanching water, plunge into iced water and drain again. Drain the haricot beans in a sieve and wash under cold running water. Put the allspice, peppercorns and cumin seeds into a spice grinder. Add the leek, green and haricot beans, bay leaf and garlic to the meat and season with the spices in the spice grinder plus salt. Simmer the vegetables for 10 more minutes, then remove and discard the whole spices. Wash and shake dry the parsley, pluck the leaves and stir into the stew.

Grate a little nutmeg into warmed deep plates and serve the stew in them.

Spicy and Sour Soup (Solyanka)

Saxony, Saxony-Anhalt and Thuringia

Preparation time:		20 minutes
Cooking time:		10 minutes
Serves:		4

9 oz	onions	250 g
2	red bell peppers	2
3½ oz	smoked bacon rashers	100 g
1 tbsp	oil	1 tbsp
½ cup/3½ oz	tomato purée (paste)	100 g
3½ cups/27 fl oz	chicken stock	800 ml
½ cup/3½ fl oz	gherkin (pickle) pickling liquid	100 ml
1	bay leaf	1
1 tsp	yellow mustard seeds	1 tsp
3½ oz	cooked beef, chicken or pork	100 g
3½ oz	salted and cured pork	100 g
3½ oz	salami	100 g
3½ oz	sausages (e.g. Jagdwurst poultry or Kochsalami)	100 g
2 oz	gherkins (dill pickles)	50 g
*	pinch of freshly ground allspice	*
*	pinch of mild chilli powder	*
*	freshly ground black pepper	*
1 tsp	sweet paprika	1 tsp
1	garlic clove	1
*	pinch of unwaxed lemon zest	*
1 tbsp	finely chopped parsley	1 tbsp
*	salt	*
4–6 tbsp	sour cream	4–6 tbsp
*	dill or parsley, to garnish	*

Peel and cut the onions into 10–15-mm (½ inch–¾-inch) thick strips. Halve the bell peppers lengthwise, seed, wash and cut into uniform large pieces. Cut the bacon into 10-mm (½-inch) wide strips.

Heat oil in a pan. Sauté the onions and bell peppers over a medium heat. Stir in the tomato purée (paste) and cook briefly over a low heat. Add the bacon, stock and pickling liquid, then add the bay leaf and mustard seeds. Bring to a simmer and cook for 5 minutes.

Meanwhile, cut the meat, salted pork, salami, sausages and gherkins (dill pickles) into 5–10-mm (¼–½-inch) cubes. Add to the stew and season with the allspice, chilli powder and black pepper.

Heat all the ingredients through, without bringing to a boil. Dissolve the paprika completely in a little water and add to the stew with the garlic. Add the lemon zest and parsley and stir into the stew. Adjust the spiciness of the stew and season with salt if needed.

Pour into warmed deep plates, top each plate with 1 tablespoon of sour cream and garnish with dill or parsley before serving.

'Baker's Oven' Meat and Potato Stew

Baden

Preparation time:		10 minutes
Marinating time:		12 hours
Cooking time:		4 hours
Serves:		4

14 oz	beef brisket	400 g
14 oz	veal chuck	400 g
14 oz	pork shoulder	400 g
3	onions	3
1	garlic clove	1
2	sprigs thyme	2
1 tsp	peppercorns	1 tsp
1 tsp	allspice berries	1 tsp
2	small bay leaves	2
*	salt	*
3½ cups/27 fl oz	riesling white wine	800 ml
2½ lbs	waxy potatoes	1.2 kg
2	large carrots	2
2	thick leeks	2
½	bunch of parsley	½
*	farmhouse bread, to serve	*

Wash, pat dry and cut the meat into 3–4-cm (1–1½-inch) cubes. Peel and dice the onions and combine with the meat, garlic (peeled and chopped), thyme, peppercorns, allspice and bay leaf in a bowl. Season with salt, add the wine, cover and marinate in the refrigerator for 12 hours.

Peel the potatoes and carrots. Trim and wash the leek. Cut the potatoes into large cubes and the carrots and leek into 3–4-cm (1–1½-inch) thick slices.

Preheat the oven to 150°C/300°F/Gas Mark 2. Alternate the marinated meat with the vegetables in an ovenproof dish or casserole (Dutch oven). Pour in the marinade, cover with a lid and wrap well with foil. Cook the stew in the oven for about 4 hours.

Wash, shake dry, pluck and finely chop the parsley. Sprinkle over the stew and serve with farmhouse bread.

Beef Stew

Baden-Württemberg

For the soup:		
1 lb 12 oz	beef brisket	800 g
2 tbsp	oil	2 tbsp
2	onions	2
7 oz	celeriac	200 g
1	carrot	1
1	bay leaf	1
3	allspice berries	3
3	juniper berries	3
*	salt	*
*	freshly ground black pepper	*

Preparation time: 30 minutes
Cooking time: 3 hours 30 minutes
Serves: 4

For the garnish:		
7 oz	small waxy potatoes	200 g
1	onion	1
2	carrots	2
7 oz	celeriac	200 g
¼	leek	¼
1 tbsp	finely chopped parsley	1 tbsp

For the spätzle:		
3½ oz	plain (all-purpose) flour	100 g
2	eggs	2
1 tsp	salt	1 tsp
1 tsp	oil	1 tsp

To serve:		
2	frankfurters (hot dogs)	2
1	large onion	1
1 tbsp	butter	1 tbsp
*	freshly grated nutmeg	*
1 tbsp	finely chopped chives	1 tbsp

For the soup: Brown the beef in a large pan with oil. Add 3 litres (12 cups/100 fl oz) of water and simmer for 3 hours. Meanwhile, halve an unpeeled onion and place cut-side down over foil in a dry frying pan until dark brown. Add it to the stock after 1 hour of cooking.

Peel the remaining half onion, celeriac and carrot. Cut into about 1-cm (½-inch) chunks. Add the vegetables and spices to the pan after 2 hours 30 minutes. At the end of the cooking, season with salt and pepper. Remove the meat, sieve the stock then return the meat to the pan.

For the garnish: Peel and quarter the potatoes. Peel the onion, carrots and celeriac. Cut into 1-cm (½-inch) chunks. Measure out 1.2 litres (5 cups/40 fl oz) stock and simmer the vegetables for 30 minutes. Cut the leek into 1-cm (½-inch) strips and add after 15 minutes. Cut the meat into 1-cm (½-inch) chunks. Add with the parsley.

For the spätzle: Work the flour with the eggs, salt and oil and knead for 5 minutes until bubbles form. Immerse the spätzle maker (p. 428) in the boiling water, fill with the dough and slide the box from side to side, dropping them into the water. Boil for a few minutes, then drain.

To serve: Slice the frankfurters and add to the stock with the spätzle. Slice the onion and fry in the butter until golden. Grate nutmeg into deep plates and serve the stew topped with onions and the chives.

Pea and Pork Belly Stew

All regions

Soaking time: 12 hours
Preparation time: 10 minutes
Cooking time: 1 hour
Serves: 4

6 oz	dried and hulled yellow peas	180 g
1	onion	1
14 oz	waxy potatoes	400 g
1–2	carrots	1–2
4 oz	celeriac	120 g
1	leek	1
11 oz	lightly smoked pork belly	300 g
1 tbsp	oil	1 tbsp
4 cups/34 fl oz	chicken stock	1 litre
1	bay leaf	1
*	dried marjoram, to season	*
*	salt	*
*	freshly ground black pepper	*
1 tbsp	finely chopped parsley	1 tbsp

Soak the peas in water to soften overnight and drain the next day.

Peel and finely chop the onion. Peel the potatoes. Trim and peel the carrots and celeriac. Cut the potatoes, carrots and celeriac into 1.5 cm (¾-inch) chunks. Trim, wash and cut the leek into 5-mm (¼-inch) thick slices. Cut the pork belly into 2-cm (1-inch) chunks.

Heat oil in a pan. Brown the pork belly. Add the onion and sauté for a few minutes. Add the peas, stock, potatoes, carrots, celeriac and bay leaf then simmer for about 1 hour. Add the leek after 45 minutes of cooking.

Season the stew with marjoram, salt and pepper and stir in the parsley before serving.

Lentil and Sausage Stew

All regions

Preparation time:		20 minutes
Cooking time:		50 minutes
Serves:		4

1	onion	1
2 tbsp	oil	2 tbsp
11 oz	small green lentils	300 g
1 tbsp	tomato purée (paste)	1 tbsp
½ cup/4 fl oz	heavy red wine	125 ml
6¼ cups/50 fl oz	chicken stock	1.5 litres
2 oz	carrots	60 g
2 oz	celeriac	60 g
2 oz	leeks	60 g
½–1 tbsp	dried marjoram	½–1 tbsp
3½ oz	smoked bacon rashers	100 g
1	garlic clove	1
*	salt	*
4	frankfurters (hot dogs)	4
1 tbsp	parsley, finely chopped	1 tbsp
1 tbsp	Beurre Noisette (p. 112)	1 tbsp

Peel and finely chop the onion. Heat 1 tablespoon oil in a pan and sauté the onion over a low heat, until translucent. Add the lentils, stir in the tomato purée (paste) and fry briefly. Deglaze the pan with the wine and simmer until thick and reduced. Add the stock and steep, rather than simmer for 45–50 more minutes.

Trim and peel the carrots and celeriac. Trim and wash the leeks. Cut the vegetables into small dice, add to the stock with a pinch of marjoram and cook together for 5 minutes.

Finely dice the bacon. Heat the remaining oil in a frying pan or skillet and fry the bacon until crispy. Drain on paper towels.

Add the garlic to the stew. Add the bacon and season with salt. Let the garlic infuse the stew for a few minutes, then remove and discard.

Slice the sausages and add to the stew to warm through. The stew needs no further cooking. Before serving, stir in the parsley and 1 tablespoon Beurre Noisette (p. 112).

Peppered Beef Stew

Westphalia

Preparation time:		15 minutes
Cooking time:		1 hour 25 minutes
Serves:		4

1 lb 12 oz	marbled beef (e.g. shank)	800 g
2 tbsp	oil	2 tbsp
14 oz	onions	400 g
3 cups/25 fl oz	meat stock	750 ml
2	bay leaves	2
1 tbsp	coarsely ground black pepper	1 tbsp
*	salt	*
1–2 tbsp	dry breadcrumbs	1–2 tbsp
*	ground allspice	*
2 tbsp	lemon juice	2 tbsp
*	Boiled Potatoes (p. 260)	*
*	Stewed Cucumbers (p. 311)	*
*	Pickled Beetroot (Beets) (p. 312)	*
*	pilsner beer, chilled, to serve	*

Wash, pat dry and cut the meat into 3-cm (1½-inch) cubes. Heat the oil in a casserole (dutch oven) and sear the meat well on all sides, in batches.

Peel, dice and add the onion to the meat. Add 500 ml (2 cups/17 fl oz) stock, the bay leaf, pepper and season with salt. Cover with the lid and braise over a low heat for about 2 hours. Top up with more stock if necessary.

Stir in the breadcrumbs to thicken the sauce. Adjust the seasoning with a pinch of allspice, lemon juice and salt, then simmer for 10 minutes.

Serve the stew with Boiled Potatoes (p. 260), Stewed Cucumbers (p. 311) and a few Pickled Beetroot (Beets) (p. 312). Accompany with a chilled pilsner.

Bean, Apple and Bacon Stew
(Pluckte Finken)

Bremen

Soaking time:	12 hours
Preparation time:	20 minutes
Cooking time:	1 hour
Serves:	4

2 cups/9 oz	dried haricot beans	250 g
4	onions	4
2 tbsp	butter	2 tbsp
1 × 14 oz	side of smoked back bacon	400 g
14 oz	waxy potatoes	400 g
14 oz	carrots	400 g
11 oz	apples	300 g
2 tbsp	apple cider vinegar	2 tbsp
*	salt	*
*	freshly ground white pepper	*
*	finely chopped parsley, optional	*

Soak the beans overnight in plenty of water, to soften.
The following morning, pour the beans into a sieve to drain.

Peel and finely chop the onions. Melt the butter in
a pan and sauté the onions over a medium-low heat. Add
the bacon and fry on all sides for about 10 minutes. Add
enough water to cover the bacon by 2.5 cm (1 inch) and
bring to a boil. Add the beans and simmer until cooked,
about 40 minutes.

Meanwhile, peel and wash the potatoes. Trim and peel
the carrots. Dice the potatoes and carrots. Peel, quarter,
core and cut the apples into pieces or wedges.

Take the bacon out of the pan and add the potatoes,
carrots and apples and simmer for 15 minutes. Season
the stew with vinegar, a little salt and pepper. Remove the
bacon, cut into slices or bite-size pieces and return to
the pan. Serve the stew in deep plates. Sprinkle with finely
chopped parsley, if you like.

Meat, Potato and Prune Stew
(Plumm un Tüffel)

Mecklenburg-Western Pomerania

Soaking time:	12 hours
Preparation time:	10 minutes
Cooking time:	45 minutes
Serves:	4

1⅔ cups/7 oz	pitted prunes	200 g
3 cups/25 fl oz	meat stock	750 ml
2	large onions	2
1	bay leaf	1
2	cloves	2
1lb 6 oz	waxy potatoes	750 g
1 tbsp	butter	1 tbsp
1 × 1lb 2 oz	side of smoked back bacon	500 g
1 tsp	sugar	1 tsp
*	salt	*
*	freshly ground black pepper	*
2–3 tbsp	lemon juice	2–3 tbsp
*	ground cinnamon	*

Soak the prunes in water overnight, to soften. The
following morning, transfer the prunes to a sieve and drain,
reserving the soaking liquid.

Heat the stock in a pan. Peel the onions. Finely
chop one onion. Attach the bay leaf to the other onion
by studding it with the cloves. Peel, wash and cut the
potatoes into 2-cm (1-inch) dice.

Heat the butter in a pan and sauté the finely chopped
onion. Add the stock, bacon, studded onion and sugar
then simmer for 25 minutes. Add the potatoes and cook
for 10 minutes.

Take the bacon out of the stock and cut into cubes.
Return the bacon to the pan and add the prunes and a little
of the soaking liquid. Cook for 10 more minutes. Season
the stew with salt, pepper and lemon juice. The seasoning
can also be adjusted with a pinch of ground cinnamon.

Green Bean Stew (Schnippelbohneneintopf)

Westphalia and
Northern Germany

Preparation time:		15 minutes
Cooking time:		25 minutes
Serves:		4

1	small onion	1
2	small carrots	2
4	waxy potatoes	4
3 cups/14 oz	flat green beans	400 g
4½ cups/37 fl oz	chicken stock	1.1 litres
1	bay leaf	1
1	garlic clove, sliced	1
1 tsp	dried savory	1 tsp
1 strip	unwaxed lemon zest	1 strip
7 oz	cured and smoked sausages	200 g
1 tbsp	parsley, finely chopped	1 tbsp
*	salt	*
*	freshly ground black pepper	*
*	freshly grated nutmeg	*

Peel the onion and cut into 1-cm (½-inch) dice. Trim, peel and slice the carrots. Peel and cut the potatoes into 1-cm (½-inch) dice. Trim, wash and cut the beans on the diagonal into 1–1.5-cm (½–¾ inch) lengths.

Boil the beans in salted water until tender but firm to the bite, then drain in a sieve, plunge into iced water and drain again.

Heat the stock in a pan with the bay leaf, then add the onion, potatoes and carrots. Simmer for 15 minutes.

Add the beans to the pan, season with the garlic, savory and lemon zest and simmer for a few more minutes. Cut the sausages into 5-mm (¼-inch) thick slices, add to the stew and heat through. Stir in the parsley, then season with salt, pepper and nutmeg. Before serving, remove and discard the bay leaf and lemon zest.

Bean, Vegetable and Ham Stew (Schnüsch)

Schleswig-Holstein

Preparation time:		20 minutes
Cooking time:		30 minutes
Serves:		4

1½ cups/7 oz	fine green beans	200 g
7 oz	carrots	200 g
12 oz	kohlrabi	350 g
11 oz	waxy potatoes	300 g
3½ cups/27 fl oz	chicken stock	800 ml
scant 1 cup/7 fl oz	milk	200 g
1⅔ cup/7 oz	frozen peas	200 g
1 tbsp	plain (all-purpose) flour	1 tbsp
*	salt	*
*	freshly ground black pepper	*
½ tsp	dried savory	½ tsp
1	garlic clove	1
2	parsley stems	2
1 strip	unwaxed lemon zest	1 strip
1½ oz	cold butter	40 g
1 tbsp	finely chopped parsley	1 tbsp
3½ oz	smoked ham, e.g Katenrauchschinken	100 g
*	freshly grated nutmeg	*
*	parsley leaves, to serve	*

Trim, wash and cut the beans into about 3-cm (1-inch) lengths. Cook until soft in a pan of heavily salted boiling water. Drain in a sieve, plunge into iced water and drain again.

Trim and peel the carrots and kohlrabi. Peel and wash the potatoes. Cut all of the vegetables into 1–1.5-cm (½–¾-inch) chunks. Combine with the stock in a pan and simmer for 20–30 minutes until tender. Add the milk, beans and peas and heat through briefly.

Dissolve the flour completely in a little cold water and gradually mix it into the gently simmering stew to slightly thicken it. Season with salt, pepper and savory. Add the garlic, parsley and lemon zest, let them infuse for a few minutes, then remove and discard.

Filter the sauce through a sieve then blend in the cold butter with a stick (immersion) blender. Return the vegetables to the sauce, adjust the seasoning if necessary and add the parsley.

Cut the ham into strips. Grate a little nutmeg into warmed deep plates and ladle the stew into them. Scatter the ham over the stew, garnish with parsley leaves, if you like, and serve.

Beurre Noisette

All regions

Preparation time:		15 minutes
Cooking:		5 minutes
Makes:		about 200 ml (¾ cup/7 fl oz)

1 cup/9 oz	butter	250 g

Put the butter in a small pan over a medium heat and slowly heat until it melts, turns golden and gives off a nutty aroma.

Remove the pan from the heat and pour the butter through a sieve lined with a paper towel. Pour into an airtight glass jar and store in the refrigerator until needed.

Broccoli Raab Stew

Westphalia

Preparation time:		15 minutes
Cooking time:		25 minutes
Serves:		4

2 lb 4 oz	floury potatoes	1 kg
2 lb 4 oz	onions	2
2¼ lbs	cime di rapa (broccoli raab)	1 kg
1 tbsp	clarified butter	1 tbsp
1½ cups/13 fl oz	chicken or vegetable stock	375 ml
⅔ cup/5 oz	sour cream	150 g
*	salt	*
*	freshly ground black pepper	*

Peel and cut the potatoes into 1-cm (½-inch) dice. Peel and finely chop the onions. Trim off the top leaves and roots from the cime di rapa (broccoli raab) stems and discard. Wash and cut the stems into about 3-cm (1-inch) lengths.

Place a large, deep frying pan or skillet over a medium heat. Melt the clarified butter and sauté the onions until translucent. Add the potatoes and the stock and simmer for 10 minutes.

Add the cime di rapa (broccoli raab) and cook for 10–15 more minutes. Crush the contents of the pan with a potato masher, adding more stock if necessary. Stir in the sour cream and season with salt and pepper.

Westphalian Stew (Westfälisches Blindhuhn)

North Rhine-Westphalia

Soaking time:	12 hours
Preparation time:	15 minutes
Cooking time:	2 hours
Serves:	4

1½ cups/7 oz	dried haricot beans	200 g
1	bay leaf	1
14 oz	side of smoked streaky bacon	400 g
2 cups/9 oz	green runner beans	250 g
9 oz	carrots	250 g
1 lb 2 oz	potatoes	500 g
9 oz	cooking apples (e.g. Bramley)	250 g
7 oz	firm pears	200 g
2	onions	2
*	salt	*
*	freshly ground black pepper	*
*	sugar	*
½	bunch parsley, finely chopped	½

Soak the haricot beans overnight in 1.5 litres (6 cups/ 50 fl oz) of water, to soften. The following day, bring the beans to a boil, in their soaking water, with the bay leaf. Add the bacon after 30 minutes, then boil for 1 more hour.

Trim, wash and cut the green beans into pieces. Trim, peel and slice the carrots. Peel and dice the potatoes. Peel, quarter and core the apples and pears. Peel and slice the onions. Take the bacon out of the stock and set aside in a warm place. Add the vegetables and fruit to the stock, then cook for 20–25 minutes. Season with salt, pepper and a pinch of sugar.

Cut the bacon into thin slices and return to the pan. Serve the stew in soup plates sprinkled with finely chopped parsley.

Creamy Chestnut Soup

Rhineland-Palatinate

Preparation time:	15 minutes
Cooking time:	10 minutes
Serves:	4

1 tsp	icing (confectioners') sugar	1 tsp
¼ cup/2 fl oz	port	50 ml
3½ cups/27 fl oz	chicken stock	800 ml
3 cups/1 lb	cooked chestnuts	450 g
½ tbsp	dark chocolate, optional	½ tbsp
*	pinch orange zest, optional	*
¼	vanilla pod (bean)	¼
¾ cup/7 fl oz	single (light) cream	200 ml
1¼ oz	cold butter	30 g
3½ oz	white mushrooms	100 g
1 tsp	Beurre Noisette (p. 112)	1 tsp
1 tbsp	finely chopped parsley	1 tbsp
*	salt	*

Sift the sugar into a frying pan or skillet and caramelise over a medium heat. Deglaze with the port and simmer to reduce by two-thirds.

Combine the stock with 350 g (2½ cups/12 oz) chestnuts in a pan and bring to a boil. If you would like to give the soup an even richer flavour, add the chopped dark chocolate and grated orange zest along with the ¼ vanilla pod (bean) and its scraped out seeds to the cream (infuse the vanilla pod for 1–2 minutes and then remove and discard), and blend. Otherwise, simply add the cream, lower the heat and blend with a stick (immersion) blender. Add the reduced port to the soup. Add the cold butter and blend again. Season with salt.

Quarter the remaining chestnuts. Clean the mushrooms, wiping with paper towels if necessary, then cut in half.

Heat the Beurre Noisette (p. 112) in a frying pan or skillet over a medium heat and briefly fry the mushrooms. Add the chestnuts and warm through. Sprinkle with parsley and season with salt.

Blend the soup again with a stick (immersion) blender until frothy. Pour the soup into warmed deep plates. Top with the mushroom and chestnut mixture.

Soups, Stews & Sauces

Remoulade

All regions

Preparation time:		10 minutes
Makes:		about 250 ml (1 cup/8 fl oz)

2	fresh egg yolks	2
1 tsp	white wine vinegar	1 tsp
½ tsp	hot mustard	½ tsp
scant 1 cup/7 fl oz	vegetable or olive oil	200 ml
1 tsp	lemon juice	1 tsp
4	anchovy fillets	4
1 tbsp	capers	1 tbsp
2 oz	gherkins (dill pickles)	50 g
3 tbsp	parsley, chervil, chopped	3 tbsp
*	salt	*
*	freshly ground black pepper	*

Allow all the ingredients to come to room temperature. Stir a pinch of salt into the egg yolks and let stand for 1 minute. Whisk in the vinegar and mustard.

Whisk the oil into the mixture, a few drops at a time at first and then in a thin stream, until creamy. Season with lemon juice, salt and pepper.

Finely chop the anchovies, capers and gherkins (dill pickles) and stir into the sauce, together with the herbs. Adjust the seasoning with salt, pepper and a little of the pickling liquid from the gerrkins (dill pickles). Store the remoulade in the refrigerator and use within 1 day, as it contains raw egg.

Mayonnaise

All regions

Preparation time:		5 minutes
Makes:		about 250 ml (1 cup/8 fl oz)

*	salt	*
2	fresh egg yolks	2
1 tbsp	red wine vinegar	1 tbsp
*	Worcestershire sauce	*
½ tsp	hot mustard	½ tsp
¾ cup/7 fl oz	oil	200 ml

Allow all the ingredients to come to room temperature. Stir a pinch of salt into the egg yolks and let stand for 1 minute. Whisk in the vinegar, Worcestershire sauce and mustard.

Whisk the oil into the mixture, a few drops at a time at first and then in a thin stream until creamy. Season with salt.

Store in the refrigerator and use within 1 day, as it contains raw egg. Delicious with French fries, fried vegetables and fish, as a salad dressing or to accompany finger food as a dip.

Herb Sauce

All regions

Preparation time:		10 minutes
Cooking time:		5 minutes
Serves:		4

1 tsp	icing (confectioners') sugar	1 tsp
1 tbsp	Noilly Prat (French vermouth)	20 ml
½ cup/4 fl oz	white wine	125 ml
2–3	garlic slices	2–3
1	bay leaf	1
½ cup/4 fl oz	vegetable stock	125 ml
½ cup/3½ fl oz	single (light) cream	100 ml
1	handful of chervil	1
1	handful of basil leaves	1
1	handful of tarragon leaves	1
2 tbsp	butter	2 tbsp
*	grated unwaxed lemon zest	*
*	freshly grated nutmeg	*
*	salt	*

Caramelise the sugar in a pan over a medium heat. Deglaze the pan with the vermouth and wine then reduce. Add the garlic and bay leaf, followed by the stock and cream and reduce for a few minutes. Remove and discard the bay leaf and transfer the sauce to a measuring jug. Wash and finely chop the herbs then add them together with the butter, a pinch of lemon zest, a little nutmeg and salt to the sauce. Blend with a stick (immersion) blender.

Chive Sauce

All regions

Preparation time:		5 minutes
Cooking time:		5 minutes
Serves:		4

1 cup/8 fl oz	vegetable stock	250 ml
2 tbsp	plain (all-purpose) flour	2 tbsp
1 dash	lemon juice	1 dash
½ strip	unwaxed lemon zest	½ strip
⅓ cup/3 fl oz	single (light) cream	80 ml
¾ oz	cold butter	20 g
*	salt	*
1–2 tbsp	finely chopped chives	1–2 tbsp

Heat the stock. Dissolve the flour completely in a little cold water, add to the stock and bring to a boil. Stir in the lemon juice and zest and simmer for 2–3 minutes. Add the cream and bring back to the boil. Remove the lemon zest and add in the butter. Season with salt and stir in the chives.

Cream Sauce

Preparation time:		5 minutes
Cooking time:		20 minutes
Makes:	about 500 ml (generous 2 cups/17 fl oz)	

1	onion	1
1 tbsp	oil	1 tbsp
1¼ cups/10 fl oz	chicken stock	300 ml
½	small bay leaf	½
2 oz	cold butter	50 g
½ cup/3½ fl oz	single (light) cream	100 ml
*	salt	*
*	cayenne pepper	*
1 strip	unwaxed lemon zest	1 strip

Peel and finely chop the onions. Sauté in the oil in a small pan until translucent. Add the stock and bay leaf and simmer for about 20 minutes.

Remove the bay leaf then blend in the butter and cream with a stick (immersion) blender. Season the sauce with salt and cayenne pepper. Add the lemon zest and let it infuse for a few minutes, then remove and discard.

Frankfurt-Style Herb Sauce

Preparation time:		15 minutes
Cooking time:		8–9 minutes
Serves:		4

4	eggs	4
⅔ cup/2 oz	borage or chervil	50 g
⅔ cup/2 oz	watercress or parsley	50 g
⅔ cup/2 oz	sorrel or chives	50 g
1 cup/8 oz	yoghurt or sour cream	250 g
1 cup/8 oz	sour cream	250 g
4–5 tbsp	sunflower oil	4–5 tbsp
*	salt	*
*	freshly ground black pepper	*
2 tsp	mustard	2 tsp
1–2 tbsp	lemon juice	1–2 tbsp
*	sugar	*

Hard-boil the eggs for 8–9 minutes. Plunge into cold water, let cool and peel. Separate the yolks from the whites. Finely chop the whites.

Wash, shake dry, pluck and finely chop the herbs (the more herbs you use, the sharper and greener the sauce will become).

Mix the herbs with the yoghurt or sour cream. Add the chopped egg whites.

Slowly add the oil to the egg yolk while stirring constantly with a whisk until smooth. Season with salt and pepper. Add the yolk mixture to the herb mixture and season with mustard, lemon juice and sugar.

Béchamel Sauce

All regions

Preparation time:	5 minutes
Cooking time:	5 minutes
Makes:	about 750 ml (3 cups/25 fl oz)

⅔ cup/2¾ oz	plain (all-purpose) flour	75 g
⅓ cup/2¾ oz	butter	75 g
1	bay leaf	1
5	peppercorns	5
3 cups/25 fl oz	cold milk	750 ml
*	salt	*
*	freshly grated nutmeg	*

Gently simmer the flour in a pan with the butter, bay leaf and peppercorns. Gradually stir in the milk, then simmer while stirring constantly for about 5 minutes. Season with salt and nutmeg, then filter the sauce through a fine sieve.

Bell Pepper Dip with Herbs

All regions

Preparation time:	10 minutes
Cooking time:	5 minutes
Serves:	4

3	spring onions (scallions)	3
1	small red bell pepper	1
1 tbsp	mild olive oil	1 tbsp
*	salt	*
¾ cup/5 oz	soft cream cheese	150 g
1 cup/7 oz	Quark	200 g
6 tbsp	milk	6 tbsp
¼ tsp	sweet paprika	¼ tsp
1 tbsp	melted Beurre Noisette (p. 112)	1 tbsp
½–1 tsp	thyme, finely chopped	½–1 tsp
1 tbsp	parsley, finely chopped	1 tbsp
*	freshly ground black pepper	*

Trim, wash and cut the spring onions (scallions) into thin rings. Halve the bell pepper lengthwise, seed, wash and finely dice. Heat the olive oil in a frying pan or skillet, sauté the diced pepper for a few minutes and season with salt.

Mix the cream cheese with the Quark and milk until smooth, then stir in the paprika. Add the spring onions (scallions), peppers, Beurre Noisette (p. 112), thyme and parsley and season well with salt and pepper.

White Wine Sauce

All regions

Preparation time:		5 minutes
Cooking time:		20 minutes
Makes:		about 300 ml (1¼ cups/10½ fl oz)

1	onion	1
1 tbsp	oil	1 tbsp
⅓ cup/2¾ fl oz	white wine	80 ml
1 tsp	Noilly Prat (French vermouth)	1 tsp
1 cup/8 fl oz	vegetable stock	250 ml

Peel and finely chop the onions. Sauté in a small pan with the oil until translucent. Deglaze the pan with the wine and vermouth, then add the stock.

Cook the onions until soft, about 15 minutes. They must be completely soft to bind the sauce.

Creamy White Wine Sauce

All regions

Preparation time:		10 minutes
Cooking time:		5 minutes
Makes:		about 400 ml (1⅔ cups/14 fl oz)

1 tbsp	icing (confectioners') sugar	1 tbsp
½ cup/3½ fl oz	dry white wine	100 ml
1 cup/8 fl oz	vegetable stock	250 ml
½ cup/3½ fl oz	single (light) cream	100 ml
2 tsp	plain (all-purpose) flour	2 tsp
1 tbsp	cold butter	1 tbsp
*	salt	*
*	freshly ground black pepper	*

Cook the sugar in a pan over a medium heat to a golden caramel, then deglaze the pan with the wine and reduce by two-thirds. Add the stock and simmer for 1–2 minutes. Add the cream and bring to a boil. Dissolve the plain flour completely in a little cold water and gradually mix it into the sauce to slightly thicken. Finally, mix in the butter with a stick (immersion) blender and season the sauce with salt and pepper.

Soups, Stews & Sauces

Hollandaise Sauce

All regions

Preparation time:		5 minutes
Cooking time:		20 minutes
Makes:		about 250 ml (1 cup/8 fl oz)

1	shallot	1
¼ cup/2 fl oz	white wine	50 ml
1 tsp	white wine vinegar	1 tsp
5	peppercorns	5
½ cup/4 fl oz	vegetable stock	125 ml
½ cup/4¼ oz	butter	125 g
3	egg yolks	3
*	salt	*
1 dash	lemon juice	1 dash

Peel and finely chop the shallot. Combine with the wine, vinegar, peppercorns and 5 tablespoons of the stock in a pan and reduce almost completely. Stir in the remaining stock and filter through a sieve into a bowl.

Heat the butter in a clean pan until it foams. Combine the egg yolks with the stock in a bowl over a bain-marie and beat until thick and frothy. The temperature should not exceed 80°C/175°F. Take the bowl out of the bain-marie, stir a few drops of warm butter into the egg mixture then add the rest in a thin stream while stirring until the sauce is thick and creamy. Season with the salt and lemon juice.

Mustard Sauce

Northern Germany

Preparation time:		5 minutes
Cooking time:		2 minutes
Serves:		4

½ cup/3½ fl oz	vegetable stock	100 ml
½ cup/3½ fl oz	single (light) cream	100 ml
2 tbsp	Dijon mustard	2 tbsp
1 tsp	sweet Bavarian mustard	1 tsp
1 pinch	grated unwaxed lemon zest	1 pinch
*	salt	*

Combine the stock with the cream in a pan and bring to a boil. Stir in the Dijon and sweet mustards and season with the lemon zest and salt.

Brown Sauce

All regions

Preparation time:		25 minutes
Cooking time:		2 hours 45 minutes
Makes:		about 600 ml (2½ cups/20 fl oz)

3 lb 4 oz	meaty veal soup bones	1.5 kg
3	onions	3
1	carrot	1
5 oz	celeriac	150 g
1 tsp	icing (confectioners') sugar	1 tsp
1 tbsp	tomato purée (paste)	1 tbsp
1¼ cups/10 fl oz	heavy red wine	300 ml
½–1 tbsp	oil	½–1 tbsp
8½ cups/68 fl oz	lightly salted chicken stock	2 litres

Preheat the oven to 220°C/425°F/Gas Mark 7. Chop the bones into small pieces. Wash the bones and rub dry, transfer to a roasting pan and place on the middle shelf inside the oven and roast for about 45 minutes. Peel and cut the onions, carrots and celeriac into 1.5-cm (¾-inch) dice.

Put the sugar into a large pan over a medium heat and lightly caramelise. Stir in the tomato purée (paste) and cook briefly. Deglaze three times with a third of the wine, slowly reducing each time.

Sauté the diced vegetables in a frying pan or skillet with oil. Add the roasted bones and sautéed vegetables to the pan and cover well with the stock. Simmer the vegetables and bones for 2 hours. Filter the sauce through a sieve.

Horseradish Sauce

All regions

Preparation time:		5 minutes
Cooking time:		10 minutes
Serves:		4

3 oz	waxy potatoes	80 g
scant 1 cup/7 fl oz	chicken stock	200 ml
1	bay leaf	1
½–1 tsp	Dijon mustard	½–1 tsp
1 tbsp	creamed horseradish	1 tbsp
¾ cup/3 fl oz	single (light) cream	80 ml
4 tsp	cold butter	4 tsp
*	salt	*

Peel and finely dice the potatoes and put in a pan with the stock and the bay leaf and cook until tender. Remove and discard the bay leaf. Stir in the mustard, creamed horseradish and cream then mix in the butter with a stick (immersion) blender. Season with salt.

Red Wine and Butter Sauce

All regions

Preparation time: 5 minutes
Cooking time: 10 minutes
Serves: 4

1 tsp	icing (confectioners') sugar	1 tsp
½ cup/3½ fl oz	port	100 ml
½ cup/3½ fl oz	heavy red wine	100 ml
½ cup/3½ oz	chilled butter	100 g
*	salt	*
*	freshly ground black pepper	*

Sift the sugar into a pan, frying pan or skillet and caramelise over a medium heat. Add the port and red wine and reduce by two-thirds.

Cut the butter into cubes. Add the butter cubes, one at a time, to the pan and stir constantly to mix into the sauce. Take the pan off the heat if necessary. Season with salt and pepper. This sauce makes a good accompaniment for seared beef.

Gravy

All regions

Preparation time: 5 minutes
Cooking time: 15 minutes
Makes: about 300 ml (1¼ cups/10½ fl oz)

1 batch	Brown Sauce (p. 122)	1 batch
1 tsp	cornflour (corn starch)	1 tsp
1 strip	unwaxed lemon zest	1 strip
2	garlic slices	2
1 pinch	dried marjoram	1 pinch
1 pinch	ground cumin	1 pinch
1 tbsp	cold butter	1 tbsp
*	salt	*

Put the Brown Sauce (p. 122) into a pan and reduce by half. Dissolve the cornflour (corn starch) completely in a little cold water, stir into the sauce and simmer for 2 minutes. Add the lemon zest, garlic, marjoram and cumin and simmer for a further few minutes. Remove and discard the lemon zest and garlic. Add the butter to the sauce in small pieces and blend using a stick (immersion) blender. Season the sauce with salt.

Pepper Sauce

All regions

1 tbsp	peppercorns	1 tbsp
*	oil, for frying	*
1 tsp	icing (confectioners') sugar	1 tsp
1 tbsp	cognac	1 tbsp
1 cup/8 fl oz	chicken stock	250 ml
½ cup/3½ fl oz	single (light) cream	100 ml
1¼ oz	cold butter	30 g
1	slice garlic	1
*	salt	*
*	cayenne pepper	*
*	pinch of freshly grated nutmeg	*

Preparation time: 10 minutes
Cooking time: 20 minutes
Makes: about 250 ml (1 cup/8 fl oz)

Lightly crush the peppercorns, sift out the fine dust and briefly sauté the crushed pepper in oil (not too hot). Drain the pepper in a sieve.

Lightly caramelise the sugar in a small pan over a medium heat. Deglaze the pan with the cognac. Add the stock, pepper and cream and reduce for 15–20 minutes.

Filter the sauce through a sieve and add the cold butter in small pieces, with the garlic and blend using a stick (immersion) blender. Season with salt, cayenne pepper and nutmeg.

Wild Game Sauce

All regions

Preparation time: 5 minutes
Cooking time: 15 minutes
Makes: about 300 ml (1¼ cups/10½ fl oz)

1 batch	Brown Sauce (p. 122)	1 batch
1 tsp	cornflour (corn starch)	1 tsp
5	juniper berries	5
1	bay leaf	1
7	allspice berries	7
1 strip	unwaxed lemon zest	1 strip
1 strip	unwaxed orange zest	1 strip
½–1 tsp	grated dark chocolate	½–1 tsp
1–2 tsp	lingonberry compote	1–2 tsp
1 tbsp	cream	1 tbsp
*	salt	*
*	freshly ground black pepper	*
1 tbsp	cold butter	1 tbsp

Put the Brown Sauce (p. 122) into a pan and reduce by half. Dissolve the cornflour (corn starch) completely in a little cold water, stir into the sauce and simmer for 2 minutes. Add the juniper berries, bay leaf, allspice and lemon and orange zest and simmer for a further 5 minutes. Season the sauce with chocolate, lingonberry compote, cream, salt and pepper. Add the cold butter in small pieces and blend using a stick (immersion) blender. Filter the sauce through a sieve.

Peppered Mackerel Mousse

Northern Germany

Preparation time:		25 minutes
Cooking time:		15 minutes
Serves 4:	about 200 ml (¾ cup/7 fl oz) per serving	

1¼ cups/10 fl oz	vegetable stock	300 ml
1	bay leaf	1
2	garlic cloves	2
1 tsp	Seven-Spice Mix (p. 438)	1 tsp
2	sheets gelatine	2
3½ oz	smoked peppered mackerel	100 g
¾ cup/7 fl oz	single (light) cream	200 ml
*	salt	*
*	lemon juice	*

Put the stock into a pan with the bay leaf, bring to a boil, then reduce to a simmer and infuse for 10 minutes. Add the garlic and Seven-Spice Mix (p. 438) and infuse for a couple more minutes, then strain through a sieve.

Soften the gelatine in cold water, squeeze well and add to the hot stock. Let the stock cool.

Remove as many bones as possible from the mackerel fillets, cut the fish into small pieces, combine with the cold stock in a measuring jug and blend with a stick (immersion) blender.

Whip the cream to soft peaks, add to the mackerel mixture and season with salt and a dash of lemon juice. Fill serving glasses with the mousse and refrigerate until set, around 2 hours.

Smoked Trout Spread

Southern Germany

Preparation time:		15 minutes
Serves:		4

1	egg	1
3	pickled anchovy fillets	3
1 tsp	capers	1 tsp
1 × 4 oz	smoked trout fillet	1 × 125 g
1⅓ cups/11 oz	cream cheese	300 g
3 tbsp	milk	3 tbsp
1 tbsp	olive oil	1 tbsp
2 tbsp	chopped chives	2 tbsp
*	lemon juice	*
½ tsp	unwaxed lemon zest	½ tsp
*	salt	*
*	freshly ground black pepper	*
*	wholegrain bread, to serve	*
*	lemon wedges, to serve	*

Hard-boil the eggs for about 10 minutes. Refresh in iced water, peel and finely chop. Drain the anchovies and capers, then finely chop. Cut the smoked trout fillet into small pieces.

Mix the cream cheese with the milk and oil until smooth. Stir in the chopped egg, anchovies, capers, trout and chives. Season the spread with a dash of lemon juice, the lemon zest, salt and pepper. Serve the spread with wholegrain bread and lemon wedges.

Fried Marinated Herring (Brathering)

Northern Germany

Preparation time:		20 minutes
Cooking time:		10 minutes
Marinating time:		12 hours
Serves:		4

5 oz	onions	150 g
1 tbsp	icing (confectioners') sugar	1 tbsp
½ cup/3¾ fl oz	mild white wine vinegar	100 ml
2 cups/17 fl oz	vegetable stock	500 ml
1	bay leaf	1
1 tsp	mustard seeds	1 tsp
1 tsp	juniper berries	1 tsp
1 tsp	coriander seeds	1 tsp
1 tsp	allspice berries	1 tsp
1 tsp	peppercorns	1 tsp
1 tbsp	dill, finely chopped	1 tbsp
1 tbsp	parsley, finely chopped	1 tbsp
1	garlic clove, sliced	1
1 oz	salt	25 g
2 tsp	granulated sugar	2 tsp
8	small fresh herring fillets	8
4–6 tbsp	cornflour (corn starch)	4–6 tbsp
2–3 tbsp	oil	2–3 tbsp
*	Pan-Fried Potatoes (p. 265)	*

Peel the onion and cut into very thin strips. Put the icing (confectioners') sugar into a pan over a medium heat and lightly caramelise. Sauté the onions and deglaze the pan with the vinegar. Add the stock, bay leaf and whole spices then bring to a boil.

Add the dill, parsley and garlic and remove from the heat. Season the marinade well with salt and sugar. Transfer to a shallow container and let cool for a short time.

Thoroughly rinse the herring under cold running water and pat dry. Dredge in cornflour (corn starch) and tap to remove the excess.

Heat the oil in a frying pan or skillet and fry the herring in batches on both sides for about 5 minutes over a medium heat. Let the herring cool a little and put into the marinade. Cover the container and marinate in the refrigerator for at least 1 hour, but preferably overnight.

Take the herring out of the marinade and serve with onions and a little of the marinade on plates, along with Pan-Fried Potatoes (p. 265).

Bismarck Herring

Northern Germany

Preparation time:		15 minutes
Marinating time:		4 days
Makes:		10

10	fresh herring fillets	10
*	salt	*
2¼ cups/18 fl oz	white wine vinegar	500 ml
2 tbsp	granulated sugar	2 tbsp
2	bay leaves	2
5	allspice berries	5
3	juniper berries	3
½ tsp	mustard seeds	½ tsp
½ tsp	peppercorns	½ tsp
2–3	onions	2–3

Sprinkle the fillets with 1–2 teaspoons of salt in a glass bowl, cover with a suitable lid and rest for 2 days in the refrigerator.

Rinse the fillets in cold water and put into a clean glass bowl. Combine the vinegar with 500 ml (2¼ cups/18 fl oz) of water, 1 tablespoon of salt, the sugar, bay leaves and spices in a pan and bring to a boil. Let cool completely.

Peel and cut the onions into rings. Add them to the herring. Pour the marinade over the herring, covering completely. Marinate for 2 days in a cool place.

Pickled Herring

Northern Germany

Preparation time:		10 minutes
Resting time:		3 hours
Steeping time:		at least 2 days
Serves:		4–6

2 lb 4 oz	fresh herring (matjes)	1 kg
*	salt	*
2¼ cups/18 fl oz	vinegar	500 ml
*	granulated sugar	*
2	onions	2

Clean and debone the herring. Rub with 3–4 tablespoons salt, coating well, then leave for 3 hours until their flesh is firm.

Combine the vinegar with 500 ml (2¼ cups/18 fl oz) water, a little salt and a pinch of sugar, then bring to a boil for a few minutes. Let cool completely. Peel and cut the onions into rings.

Combine the herring with the onion rings in a stoneware pickling crock or a large Mason jar. Fill the crock or jar with the cold pickling liquid, making sure to cover the contents completely with the liquid. Cover with the lid and let steep for at least 2 days in a cool place.

Herring in Aspic

Bremen

Preparation time:		1 hour
Cooling time:		6 hours
Serves:		4

2¼ cups/18 fl oz	clear fish stock	500 ml
9	gelatine sheets	9
1	small bunch of dill	1
½	bunch of chervil	½
1 × 8 oz	floury potato	1 × 225 g
¾ cup/7 fl oz	single (light) cream	200 ml
*	salt	*
*	freshly ground pepper	*
*	freshly grated nutmeg	*
4	salted herring (matjes) fillets	4
*	Green Salad (p. 54), to serve	*

Gently heat the fish stock. Soften 7 gelatine sheets in cold water, squeeze well and dissolve in the fish stock. Wash, shake dry and finely chop the dill and chervil and add to the stock.

Chill a 1-litre (4-cups/34-fl oz) capacity terrine mould or loaf pan for 1 hour in the refrigerator. Pour about 250 ml (1 cup/8 fl oz) of the fish aspic mixture into the mould, tilting so that the sides are well covered and return to the refrigerator. Repeat this operation two or three times until the aspic has a thickness of about 1 cm (½ inch).

Boil the potato until cooked, then peel and press through a ricer. Mix with 3–4 tablespoons of the cream. Soften the remaining gelatine sheets in cold water, squeeze well, then stir into the tepid mashed potato. Let cool a little. Whip the remaining cream to stiff peaks and mix into the now cooled mashed potato. Season with salt, pepper and nutmeg.

Skin and fillet the salted herring. Cut the fillets into small cubes and mix with about 150 ml (⅔ cup/5 fl oz) of the fish aspic mixture.

Fill the terrine mould with a little of the mashed potato mixture and refrigerate for about 10 minutes. Make a 1–1.5-cm (½–¾-inch) thick layer of herring and aspic mixture in the mould and refrigerate for another 5–10 minutes. Repeat this process as many times as needed until all of the mashed potato and herring and aspic mixtures are used up. Finally, pour in the rest of the plain fish aspic.

Place the aspic in the refrigerator to set for 4–6 hours. Remove the aspic from the mould and cut into about 2-cm (1-inch) slices using an electric carving knife. Serve with a green salad.

Smoked Eel Terrine

Franconia

Preparation time:		12 hours
Cooking time:		30 minutes
Cooling time:		12 hours
Serves:		10

For the terrine:		
2 lb 4 oz	small waxy potatoes	1 kg
2	pinches of saffron threads	2
*	salt	*
2	leeks	2
1 lb 12 oz	smoked eel	800 g
*	oil, for greasing	*

For the aspic:		
3 cups/25 fl oz	vegetable stock	750 ml
12	gelatine sheets	12
3 tbsp	red wine vinegar	3 tbsp
2 tsp	Dijon mustard	2 tsp
*	salt	*
*	sugar	*
*	cayenne pepper	*

For the tomato vinaigrette:		
5	tomatoes	5
5	spring onions (scallions)	5
½ cup/3½ fl oz	vegetable stock	100 ml
2 tbsp	red wine vinegar	2 tbsp
1 tsp	hot mustard	1 tsp
*	salt	*
*	freshly ground black pepper	*
*	sugar	*
4 tbsp	olive oil	4 tbsp

For the terrine: The day before cooking, peel and halve the potatoes crosswise, or cut into slices. Boil with the saffron in salted water until tender. Cool in the liquid.

Trim, halve lengthwise and wash the leeks. Blanch in salted water until tender. Plunge into iced water and drain.

Remove the skin from the eel and set aside to infuse the stock. Detach the fillets from the backbone, remove all bones and cut the fillets into pieces as long as the mould.

For the aspic: Heat the stock with the eel skin and leave to infuse for 4–5 minutes. Soften the gelatine in cold water. Remove the eel skin from the stock. Mix the vinegar and mustard in and season with salt, sugar and cayenne. Add the gelatine to the stock. Cool to room temperature.

Grease a 1.5-litre (50-fl oz) terrine mould or loaf pan with oil and line with clingfilm (plastic wrap). Lay the leek layers side by side, crosswise, so they hang over both sides. Cover with potatoes, arrange half the eel pieces in the middle and cover with another layer of potatoes. Repeat with another layer of each. Fold the leek over, then cover with clingfilm (plastic wrap). Chill to set overnight.

For the tomato vinaigrette: Blanch the tomatoes in boiling water for 3 minutes. Plunge into iced water, then peel, quarter, seed and finely dice. Trim, wash and finely slice the spring onions (scallions). Combine the stock, vinegar, mustard, salt, pepper and a pinch of sugar and blend with a stick (immersion) blender. Gradually pour in the olive oil while blending. Add the vegetables. Unmould the terrine, cut into slices and serve with the vinaigrette.

Matjes Herring

Northern Germany

Preparation time:		15 minutes
Serves:		4

1	onion	1
1	large apple	1
2	Pickled Cucumbers (p. 29)	2
1⅔ cups/14 fl oz	sour cream	400 ml
*	salt	*
*	freshly ground black pepper	*
*	sugar	*
*	lemon juice	*
8 × 3½ oz	pickled herring double fillets	8 × 100 g
*	Boiled Potatoes (p. 260), to serve	*

Peel, halve and slice the onion. Wash, quarter and core the apple. Halve the apple quarters, then cut crosswise into 3–4-mm (⅛-inch) slices. Slice the Pickled Cucumbers.

Season the sour cream with salt, pepper, a pinch of sugar and a dash of lemon juice. Mix in the onion, apple and Pickled Cucumbers (p. 29).

Wash and pat dry the herring fillets, arrange on plates and pour the apple and onion sauce over the top. Accompany with Boiled Potatoes (p. 260).

Matjes Herring
with Green Beans

Northern Germany

Preparation time:		20 minutes
Cooking time:		15 minutes
Serves:		4

8	pickled herring (matjes) fillets	8
½	lemon, juiced	½
2 tbsp	oil	2 tbsp
2½ oz	fine green beans	600 g
2	sprigs of savory	2
½ cup/1½ oz	butter	40 g
*	salt	*
*	freshly ground black pepper	*
6	thin slices smoked bacon	6
1 tbsp	finely chopped parsley	1 tbsp
*	Boiled Potatoes (p. 260), to serve	*

Briefly wash and pat dry the herring fillets, then arrange side-by-side in a dish. Mix the lemon juice with the oil, drizzle the mixture over the fillets, cover with clingfilm (plastic wrap) and refrigerate.

Wash and trim the ends of the green beans. Bring salted water to a boil with the savory, add the beans and cook for 6–8 minutes until tender but firm to the bite. Plunge briefly into iced water and drain. Melt the butter in a pan and toss the beans in the butter. Season with salt and pepper.

Cut the bacon slices crosswise into thin strips and fry in a frying pan or skillet until crispy.

Arrange the herring fillets on plates with the beans and sprinkle with the bacon strips and parsley. Accompany with Boiled Potatoes (p. 260).

Smoked Mackerel

Northern Germany

Marinating time:		12 hours
Preparation time:		10 minutes
Cooking time:		1 hour 40 minutes
Serves:		4

5 oz	salt	150 g
1 tsp	juniper berries	1 tsp
1 tsp	peppercorns	1 tsp
½ tsp	coriander seeds	½ tsp
1	bay leaf	1
4	mackerel, cleaned, scaled	4
*	bread, to serve	*
*	Potato Salad (p. 62), to serve	*
*	creamed horseradish, to serve	*

To make this recipe, you will need a smoker and around 4 tablespoons wood chips, preferably beech or alder.

Combine the salt with the whole spices and the bay leaf in a pan, add 2 litres (8½ cups/67½ fl oz) water, bring to a boil and let cool.

Wash and pat dry the fish, lay in a deep container and fill with the brine. The fish should be completely covered. Marinate for 10–12 hours in the refrigerator.

The following day, take the fish out of the brine, wash in cold water and pat dry. Stick the smoking hooks into the fish, about 1 cm (½inch) behind the head, to the right and left of the backbone.

Preheat an electric or gas smoker oven to 50°C/125°F. Hang the fish inside the smoker, spaced at least 3 cm (1 inch) apart and let dry until the skin feels a bit like parchment, about 40 minutes. Leave the vent and door slightly open.

Close the smoker oven, raise the temperature to 100°C/200°F and cook the fish for 30 minutes.

Reduce the heat to 65°C/150°F, put the wood chips into the wood-chip container, close the smoker oven and smoke the fish for about 1 hour. The fish are done when the dorsal fin can be pulled out easily. Serve the smoked mackerel hot or cold. Accompany with bread, Potato Salad (p. 62) and creamed horseradish.

Herring and Corned Beef Hash (Labskaus)

Northern Germany

Preparation time:		30 minutes
Cooking time:		1 hour 30 minutes
Serves:		4

1 lb 5 oz	corned beef	600 g
3	onions	3
2	bay leaves	2
2	cloves	2
2 lb 4 oz	floury potatoes	1 kg
4 large	Pickled Cucumbers (p. 29)	4 large
*	salt	*
*	freshly ground black pepper	*
3½ oz	pickled beetroot (beets)	100 g
4	pickled herring (matjes) fillets	4
1 tbsp	oil	1 tbsp
4	eggs	4
1 tbsp	finely chopped parsley	1 tbsp

Put the corned beef in a pan and cover with cold water. Peel the onions and attach a bay leaf to each with a clove. Add to the meat in the pan and simmer for about 1 hour 30 minutes.

Peel and cut the potatoes into chunks. Cook in a little water without adding salt. Drain, let steam and coarsely mash with a potato masher.

Remove the cloves and bay leaves from the onions and grind the meat and onions together in a meat grinder using a coarse plate. Mix with the mashed potatoes and add enough of the cooking liquid to form a mushy paste.

Finely dice the Pickled Cucumbers (p. 29) and add to the hash. Briefly reheat and season with salt and pepper.

Cut the beetroot (beets) into strips. Arrange the herring fillets and hash on plates. Heat the oil in a frying pan or skillet and fry the eggs. Put one fried egg on the hash, season with salt and pepper, sprinkle with parsley and garnish with beetroot (beets) strips.

Fish Grilled on a Stick (Steckerlfisch)

Bavaria

Preparation time:		1 hour
Soaking time:		24 hours
Marinating time:		3 hours
Cooking time:		15 minutes
Serves:		4

11 oz	4 trout or mackerel	300 g
1 tsp	freshly ground black pepper	1 tsp
1 tsp	ground coriander seeds	1 tsp
1 tsp	sweet paprika	1 tsp
½ tsp	garlic powder	½ tsp
½ tsp	ground fennel seeds	½ tsp
½ tsp	dried thyme	½ tsp
½ tsp	savory	½ tsp
½ tsp	oregano	½ tsp
½ tsp	marjoram	½ tsp
½ tsp	rosemary	½ tsp
6 tbsp	oil	6 tbsp
*	salt	*
½ cup/4¼ oz	melted butter	125 g

To make this recipe, you will need an open grill and charcoal.

Soak four square wooden skewers or rods, measuring 8–10 mm (½ inch) thick and 50–60 cm (18–24 inches) long, in water for 24 hours. Sharpen one end of each to a point.

Scale, wash and pat dry the fish. Mix the herbs and spices with the oil and rub the fish with the mixture inside and out. Marinate for a few hours in the refrigerator.

Take the fish out of the refrigerator 20 minutes before grilling. Thread the sticks through the mouth of each fish, along the backbone and out through the tail, leaving a good length sticking out at both ends. Season the fish with salt.

Light some charcoal in an open grill, burn it down to glowing embers and remove the grill grate. Position the sticks, spaced apart, over the edges of the grill so that the fish are over the embers. Grill the fish on all sides, about 15 minutes depending on their exposure to the heat. Ideally, the grill should have a holder for the sticks with 1-cm (½-inch) square notches, allowing the sticks to be manually turned, inserted and held in place on all four sides, so the fish can cook evenly. Brush the fish with melted butter from time to time. The fish are done when the dorsal fin can be pulled out easily.

Fish & Seafood

Pike Dumplings

Baden-Württemberg

Preparation time:		20 minutes
Cooking time:		15 minutes
Serves:		4

7 oz	skinless pike fillets	200 g
3½ oz	skinless perch fillets	100 g
1¼ cups/10 fl oz	single (light) cream	300 ml
1–2 tsp	hot mustard	1–2 tsp
*	freshly grated nutmeg	*
1 tsp	aniseeds	1 tsp
1 tsp	peppercorns	1 tsp
1–2 tsp	dill, finely chopped	1–2 tsp
1 tsp	dried tarragon	1 tsp
1	bay leaf	1
*	salt	*
*	Creamy White Wine Sauce (p. 120)	*
*	Boiled Potatoes (p. 260), to serve	*

Wash, pat dry and cut the fish fillets into cubes. Season with salt and pepper. Put the fish and cream in the freezer for about 5 minutes to chill well. Put the fish in a blender and add 100 g (scant ½ cup/3½ fl oz) of the cream, the mustard, salt and nutmeg. Put the aniseeds and peppercorns in a spice grinder. Blend the fish with a stick (immersion) blender to a smooth paste.

Blend in the rest of the cream, half at a time. Finally, add the dill and tarragon and season the dumpling mixture with the freshly ground spices. The mixture should be smooth and glossy. Transfer to a bowl and keep cold.

Bring 1 litre (4 cups/34 fl oz) water to a boil in a pan. Add the bay leaf and 1½ tablespoon salt. Reduce the heat to a temperature of 80–90°C/175–200°F. Use 2 tablespoons to shape 16 dumplings, regularly dipping the spoons in warm water. Simmer the dumplings in the cooking liquid for 15 minutes. The dumplings can be served with Creamy White Wine (p. 120) and accompanied by Boiled Potatoes (p. 260).

Rhenish–Style Mussels

Rhineland-Palatinate

Preparation time:		15 minutes
Cooking time:		15 minutes
Serves:		4

1	small white onion	1
1–2	carrots	1–2
1	stalk celery	1
2 oz	leeks	50 g
1	garlic clove	1
1 tbsp	oil	1 tbsp
½ cup/3½ fl oz	white wine	100 ml
1½ cups/12 fl oz	fish stock	350 ml
*	grated unwaxed lemon zest	*
*	grated unwaxed lime zest	*
3	sprigs of parsley	3
*	salt	*
½	lime, juiced	½
½–1 tsp	hot mustard	½–1 tsp
¼ cup/2 fl oz	single (light) cream	50 ml
2 tbsp	cold butter	2 tbsp
4½ lb	mussels	2 kg
1	bay leaf	1
1 tsp	juniper berries	1
1 tbsp	finely chopped parsley	1 tbsp
*	toast, to serve	*

Trim, peel, wash and finely dice the onion, carrot, celery and leek. Peel and slice the garlic. Sauté the vegetables in a pan with oil over a low heat. Deglaze with half of the wine and reduce by two-thirds. Add the stock, and a pinch each of lemon and lime zest.

Wash, shake dry, pluck and finely chop the parsley leaves. Season the stock with salt and lime juice and simmer for 1–2 minutes. Filter the stock through a sieve and set aside the vegetables. Add the mustard, cream and butter to the stock and whisk to a frothy sauce.

Thoroughly brush the mussels under cold running water and discard any open ones.

Combine 200 ml (¾ cup/7 fl oz) water in a pan with the rest of the wine and bring to a simmer. Add the bay leaf and juniper berries. Put the mussels in the pan, cover with a lid and cook over a low heat for 4–5 minutes until they open. Take out the mussels, discarding any unopened ones. Arrange the mussels on warmed, deep plates and scatter with diced vegetables and parsley. Whisk the stock until frothy and pour over the mussels. Serve with toast.

Fish & Seafood

Marinated Catfish with Horseradish

Southern Germany

Preparation time:		30 minutes
Cooking time:		30 minutes
Marinating time:		12 hours
Serves:		4

2	onions	2
1	carrot	1
5 oz	celeriac	150 g
1 tbsp	icing (confectioners') sugar	1 tbsp
3 cups/25 fl oz	vegetable stock	750 ml
1	bay leaf	1
½–1 tsp	yellow mustard seeds	½–1 tsp
5	juniper berries	5
5	allspice berries	5
1 tsp	peppercorns	1 tsp
1 strip	unwaxed lemon zest	1 strip
2	garlic cloves	2
⅔ cup/5 fl oz	red wine vinegar	150 ml
*	salt	*
2 tsp	granulated sugar	2 tsp
4 × 4 oz	catfish fillets, skinless	4 × 120 g
1 tbsp	horseradish (from a jar)	1 tbsp
2 tbsp	butter	2 tbsp
1	small piece horseradish root	1
1 tbsp	finely chopped chives	1 tbsp
*	Boiled Potatoes (p. 260), to serve	*

Peel and cut the onion into very thin rings. Trim, peel and cut the carrot and celeriac into thin strips. Lightly caramelise the icing (confectioners') sugar in a pan, add the vegetables and sauté for a few minutes.

Add the stock, bay leaf and mustard seeds. Put the juniper, allspice berries and peppercorns into a spice bag, close and add to the stock. Bring the stock to a boil, reduce the heat and simmer for 10 minutes. Add the lemon zest, garlic and vinegar and season the marinade with salt and sugar. Remove the pan from the heat and let cool. Remove the spice bag.

Wash and pat dry the fish fillets, lay in an ovenproof dish and fill with the cold marinade. Cover the dish and marinate overnight in the refrigerator.

The following day, take out the fillets, filter the marinade through a sieve into a wide pan and bring to a boil. Skim off any froth. Take out 200 ml (¾ cup/7 fl oz) of the marinade and blend with the horseradish and butter using a stick (immersion) blender. Season the sauce with salt. Warm the vegetable strips in a frying pan or skillet.

Remove the pan with the rest of the hot marinade from the heat and immerse the fish fillets in it, for 6–8 minutes, until cooked. Arrange the fillets with the vegetable strips in deep plates and cover with the sauce. Grate fresh horseradish over the top and sprinkle with chives. Accompany with Boiled Potatoes (p. 260), which can be briefly fried in a frying pan or skillet.

Braised Halibut

Northern Germany

Preparation time:		5 minutes
Cooking time:		10 minutes
Serves:		4

1	unwaxed lemon	1
1	onion	1
1	bay leaf	1
*	salt	*
4 × 5 oz	halibut fillets, skinless	4 × 150 g
*	Horseradish Sauce (p. 122)	*
*	Creamy White Wine Sauce (p. 120)	*
*	Spinach (p. 303), to serve	*

Wash, pat dry and cut the lemon into slices. Don't peel, but halve the onion. Put the skin-on onion halves, bay leaf and 2 lemon slices into a pan with 1.5 litres (6¼ cups/50 fl oz) water and bring to a boil. Season with salt.

Add the fish fillets, reduce the heat and simmer for 10 minutes. Take out the fish and serve with the remaining lemon slices. Drizzle with Horseradish Sauce (p. 122), Creamy White Wine Sauce (p. 120) and serve with Spinach (p. 303).

Pike with Caper Sauce

Mecklenburg-Western Pomerania

Preparation time:		20 minutes
Cooking time:		10 minutes
Serves:		4

1	bay leaf	1
½ tsp	allspice berries	½ tsp
½ tsp	yellow mustard seeds	½ tsp
½ tsp	peppercorns	½ tsp
2 oz	carrot	60 g
3½ oz	celeriac	100 g
2	onions	2
3 oz	leek	80 g
4¼ cups/34 fl oz	vegetable stock	1 litre
5 tbsp	red wine vinegar	5 tbsp
*	salt	*
1–2 tsp	sugar	1–2 tsp
4 × 4 oz	skinless pike fillets	4 × 120 g
½ cup/3½ fl oz	single (light) cream	100 ml
2 tsp	cornflour (corn starch)	2 tsp
2–3	anchovy fillets in oil	2–3
3 tbsp	cold butter	3 tbsp
1–2 tsp	capers	1–2 tsp
1 strip	unwaxed lemon zest	1 strip
1	garlic clove	1
1 tbsp	butter	1 tbsp
1 tsp	finely chopped dill	1 tsp
*	Mashed Potato (p. 261), to serve	*
*	Boiled Potatoes (p. 260), to serve	*

Put the bay leaf, allspice, mustard seeds and peppercorns into a spice bag and close. Trim and peel the carrot, peel the celeriac and onions and trim and wash the leek. Cut all the vegetables into very thin strips.

Heat the stock with the carrot, celeriac and onion strips with the spice bag and vinegar in a pan and simmer for 5 minutes. Season with salt and sugar. Wash and pat dry the pike fillets. Add the fillets and leek strips to the stock and simmer for 3–5 minutes until cooked. Use a slotted spoon or skimmer to carefully take the fillets out of the pan. Remove any remaining bones, cover with clingfilm (plastic wrap) and keep warm in the oven at 50°C/125°F.

Remove the spice bag and filter the stock through a sieve. Measure out 300 ml (1¼ cups/10 fl oz) stock and heat in a pan with the cream. Dissolve the cornflour (corn starch) completely in a little cold water and gradually mix it into the lightly simmering sauce to thicken. Drain and finely chop the anchovies. Blend with the cold butter into the sauce. Stir in the capers. Add the lemon zest and garlic, leave to infuse for a few minutes, then remove and discard.

Heat the vegetable strips in the butter, season with salt and stir in the dill. Lightly flake the pike and arrange on warmed plates. Cover with the sauce and garnish with the vegetable strips. This dish can be accompanied with Mashed Potato (p. 261) or Boiled Potatoes (p. 260).

Blue Trout

All regions

Preparation time:		10 minutes
Cooking time:		10 minutes
Serves:		4

4	river or sea trout	4
1	small carrot	1
½	parsnip	½
4 oz	celeriac	120 g
1	small onion	1
1 cup/8 fl oz	white wine vinegar	250 ml
2 cups/17 fl oz	dry white wine	500 ml
*	salt	*
1 tbsp	sugar	1 tbsp
1	garlic clove	1
1 strip	unwaxed lemon zest	1 strip
*	Potato Salad (p. 62), to serve	*
*	Chive Sauce (p. 115), to serve	*

Thoroughly wash the inside of the fish and pat dry, but do not wipe or wash off the thin film from the skin, as this gives the fish its blue sheen once cooked. Peel and cut the carrot, parsnip (parsley root), celeriac and onion into very thin strips.

Combine 1.5 litres (6 cups/50 fl oz) water with the vinegar and wine in a large pan. Add the vegetable strips, 1 tablespoon salt and the sugar. Heat the liquid to a gentle simmer. Add the garlic and lemon zest. Add the fish to the pan and poach, uncovered, about 10 minutes.

Carefully take the fish out of the pan. Either take the flesh off the bone and serve as fillets, or serve the fish whole with Potato Salad (p. 60) and Chive Sauce (p. 115).

Blue Tench

All regions

Preparation time:		10 minutes
Cooking time:		15 minutes
Serves:		2

17 cups/135 fl oz	vegetable stock	4 litres
2	bay leaves	2
1–2 tsp	juniper berries	1–2 tsp
1–2 tsp	peppercorns	1–2 tsp
4 sprigs	dill	4 sprigs
4 sprigs	parsley	4 sprigs
⅔ cup/5 fl oz	wine vinegar	150 ml
11 oz	freshwater tench or trout	300 g
⅓ cup/3 oz	melted butter	80 g
*	Boiled Potatoes (p. 260), to serve	*
*	Hollandaise Sauce (p.122)	*
*	salad, to serve	*

Combine the stock with the spices, herbs and vinegar in a suitable pan and heat to about 90°C/200°F.

Thoroughly wash the inside of the fish and briefly drain, but do not wipe or wash off the thin film from the skin, as this gives the fish its blue sheen once cooked. Immerse the prepared fish in the stock, making sure they are completely covered. Add a little water if necessary. Poach at a temperature of about 80°C/175°F for 10–15 minutes.

Take the fish out of the stock, drain and arrange on warmed plates. Serve the melted butter separately. Accompany with Boiled Potatoes (p. 260) and a salad. Instead of melted butter, the fish can be served with Hollandaise Sauce (p. 122) and a little creamed horseradish, if you like, alongside a salad.

Eel with Herb Vinaigrette

Berlin

Preparation time:		15 minutes
Cooking time:		10 minutes
Serves:		4

1½ lb	fresh eels, heads removed	750 g
1–2 tbsp	lemon juice	1–2 tbsp
*	salt	*
*	freshly ground pepper	*
*	hot paprika	*
2 tbsp	light vegetable oil	2 tbsp
1 cup/8 fl oz	dry white wine	250 ml
1	bunch of rocket	1 bunch
1	bunch of chervil	1 bunch
3 tbsp	white wine vinegar	3 tbsp
4 tbsp	walnut oil	4 tbsp
*	Boiled Potatoes (p. 260), to serve	*
*	butter, to serve	*

Skin the eels and cut into 2-cm (¾-inch) slices. Drizzle with lemon juice and season with salt, pepper and a pinch of paprika. Heat the oil in a frying pan or skillet and sear the eel well. Deglaze the pan with the wine, cover with a lid and cook for 10 minutes.

Wash and shake dry the rocket and chervil. Remove the large stems from the rocket and cut the leaves into strips. Do not leave any whole. Coarsely chop the chervil.

Make a vinaigrette by mixing the vinegar with salt, pepper and walnut oil. Stir in the herbs and pour into four deep plates. Arrange the eel slices over the vinaigrette and pour the cooking liquid over the top. Accompany with Boiled Potatoes (p. 260) briefly sautéed in butter.

Fish & Seafood

Pan-Fried Vendace Fillets

All regions

Preparation time:		2 minutes
Cooking time:		5 minutes
Serves:		4

4 × 3½ oz	vendace fillets, skin-on	4 × 100 g
1 tbsp	oil	1 tbsp
5 tbsp	olive oil	5 tbsp
*	salt	*
*	freshly ground black pepper	*
½ tsp	unwaxed lemon zest	½ tsp
½ tsp	unwaxed orange zest	½ tsp
*	Boiled Potatoes (p. 260), to serve	*
*	Spinach (p. 303), to serve	*

Wash and pat dry the fish fillets. Heat the oils in a frying pan or skillet over a medium heat and fry the fillets on their skin sides for 2–3 minutes until golden. Turn the fish over, remove the pan from the heat and finish cooking the fish with the residual heat for about 1 minute. Drain on paper towels and season with salt and pepper.

Sprinkle the vendace fillets with the grated zests. They can be accompanied with Boiled Potatoes (p. 260) and Spinach (p. 303).

Sweet and Sour Salmon Trout

All regions

Preparation time:		20 minutes
Marinating time:		1 hour
Cooking time:		20 minutes
Serves:		4

For the marinade:		
2	onions	2
1 tsp	butter	1 tsp
1 tbsp	sugar	1 tbsp
½ cup/3½ fl oz	red wine vinegar	100 ml
4¼ cups/34 fl oz	meat stock	1 litre
1	bay leaf	1
3	juniper berries	3
2	cloves	2

For the fish:		
1 × 1 lb 5 oz	salmon trout fillet	1 × 600 g
1¼ cups/10 fl oz	single (light) cream	300 ml
*	sugar	*
*	salt	*
*	vinegar	*
1	carrot	1
1	celeriac	1
1	leek	1
*	Green Salad (p. 54), to serve	*

For the marinade: Peel and cut the onions into strips. Heat the butter in a pan and sauté the onions until translucent. Add the sugar, deglaze with vinegar and fill the pan with the stock. Add the bay leaf, juniper berries and cloves. Simmer for 10 minutes, then let cool.

For the fish: Cut the fish fillet into 4. Cover with the marinade and leave for 1 hour.

After the hour is up, take out the fish pieces, pour the marinade through a sieve. Put half of the marinade into a pan over a medium heat and reduce by half. Stir in the cream. Season with sugar, salt and vinegar.

Bring the other half of the marinade to a simmer and poach the fish in it for 5–8 minutes.

Trim, peel and cut the vegetables into thin strips. Blanch in boiling salted water and drain.

Take the fish out of the pan. Arrange on plates with the vegetables and sauce. Serve with a Green Salad (p. 54).

Pan-Fried Trout Fillets

All regions

Preparation time:		5 minutes
Cooking time:		10 minutes
Serves:		4

6 × 3½ oz	trout fillets, skin-on	6 × 100 g
*	cornflour (corn starch)	*
1 tbsp	oil	1 tbsp
2 tbsp	Beurre Noisette (p. 112)	2 tbsp
1 tsp	mixed pepper and paprika	1 tsp
*	salt	*
*	Creamed Savoy Cabbage (p. 310)	*
*	Cucumber Salad (p. 56)	*

Wash, pat dry and halve the fish fillets. Dredge the skin side in the cornflour (corn starch) and tap to remove the excess. Heat the oil in a frying pan or skillet over a medium heat. Lightly fry the fillets on their skin sides for 2–3 minutes. Turn the fish over, remove the pan from the heat and finish cooking the fish using the residual heat while keeping the fillets moist.

In a second frying pan or skillet, warm the Beurre Noisette (p. 110) over a low heat and sprinkle in the mixed pepper and paprika. Put in the fillets and turn in the butter. Season with salt.

Serve the trout fillets drizzled with the butter and accompanied with Creamed Savoy Cabbage (p. 310) or Cucumber Salad (p. 56).

Glazed Pan-Fried Mackerel with Vegetables

All regions

Preparation time:		10 minutes
Cooking time:		25 minutes
Serves:		4

5 oz	leeks	150 g
1	black salsify root	1
2 × 5½ oz	carrots	2 × 170 g
1 tsp	juniper berries	1 tsp
1 tsp	yellow mustard seeds	1 tsp
1 tsp	allspice berries	1 tsp
1 tsp	peppercorns	1 tsp
1 tbsp	icing (confectioners') sugar	1 tbsp
¼ cup/2 fl oz	lemon juice	50 ml
1⅔ cups/14 fl oz	vegetable stock	400 ml
1	bay leaf	1
2	sprigs of dill	2
2	sprigs of parsley	2
1	garlic clove	1
2–3 strips	unwaxed lemon zest	2–3 strips
*	salt	*
*	freshly ground black pepper	*
1 tbsp	sugar	1 tbsp
4 × 3½ oz	mackerel fillets, skin-on	4 × 100 g
4 tbsp	cornflour (corn starch)	4 tbsp
1–2 tbsp	oil, for frying	1–2 tbsp
*	olive oil, to serve	*
*	dill or parsley, to garnish	*

Trim, wash and cut the leek crosswise into 5-mm (¼-inch) strips. Brush the salsify under cold running water, then peel and cut on the diagonal into thin slices. Trim, peel and cut the carrots on the diagonal into thin slices.

Toast the juniper berries, mustard seeds, allspice berries and peppercorns in a dry pan over a low heat for about 1 minute, until they begin to release their aromas. Put the spices into a spice bag and close.

Lightly caramelise the icing (confectioners') sugar in a wide, deep frying pan or skillet, add the vegetables and sauté until glazed. Deglaze the pan with the lemon juice, then add the stock. Add the bay leaf, spice bag, dill, parsley, garlic and lemon zest, bring to a simmer and cook for 10 minutes. Remove the spice bag and season well with salt, pepper and sugar.

Wash, pat dry and halve the mackerel fillets. Sprinkle the skin side with cornflour (corn starch). Heat the oil in a frying pan or skillet and fry the fillets on their skin sides over a medium heat until crispy, about 2 minutes. Take the fillets out of the pan, place skin side up in the hot lemon-flavored stock and leave to stand for 4–5 minutes until glazed.

Arrange 2 pieces of fish on each plate with a serving of vegetables and drizzle with a little olive oil. Garnish with dill and parsley if desired.

Pan-Fried Fish with Mustard Sauce

Hamburg

	For the mustard sauce:	
1	shallot	1
1–2 tsp	oil	1–2 tsp
½ cup/3½ fl oz	vegetable stock	100 ml
½ cup/3½ fl oz	single (light) cream	100 ml
1–2 tbsp	hot mustard	1–2 tbsp
1 tbsp	cold butter	1 tbsp
*	salt	*
*	freshly ground black pepper	*

	For the fish:	
1 lb 2 oz	assorted fish fillets (e.g. haddock, plaice, cod)	500 g
1–2 tbsp	oil	1–2 tbsp
*	lemon juice	*
1 tbsp	finely chopped chives	1 tbsp
*	Pan-Fried Potatoes (p. 265)	*
*	fried bacon slices, to serve	*
*	chopped cucumbers, to serve	*

Preparation time: 5 minutes
Cooking time: 15 minutes
Serves: 4

For the mustard sauce: Peel and finely chop the shallot. Heat the oil in a frying pan or skillet and sauté the shallot over a low heat until translucent. Add the stock and cream, stir in the mustard and heat to a simmer. Mix in the butter with a stick (immersion) blender and season the sauce with salt and pepper.

For the fish: Wash, pat dry and cut the fish into 3-cm (1-inch) pieces. Heat 1–2 tablespoons oil in a frying pan or skillet and fry the fish for 3–4 minutes on each side. Remove the pan from the heat and drizzle the fish with lemon juice.

Blend the sauce again and arrange the fish and sauce on plates. Sprinkle with chives. Accompany with Pan-Fried Potatoes (p. 265), bacon and cucumbers.

Salmon with Dill Sauce

All regions

Preparation time: 20 minutes
Cooking time: 10 minutes
Serves: 4

1–2 tbsp	oil	1–2 tbsp
4 × 4 oz	salmon fillets, skin-on	4 × 120 g
*	salt	*
*	freshly ground black pepper	*
1 tbsp	icing (confectioners') sugar	1 tbsp
½ cup/3½ fl oz	dry white wine	100 ml
1 cup/8 fl oz	chicken or vegetable stock	250 ml
½ cup/3½ fl oz	single (light) cream	100 ml
2 tsp	cornflour (corn starch)	2 tsp
1 tbsp	cold butter	1 tbsp
1 tbsp	finely chopped dill tips	1 tbsp
*	Boiled Potatoes (p. 260), to serve	*

Preheat the oven to 100°C/200°F/Gas Mark ¼. Heat the oil in a frying pan or skillet and fry the fillets on their skin sides over a medium heat until crispy, about 4 minutes. Turn the fillets over and cook for another 30 seconds.

Transfer to a baking sheet, place on the middle shelf of the oven and cook for 10 minutes, keeping moist. Season with salt and pepper.

Cook the sugar in a pan over a medium heat to a golden caramel, then deglaze the pan with the wine and simmer until reduced by two-thirds. Add the stock and simmer for 1–2 minutes. Add the cream, bring to a boil, then reduce the heat to a simmer.

Dissolve the cornflour (corn starch) completely in a little cold water and gradually mix it into the simmering sauce to lightly thicken. Finally, mix in the butter with a stick (immersion) blender, stir in the dill and season the sauce with salt.

Pour the dill sauce into warmed deep plates and arrange the salmon fillets on top. Accompany with Boiled Potatoes (p. 260) and serve any remaining sauce on the side.

Pan-Fried Perch Fillets

Berlin and Brandenburg

Preparation time:		5 minutes
Cooking time:		10 minutes
Serves:		4

1 lb 2oz	perch fillets, skin-on	500 g
*	cornflour (corn starch)	*
1 tbsp	oil	1 tbsp
1 tbsp	butter	1 tbsp
1 tbsp	Beurre Noisette (p. 112)	1 tbsp
*	salt	*
*	Braised Cucumbers (p. 297)	*

Wash and pat dry the fish fillets. Cut into 8 equal portions and dredge the skin sides in the cornflour (corn starch).

Heat the oil in a frying pan or skillet and fry the fish pieces on their skin sides over a medium heat for 3–4 minutes until crispy. Turn the fish over, remove the pan from the heat and finish cooking the fish with the residual heat, until glazed.

Drain on paper towels. Wipe the frying pan or skillet dry and melt the butter and Beurre Noisette (p. 112). Season the fish with a little salt and serve drizzled with the dark melted butter. Accompany with Braised Cucumbers (p. 297).

Pollack au Gratin

All regions

Preparation time:		10 minutes
Cooling time:		1 hour
Cooking time:		5 minutes
Serves:		4

½ cup/4¼ oz	soft butter	125 g
2 tsp	Dijon mustard	2 tsp
1 tbsp	preserved horseradish	1 tbsp
1 tbsp	finely chopped parsley	1 tbsp
5 tsp	finely chopped tarragon	5 tsp
⅔ cup/1¾ oz	toasted breadcrumbs	45 g
*	salt	*
*	freshly ground black pepper	*
1 × 14 oz	pollack fillet	1 × 400 g
*	oil, for greasing	*

Beat the butter until fluffy, then mix in the mustard, horseradish, parsley, tarragon and breadcrumbs. Season with salt and pepper. Use baking paper to roll the mixture up into a cylinder about 3 cm (1¼ inches) in diameter and refrigerate for 30 minutes–1 hour.

Turn on the oven grill. Wash, pat dry and cut the fish fillet into 4 equal portions. Season with salt and place on a lightly oiled baking sheet. Slice the butter cylinder into disks and arrange over the fish, slightly overlapping.

Place the baking sheet on the lowest shelf of the oven and grill the fish for about 4 minutes, until golden brown. Take out of the oven and rest on the hot baking sheet for another 1–2 minutes before serving.

Pan-Fried Char
with Lemon Butter

All regions

Preparation time:		15 minutes
Cooking time:		15 minutes
Serves:		4

For the fish:		
4	Arctic char	4
*	salt	*
4	sprigs of parsley	4
4 strips	unwaxed lemon zest	4 strips
3 tbsp	plain (all-purpose) flour	3 tbsp
4 tbsp	oil	4 tbsp

For the lemon butter:		
3 tbsp	butter	3 tbsp
3 tbsp	Beurre Noisette (p. 112)	3 tbsp
1	garlic clove	1
1 tsp	grated unwaxed lemon zest	1 tsp
*	salt	*
4 tbsp	lemon juice, for drizzling	4 tbsp
1 tbsp	finely chopped parsley	1 tbsp
*	Parsley Potatoes (p. 260), to serve	*

For the fish: Preheat the oven to 100°C/200°F/Gas Mark ¼. Wash the fish inside and out, pat dry and season with salt. Wash and shake dry the parsley. Put 1 parsley sprig and 1 strip lemon zest inside the belly cavity of each fish.

Put the flour onto a plate and dredge the fish. Heat the oil in a large frying pan or skillet and fry the fish, in batches if necessary, on both sides over a low heat. Transfer the fish to a baking pan lined with baking paper or a roasting pan, place on the middle shelf of the oven and cook for about 15 minutes, keeping moist.

For the lemon butter: Use paper towels to wipe the frying pan or skillet clean of the butter and oil used to fry the fish, then melt the butter and Beurre Noisette (p. 110) in the pan. Add the garlic and lemon zest and infuse for a few minutes. Season with salt, then put the fish in the lemon butter to coat.

Serve the fish drizzled with lemon butter and lemon juice. Sprinkle with parsley. The fish can be accompanied with Parsley Potatoes (p. 260).

Breaded Rosefish

All regions

Preparation time:		20 minutes
Cooking time:		10 minutes
Serves:		4

2	eggs	2
1 tsp	Dijon mustard	1 tsp
*	grated unwaxed lemon zest	*
½ cup/2 oz	plain (all-purpose) flour	55 g
1½ cups/4 oz	breadcrumbs	110 g
1 × 1lb 2oz	skinless rosefish fillet	1 × 500 g
*	salt	*
*	oil, for frying	*
*	a few lettuce or herb leaves	*
1	unwaxed lemons, quartered	1
*	Potato Salad (p. 62), to serve	*

Whisk the eggs briskly in a deep plate with the mustard and a pinch of lemon zest. Put the flour into another deep plate and put the breadcrumbs into a third.

Wash and pat dry the fish and cut into pieces if necessary. Season with salt. Dredge the fish in flour first, then dip in the beaten egg and dredge in the breadcrumbs.

Heat a frying pan or skillet over a medium heat and add enough oil to cover the bottom well. Fry the breaded fish on both sides until golden brown. Drain on paper towels and lightly season with salt. Serve with lemon wedges, lettuce leaves and Potato Salad (p. 62) if you like.

Beer-Battered Carp

Bavaria

Preparation time:		10 minutes
Cooking time:		10 minutes
Serves:		4

1 tbsp	allspice berries	1 tbsp
1 tbsp	juniper berries	1 tbsp
1 tbsp	cumin seeds	1 tbsp
1 tbsp	peppercorns	1 tbsp
1½ cups/6 oz	cornflour (corn starch)	160 g
1 cup/8 fl oz	beer	250 ml
1 × 1 lb 12 oz	skinless carp fillet	1 × 800g
*	salt	*
¼ cup/2 fl oz	clarified butter, for frying	70 ml
¼ cup/2 fl oz	oil, for frying	70 ml
*	a few dashes of lemon juice	*
*	Chive Sauce (p. 115), to serve	*

Fill a spice grinder with the allspice and juniper berries, cumin seeds and peppercorns. Mix the flour with the cornflour on a plate and season with the freshly ground spices. Put the beer into a bowl.

Wash and pat dry the fish fillet. Cut into 4–5-cm (1½–2-inch) pieces and remove the bones using a sharp knife. Season with salt, then dredge first in the flour mixture, dip in the beer and then dredge again in the flour mixture. Repeat the process with all the fish pieces.

Heat the clarified butter with the oil in a frying pan or skillet. Fry the fish pieces in batches over a low heat until golden. Take the fish out of the pan with a slotted spoon or skimmer, then drain on paper towels and drizzle with lemon juice. Accompany with Chive Sauce (p. 115).

Baked Salmon Trout Fillets

All regions

Preparation time:		5 minutes
Cooking time:		20 minutes
Serves:		4

4	skinless salmon trout fillets	4
*	oil, for greasing	*
1 oz	Beurre Noisette (p. 112)	30 g
1	garlic clove	1
*	salt	*
*	Kohlrabi (p. 292), to serve	*

Preheat the oven to 80°C/175°F. Wash, pat dry and halve the fish fillets. Grease a baking sheet with oil. Lay the fillets side-by-side on the baking sheet. Cover with aluminum foil and cook in the oven for 10–20 minutes, depending on the thickness of the fillets.

Heat the Beurre Noisette (p. 112) in a frying pan or skillet with the garlic. Season with salt. Take the fillets out of the oven and brush with the seasoned butter. Accompany with Kohlrabi (p. 292).

Whitefish en Papillote

Baden-Württemberg and Bavaria

Preparation time:		10 minutes
Cooking time:		25 minutes
Serves:		4

4 × 11 oz	European whitefish	4 × 300 g
*	salt	*
*	freshly ground black pepper	*
4 tbsp	olive oil	4 tbsp
4	garlic slices	4
4	unwaxed lemon slices	4
1 tsp	fennel seeds	1 tsp
4	sprigs of dill	4
4	bay leaves	4
*	a few parsley leaves	*
4 tbsp	white wine	4 tbsp
3 tbsp	butter	3 tbsp

For the dip:		
⅔ cup/5 oz	crème fraîche	150 g
2 tbsp	single (light) cream	2 tbsp
1 tsp	finely chopped tarragon	1 tsp
1 tbsp	lime juice	1 tbsp
1	unwaxed lime, zested	1
*	sugar	*
*	salt	*
*	freshly ground black pepper	*

Preheat the oven to 180°C/350°C/Gas Mark 4. Thoroughly wash the fish inside and out. Pat dry and season with salt and pepper.

Brush four sheets of aluminum foil with olive oil. Lay a fish on each sheet and fill the belly cavity of each with 1 garlic and lemon slice, ¼ teaspoon fennel seeds, 1 dill sprig, 1 bay leaf and parsley leaves. Pour 1 tablespoon wine over each fish. Cut the butter into small pieces and distribute them over the fish and then fold the foil over into sealed parcels. Cook the fish on the middle shelf of the oven for about 25 minutes.

For the dip: Mix the crème fraîche with the cream until smooth and stir in the tarragon. Season with lime juice and zest, salt and pepper. Open the foil parcels at the table and serve the fish with the dip.

Battered Fish Fillets (Backfisch)

All regions

Preparation time:		20 minutes
Cooking time:		20 minutes
Serves:		4

1 tbsp	peppercorns	1 tbsp
2	eggs	2
1 cup/3½ oz	all-purpose (plain) flour	100 g
⅔ cup/5 fl oz	beer	150 ml
*	freshly ground black pepper	*
4 tbsp	Beurre Noisette (p. 112)	4 tbsp
*	salt	*
*	oil, for deep-frying	*
1 lb 2 oz	skinless pollack fillets	500 g
*	a few drops of lemon juice	*
*	cornflour (corn starch)	*
*	lemon wedges, to serve	*
*	Potato Salad (p. 62), to serve	*
*	Remoulade (p. 114), to serve	*

Put the peppercorns in a spice grinder. Separate the eggs. Mix the flour with the beer and egg yolks to a smooth batter and season with the freshly ground pepper. Mix in the Beurre Noisette (p. 112). Beat the egg whites, with a pinch of salt, to soft peaks and fold evenly into the batter.

Heat plenty of oil in a pan to 170°C/350°F. Wash and pat dry the fish fillets and season with salt and lemon juice. Put the cornflour (corn starch) into a deep plate. Dredge the fillets in the flour, then dip into the batter.

Fry in the hot oil for 4–5 minutes until golden brown, turning over once and drain on paper towels. Serve the fish with lemon wedges accompanied by a Potato Salad (p. 62) and Remoulade (p. 114).

Haddock with Mustard Dip

Northern Germany

Preparation time:		5 minutes
Cooking time:		20 minutes
Serves:		4

4	skinless haddock fillets	4
4 tsp	olive oil	4 tsp
*	salt	*
⅔ cup/5 oz	Greek yoghurt	150 g
2 tbsp	chicken stock	2 tbsp
2 tsp	Dijon mustard	2 tsp
2 tsp	Bavarian sweet mustard	2 tsp
*	grated unwaxed orange zest	*
*	Spinach (p. 303), to serve	*

Preheat the oven to 100°C/210°C/Gas Mark ¼. Put each fish fillet on a heatproof plate, cover with aluminum foil and cook in the oven for 15–20 minutes, keeping moist. Remove the foil, brush each fillet with 1 teaspoon olive oil and season with salt.

For the mustard dip: Mix the yoghurt with the stock, both mustards and a pinch of orange zest until smooth. Serve the fillets on plates and drizzle over the dip. The fish can be accompanied by Spinach (p. 303).

Marinated Char with Asparagus

All regions

Preparation time:		30 minutes
Marinating time:		12 hours
Serves:		4

For the fish:		
2 tsp	coriander seeds	2 tsp
1 tsp	peppercorns	1 tsp
1 tbsp	juniper berries	1 tbsp
1 tsp	fennel seeds	1 tsp
1 tsp	mustard seeds	1 tsp
4 × 3 oz	Arctic char fillets, skin-on	4 × 80 g
¼ cup/2 oz	salt	50 g
3 tbsp	sugar	3 tbsp
1 tbsp	finely chopped parsley	1 tbsp
1 tbsp	finely chopped dill	1 tbsp
1 tbsp	grated unwaxed lemon zest	1 tbsp
1 tbsp	grated unwaxed orange zest	1 tbsp

For the asparagus:		
8	white asparagus spears	8
1–2 tbsp	salt	1–2 tbsp
1 tbsp	sugar	1 tbsp

For the vinaigrette:		
2	eggs	2
⅓ cup/2½ fl oz	vegetable stock	80 ml
½ tsp	hot mustard	½ tsp
1–2 tbsp	red wine vinegar	1–2 tbsp
3–4 tbsp	mild olive oil	3–4 tbsp
*	salt	*
*	freshly ground black pepper	*
*	sugar	*
1 tbsp	finely chopped chives	1 tbsp

For the fish: Toast the coriander seeds, peppercorns, juniper berries, fennel seeds and mustard seeds in a dry frying pan or skillet. Finely grind the spices in a food processor or mortar.

Wash and pat dry the fish fillets. Mix together the salt, sugar, spice mixture, parsley, dill, and orange and lemon zests in a small bowl. Coat the fish fillets with the mixture on both sides, cover each fillet in clingfilm (plastic wrap) and rest overnight in the refrigerator.

For the asparagus: The following day, peel the spears and cut off the woody ends. Bring 2 litres (8½ cups/70 fl oz) of water to a boil in a large pan and add the salt and sugar. Boil the asparagus for 8–10 minutes, depending on their thickness. Take them out of the pan, plunge into iced water then drain. Cover the asparagus and set aside to come to room temperature.

For the vinaigrette: Hard-boil the eggs, then peel and cut in half. Separate the yolks from the whites and finely chop both, separately.

Put the stock into a small bowl and use a whisk to mix in the mustard, vinegar and olive oil. Season well with salt, pepper and a pinch of sugar and then mix in the eggs.

Take the fish out of the refrigerator, scrape off the marinade with the back of a knife and remove the skin. Cut the fillets into slices. To serve, arrange 2 asparagus spears on each plate, drizzle with the vinaigrette and sprinkle with chives. Arrange the char pieces next to them on the plate.

Finkenwerder-Style Plaice with Bacon

Hamburg and Lower Saxony

Preparation time:		25 minutes
Cooking time:		10 minutes
Serves:		4

4 oz	streaky bacon slices	120 g
5 tbsp	oil	5 tbsp
2–3	spring onions (scallions)	2–3
4 × 1lb 2 oz	whole plaice	4 × 500g
¾ cup/3½ oz	plain (all-purpose) flour	100 g
*	salt	*
*	freshly ground black pepper	*
*	lemon wedges, to serve	*

Finely dice the bacon. Heat 1 tablespoon oil in a frying pan or skillet and fry the bacon over a medium heat until crispy. Drain on paper towels.

Trim and wash the spring onions (scallions), remove the dark green leaves and cut the rest, on the diagonal, into thin rings.

Preheat the oven to 100°C/200°F/Gas Mark ¼. Wash and pat dry the fish. Put the flour on a shallow plate. Dredge the fish in the flour. Heat 3 tablespoons oil in a frying pan or skillet and sear the fish, one after the other, for 1–2 minutes on each side. Transfer the fish to a baking sheet, place on the middle shelf of the oven and cook for 10 minutes, keeping moist. Take the fish out and season with salt and pepper.

In the meantime, heat 1 tablespoon oil in a frying pan or skillet and sauté the spring onions (scallions) over a low heat for 1–2 minutes.

Arrange the fish on warmed plates and drizzle with the oil from the pan. Scatter the bacon and spring onions over the fish. Serve with lemon wedges.

Oven-Baked Cod Fillets

North Sea and Baltic Coast

Preparation time:		5 minutes
Cooking time:		20 minutes
Serves:		4

1 tbsp	butter or oil, for greasing	1 tbsp
4	cod fillets	4
1½ oz	Beurre Noisette (p. 112)	40 g
1 tsp	grated unwaxed lemon zest	1 tsp
1 tsp	grated unwaxed orange zest	1 tsp
1	garlic clove	1
*	salt	*
*	Mustard Sauce (p. 121), to serve	*
*	lemon wedges, to serve	*

Preheat the oven to 80°C/175°F and grease a baking sheet with oil. Wash, pat dry and cut the fish fillets into pieces. Lay side-by-side on the baking sheet. Cover the fish with aluminum foil, place on the middle shelf of the oven and cook for 15–20 minutes, keeping moist.

Heat the Beurre Noisette (p. 112) with the lemon and orange zests and garlic. Leave to infuse for a few minutes. Brush the fish with the seasoned butter. Serve with Mustard Sauce (p. 121) and lemon wedges.

Fish & Seafood

Pan-Fried Perch with Herb Foam

Baden

Preparation time:		15 minutes
Cooking time:		5 minutes
Serves:		4

8 × 3½ oz	European perch fillets	8 × 100 g
*	salt	*
*	freshly ground white pepper	*
2 tbsp	lemon juice	2 tbsp*
*	cornflour (corn starch), for dredging	*
1	shallot	1
3 tbsp	butter	3 tbsp
1	bunch of assorted spring herbs	1
¾ cup/7 fl oz	fish stock	200 ml
½ cup/3½ fl oz	single (light) cream	100 ml
*	freshly grated nutmeg	*
3 tbsp	neutral vegetable oil	3 tbsp
*	Boiled Potatoes (p. 260), to serve	*
*	Green Salad (p. 54), to serve	*

Briefly wash and pat dry the fish fillets. Season with salt and white pepper and drizzle with lemon juice. Dredge the fillets in flour and tap lightly to remove the excess.

Peel and dice the shallot and sauté in a pan with 1 tablespoon of butter until translucent. Add the herbs, briefly sauté and add the stock. Bring to a boil, remove from the heat and finely blend using a stick (immersion) blender.

Press through a sieve into the pan and add the cream. Season with salt, white pepper and nutmeg and reduce a little. Cut 1 tablespoon of butter into small pieces and whisk into the sauce. Shortly before serving, beat to a foam with a stick (immersion) blender.

Heat the oil and remaining butter in a frying pan or skillet and lay the fillets skin-side down in the hot fat. Fry for a few minutes, carefully turn over and fry the other side. Arrange 2 fillets on each warmed plate and cover with the herb foam. Serve with Boiled Potatoes (p. 260) and the Green Salad (p. 54).

Smoked Pike with Turnip Sauce

All regions

Preparation time:		25 minutes
Cooking time:		10 minutes
Serves:		4

For the turnip sauce:		
1 lb 5 oz	turnips	600 g
*	salt	*
1	onion, peeled and diced	1
2 tbsp	oil	2 tbsp
½ cup/3½ fl oz	sweet white wine	100 ml
1¼ cups/10 fl oz	fish or meat stock	300 ml
1 tbsp	sugar	1 tbsp
*	freshly ground pepper	*
1	garlic clove	1
1 tbsp	butter	1 tbsp
2 tbsp	parsley or turnip greens	2 tbsp

For the fish:		
about 3 lb 4 oz	pike	about 1.5 kg
*	salt	*
*	freshly ground black pepper	*
2 tbsp	lemon juice	2 tbsp
1 tbsp	oil, for frying	1 tbsp
2 tbsp	Beurre Noisette (p.112)	2 tbsp

To make this recipe, you will need a smoker oven.

For the turnip sauce: Peel and cut the turnips into thin slices or shred into strips. Sprinkle with salt. Peel and dice the onion.

Heat the oil in a pan. Sauté the onion. Add the turnips and sauté. Add the wine and stock. Season with sugar, salt and pepper. Crush and add the garlic then cook for 20 minutes.

Drain the vegetables in a sieve and reserve the liquid to make the sauce. Adjust the seasoning if necessary and add the butter using a stick (immersion) blender.

Add the vegetables to the sauce. Sprinkle with finely chopped parsley or turnip greens.

For the fish: Thoroughly wash the pike inside and out and pat dry. Run a sharp knife along the backbone and separate the fillets, remove any visible bones with tweezers and carefully remove the skin (or have your fishmonger prepare the fillets for you).

Prepare the smoker oven following the manufacturer's instructions.

Cut the fillets into 4-cm (1½-inch) wide strips. Season with salt, pepper and lemon juice.

Heat the oil in a frying pan or skillet. Lightly fry the fish pieces on both sides. Lay the pieces on the smoker-oven rack and smoke for 8–10 minutes.

Heat the Beurre Noisette (p. 112) in a frying pan or skillet. Take the smoked fish out of the oven. Arrange on warmed plates, drizzle with the Beurre Noisette and serve with the turnip sauce.

Catfish with Dill-Infused Cucumbers and Lemon Sauce

All regions

For the sauce:

1 × 3½ oz	waxy potato	1 × 100 g
1½ cups/12 fl oz	vegetable stock	350 ml
1	bay leaf	1
*	grated unwaxed lemon zest	*
2 tbsp	Beurre Noisette (p. 112)	2 tbsp
⅓ cup/3 fl oz	single (light) cream	80 ml
*	salt	*
*	a few dashes of lemon juice	*

For the cucumbers:

2	small cucumbers	2
*	salt	*
3 tbsp	Beurre Noisette (p. 112)	3 tbsp
1 tbsp	finely chopped dill	1 tbsp

For the fish:

3–4	small waxy potatoes	3–4
4 × 4 oz	catfish (wels catfish) fillets	4 × 120 g
*	salt	*
3 tbsp	Beurre Noisette (p. 112)	3 tbsp

For the sauce: Peel and wash the potatoes and cut into 5-mm (¼-inch) slices. Put the potato slices in a pan with the stock and bay leaf and simmer for 15–20 minutes until cooked. Remove and discard the bay leaf.

Transfer the potatoes and stock to a measuring jug with the Beurre Noisette (p. 112) and cream then finely blend with a stick (immersion) blender. Season the sauce with salt and lemon juice.

For the cucumbers: Peel and halve the cucumbers lengthwise and remove the seeds with a spoon. Slice the cucumber halves and blanch in heavily salted boiling water until tender but firm to the bite. Drain in a sieve, plunge into iced water then drain again. Heat the Beurre Noisette (p. 112) in a frying pan or skillet and sauté the cucumber slices. Then add the dill.

For the fish: Peel and finely slice the potatoes. Wash, pat dry and season the fish fillets with salt. Cover the tops of the fillets with the potato slices, overlapping to resemble fish scales.

Heat the Beurre Noisette (p. 112) in a frying pan or skillet and fry the fillets over a medium heat, first on the potato side, then turn over and fry the flesh side, over a low heat, for about 3 minutes. Take the fillets out of the pan and drain on paper towels.

Arrange the dill-infused cucumbers on warmed plates and lay one fillet, with the potato side facing upward, on top. Blend the sauce with a stick (immersion) blender until frothy and drizzle over the cucumbers.

Sylt Oysters

Schleswig-Holstein

24	Pacific oysters	24
1	shallot	1
2 tbsp	white wine vinegar	2 tbsp
4 tbsp	vegetable stock	4 tbsp
1 tbsp	finely chopped chives, basil, chervil, parsley, dill	1 tbsp
1 tbsp	olive oil	1 tbsp
*	salt	*

Use an oyster knife to carefully shuck the oysters. Remove the oysters and collect the liquid. If necessary, filter through a small sieve to remove any shell fragments. Carefully remove any shell fragments from the oysters using a brush dipped in salted water.

Peel and finely chop the shallot. Make a vinaigrette with the oyster liquor, shallots, vinegar, stock, herbs and olive oil and season with a pinch of salt.

Arrange the oysters on plates, in their shells if you like, nestled in a bed of coarse sea salt. Drizzle the oysters with the herb vinaigrette.

Fish Patties

Preparation time:		30 minutes
Cooking time:		6 minutes
Serves:		4

2 oz	white bread	50 g
¼ cup/2 fl oz	milk	50 ml
½ bunch	spring onions (scallions)	½ bunch
½	garlic clove	½
1 lb 2 oz	firm white fish fillet (e.g. cod)	500 g
1	egg yolk	1
*	salt	*
*	freshly ground black pepper	*
½ tsp	grated unwaxed lemon zest	½ tsp
*	lemon juice	*
*	white breadcrumbs	*
4 tbsp	oil, for frying	4 tbsp
*	Potato and Leek Casserole (p. 278), to serve	*

Cut the bread into small cubes and put in a bowl. Add the milk, cover and let soak.

Trim, wash and cut the spring onions (scallions) into thin rings. Peel and finely chop the garlic.

Wash and pat dry the fish fillet. Dice the flesh as finely as possible and put into a bowl. Add the egg yolk, soaked bread and spring onion (scallion) rings and mix thoroughly with your hands. Season the mixture with salt, pepper, garlic, lemon zest, a dash of lemon juice, and mix well.

Wet your hands, shape the mixture into small patties and dredge in the breadcrumbs. Heat the oil in a frying pan or skillet and fry the fish patties on both sides over a low heat for 5–6 minutes, until golden. Take the patties out of the pan and drain on paper towels. Serve on plates with Potato and Leek Casserole (p. 278).

River Fish Ragout

Preparation time:		25 minutes
Cooking time:		20 minutes
Serves:		4

2¼ lb	assorted freshwater fish, (e.g. pike, tench, carp)	1 kg
3	large onions	3
3	white potatoes	3
2 tbsp	light vegetable oil	2 tbsp
2 tbsp	sweet paprika	2 tbsp
4	large beefsteak tomatoes	4
1½ cups/13 fl oz	fish stock	375 ml
*	salt	*
*	freshly ground black pepper	*
1	bunch of dill	1
*	Boiled Potatoes (p. 260), to serve	*

If possible, have your fishmonger fillet and debone the fish. Cut the fillets into chunks. Peel the onions and potatoes. Finely chop the onions and cut the potatoes into 1-cm (½-inch) dice.

Heat oil in a casserole (Dutch oven). Sauté the onions and potatoes for 10 minutes, stirring constantly and sprinkle with paprika.

Blanch, peel, halve and seed the tomatoes. Coarsely chop the flesh and add to the pan. Add the fish stock, bring to a boil, reduce the heat and season with salt and pepper. Mix in the fish pieces, cover with the lid and simmer for 8–10 minutes.

Wash and shake dry the dill, then pluck the tips and finely chop. Mix the dill into the ragout. Serve with Boiled Potatoes (p. 260).

Roast Chicken

All regions

Preparation time:		10 minutes
Cooking time:		1 hour 45 minutes
Serves:		4

1 × 3 lb 4 oz	stewing chicken	1.5 kg
*	salt	*
*	freshly ground black pepper	*
3	sprigs of parsley	3
3	strips of unwaxed lemon zest	3
3 oz	Beurre Noisette (p. 112)	80 g
*	Green Salad (p. 54), to serve	*

Season the inside of the chicken with salt and pepper. Wash and pat dry the parsley sprigs and put inside the cavity with the lemon zest.

Preheat the oven to 160°C/325°F/Gas Mark 3. Warm and season the Beurre Noisette (p. 112) with salt. Put the chicken in a roasting pan and brush all over with the Beurre Noisette.

Place the pan on the lowest shelf inside the oven and roast for about 1 hour 15 minutes, regularly basting with Beurre Noisette. Then raise the oven temperature to 200°C/400°F/Gas Mark 6 and roast the chicken for another 20–25 minutes to crisp the skin.

Take the chicken out of the oven, carve and serve. Accompany with a Green Salad (p. 54).

Chicken Cooked in Riesling

Southwestern Germany

Preparation time:		15 minutes
Cooking time:		1 hour
Serves:		4

1 × 3 lbs 4 oz	chicken	1.5 kg
*	salt	*
*	freshly ground black pepper	*
1	sprig of tarragon	1
3	sprigs of parsley	3
2 tbsp	oil	2 tbsp
1 cup/8 fl oz	Riesling dry white wine	250 ml
1 cup/8 fl oz	chicken stock	250 ml
2	onions	2
1	bay leaf	1
¼ oz	cold butter	30 g
1 tbsp	chopped tarragon leaves	1 tbsp

Season the chicken inside and out with salt and pepper. Wash and pat dry the tarragon and parsley sprigs and put inside the cavity. Preheat the oven to 180°C/350°F/Gas Mark 4.

Heat the oil in a casserole (dutch oven) over a medium heat and brown the chicken on all sides until golden brown. Deglaze the pan with the wine and stock and simmer for a few minutes.

Peel and cut the onions into rings and add to the chicken together with the bay leaf. Cover with the lid and braise in the oven for 50 minutes–1 hour.

Take the chicken out of the pan and keep warm. Skim the fat off the cooking liquid and blend with the onions using a stick (immersion) blender. Press the sauce through a sieve, cut the butter into small pieces and whisk into the sauce.

Finally, stir in the chopped tarragon and let infuse for a few minutes. Carve the chicken into portions and serve with the sauce.

Cheese-Stuffed Chicken

Southern Germany

Preparation time:		25 minutes
Cooking time:		1 hour 15 minutes
Serves:		4

1 × 2 lb 8 oz	chicken	1 × 1.2 kg
*	salt	*
*	freshly ground black pepper	*
2	shallots	2
1	garlic clove	1
1	leek	1
1	carrot	1
3½ oz	button (white) mushrooms	100 g
2	savoy or white cabbage leaves	2
3 tbsp/1½ oz	butter	40 g
5 oz	smoked cheese	150 g
1 tbsp	white peppercorns	1 tbsp
3 tbsp	olive oil	3 tbsp
1 cup/8 fl oz	chicken stock	250 ml

Season the chicken inside and out with salt and pepper.

Peel the shallots and garlic clove, thoroughly clean the leek and peel the carrot. Clean the mushrooms and wipe dry if necessary. Cut everything into small dice. Blanch the cabbage leaves for 3 minutes in boiling salted water, plunge into iced water, drain and cut into thin strips.

Heat the butter in a pan over a medium heat and sauté the diced vegetables and cabbage strips. Remove from the heat and let cool.

Cut the cheese into small cubes and mix with the cold vegetables. Season with salt and pepper and stuff the prepared chicken with the mixture. Close the cavity and secure with wooden toothpicks. Preheat the oven to 180°C/350°C/Gas Mark 4.

Crush the peppercorns in a mortar, with a pestle, or use the blade of a wide knife. Heat the oil in a large casserole (dutch oven) and lightly toast the peppercorns.

Brown the chicken on all sides, then turn breast-side up and pour over the stock. Cover with the lid and cook in the oven for about 50 minutes. Then remove the lid and cook for another 15–20 minutes, until golden brown.

Take the chicken out of the pan and rest before carving. The cooking liquid can be reduced a little and served together with the chicken as a sauce.

Stuffed Chicken Breasts

All regions

Preparation time:		20 minutes
Cooking time:		20 minutes
Serves:		4

4 × 5 oz	chicken breasts	4 × 150 g
*	salt	*
*	freshly ground black pepper	*
8	sage leaves	8
4	thin slices ham	4
2 tbsp	plain (all-purpose) flour	2 tbsp
3 tbsp	oil	3 tbsp
4 tsp	Madeira wine	4 tsp
½ cup/4 fl oz	chicken stock	120 ml
1½ oz	cold butter	40 g
*	white bread, to serve	*

Using a sharp knife, cut a pocket into each chicken breast. Season with salt and pepper.

Wash and pat dry the sage leaves. Put 1 thin ham slice and 2 sage leaves into each breast pocket. Close the pockets and secure with wooden toothpicks. Dredge the chicken breasts in flour.

Heat the oil in a frying pan or skillet over a medium heat and brown the chicken for 3–4 minutes on each side. Remove from the pan and keep warm. Deglaze the pan with the wine and add the stock. Reduce to a thick sauce. Cut the butter into small pieces and stir into the sauce. Serve the stuffed breasts in the sauce, accompanied by white bread if desired.

Pan-Fried Chicken Breasts

All regions

Preparation time:	10 minutes
Cooking time:	40 minutes
Serves:	4

4 × 5 oz	chicken breasts, skin on	4 × 150 g
1	handful of parsley, basil, sage	1
1 tbsp	oil	1 tbsp
*	salt	*
*	freshly ground black pepper	*
*	Stewed Leeks and Mushrooms (p. 297)	*
*	Mixed Vegetables (p. 295)	*

Preheat the oven to 100°C/210°F/Gas Mark ¼. Put a shelf on the middle oven rail and put a drip tray under it. Lightly lift the skin from the chicken breasts and push a few herb leaves between the skin and the meat.

Heat the oil in a frying pan or skillet over a medium heat and fry the chicken breasts on their skin side over a medium heat, until crispy, about 3 minutes. Turn over and briefly brown the meat side, then transfer directly onto the oven shelf and cook for 40 minutes.

Take the breast halves out of the oven and season with salt and pepper. Serve accompanied with Stewed Leeks and Mushrooms (p. 297) or Mixed Vegetables (p. 295).

Beer-Braised Chicken

Rhineland

Marinating time:	24 hours
Preparation time:	20 minutes
Cooking time:	30 minutes
Serves:	4

1 × 3 lbs 4 oz	chicken	1 × 1.5 kg
*	salt	*
*	freshly ground black pepper	*
4 cups/34 fl oz	pilsner lager	1 litre
1	sprig thyme	1
2	onions	2
7 oz	smoked back bacon slices	200 g
2 oz	clarified butter	50 g
*	flour, for dusting	*
½ tsp	marjoram leaves	½ tsp
½ cup/4 fl oz	single (light) cream	125 ml
1 tbsp	finely chopped parsley	1 tbsp

Cut the chicken into 8 pieces using a sharp knife or kitchen shears. Rub with salt and pepper. Pour the lager into a bowl, add the thyme, immerse the chicken pieces and cover the bowl. Marinate for 24 hours. The chicken should be completely covered by the lager.

Peel and finely chop the onions. Cut half of the bacon into small cubes. Melt the clarified butter in a pan and fry the bacon and onion until translucent.

Remove the chicken pieces from the marinade, add to the pan and cook on all sides until light golden. Sprinkle with flour, braise lightly, then deglaze the pan with half of the lager marinade. Bring to a boil, season with salt, pepper and marjoram and add the rest of the marinade and cream.

Cover with a lid and braise over low heat for about 10–15 minutes. Remove the lid and simmer the chicken in the sauce for 10–15 minutes.

Cut the rest of the bacon into small strips and toast in a dry pan until crispy. Arrange the chicken pieces in a serving dish and sprinkle with the bacon strips and parsley. The sauce can be reduced a little and served with the chicken.

Chicken Legs
with Mustard Sauce

All regions

Preparation time:		15 minutes
Cooking time:		20 minutes
Serves:		4

8	chicken legs	8
2 tbsp	oil	2 tbsp
2 tbsp/1 oz	butter	30 g
*	salt	*
*	freshly ground white pepper	*
4	shallots	4
½ cup/4 fl oz	chicken stock	125 ml
½ cup/4 fl oz	single (light) cream	125 ml
3 tsp	hot grain mustard	3 tsp
*	lemon juice, to season	*

Heat the oil and butter in a pan and cook the chicken legs on all sides over a medium heat until golden brown. Take them out of the pan and season with salt and pepper.

Peel and finely chop the shallots and sauté in the remaining fat in the pan until translucent.

Return the legs to the pan. Deglaze with the stock and cream and stir in the mustard. Cover with a lid and cook over a low heat for 15–20 minutes.

Take the chicken legs out of the pan and reduce the sauce a little if necessary. Season well with salt, pepper and lemon juice.

Chicken Legs
with Aromatic Potatoes

All regions

Preparation time:		15 minutes
Cooking time:		45 minutes
Serves:		4

For the potatoes:		
2 lbs 4 oz	small waxy potatoes	1 kg
2–3 tbsp	olive oil	2–3 tbsp
*	salt	*
2	garlic cloves	2
2–3	small sprigs of rosemary	2–3
3	strips of unwaxed lemon zest	3
3	strips of unwaxed orange zest	3
½ bunch	spring onions (scallions)	½ bunch
5 oz	small cherry tomatoes	150 g
3 tbsp	vegetable stock	3 tbsp

For the chicken legs:		
1	garlic clove	1
½ tsp	ground coriander seeds	½ tsp
1 tsp	sweet paprika	1 tsp
½ tbsp	dried oregano	½ tbsp
1 tsp	salt	1 tsp
1 tsp	freshly ground black pepper	1 tsp
½ tsp	sugar	½ tsp
7 tbsp	olive oil	7 tbsp
1 tsp	honey	1 tsp
4 × 7oz	chicken legs, skin on	4 × 200 g

For the potatoes: Preheat the oven to 200°C/400°F/Gas Mark 6. Wash and halve the potatoes, mix with the olive oil and season with salt. Spread the potatoes out in a roasting pan.

For the chicken legs: Peel and finely chop the garlic. Make a basting marinade by mixing the coriander seeds, paprika, oregano, salt, pepper and sugar with the olive oil and honey.

Lightly season the chicken legs on all sides with salt. Lay the legs over the potatoes. Put the roasting pan on the middle shelf of the oven and cook for 35 minutes. Raise the oven temperature to 220°C/425°F/Gas Mark 7. Add the garlic, rosemary, lemon and orange zest to the potatoes and mix. Baste the legs with the marinade and roast for another 10 minutes.

Trim, wash and slice the spring onions (scallions) on the diagonal. Wash and halve the cherry tomatoes. Heat the spring onions (scallions) and tomatoes briefly in the stock, season with salt and mix with the potatoes shortly before serving.

When cooked, remove the whole aromatics from the potatoes. Arrange the potatoes on warmed plates and lay the chicken legs on top.

Poultry & Game Birds

Roast Turkey

All regions

Preparation time:	30 minutes
Cooking time:	4 hours 30 minutes
Serves:	4–6

For the sauce:

2	onions	2
1	carrot	1
5 oz	celeriac	150 g
1 tbsp	oil	1 tbsp
1–2 tsp	icing (confectioners') sugar	1–2 tsp
½–1 tbsp	tomato purée (paste)	½–1 tbsp
1 cup/8 fl oz	heavy red wine	250 ml
3 cups/25 fl oz	chicken stock	750 ml
1	bay leaf	1
1 tsp	cornflour (corn starch)	1 tsp
1	garlic clove	1
1	strip of unwaxed lemon zest	1
1	sprig of rosemary	1
½ tbsp/¼ oz	cold butter	10 g

For the turkey:

1	onion	1
1 tbsp	oil	1 tbsp
4 oz	cooked ham	120 g
1	apple	1
2	carrots	2
11 oz	day-old white bread	300 g
1½ cups/12 fl oz	milk	350 ml
4	eggs	4
*	salt	*
*	freshly ground black pepper	*
*	freshly grated nutmeg	*
5 oz	corn kernels (from a can)	150 g
2 oz	semolina	50 g
2 oz	raisins	50 g
6 lbs 8 oz	(small) turkey	3 kg
3½ oz	melted butter	100 g

For the sauce: Peel and cut the onions, carrot and celeriac into 1-cm (½-inch) dice. Heat the oil and sauté until tender.

Lightly caramelise the sugar in a pan over a low heat. Stir in the tomato purée (paste) and cook briefly. Deglaze the pan with half the wine. Simmer until reduced, then repeat with the rest of the wine. Add the stock and transfer to a large roasting pan. Add the vegetables. Preheat the oven to 150°C/300°F/Gas Mark 3.

For the turkey: Peel and chop the onion. Sauté in the oil until translucent. Dice the ham. Peel and dice the apple and carrots, and cube the bread. Heat the milk in a pan and whisk in the eggs. Season with salt, pepper and nutmeg. Add the bread, mix in the fruit and vegetables, ham, semolina, and seasoning. Rest for 10 minutes.

Salt the turkey cavity, fill with stuffing, then secure with a skewer. Tie the legs and lay breast-side down over the vegetables. Season the butter with salt and baste the turkey. Roast for 4 hours 15 minutes, regularly basting. Add the bay after 4 hours. To crisp the skin, raise to 200°C/400°F/Gas Mark 6 for the last 15 minutes.

Sieve the sauce into a pan. Heat through, dissolve the flour in water, stir into the sauce and simmer for 2 minutes. Add the garlic, lemon and rosemary, allow to infuse then discard. Add the butter and season. Serve with the turkey.

Chicken Fricassee with Morels

All regions

Preparation time:	20 minutes
Cooking time:	15 minutes
Serves:	4

4 × 5 oz	chicken breasts	4 × 150 g
*	salt	*
*	freshly ground black pepper	*
1	carrot	1
1	leek	1
1	celery stalk	1
4 tbsp/2 oz	butter	50 g
1 cup/9 fl oz	chicken stock	250 ml
½ cup/1¼ oz	dried morels	30 g
½ cup/4 fl oz	single (light) cream	125 ml
*	lemon juice, to season	*
1½ tbsp	chilled butter	1½ tbsp
3½ oz	small button mushrooms	100 g
*	boiled rice, to serve	*

Season the chicken breasts with salt and pepper. Trim, wash and chop the carrot, leek and celery into small pieces. Heat half the butter in a pan over a medium heat and brown the chicken on all sides.

Deglaze the pan with the stock, add the morels and simmer for 15 minutes. Use a slotted spoon or skimmer to take the chicken and morels out of the pan. Keep warm. Cut the chicken into bite-sized pieces.

Filter the cooking liquid through a sieve, add the cream and reduce a little. Season with salt, pepper and lemon juice. Cut the cold butter into small pieces and whisk into the sauce.

Clean the mushrooms, wiping dry if necessary, and sauté in a pan over a medium heat with the rest of the butter. Add to the sauce with the chicken and morels and briefly heat everything again. Serve with boiled rice.

Roast Young Turkey with Stuffing

Southern Germany

Preparation time:		30 minutes
Cooking time:		3 hours 45 minutes
Serves:		4–6

1½ oz	dried lingonberries	40 g
2 tbsp	brandy	2 tbsp
9 oz	day-old white bread	250 g
1 cup/8 fl oz	milk	250 ml
2	eggs	2
*	salt	*
*	freshly ground black pepper	*
*	freshly grated nutmeg	*
1	onion	1
1 tbsp	butter	1 tbsp
2 tbsp	dried horn of plenty mushrooms	2 tbsp
9 oz	finely minced ground veal	250 g
5 tbsp	single (light) cream	5 tbsp
1½ oz	pistachio nuts	40 g
3 oz	ham	80 g
3 oz	corn kernels (from a can)	80 g
1 tbsp	chopped parsley leaves	1 tbsp
1	pinch lemon zest	1
1	pinch orange zest	1
6 lbs 8 oz	young turkey	3kg
*	Savoy Cabbage (p. 308), to serve	*

For the stuffing: Soak the berries in the brandy until softened, around 20 minutes. Cut the bread into 1-cm (½-inch) cubes. Heat the milk through and whisk in the eggs. Season with salt, pepper and nutmeg and mix thoroughly with the bread. Peel and finely chop the onion and sauté in a frying pan or skillet with the butter, over a low heat, until translucent. Mix with the bread mixture and let cool.

Put the mushrooms into a pan with water, bring to a boil, then reduce the heat and simmer for a few minutes. Drain, let cool and finely slice. Mix the minced (ground) veal with the cream. Add in the mushrooms, pistachios, ham, corn and soaked berries. Season with parsley, nutmeg, lemon and orange zest, salt and pepper.

Preheat the oven to 120°C/250°F/Gas Mark ½. Put a shelf on the second lowest oven rail and put a drip tray under it. Season the turkey with salt, then stuff the cavity with the mixture (any leftover stuffing can be shaped into patties and fried). Put the turkey directly onto the shelf in the oven and roast for 3 hours, then raise the oven temperature to 160°C/325°F/Gas Mark 3 and roast until the skin is crispy and brown, about 40 minutes.

Just before serving, take out the stuffing, slice it, then carve the turkey. Serve the turkey with the stuffing. Accompany with Savoy Cabbage (p. 308).

Turkey Rolls with Herb Sauce

Southern Germany

Preparation time:		15 minutes
Cooking time:		20 minutes
Serves:		4

4 × 4 oz	turkey breast cutlets	4 × 120 g
*	oil, for greasing and frying	*
*	salt	*
*	freshly ground black pepper	*
4	slices of ham	4
4	slices of gouda cheese	4
1 tsp	icing (confectioners') sugar	1 tsp
4 tsp	Noilly Prat (French vermouth)	4 tsp
½ cup/4 fl oz	white wine	125 ml
2–3	garlic slices	2–3
1	bay leaf	1
½ cup/4 fl oz	vegetable stock	125 ml
½ cup/3½ fl oz	single (light) cream	100 ml
1	handful of chervil	1
1	handful of tarragon	1
1	handful of basil leaves	1
2 tbsp	butter	2 tbsp
*	grated unwaxed lemon zest	*
*	freshly grated nutmeg	*
*	Mashed Potatoes (p. 261), to serve	*

Preheat the oven to 160°C/325°F/Gas Mark 3. Lay the cutlets between two sheets of oiled clingfilm (plastic wrap) and pound until very thin. Season with salt and pepper. Cover each cutlet with 1 slice of ham and 1 slice of cheese, fold over the edges along the length of the cutlet and lightly pound, then roll up the cutlet from the shorter end. Secure with metal or bamboo skewers.

Heat 1 tablespoon of oil in a frying pan or skillet over a medium heat and brown the rolls on all sides. Put the frying pan or skillet into the hot oven and cook through for about 20 minutes, keeping moist. Take out the skewers and season the rolls with salt and pepper.

Caramelise the sugar in a pan over a medium heat. Deglaze the pan with the vermouth and wine and reduce. Add the garlic and bay leaf, followed by the stock, juices from the frying pan or skillet and cream then reduce for a few minutes. Remove and discard the bay leaf and transfer the sauce to a measuring jug.

Wash, shake dry and finely chop the assorted herbs. Add the herbs, butter, a pinch of lemon zest and a little nutmeg to the sauce. Blend with a stick (immersion) blender.

Pour the sauce onto heated plates and arrange the rolls on top. Serve with Mashed Potatoes (p. 261).

Lübeck-Style Roast Duck

Schleswig-Holstein

Preparation time:		15 minutes
Cooking time:		2 hours 30 minutes
Serves:		4

1 × 5 lbs 8 oz	duck	1 × 2.5kg
*	salt	*
*	freshly ground black pepper	*
3	small apples	3
7 oz	white bread	cut 200 g
3 tbsp	Rum-Soaked Raisins (p. 362)	3 tbsp
1	pinch of ground cinnamon	1
2 cups/17 fl oz	chicken stock	500 ml

Rub the duck inside and out with salt and pepper. Preheat the oven to 160°C/325°F/Gas Mark 3. Peel, quarter, core and dice the apples. Cut the bread into small cubes and mix with the raisins and half the apple. Season with salt, pepper and cinnamon and stuff the duck with the mixture. Close the cavity and secure with small bamboo skewers or wooden toothpicks.

Put the duck into a shallow roasting pan, add a little stock, and roast in the oven for 2 hours 30 minutes, basting regularly with the remaining stock, as necessary.

Take out the duck and keep warm. Filter the stock from the pan through a sieve and reduce a little. Carve the duck and serve with the stuffing and sauce.

Veal-Stuffed Boneless Duck

Southern Germany

Preparation time:		30 minutes
Cooking time:		3 hours
Serves:		4

For the duck:		
5 lbs 8 oz	duck, ready to cook	2.5 kg
2 slices	bread	2 slices
1 tbsp	butter	1 tbsp
1 tbsp	horn of plenty mushrooms	1 tbsp
9 oz	finely minced (ground) veal	250 g
4 tbsp	single (light) cream	4 tbsp
¾ oz	pistachio nuts	20 g
1½ oz	veal tongue, chopped	40 g
*	freshly grated nutmeg	*
*	grated unwaxed lemon zest	*
*	grated unwaxed orange zest	*
*	salt	*
*	freshly ground black pepper	*

For the sauce:		
2	onions	2
1	small carrot	1
3½ oz	celeriac	100 g
1 tbsp	oil	1 tbsp
2 tsp	icing (confectioners') sugar	2 tsp
1 tbsp	tomato purée (paste)	1 tbsp
1 cup/8 fl oz	red wine	250 ml
5 cups/40 fl oz	duck or chicken stock	1.2 litres
1	bay leaf	1
1 tsp	juniper berries	1 tsp
1 tsp	allspice berries	1 tsp
1 tsp	cornflour (corn starch)	1 tsp

Cut wings off the duck, leaving 2–3 cm (¾–1 inch). Lay, back-side upwards, and cut along the backbone and detach the meat from the carcass and the leg meat from the joints. Repeat on the other side. Preheat the oven to 220°C/425°F/Gas Mark 7. Run the knife, inside the duck, along the breastbone, without damaging the skin, and remove the carcass. Remove the thigh and wing bones. Chop the carcass and roast for 20–30 minutes.

For the duck: Cube the bread and fry in the butter until brown. Combine the mushrooms with water and bring to a boil, then drain and chop. Mix the veal with the cream. Add the mushrooms, pistachios and tongue. Season with nutmeg, and a pinch each of the zests.

Season the duck inside and out with salt and pepper. Stuff the duck, spreading the stuffing along the middle. Fold the meat over, overlapping the edges. Secure with skewers. Turn the duck onto its back and reshape. Tie the legs together with string. Roast for 2 hours at 150°C/300°F/Gas Mark 2. Increase to 200°C/400°F/Gas Mark 6 and roast for 1 hour until crispy and brown.

For the sauce: Peel and dice the vegetables and sauté in the oil. Caramelise the sugar over a low heat. Stir in the purée and cook briefly. Deglaze the pan with the wine and simmer to thicken. Add the bones, vegetables, stock and spices, then simmer for 3 hours. 30 minutes before the end of the cooking, sieve the sauce into a pan, return the vegetables and simmer. Dissolve the cornflour (corn starch) in water, stir into the sauce, and simmer for 2 minutes. Remove the vegetables, slice the duck, and serve.

Duck Legs with Teltow Turnips

Berlin

Preparation time:		30 minutes
Cooking time:		2 hours
Serves:		4

8	shallots	8
2	carrots	2
2	bundles turnips	2
4	duck legs	4
*	salt	*
*	freshly ground black pepper	*
2 tbsp	oil	2 tbsp
2 cups/17 fl oz	chicken stock	500 ml
1 cup/8 fl oz	dry red wine	250 ml
1	garlic clove	1
1	sprig of thyme	1
1½ tbsp/¾ oz	butter	20 g

Peel the shallots and carrots, halve the shallots and cut the carrots into pieces. Wash, trim and peel the turnips.

Rub the duck legs with salt and pepper. Heat the oil in a casserole (dutch oven) over a medium heat and sear the legs well on all sides.

Take out the legs and briefly sauté the carrots and shallots. Deglaze the pan with a little stock, bring to a boil, then remove the carrots and shallots with a slotted spoon or skimmer and set aside.

Return the legs to the pan, add the wine and the rest of the stock, cover with the lid and braise, about 1 hour 30 minutes.

When the meat is cooked and comes off the bone, add the shallots and carrots. Peel, crush and finely chop the garlic and mix into the vegetables together with the thyme. Simmer, uncovered, for a further 15 minutes.

Heat the butter in a frying pan or skillet over a medium heat and sauté the turnips. Moisten with a little water, season with salt and pepper, cover with a lid and cook for 10–15 minutes.

Take the legs out of the pan, let cool a little and remove the skin. Transfer the shallots and carrots to a sieve and let drain, collecting the sauce. Arrange the shallots, carrots and turnips in a serving dish or on four plates. Cover the vegetables with the legs and pour over the sauce.

Smoked Duck Breast with Pearl Barley

All regions

Preparation time:		30 minutes
Cooking time:		1 hour
Serves:		4

4 × 6 oz	duck breasts, skin on	4 × 180 g
*	salt	*
*	freshly ground black pepper	*
7 oz	pearl barley	200 g
4½ cups/34 fl oz	chicken stock	1 litre
1 tbsp	oil	1 tbsp
1	leek	1
1	carrot	1
1	parsnip	1
2 stalks	celery	2 stalks
3 tbsp/1½ oz	butter	40 g
3–4 tbsp	single (light) cream	3–4 tbsp
1	bunch of chives, to garnish	1

To make this recipe, you will need a smoker oven or stovetop smoker, and wood chips, ideally beech.

Carefully score the skin sides of the duck breasts. Rub with salt and pepper.

Put the barley in a sieve and wash under cold running water. Let drain thoroughly, then combine with the stock in a pan and bring to a boil. Cover with a lid and let swell for 45–55 minutes over a low heat.

Heat the oil in a frying pan or skillet over a medium heat and sear the breasts well on their skin sides, about 2 minutes, then turn over and sear on the other side for 1 minute. Transfer to a rack over a dish to drain.

Heat the wood chips in a smoker oven or a stovetop smoker. Put the duck breasts on a rack in the smoker and hot-smoke slowly for 5–6 minutes. Preheat the oven to 160°C/325°F/Gas Mark 3.

Cut off the roots and green leaves from the leek, cut the white part in half lengthwise and wash thoroughly. Peel the carrot and parsnip. Cut the leek, carrot and celery stalks into small dice. Heat the butter in a casserole (dutch oven) and sauté the vegetables. Deglaze the pan with the cream, cover with the lid and cook for a few minutes until the vegetables are tender but firm to the bite. Stir in the barley and season with salt and pepper.

Take the breasts out of the smoker and rest in the oven for about 5 minutes. Wash, shake dry and finely chop the chives.

Cut the breasts into thin slices. Arrange the vegetables and pearl barley on warmed plates, sprinkle with chives and cover with the duck breast slices.

Grilled (Broiled) Duck Legs with Riesling Sauce

Southwestern Germany

Preparation time:		30 minutes
Cooking time:		2 hours 30 minutes
Serves:		4

For the duck legs:		
4	duck legs, skin on	4
9 cups/68 fl oz	chicken stock	2 litres
1	carrot	1
7 oz	celeriac	200 g
½	onion	½
1	bay leaf	1
½–1 tsp	juniper berries	½–1 tsp
5	allspice berries	5
½ tsp	black peppercorns	½ tsp
*	salt	*

For the sauce:		
1 tbsp	icing (confectioners') sugar	1 tbsp
½ cup/3½ fl oz	Riesling white wine	100 ml
½ cup/3½ fl oz	single (light) cream	100 ml
2 tsp	cornflour (corn starch)	2 tsp
1 tbsp	cold butter	1 tbsp
*	salt	*
*	cayenne pepper	*
*	Potato Dumplings (p. 268), to serve	*
*	Savoy Cabbage (p. 308), to serve	*

For the duck legs: Use a sharp knife to remove the thigh bone from the duck legs and run the knife lightly between the meat and the leg bones. Pour the stock into a pan, bring to a boil over a high heat and add the legs. The legs should be completely covered by the stock, add more if necessary. Simmer the legs until tender, about 2 hours 30 minutes.

Trim, peel and halve the carrot and celeriac. Peel the onion. After about 1 hour 30 minutes of cooking time, add the vegetables, bay leaf, juniper berries, allspice and peppercorns to the stock. When finished cooking, skim off the fat from the cooking liquid (reserve for other uses). Measure out 250 ml (1 cup/8 fl oz) of the cooking liquid and set aside.

Turn on the oven grill. Take the legs out of the pan and lay in a deep baking pan with the skin sides facing upwards. Add 1 ladle of stock to the pan and place on the lowest shelf of the oven. Grill (broil) for 15–20 minutes until crispy. Season with salt.

For the sauce: Lightly caramelise the sugar in a pan over a medium heat. Deglaze with the wine and simmer until reduced by two-thirds. Add the set-aside cooking liquid and bring to a boil, then reduce the heat. Dissolve the cornflour (corn starch) completely in a little cold water and gradually mix it into the sauce to lightly thicken. Finally, mix in the butter with a stick (immersion) blender and season the sauce with salt and cayenne pepper.

Arrange the duck legs on plates. Blend the sauce until frothy with a stick (immersion) blender and drizzle over the legs. This dish can be accompanied with Potato Dumplings (p. 268) and Savoy Cabbage (p. 308).

Roast Goose with Apples and Onions

All regions

Preparation time:		25 minutes
Cooking time:		3 hours 30 minutes
Serves:		6–8

For the goose:		
1 × 9 lb	goose	1 × 4 kg
2	onions	2
½	apple	½
10½ cups/84 fl oz	chicken stock	2.5 litres
4 tbsp/2 oz	melted butter	50 g
*	salt	*

For the sauce:		
1 tsp	icing (confectioners') sugar	1 tsp
2	onions	2
1	small carrot	1
3½ oz	celeriac	100 g
1 tbsp	tomato purée (paste)	1 tbsp
1 cup/8 fl oz	heavy red wine	250 ml
1 tsp	allspice berries	1 tsp
1	bay leaf, optional	1
1 sprig	mugwort, optional	1 sprig
1	small garlic clove	1
1 tsp	dried marjoram	1 tsp
2 tsp	cornflour (corn starch)	2 tsp
*	salt	*
*	freshly ground black pepper	*
*	Potato Dumplings (p. 268), to serve	*
*	Red Cabbage (p. 308), to serve	*

Preheat the oven to 150°C/300°F/Gas Mark 2.

For the goose: Cut the wings off and coarsely chop. Peel and quarter the onions. Wash the apple, leaving the core in, and cut into wedges. Spread out the wing pieces with the onions and apples in a large roasting pan, pour in the stock and put in the goose. Cover with foil and cook for 2 hours 30 minutes.

Raise the oven temperature to 200°C/400°F/Gas Mark 6. Put a shelf on the middle oven rail and put a drip tray under it. Carefully lift the goose out of the cooking liquid and place directly on the shelf. Line the shelf with a small sheet of baking paper if necessary. Roast the goose until the skin is crispy and brown, about 1 hour. Mix the butter with ½ teaspoon of salt and baste the goose regularly.

Meanwhile, skim the cooking liquid, sieve and let stand for 5 minutes. Skim off the fat and set aside. Measure out 750 ml (3 cups/25 fl oz) cooking liquid.

For the sauce: Lightly caramelise the sugar in a pan over a low heat. Peel the onions, carrot and celeriac. Cut into 1 cm (½ inch) dice. Add the vegetables and sauté. Stir in the purée and cook until a brown layer forms on the bottom. Add the wine a little at a time, and thicken.

Add the goose wings and the 750 ml (3 cups/25 fl oz) cooking liquid. Add the allspice berries, the bay leaf and mugwort, and simmer for 30 minutes. Add the garlic and marjoram and let infuse for 5 minutes.

Filter the sauce through a sieve into a clean pan. Dissolve the cornflour (corn starch) in a little water, add to the sauce and simmer for 2 minutes to thicken, then stir in 1 tablespoon of goose fat. Season with salt and pepper.

Carve the goose and serve with the sauce, Potato Dumplings (p. 268) and Red Cabbage (p. 308).

Poultry & Game Birds

Pomeranian-Style Goose Legs

Preparation time:		30 minutes
Cooking time:		2 hours 30 minutes
Serves:		4

2	onions	2
1	carrot	1
4 oz	celeriac	120 g
¼	apple	¼
1 tbsp	icing (confectioners') sugar	1 tbsp
1 tbsp	tomato purée (paste)	1 tbsp
1 cup/8 fl oz	red wine	250 ml
2 cups/17 fl oz	chicken stock	500 ml
1 tbsp	oil	1 tbsp
4 × 1 lb	goose legs	4 × 450 g
2 tbsp	melted butter	2 tbsp
1	bay leaf	1
5	allspice berries	5
½ tsp	peppercorns	½ tsp
4 tsp	rum	4 tsp
12	prunes	12
1	garlic clove	1
1	strip of unwaxed lemon zest	1
1	strip of unwaxed orange zest	1
*	salt	*
*	freshly ground black pepper	*
*	pinch dried marjoram pinch	*
*	Potato Dumplings (p. 268), to serve	*
*	Bread Dumplings (p. 286), to serve	*

Peel the onions and carrot and trim and peel the celeriac. Cut into 1-cm (½-inch) dice. Core and dice the apple.

Lightly caramelise the sugar in a pan, stir in the tomato purée (paste) and cook briefly. Deglaze the pan with half of the wine and reduce until thick. Add the remaining wine and let simmer, then add the stock. Preheat the oven to 150°C/300°F/Gas Mark 2. Heat the oil in a frying pan or skillet over a medium heat and sauté the vegetables. Spread out the vegetables inside a baking pan and pour the sauce base over them.

Brush the goose legs with melted butter, season with salt and arrange skin-side up over the vegetables. Place the pan on the middle shelf inside the oven and braise until soft, about 2 hours 30 minutes. After 2 hours of the cooking time, combine the bay leaf, allspice berries and peppercorns in a spice bag, close and add to the sauce.

Bring 100 ml (½ cup/3½ fl oz) water to a boil and add the rum and prunes.

At the end of the cooking time, take out the legs, skimming off the fat from the surface of the sauce if necessary. Filter the sauce through a sieve, pressing on the vegetables.

Stir the prunes and soaking liquid into the sauce. Add the garlic and citrus zests and let infuse for a few minutes. Remove the spices from the sauce and season with salt, pepper and a pinch of marjoram.

Serve the goose legs with the sauce and accompany with Potato Dumplings (p. 268) or Bread Dumplings (p. 286).

Saint Martin's Goose

Preparation time:		30 minutes
Cooking time:		5 hours
Serves:		6–8

1	apple	1
3	onions	3
*	salt	*
*	freshly ground black pepper	*
1 tsp	dried marjoram	1 tsp
1 × 9 lb 12 oz	goose	1 × 4.5 kg
6½ cups/54 fl oz	chicken stock	1.6 litres
1	carrot	1
5 oz	celeriac	150 g
2 tsp	icing (confectioners') sugar	2 tsp
1 tbsp	tomato purée (paste)	1 tbsp
1⅔ cup/14 fl oz	red wine	400 ml
3	sprigs of parsley	3
2	garlic slices	2
1	strip of unwaxed orange zest	1
1	strip of unwaxed lemon zest	1
2 tbsp	cold butter	2 tbsp

Wash, quarter and core the apple. Peel 1 onion. Coarsely chop the apple and onion and season with salt, pepper and ½ teaspoon marjoram.

Preheat the oven to 140°C/275°F/Gas Mark 1. Cut the wing bones off the goose. Stuff the cavity with the onion and apple mixture and put into a large roasting pan. Add 300 ml (1¼ cups/10½ fl oz) stock to the pan, cover with a lid or foil and cook in the oven for about 4 hours 30 minutes. The skin should remain light and the meat become soft. Regularly skim the fat released by the goose and set aside.

Cut the breast and legs off the goose and remove the thigh bones from the legs. Take out the stuffing. Use kitchen shears to cut up the carcass and wing bones. Peel and cut the remaining onions, the carrot and celeriac into 1-cm (½-inch) dice.

Lightly caramelise the sugar in a pan, stir in the tomato purée (paste) and briefly cook. Deglaze the pan with half of the wine and reduce until thick. Add the remaining the wine and reduce again. Add the bones, vegetables and half the stuffing, then add the goose cooking liquid and 1.2 litres (5 cups/40 fl oz) stock.

Let simmer for 1 hour, then filter through a sieve and reduce by half. Add the rest of the marjoram, the parsley, garlic and citrus zests and let infuse for a few minutes. Remove and discard the parsley, garlic and zests, mix in a little goose fat and the butter with a stick (immersion) blender. Season the sauce with salt.

Meanwhile, turn on the oven grill. Arrange the breast and legs skin-side up in a roasting pan, add the remaining stock, place the pan on the lowest shelf inside the oven and grill (broil) for 15–20 minutes until crispy. Serve with the sauce.

Pheasant with Sweetheart Cabbage and Chestnut Puree

Saarland

Preparation time:		15 minutes
Cooking time:		30 minutes
Serves:		4

8	pheasant breasts	8
*	salt	*
*	freshly ground black pepper	*
1 tbsp	oil	1 tbsp
1 tsp	granulated sugar	1 tsp
10	peeled chestnuts	10
4 tbsp	single (light) cream	4 tbsp
7 oz	white muscat grapes	200 g
2 oz	butter	50 g
1	small sweetheart cabbage	1
½ cup/3½ fl oz	Gewürztraminer wine	100 ml
½ cup/4 fl oz	chicken stock	120 ml

Rub the pheasant breasts with salt and pepper. Preheat the oven to 160°C/325°F/Gas Mark 3.

Heat the oil in a pan over a medium heat and lightly caramelise the sugar. Add the chestnuts, briefly toss in the caramelised sugar and then deglaze the pan with the cream and a little water. Braise the chestnuts over a low heat until cooked, then purée in a blender and press through a sieve.

Peel, halve and seed the grapes. Melt 10 g (½ tbsp/¼ oz) butter in a pan and briefly toss the grapes in it. Halve the cabbage, remove the stem and cut the halves into thin strips. Blanch in boiling salted water, then drain well. Melt 20 g (1 tbsp/¾ oz) butter in a pan over a medium heat and briefly sauté the cabbage. Season with salt and pepper.

Sauté the pheasant breasts in the rest of the butter over a medium heat without colouring. Take out of the pan, transfer directly onto an oven shelf and place a drip tray under it. Roast the breasts in the oven for 15 minutes. Combine the juices collected in the drip tray with the wine and chicken stock in a pan and reduce a little.

Cut the pheasant breasts into slices. Make a bed of cabbage on warmed plates, cover with the breast slices and serve with the grape and chestnut purée. Serve the sauce separately.

Bread-Wrapped Pheasant Breast

All regions

Preparation time:		20 minutes
Cooking time:		30 minutes
Serves:		4

8	thin slices day-old brown bread	8
5 oz	finely minced (ground) veal	150 g
3 tbsp	single (light) cream	3 tbsp
1 tbsp	sherry	1 tbsp
2–3 tbsp	chopped parsley	2–3 tbsp
*	freshly ground black pepper	*
4 × 3–3½ oz	pheasant breasts	4 × 80–100 g
1 tbsp	oil	1 tbsp
3½ oz	chestnuts, to serve, optional	100 g
1 tbsp	butter, to serve, optional	1 tbsp

Preheat the oven to 80°C/175°F/Gas Mark ¼. Put a shelf in the middle of the oven and place a drip tray under it. Mix the veal with the cream and sherry until smooth. Lay 2 slices of bread next to each other, slightly overlapped. Repeat with all of the slices. Spread the mixture over the bread, sprinkle with parsley and season with pepper.

Roll up each pheasant breast in the bread. Heat oil in a frying pan or skillet and sear the rolls over a medium heat, first on the seam side, then all over until golden brown. Transfer the rolls directly onto the oven shelf and cook for 25–30 minutes.

If desired, heat 1 tablespoon butter in a frying pan or skillet over a medium heat and warm 100 g (3½ oz) chestnuts in the butter. Season with salt. Cut the rolls into slices and serve with the chestnuts.

Braised Squab

Preparation time:		30 minutes
Cooking time:		20 minutes
Serves:		4

4	squabs, with giblets	2
*	salt	*
*	freshly ground black pepper	*
2	stale buns	2
½ cup/4 fl oz	hot milk	120 ml
2	shallots	2
3½ oz	butter	100 g
4	sprigs of thyme	4
1	bunch of parsley	1
2	egg yolks	2
*	freshly grated nutmeg	*
1 cup/8 fl oz	chicken stock	250 ml

Rub the squabs inside and out with salt and pepper. Preheat the oven to 160°C/325°F/Gas Mark 3.

Cut the buns into cubes and soak in the milk. Peel and finely chop the shallots. Sauté in a pan with 4 teaspoons of the butter until translucent. Cut the squab livers into small pieces, add to the pan, and cook briefly. Wash and shake dry the herbs. Finely chop the parsley. Pluck the leaves from 2 thyme sprigs and add to the pan with half the parsley. Squeeze the bread and work together with the egg yolks and shallot and liver mixture into a smooth stuffing. Season with salt, pepper, and nutmeg, and stuff the squabs with the mixture. Close the cavities and secure with small bamboo skewers or wooden toothpicks.

Heat 2 tablespoons of butter in a casserole (dutch oven) and sear the squabs well on all sides. Chill the remaining butter. Add the remaining thyme and parsley and the stock. Cover with the lid and cook in the oven for about 20 minutes.

Take out the squabs and keep warm. Filter the stock from the pan through a sieve and reduce a little. Cut the cold butter into small pieces, and beat into the sauce until slightly thickened. Serve the squabs with the sauce.

Braised Guinea Fowl Legs

Preparation time:		30 minutes
Cooking time:		50 minutes
Serves:		4

2	onions	2
1	carrot	1
5 oz	celeriac	150 g
4 × 7oz	guinea fowl legs, skin on	4 × 200 g
2–3 tbsp	oil	2–3 tbsp
2 tsp	icing (confectioners') sugar	2 tsp
1 tbsp	tomato purée (paste)	1 tbsp
2 tbsp	cognac	2 tbsp
3 tbsp	port	3 tbsp
1 cup/7 fl oz	heavy red wine	200 ml
2½ cups/20 fl oz	chicken stock	600 ml
1	bay leaf	1
5	juniper berries	5
½ tsp	peppercorns	½ tsp
1 tbsp	dried white mushrooms	1 tbsp
*	salt	*
*	freshly ground black pepper	*
1	garlic clove	1
1	strip of unwaxed orange zest	1
1	small sprig of thyme	1
1 tbsp/¾ oz	cold butter	20 g
*	Mashed Potatoes (p. 261), to serve	*

Peel and cut the onions, carrot, and celeriac into 1–1.5-cm (½–¾-inch) dice. Use a knife tip to remove the thigh bones from the guinea fowl legs.

Heat 1–2 tablespoons oil in a wide casserole (dutch oven), put the legs inside, skin-side down, and brown over a medium heat. Turn over and briefly sear the other sides. Take the legs out of the pan and wipe clean of any oil.

Sift the sugar into the pan and lightly caramelise. Stir in the tomato purée (paste) and cook briefly. Deglaze the pan with the cognac, port, and half of the red wine, and simmer the liquid until reduced to a syrup. Add the rest of the wine and simmer to reduce.

Preheat the oven to 160°C/325°F/Gas Mark 3. Heat the remaining oil in a frying pan or skillet and sauté the diced vegetables over a medium heat. Add the vegetables to the wine reduction in the pan and add the stock. Return the legs to the pan with the skin side facing upward, taking care not to let the skin become immersed in the sauce.

Place the pan, uncovered, on the middle shelf of the oven and braise for 45–50 minutes until soft. After 30 minutes of the cooking time, add the bay leaf, lightly crushed juniper berries, peppercorns, and dried white mushrooms and continue cooking until done. Take the braised legs out of the pan, season with salt and pepper if desired, and keep warm.

Put the pan with the cooking liquid on the hob stove or top and reduce a little over a low heat. Peel and halve the garlic clove. Add the garlic, orange zest, and thyme, and let infuse for a few minutes in the sauce. Filter the sauce through a sieve, pressing well on the vegetables. Stir the cold butter into the sauce and season with salt and pepper. Accompany with Mashed Potatoes (p. 261).

Partridge with Brussels Sprouts and Black Salsify

All regions

Preparation time:		40 minutes
Cooking time:		40 minutes
Serves:		4

For the partridge:		
2 × 14 oz	partridges	2 × 400 g
2	onions	2
2	carrots	2
7 oz	celeriac	200 g
*	salt	*
*	freshly ground black pepper	*
1–2 tbsp	oil	1–2 tbsp
1 tbsp	tomato purée (paste)	1 tbsp
1 cup/7 fl oz	red wine	200 ml
2 cups/17 fl oz	port	500 ml
4 tsp	cognac	4 tsp
1	pinch of granulated sugar	1
2½ cups/20 fl oz	chicken stock	600 ml
1	strip of unwaxed orange zest	1
1	bay leaf	1
1	small sprig of thyme	1
5	juniper berries	5
½ tsp	peppercorns	½ tsp
¼ oz	dried mushrooms	10 g
2 tsp	cornflour (corn starch)	2 tsp
1 tbsp	lingonberries (from a jar)	1 tbsp
1 tbsp/¾ oz	cold butter	20 g

For the vegetables:		
1–2	black salsify (scorzonera)	1–2
2	carrots	2
3½ oz	Brussels sprouts	100 g
½ cup/3½ fl oz	vegetable stock	100 ml
*	salt	*
*	freshly ground black pepper	*
*	freshly grated nutmeg	*
2 tbsp	Beurre Noisette (p. 112)	2 tbsp
1 tbsp	finely chopped parsley	1 tbsp

For the partridge: Cut off the legs and wings. Use a sharp knife to remove the thigh bone from the legs. Leave the breasts attached to the carcass.

Peel the onions, carrots and celeriac, then dice. Lightly season. Heat a little oil in a pan and sear the legs and wings over a medium heat, skin-side down. Turn over and sear the other side. Sauté the vegetables for 1–2 minutes, then stir in the purée and cook briefly. Deglaze the pan with the alcohol, and reduce until syrupy. Season with sugar. Return the legs and wings to the pan, add the stock, and braise for 45 minutes. After 25 minutes, add the zest, bay, thyme, juniper, pepper and mushrooms.

Preheat the oven to 130°C/250°F/Gas Mark ¾. Put a drip tray under the oven shelf. Season the breasts. Sear in a pan over a medium heat, then roast for 20–25 minutes.

For the vegetables: Peel and slice the salsify and carrots. Separate the sprout leaves. Cook the vegetables separately in boiling salted water. Heat the stock in a pan. Season with a pinch of nutmeg. Add the Beurre Noisette (p. 112) and parsley. Remove the legs, sieve the sauce and reduce by half. Stir in the flour, then add the lingonberries and cold butter. Serve the partridge pieces with the sauce and vegetables.

Roast Guinea Fowl with Stuffing

All regions

Preparation time:		30 minutes
Cooking time:		1 hour 15 minutes
Serves:		4

1 × 2 lbs 4 oz	guinea fowl	1 × 1 kg
*	salt	*
*	freshly ground black pepper	*
1	shallot	1
2 oz	butter	50 g
3 slices	white bread	3 slices
5–6 tbsp	milk	5–6 tbsp
½	bunch of parsley	½
2–3	tarragon leaves	2–3
9 oz	finely minced (ground) veal	250 g
1	egg	1
1	leek	1
1	carrot	1
1	celery stalk	1
1	onion	1
½ cup/4 fl oz	dry white wine	120 ml
½ cup/4 fl oz	chicken stock	120 ml
2 tbsp	crème fraîche	2 tbsp

Rub the guinea fowl inside and out with salt and pepper.

Peel and dice the shallot and sauté in a pan with 2 teaspoons of butter over a medium heat until translucent. Cut the crusts off the bread slices, cut the slices into cubes and soak in the milk for 5 minutes. Wash, shake dry and pluck the parsley (set aside the stems for using another time) and finely chop the leaves with the tarragon.

Preheat the oven to 160°C/325°F/Gas Mark 3. Squeeze the bread and mix with the shallot, herbs and minced (ground) veal. Add the egg and work until smooth. Season the stuffing with salt and pepper, then stuff the guinea fowl.

Heat the remaining butter in a roasting pan and brown the guinea fowl on all sides until golden. Trim and wash the leek, carrot and celery and peel the onion. Cut all of the vegetables into small pieces, add to the pan and brown with the guinea fowl. Turn the guinea fowl onto its back, pour over the wine and stock, cover with a lid or foil and cook in the oven for 50–60 minutes. Then remove the lid and cook for 15 more minutes until it turns golden brown.

Take out the guinea fowl and press the cooking liquid through a sieve. Stir in the crème fraîche and reduce the sauce for a few minutes to thicken.

Carve the guinea fowl. Take out the stuffing and cut into slices. Serve the sauce separately.

Partridge Wrapped in Vine Leaves

Palatinate and North Western Germany

Preparation time:		30 minutes
Cooking time:		30 minutes
Serves:		4

4	young partridges	4
*	salt	*
*	freshly ground black pepper	*
8	very thin slices smoked bacon	8
8	fresh vine leaves	8
2 tbsp	oil	2 tbsp
1 lb 5 oz	grapes, deseeded	600 g
½ cup/4 fl oz	chicken stock	120 ml
½ cup/4 fl oz	gewürztraminer wine	120 ml
2	juniper berries	2
4 tsp	grappa	4 tsp
4 tbsp/2 oz	cold butter	50 g

Rub the partridges with salt and pepper. Wrap each partridge with 2 slices of bacon and 2 vine leaves and secure with string. Preheat the oven to 180°C/350°F/Gas Mark 4.

Heat the oil in a casserole (dutch oven) and sear the wrapped partridges on all sides. Cook in the oven for 20 minutes, basting regularly with the pan juices. Wash, halve and deseed the grapes and add to the partridges once cooked. Mix with the pan juices and cook for a further 8 minutes. Take the partridges and grapes out of the pan and keep warm.

Add the stock and wine to the juices in the pan. Add the crushed juniper berries and simmer, about 5 minutes. Filter the sauce through a sieve and add the grappa. Cut the cold butter into small pieces and stir into the sauce. Serve the partridges with the grapes and sauce.

Stuffed Quail

All regions

Preparation time:		30 minutes
Cooking time:		25 minutes
Serves:		4

4	quails	4
4 ¼ oz	finely minced (ground) veal	125 g
1 tbsp	single (light) cream	1 tbsp
2 tbsp	croutons	2 tbsp
*	finely diced black truffle	*
1	pinch of dried marjoram	1
1	pinch of grated unwaxed lemon zest	1
1 tsp	port	1 tsp
*	salt	*
*	freshly ground black pepper	*
*	oil	*
*	melted butter, for basting	*
*	Sweetheart Cabbage (p. 303)	*

Prepare each quail one at a time. Put a quail, with its wings upward, on a clean work counter and run a small sharp knife along its backbone. Carefully run the knife along the carcass to detach the meat from the bones. Cut off the wings and the legs at the first joint. Remove the carcass from the meat. Lay the boned quail flat on the work counter skin-side down. Preheat the oven to 140°C/275°F/Gas Mark 1.

Mix the minced (ground) veal with the cream, stirring vigorously until the mixture becomes glossy. Add the croutons, truffle, a pinch of marjoram, a little lemon zest, and the port and mix well.

Season the quails with salt and pepper, then put 1 tablespoon of the stuffing in the middle of each quail. Fold the meat over, overlapping the edges a little, turn over, reshape, and season the outside with salt and pepper.

Fold foil into small, square parcels. Lightly grease the parcels with oil, place 1 stuffed quail in each, with the breast facing upward, and fold the foil tightly over the quail.

Roast the quail in the oven for about 25 minutes. Baste with butter from time to time. Serve the quails whole or cut into slices. Accompany with Sweetheart Cabbage (p. 303).

Poultry & Game Birds

Veal & Beef

Veal Schnitzel

All regions

Preparation time:		5 minutes
Cooking time:		20 minutes
Serves:		2

½ tsp	oil	½ tsp
4 × 2 oz	veal cutlets	4 × 60 g
5 tbsp	chicken stock	5 tbsp
*	salt	*
*	freshly ground black pepper	*
1 tsp	cold butter	1 tsp

Heat a frying pan or skillet over a medium heat and brush with the oil. Sear the veal cutlets on both sides, about 3 minutes, and remove from the pan.

Deglaze the pan with the stock, season with salt and pepper, and simmer until only 3–4 tablespoons liquid remains. Remove the pan from the heat and incorporate the cold butter. Coat the schnitzels with the sauce and adjust the seasoning if necessary.

Stuffed Veal Schnitzel

Bavaria

Preparation time:		40 minutes
Cooking time:		25 minutes
Serves:		4

For the stuffing:		
2	handfuls of spinach leaves	2
1	bunch of parsley	1
*	salt	*
⅓ cup	Bergkäse (hard alpine) cheese	40 g
¼	onion	¼
3	bacon slices	3
¼ cup	walnuts	30 g
⅛	pear	⅛

For the schnitzel:		
½ tsp	fennel seeds	½ tsp
½ tsp	coriander seeds	½ tsp
½ tsp	peppercorns	½ tsp
2	eggs	2
2 tbsp	single (light) cream	2 tbsp
½ tsp	hot mustard	½ tsp
¾ cup/3 oz	plain (all-purpose) flour	80 g
2¾ cups/7 oz	white breadcrumbs	200 g
8 × 2 oz	veal cutlets	8 × 60 g
*	salt	*
⅔ cup 5 fl oz	oil, for frying	150 ml
4	lemon wedges, to serve	4

For the stuffing: Select the best spinach leaves and remove the large stems from the parsley. Wash the spinach and parsley and blanch both in boiling salted water for 1 minute, drain, then plunge into iced water, and drain again. Squeeze out the excess water and mince everything. Cut the cheese into small dice. Peel and mince the onion, and cook in a frying pan or skillet with 80 ml (⅓ cup/2 fl oz) water until soft and the liquid evaporates completely. Cut the bacon into small cubes and fry in a dry frying pan or skillet over a low heat to melt the fat, then transfer to a strainer and let drain. Coarsely chop the walnuts. Wash, core and cut the pear into small dice.

For the schnitzel: Put the fennel and coriander seeds and peppercorns into a spice grinder. Mix the eggs with the cream and mustard in a mixing beaker, season with the spices from the grinder, and blend with a stick (immersion) blender. Transfer to a deep plate. Put the flour and breadcrumbs separately into deep plates.

Lay the cutlets out on a work surface, season with salt, and cover half of each with the parsley and spinach stuffing mixture. Sprinkle with the cheese, onion, bacon, walnuts, and pear, then fold each of the cutlets over.

Dredge the stuffed schnitzels one at a time in the flour and tap to remove the excess. Then dip in the egg mixture and finally dredge in the breadcrumbs, pressing only lightly.

Heat the oil in a deep frying pan and fry the schnitzels over a medium heat, first on one side, until golden brown, then turn over, adding more oil if needed, and fry the other side. Drain on paper towels and serve on plates with the lemon wedges.

Veal Schnitzel with Cream Sauce

All regions

Preparation time:		10 minutes
Cooking time:		15 minutes
Serves:		4

4 × 2 oz	veal cutlets	4 × 60 g
1 tbsp	oil, plus extra for greasing	1 tbsp
1 tbsp	cognac	1 tbsp
½ cup/ 3½ fl oz	veal or vegetable stock	100 ml
6 tbsp	single (light) cream	6 tbsp
1 tsp	Dijon mustard	1 tsp
1	bay leaf	1
1 tbsp	cold butter	1 tbsp
*	salt	*
*	freshly ground black pepper	*
½	grated unwaxed lemon, zested	½
11 oz	button (white) mushrooms	300 g
4	spring onions (scallions)	4
1 tbsp	Beurre Noisette (p. 112)	1 tbsp

Lay the cutlets between two sheets of oiled clingfilm (plastic wrap) and pound flat. Heat the oil in a frying pan or skillet and fry the cutlets on both sides over a medium heat. Transfer the cutlets to a heated plate and set aside.

Deglaze the pan with the cognac and stock. Add the cream, mustard and bay leaf, bring to a boil, then simmer for a few minutes.

Mix in the cold butter and season the sauce with salt, pepper and a pinch of lemon zest. Remove and discard the bay leaf. Return the cutlets to the sauce and let simmer.

Wash, wipe dry and slice the mushrooms. Trim, wash and cut the spring onions (scallions) into rings.

Heat the Beurre Noisette (p. 112) in a frying pan or skillet and fry the mushrooms and spring onions (scallions). Season with salt, pepper, and the remaining lemon zest.

Add the mushrooms and onions to the sauce and mix well. Serve the schnitzel on warmed plates with the sauce.

Veal Schnitzel with Bell Pepper Sauce

All regions

Preparation time:		15 minutes
Cooking time:		20 minutes
Serves:		4

For the sauce:		
1	red bell pepper	1
1 tbsp	oil	1 tbsp
½	onion	½
1 tsp	icing (confectioners') sugar	1 tsp
1 cup/8 fl oz	vegetable stock	250 ml
6 tbsp	single (light) cream	6 tbsp
*	salt	*
*	cayenne pepper	*
½ tsp	sweet paprika	½ tsp
1	strip of unwaxed lemon zest	1
2	slices garlic	2
1 tbsp	cold butter	1 tbsp

For the schnitzel:		
8 × 2 oz	veal cutlets	8 × 60g
1–2 tsp	oil, plus extra for greasing	1–2 tsp
*	salt	*
*	freshly ground black pepper	*

For the sauce: Turn on the oven grill. Quarter the bell pepper lengthwise, seed and wash. Put the pepper quarters skin-side up on a baking sheet and brush with the oil. Put the baking sheet on the top shelf inside the oven and cook until the skin turns dark and bubbles form. Take out of the oven, let cool briefly, and peel off the skin. Cut into small pieces.

Peel and finely chop the onion. Put the sugar into a pan over a medium heat and lightly caramelise. Sauté the onion until glazed and add the pepper pieces. Add the stock and simmer for 10–15 minutes until cooked.

Add the cream, lower the heat, and blend to a sauce with a stick (immersion) blender. Return the sauce to the heat and season well with salt, a pinch of cayenne pepper and the paprika. Add the lemon zest and garlic, let infuse for a few minutes, then remove and discard. Blend the cold butter into the sauce and adjust the seasoning if necessary.

For the schnitzel: Lay the cutlets between two sheets of oiled clingfilm (plastic wrap) and pound very thin, then season with salt and pepper. Heat the oil in a frying pan or skillet and fry the cutlets on both sides over a medium heat. Serve the cutlets on warmed plates with the sauce.

Veal Fricassee

All regions

Preparation time:		1 hour
Cooking time:		1 hour 30 minutes
Serves:		4

11 oz	veal tongue, corned	300 g
1	onion	1
1	bay leaf	1
2	cloves	2
1	sprig of thyme	1
9 oz	veal sweetbreads	250 g
11 oz	veal tenderloin	300 g
9 oz	white asparagus spears	250 g
9 oz	green asparagus spears	250 g
*	salt	*
*	granulated sugar	*
½ cup/2¼ oz	butter	60 g
5	large white mushrooms	5
*	freshly ground black pepper	*
2 tbsp	sour cream	2 tbsp
½ cup/4 fl oz	single (light) cream	120 ml
1	strip of unwaxed lemon zest	1
2 tbsp	double (heavy) cream	2 tbsp
*	boiled rice, to serve	*

Wash the tongue and put it in a pan. Cover with cold water, bring to a boil, and skim off the foam. Peel the onion and attach the bay leaf by studding with the cloves and add to the pan with the tongue, along with the thyme. Simmer for 1 hour.

In the meantime, clean the sweetbreads and soak in iced water, changing the water often. At the end of the cooking time, add the sweetbreads to the pan and simmer for 20 more minutes.

Wash, pat dry and cut the tenderloin into cubes. Take the tongue and sweetbreads out of the pan. Peel the tongue and remove the membrane and nerves. Filter the cooking liquid through a muslin (cheese) cloth and set aside.

Peel the white asparagus spears, and peel only the bottom thirds of the green ones. Cut the woody ends off both. Combine a little salted water with a pinch of sugar and 1 tablespoon butter in a pan and bring to a boil. Cook the asparagus for 5–10 minutes. Take out, let cool a little and cut into equal pieces.

Clean the mushrooms, wiping dry if necessary, and quarter. Melt 20 g (7½ tbsp/¾ oz) of butter in a frying pan or skillet and briefly sauté the mushrooms over a medium heat. Season with salt and pepper.

Bring 500 ml (generous 2 cups/17 fl oz) of the tongue and sweetbread cooking liquid to a boil and reduce a little. Add the sour cream, cream, remaining butter and lemon zest, and season with salt and pepper. Add the tongue, sweetbreads, asparagus and mushrooms to the sauce.

Bring the rest of the cooking liquid to a boil and poach the tenderloin for 4 minutes. Take out, let drain, and mix into the fricassee. Let simmer for a few minutes. Remove the lemon zest and add in the whipped cream. Adjust the seasoning and serve the fricassee with boiled rice.

Stuffed Breast of Veal

Southern Germany

Preparation time:		30 minutes
Cooking time:		3 hours
Serves:		6–8

1 tsp	icing (confectioners') sugar	1 tsp
2 tbsp	tomato pureé (paste)	2 tbsp
1 cup/8 fl oz	red wine	250 ml
2 cups/17 fl oz	chicken stock	500 ml
2	carrots	2
7 oz	celeriac	200 g
3	onions	3
4 lb 4 oz	milk-fed veal breast	2 kg
1 tbsp	oil	1 tbsp
1	bay leaf	1
½ tsp	peppercorns	½ tsp
2	strips of unwaxed lemon zest	2
2	cloves garlic	2
1	sprig of rosemary	1
1 tsp	cornflour (corn starch)	1 tsp
*	salt	*
*	freshly ground black pepper	*

For the stuffing:		
5 oz	day-old pretzel rolls	150 g
⅔ cup/5 fl oz	milk	150 ml
2	small eggs	2
*	salt	*
*	freshly ground black pepper	*
*	freshly grated nutmeg	*
½	onion	½
3½ oz	finely minced (ground) veal	100 g
3 tbsp	single (light) cream	3 tbsp
1 tbsp	finely chopped parsley	1 tbsp
1–2 tsp	grated unwaxed lemon zest	1–2 tsp
*	seasonal vegetables, to serve	*

Caramelise the sugar over a medium heat. Add the pureé and cook briefly. Deglaze with the wine three times, slowly reducing. Add the stock and simmer. Peel and cut the vegetables into 5–10-mm (¼–½-inch) dice. Sauté in a dry roasting pan, then add to the sauce.

For the stuffing: Scrape the salt off the rolls, cut into 1-cm (½-inch) cubes, and put in a bowl. Bring the milk to a boil, take off the heat and stir in the eggs. Season the mix with salt, pepper and nutmeg and mix with the bread. Peel and finely chop the onion. Combine with 100 ml (scant ½ cup/3½ fl oz) water in a pan and cook until soft, boiling down completely. Add the onion to the bread. Mix the veal with the cream, then mix into the bread with the parsley. Season with salt, pepper, and nutmeg.

Preheat the oven to 150°C/300°F/Gas Mark 2. Cut a pocket in the veal. Fill with stuffing and close with a skewer. Sear in a pan with oil over a medium heat. Add to the pan with the sauce and braise for 3 hours, basting often. 45 minutes before the end, add the bay, pepper, lemon zest and garlic. Add the rosemary at the end and infuse briefly.

Keep the veal warm. Sieve the sauce and heat to a simmer. Discard the vegetables. Dissolve the cornflour (corn starch) in water, add to the sauce, and simmer to thicken and season. Slice the veal, drizzle with the sauce.

Roast Veal Tenderloin

Preparation time:	10 minutes
Cooking time:	2 hours
Serves:	4

1–2 tsp	oil	1–2 tsp
2¼ lb	veal fillet (tenderloin)	1 kg
4 tbsp	butter	4 tbsp
1	sprig of thyme	1
*	salt	*
*	freshly ground black pepper	*

Preheat the oven to 100°C/200°F/Gas Mark ¼. Put a shelf on the middle rail of the oven and place a drip tray under it.

Heat the oil in a frying pan or skillet. Sear the veal on all sides over a medium heat. Transfer to the oven shelf and roast until medium rare, about 2 hours.

Melt the butter in a frying pan or skillet over a low heat. Add the thyme, let infuse for 3–4 minutes, then remove and discard. Take the veal out of the oven, coat with the thyme-infused butter, and season with salt and pepper.

Veal Cheeks

Bavaria

Preparation time:	30 minutes
Cooking time:	3 hours
Serves:	4

2–3 tbsp	oil	2–3 tbsp
12 × 5 oz	veal cheeks	12 × 150 g
1 tsp	icing (confectioners') sugar	1 tsp
1 tbsp	tomato pureé (paste)	1 tbsp
1¼ cups/10 fl oz	red wine	300 ml
2	onions	2
1	carrot	1
1	parsnip	1
4 oz	celeriac	120 g
4¼ cups/34 fl oz	chicken stock	1 litre
½ tsp	mustard seeds	½ tsp
1 tsp	cornflour (corn starch)	1 tsp
1	sprig of thyme	1
1	strip of lemon zest	1
1	garlic clove	1
*	salt	*
*	freshly ground black pepper	*
*	Boiled Potatoes (p. 260), to serve	*

Heat 1–2 tablespoons oil in a casserole (dutch oven) and sear the veal cheeks over a medium heat, then remove. Sprinkle the sugar into the pan and lightly caramelise. Stir in the tomato pureé (paste) and cook briefly. Deglaze three times with a third of the wine, slowly reducing each time.

Peel and cut the onions, carrot, parsnip and celeriac into 1-cm (½-inch) dice.

Heat the rest of the oil in a frying pan or skillet and sauté the vegetables, then transfer to the casserole (dutch oven) with the cheeks and add the stock. The cheeks should be completely covered by the liquid. Cover with the lid, leaving a small gap. Braise the cheeks over a low heat until tender, about 3 hours. Remove the lid after 2 hours of cooking.

Take out the meat and set aside. Add the mustard seeds to the pan and simmer to reduce the sauce. Dissolve the cornflour (corn starch) completely in a little cold water, stir into the sauce, and simmer for 2 minutes. Add the thyme, lemon zest, and garlic and let infuse for a few minutes.

Filter the sauce through a sieve into a pan, pressing lightly on the vegetables. Season the sauce with salt and pepper. Return the cheeks to the sauce and warm through.

Arrange the veal cheeks on warmed plates with the shallots and a little sauce. Accompany with small Boiled Potatoes (p. 260).

Braised Veal Roast with Cream Sauce

All regions

Preparation time:		25 minutes
Cooking time:		3 hours
Serves:		4

2	onions	2
1	carrot	1
3½ oz	celeriac	100 g
2	ripe tomatoes	2
2–3 tbsp	oil	2–3 tbsp
3 lb 4 oz	veal knuckle	1.5 kg
1 tsp	icing (confectioners') sugar	1 tsp
1 tbsp	tomato pureé (paste)	1 tbsp
⅔ cup/5 fl oz	heavy red wine	150 ml
2 cups/17 fl oz	chicken stock	500 ml
¼ oz	chestnut (cremini) mushrooms	10 g
1	bay leaf	1
3	juniper berries	3
½ cup/ 3½ fl oz	single (light) cream	100 ml
2	sprigs of parsley	2
1	garlic clove	1
1	strip unwaxed lemon zest	1
*	salt	*
1	pinch of cayenne pepper	1

Preheat the oven to 150°C/300°F/Gas Mark 2. Peel and cut the onions, carrot and celeriac into 1–2 cm (½–1 inch) dice. Wash and halve the tomatoes, removing the stems, then divide into eighths.

Heat 1–2 tablespoons oil in a roasting pan and sear the meat on all sides over a medium heat. Take out the meat and wipe the pan dry with paper towels. Sprinkle the sugar into the roasting pan and lightly caramelise. Stir in the tomato pureé (paste) and cook briefly. Deglaze the pan with half of the red wine, and simmer the liquid until reduced to a syrup. Add the remaining wine, reduce again and add the stock.

Heat the rest of the oil in a frying pan or skillet. Sauté the onions, carrot and celeriac, then add to the roasting pan with the tomatoes. Lay the meat on top of the vegetables, cover with a lid or foil, put the roasting pan on the middle shelf of the oven and braise for about 3 hours, turning the meat over from time to time.

About 20 minutes before the end of the cooking time, add the mushrooms, bay leaf and juniper berries. At the end of the cooking time, stir in the cream. Add the parsley, garlic and lemon zest and let infuse for a few minutes in the sauce.

Take out the meat and cut into slices. Filter the sauce through a sieve, pressing down firmly on the vegetables, and season with salt and a pinch of cayenne pepper. Heat the meat through in the sauce.

Veal Ragout

All regions

Preparation time:		20 minutes
Cooking time:		1 hour
Serves:		4

For the meat:		
2 lb 8 oz	veal shoulder	1.2 kg
*	salt	*
1	onion	1
1	bay leaf	1
2	cloves	2
1–2 tsp	icing (confectioners') sugar	1–2 tsp
½ cup/3½ fl oz	dry white wine	100 ml
4¼ cups/34 fl oz	vegetable stock	1 litre
½ tsp	peppercorns	½ tsp
½ cup/4 fl oz	single (light) cream	120 ml
1–2 tsp	cornflour (corn starch)	1–2 tsp
3	sprigs of parsley	3
1	garlic clove	1
2	strips of unwaxed lemon zest	2
1	pinch of cayenne pepper	1
*	lemon juice	*
1½ tbsp	cold butter	20 g
1 tbsp	tarragon, chervil, parsley	1 tbsp

For the rice:		
7 oz	long-grain rice	200 g
*	salt	*
¾ oz	butter	20 g
½ tbsp/¼ oz	Beurre Noisette (p. 112)	10 g
8	lemon slices, to serve	8

For the meat: Trim the fat and sinew from the meat if necessary, and cut into 15–20-mm (¾–1-inch) chunks. Bring plenty of salted water to a simmer in a pan and cook the meat for 3–4 minutes. Drain in a colander. Peel the onion and attach the bay leaf by studding with the cloves.

Lightly caramelise the sugar in a pan, then deglaze the pan with the wine and simmer until reduced by two-thirds. Add the stock, meat, onion and peppercorns. Cover with a lid, leaving a small gap, and steep rather than simmer over a low heat for 1 hour.

For the rice: Put the rice into a sieve and rinse under cold running water until the water runs clear. Put into a pan and add enough water to cover the rice by a finger's width. Season with salt, bring to a boil, cover with a lid and simmer until the rice swells, about 15 minutes.

Filter the stock through a sieve into a pan. Remove and discard the onion and set aside the meat. Add the cream to the stock. Dissolve the cornflour (corn starch) completely in a little cold water, stir into the sauce and simmer for 2 minutes.

Wash and pat dry the parsley. Add the parsley, garlic and lemon zest to the sauce, let infuse for a few minutes, then remove and discard. Season with salt, a pinch of cayenne pepper and a dash of lemon juice. Blend in the butter with a stick (immersion) blender then add the meat to the sauce and heat through. Spoon the ragout onto warmed plates. Stir the butter and Beurre Noisette (p. 112) into the rice and add to the plates. Garnish with herbs and serve with lemon slices.

Swabian-Style Veal Roulade (Schwäbische Kalbsvögerl)

Baden-Württemberg

½	small carrot	½
3½ oz	celeriac	100 g
2	small onions	2
2 oz	smoked ham	50 g
3 tbsp	oil	3 tbsp
1–2 tbsp	tomato pureé (paste)	1–2 tbsp
1⅔ cups/14 fl oz	chicken stock	400 ml
3 oz	canned chopped tomatoes	80 g
1 tbsp	allspice berries	1 tbsp
1 tbsp	coriander seeds	1 tbsp
1 tbsp	peppercorns	1 tbsp
1 tsp	crushed cinnamon stick	1 tsp
1	bay leaf	1
4	eggs	4
4 × 4 oz	veal cutlets	4 × 120 g
*	salt	*
1–2 tbsp	hot mustard	1–2 tbsp
4	slices of Black Forest ham	4
1 tsp	cornflour (corn starch)	1 tsp
1 tbsp	cold butter	1 tbsp
1	pinch of cayenne pepper	1
1	garlic clove	1
1	strip of unwaxed lemon zest	1
*	Mashed Potatoes (p. 261), to serve	*
*	Spätzle (p. 288), to serve	*

Trim and peel the carrot and celeriac. Halve the carrot lengthwise and cut into thin slices. Cut the celeriac into strips, and then into thin slices. Peel and cut the onions into 1-cm (½-inch) dice. Cut the smoked ham into strips.

Heat 2 tablespoons oil in a deep frying pan or skillet and sauté the vegetables with the ham. Add the tomato pureé (paste) and cook briefly. Add 300 ml (1¼ cups/10½ fl oz) stock with the tomatoes and braise for 30 minutes.

Grind the whole spices and bay leaf in a spice grinder. Hard-boil the eggs for 8 minutes, plunge into iced water, then peel. Lay the cutlets between two sheets of clingfilm (plastic wrap) and pound flat. Season with salt, spread with mustard, and season with the ground spices. Lay 1 slice of ham on each cutlet and top with an egg. Roll up the cutlets and secure with skewers.

Heat the remaining oil in a frying pan or skillet, sear the roulades on all sides over a medium heat, and put into the sauce. Wipe the frying pan or skillet dry with paper towels. Deglaze the caramelised juices in a frying pan or skillet with 100 ml (scant ½ cup/3½ fl oz) stock, then add that liquid to the sauce. Cover the roulades with a lid and braise in the sauce, over a low heat, for about 1 hour.

Take the roulades out of the sauce and remove the skewers. Dissolve the cornflour (corn starch) in a little water and mix it into the simmering sauce to lightly thicken. Incorporate the butter, and season with salt, a pinch of cayenne and the spice mixture. Add the garlic and lemon zest, infuse for a few minutes, then remove. Return the roulades to the sauce and warm through. Serve with the sauce. Accompany with Mashed Potatoes (p. 261) and Spätzle (p. 288).

Braised Veal Shank

Bavaria

2	onions	2
1	carrot	1
4 oz	celeriac	120 g
2–3 tbsp	oil	2–3 tbsp
6 lbs 12 oz	veal shank	3 kg
2 tsp	icing (confectioners') sugar	2 tsp
1 tbsp	tomato pureé (paste)	1 tbsp
⅔ cup/5 fl oz	red wine	150 ml
2 cups/17 fl oz	chicken stock	500 ml
1	bay leaf	1
½ tsp	peppercorns	½ tsp
1	garlic clove	1
1	strip of unwaxed lemon zest	1
1	sprig of thyme	1
*	salt	*
*	freshly ground black pepper	*

Preheat the oven to 160°C/325°F/Gas Mark 3. Peel the onions, carrot and celeriac. Finely chop the onion and cut the carrot and celeriac into small pieces.

Heat 1–2 tablespoons oil in a roasting pan. Sear the shank on all sides over a medium heat and take out of the pan. Wipe the oil and fat from the pan with paper towels. Sprinkle the sugar into the pan and lightly caramelise. Stir in the tomato pureé (paste) and cook briefly. Deglaze the pan with half the red wine and simmer until reduced to a syrup. Add the rest of the wine and simmer to reduce.

Heat the remaining oil in a frying pan or skillet and sauté the vegetables over a medium heat. Add the vegetables to the roasting pan with the stock. Lay the meat on top of the vegetables, cover with a lid or foil and put the roasting pan on the middle shelf of the oven and braise for 4 hours 30 minutes, turning over regularly. After 2 hours, remove the lid and baste the meat with the sauce from time to time.

Take the meat out of the pan and set aside. Add the bay leaf and peppercorns to the pan and simmer over a medium heat to reduce the sauce. Add the garlic, lemon zest and thyme, and let infuse for a few minutes in the sauce. Filter the sauce through a sieve, pressing firmly on the vegetables. Season the sauce with salt. Cut the shank into slices, season with salt and pepper, and serve on plates with the sauce.

Veal & Beef

Corned Beef Tongue with Horseradish Sauce

All regions

Preparation time:		20 minutes
Cooking time:		4 hours
Serves:		4–6

For the tongue:		
*	salt	*
1	onion	1
1	bay leaf	1
2	cloves	2
3 lb 6 oz	corned beef tongue	1.6 kg
1 tsp	peppercorns	1 tsp
For the sauce:		
5½ oz	floury potatoes	160 g
1–2 tsp	icing (confectioners') sugar	1–2 tsp
½ cup/3½ fl oz	dry white wine	100 ml
¾ cup/7 fl oz	cream	200 ml
1 tbsp	creamed horseradish	1 tbsp
1½ tbsp/¾ oz	cold butter	20 g
*	salt	*
1	pinch of granulated sugar	1
*	Mashed Potatoes (p. 261), to serve	*
*	Boiled Potatoes (p. 260), to serve	*

For the tongue: Bring plenty of water to a boil in a pan and salt lightly. Peel the onion and attach the bay leaf by studding with the cloves. Thoroughly wash the tongue, put into the boiling water, add the peppercorns and studded onion and simmer for 3 hours 30 minutes until soft.

Filter the resulting stock through a sieve into a clean pan. Refresh the tongue in iced water, peel and return to the stock.

For the sauce: Measure out 500 ml (2 cups/17 fl oz) of the tongue cooking liquid and put into a small pan. Peel and cut the potatoes into 5-mm (½-inch) dice. Simmer in the stock for 10–15 minutes until soft.

Lightly caramelise the icing (confectioners') sugar in a small pan, then deglaze the pan with the wine and simmer until reduced by two-thirds. Add the stock with the diced potatoes, cream and horseradish to the pan and blend until smooth with a stick (immersion) blender. Blend the cold butter into the sauce and season with salt and a pinch of sugar.

Cut the tongue into 5–10-mm (¼–½-inch) thick slices and heat through in the stock, without boiling. Arrange the tongue slices on plates with the horseradish sauce. Serve with Mashed Potatoes (p. 261) or Boiled Potatoes (p. 260).

Lübeck-Style 'Swallows' Nests'

Schleswig-Holstein

Preparation time:		30 minutes
Cooking time:		20 minutes
Serves:		4

4	eggs	4
4 × 4 oz	veal cutlets	4 × 120 g
*	salt	*
*	freshly ground black pepper	*
1–2 tbsp	hot mustard	1–2 tbsp
4	thin slices ham	4
1 tsp	oil	1 tsp
1 tbsp	icing (confectioners') sugar	1 tbsp
½ cup/ 3½ fl oz	dry white wine	100 ml
1 cup/8 fl oz	chicken or vegetable stock	250 ml
½ cup/ 3½ fl oz	single (light) cream	100 ml
2 tsp	cornflour (corn starch)	2 tsp
1	bay leaf	1
1 tbsp	cold butter	1 tbsp
*	Parsley Potatoes (p. 260), to serve	*

Hard-boil the eggs for 8 minutes, plunge into iced water, then peel when they're cold enough to handle. Lay the cutlets between two sheets of oiled clingfilm (plastic wrap) and pound flat. Season with salt and pepper and spread with mustard. Lay 1 slice ham on each cutlet and top with a boiled egg. Roll up the cutlets and secure the ends with skewers.

Heat the oil in a frying pan or skillet, sear the roulades on all sides over a medium heat and set aside on a warmed plate.

For the sauce: Sprinkle the sugar over the caramelised juices in the frying pan or skillet and caramelise over a medium heat until golden brown. Deglaze the pan with the wine and simmer until reduced by two-thirds. Add the stock and simmer for 1–2 minutes. Add the cream, bring to a boil, and reduce the heat. Dissolve the cornflour (corn starch) completely in a little cold water and gradually mix it into the simmering sauce to lightly thicken.

Add the seared roulades and bay leaf to the sauce, cover with a lid, and let simmer for about 20 minutes, turning over from time to time.

Take the roulades out of the sauce and remove the skewers. Stir the butter into the sauce, remove and discard the bay leaf, and season with salt and pepper.

Pour the sauce onto warmed plates. Halve the roulades and arrange over the sauce. Accompany with Parsley Potatoes (p. 260).

Münsterland-Style Veal Stew

Münsterland

Preparation time:		30 minutes
Cooking time:		2 hours
Serves:		4

1	veal tongue	1
3	onions	3
1	bay leaf	1
3	cloves	3
1	leek	1
1	carrot	1
1	celery stalk	1
1 lb 2 oz	veal shoulder	500 g
1 tsp	peppercorns	1 tsp
1	pinch of dried thyme	1
1 tbsp	butter	1 tbsp
2 tbsp	plain (all-purpose) flour	2 tbsp
⅔ cup/5 fl oz	dry white wine	150 ml
1 tsp	vinegar	1 tsp
*	granulated sugar	*
1 tsp	hot mustard	1 tsp
*	salt	*
*	freshly ground black pepper	*
*	capers (optional)	*
*	single (light) cream (optional)	*
*	pumpernickel, to serve	*
*	Parsley Potatoes (p. 260), to serve	*

Thoroughly wash the tongue. Peel 1 onion and attach the bay leaf by studding with the cloves. Trim, peel and coarsely chop the leek, carrot and celery. Bring 1.5 litres (6¼ cups/50 fl oz) salted water to a boil in a pan and add the studded onion, veal shoulder and tongue, vegetables, peppercorns, and the pinch of dried thyme. The meat should be completely covered with water. Cook the meat for 1 hour 30 minutes–2 hours, until soft.

Take the meat out of the cooking liquid. Peel the tongue and cut the meat into small cubes. Filter the cooking liquid through a fine sieve and set aside. Peel and dice the remaining onions. Heat the butter in a pan and sauté the onions until translucent. Sprinkle in the flour, lightly cook, and then deglaze the pan with the wine. Add enough of the reserved cooking liquid to produce a thick sauce. Simmer the sauce for about 15 minutes.

Season the sauce with vinegar, a little sugar, mustard and salt and pepper. Add more cooking liquid if necessary. Adjust the flavour and consistency of the sauce with capers and cream if preferred.

Return the meat cubes to the sauce and warm through. Serve the stew with pumpernickel or Parsley Potatoes (p. 258).

Berlin-Style Liver with Apples and Fried Onion Rings

Berlin

Preparation time:		30 minutes
Cooking time:		2½ hours
Serves:		4

For the fried onion rings:

scant 1 cup/7 fl oz	oil, for deep-frying	200 ml
2	onions	2
⅔ cup/2¾ oz	cornflour (corn starch)	70 g
1 tsp	sweet paprika	1 tsp

For the liver:

1 lb 5 oz	calves' liver	600 g
3 tbsp	plain (all-purpose) flour	3 tbsp
2 tbsp	oil	2 tbsp
3 tbsp	sherry	3 tbsp
⅔ cup/5 fl oz	meat stock	150 ml
2–3 tbsp	butter	2–3 tbsp
1	sage leaf	1
1	pinch of dried marjoram	1
1	large apple	1
1 tbsp	butter	1 tbsp
*	Mashed Potatoes (p. 261), to serve	*
*	Mashed Peas (p. 306), to serve	*

For the fried onion rings: Heat the oil to 170°C/350°F. Peel and slice the onion into rings. Mix the cornflour (corn starch) with the paprika, dredge the onion rings and shake off the excess. Deep-fry the onion rings in the hot oil until golden brown. Take them out of the pan with a slotted spoon or skimmer and drain on paper towels.

For the liver: Wash, pat dry and cut the liver into about 5-mm (½-inch) thick slices. Dredge in the flour.

Heat the oil in a frying pan or skillet over a medium heat and sear the liver slices on one side until liquid appears on the top. Turn them over and fry on the other side until liquid appears again. Take out of the pan and set aside.

Deglaze the caramelised juices in the frying pan or skillet with sherry. Add the stock, butter, sage, and a pinch of marjoram. Return the fried liver to the pan and briefly simmer in the sauce.

Wash, quarter, and core the apple, then cut the quarters into wedges. Heat the butter in a frying pan or skillet and fry the apple wedges over a low heat.

Arrange the fried liver on warmed plates, drizzle with the sauce and arrange the apple wedges on the side. Serve with the fried onion rings.

Accompany with Mashed Potatoes (p. 261) and Mashed Peas (p. 306).

Veal & Beef

Sour Veal Liver

Southern Germany

Preparation time:		15 minutes
Cooking time:		15 minutes
Serves:		4

2	onions	2
3 tbsp	butter	3 tbsp
½–1 tsp	tomato pureé (paste)	½–1 tsp
5 tbsp	red wine vinegar	5 tbsp
½ cup/4 fl oz	red wine	120 ml
1⅔ cup/14 fl oz	chicken stock	400 ml
1	small bay leaf	1
1 tsp	cornflour (corn starch)	1 tsp
*	salt	*
*	freshly ground black pepper	
1	pinch of sugar	1
1	pinch of dried marjoram	1
1	strip of unwaxed lemon zest	1
½	garlic clove	½
1 lb 8½ oz	calves' liver	700 g
1–2 tbsp	oil	1–2 tbsp
*	Mashed Potatoes (p. 261), to serve	*
*	Boiled Potatoes (p. 260), to serve	*

Peel, halve and cut the onions crosswise into strips. Fry in a saucepan with 1–2 tablespoons butter over a low heat. Stir in the tomato pureé (paste), deglaze the pan with the vinegar and wine and reduce until thick. Add the stock and bay leaf. Simmer the sauce for 10 minutes.

Dissolve the cornflour (corn starch) completely in a little cold water, stir into the sauce and lightly simmer for 2 minutes. Season with salt, pepper, and a pinch each of sugar and marjoram. Add the lemon zest and garlic, let infuse for a few minutes, then remove and discard the bay leaf. Melt the remaining butter in the sauce.

Wash, pat dry and cut the liver into 5-mm (¼-inch) thick slices. Then cut on a diagonal into 5–10-mm (¼–½-inch) strips. Sear the liver in batches in a frying pan or skillet with oil over a medium heat, about 1 minute. Add to the sauce and steep without cooking for about 2 minutes. Serve with Mashed Potatoes (p. 261) or Boiled Potatoes (p. 260).

Sour Calves' Lung

Bavaria

Preparation time:		45 minutes
Resting time:		2 days
Cooking time:		1 hour 30 minutes
Serves:		4

For the calves' lung:		
1lb 12 oz	calves' lung	800 g
1	onion	1
1	carrot	1
1	thin leek	1
*	salt	*
½ tsp	granulated sugar	½ tsp
4	peppercorns	4
2	cloves	2
2	juniper berries	2
2	bay leaves	2
⅔ cup/5 fl oz	red wine vinegar	150 ml
1 tbsp	lard	1 tbsp
1 tbsp	butter	1 tbsp
1 tsp	tomato purée (paste)	1 tsp
1 cup/8 fl oz	veal stock	250 ml
½ cup/4 fl oz	Riesling white wine	120 ml
6 tbsp	single (light) cream	6 tbsp

For the vegetables:		
1	parsnip	1
2	carrots	2
1	leek	1
2 tbsp	finely chopped parsley	2 tbsp
*	Bread Dumplings (p. 286), to serve	*

Soak the lung in plenty of cold water for about 1 hour. Drain, cover with fresh cold water in a pan and bring to a boil.

Peel the onion and cut into large pieces. Peel the carrot. Cut off the root and green leaves from the leek. Halve the leek lengthwise and wash thoroughly. Add the vegetables, a pinch of salt, sugar, peppercorns, cloves, juniper berries, bay leaves and vinegar to the pan with the lung. Simmer for about 1 hour 30 minutes. Cover and marinate the lung for 1–2 days in the refrigerator.

Take the lung out of the marinade and cut into very thin strips, removing any gristle.

Heat the lard and butter in a casserole (dutch oven) add the lung strips and tomato pureé (paste), and fry lightly. Deglaze the pan with the stock and add the wine and cream. Simmer for about 10 minutes.

For the vegetables: Wash and peel the parsnip and carrots. Cut off the root and green leaves from the leek. Halve the leek lengthwise and wash thoroughly. Cut the vegetables into large, equal pieces and cook in lightly salted water until tender but firm to the bite. Drain the vegetables in a sieve, then add to the casserole with the lung. Simmer gently for a few minutes. Serve sprinkled with parsley and with Bread Dumplings (p. 286).

Veal Kidneys

All regions

Preparation time:		30 minutes
Cooking time:		20 minutes
Serves:		4

4	small veal kidneys	4
3	onions	3
1	bay leaf	1
1	clove	1
1	carrot	1
1	leek	1
2 tbsp	oil	2 tbsp
*	salt	*
*	freshly ground black pepper	*
1 tsp	mustard	1 tsp
1 scant cup/7 fl oz	red wine	200 ml
1 scant cup/7 fl oz	veal stock	200 ml
1–2 tbsp	finely chopped parsley	1–2 tbsp
*	Mashed Potatoes (p. 261), to serve	*
*	Celeriac Mash (p. 312), to serve	*

Have your butcher prepare the kidneys and cut a pocket into each one.

Peel 1 onion and attach the bay leaf by studding with the clove. Poach the kidneys with the studded onion in boiling salted water, then briefly refresh in cold water, drain and let cool.

Peel and finely chop the remaining onions. Peel and cut the carrot into small dice. Cut off the root and green leaves from the leek. Halve lengthwise, thoroughly wash and dice the leek.

Sauté the onions in a pan with 1 tablespoon oil and season with salt and pepper. Cook the leek and carrot in boiling salted water, let drain and then mix with the onion and a little mustard. Stuff the pockets in the kidneys with the vegetable mixture.

Reduce the wine to 3 tablespoons. Preheat the oven to 180°C/350°F/Gas Mark 4.

Sear the kidneys over a high heat in an ovenproof frying pan or skillet with the remaining oil, then transfer to the oven and cook for 10–12 minutes. Take out of the oven and set aside in a warm place. Deglaze the caramelised juices with the wine reduction and stock. Reduce in the frying pan or skillet by two-thirds and season well. Arrange the kidneys on four plates, drizzle with sauce and sprinkle with parsley. Accompany with Mashed Potatoes (p. 261) or Celeriac Mash (p. 312).

Battered Veal Sweetbreads (Bries)

Berlin and Brandenburg

Preparation time:		10 minutes
Cooking time:		20 minutes
Resting time:		1 hour
Serves:		4

7 oz	veal sweetbreads	200 g
1 cup/4 oz	plain (all-purpose) flour	120g
1	egg yolk	1
½ cup/4 fl oz	lager	120 ml
1	pinch of granulated sugar	1
*	salt	*
1	pinch of freshly grated nutmeg	1
1 tbsp	melted butter	1 tbsp
1	egg white	1
2 tbsp/1¼ oz	butter	30 g
*	freshly ground black pepper	*
*	oil, for deep-frying	*
*	lettuce leaves, to serve	*

Soak the sweetbreads for 1 hour in cold water, changing the water often. Cut the sweetbreads into about 2-cm (¾-inch) chunks, removing the membranes and veins.

Combine the flour, egg yolk, lager and a pinch each of sugar, salt and nutmeg. Blend to a smooth batter using a stick (immersion) blender. Mix in the melted butter and then rest the batter for 30 minutes.

Beat the egg white to stiff peaks and fold evenly into the batter.

Melt the butter in a frying pan or skillet and sear the sweetbreads briefly over a medium heat. Season with salt and pepper. Drain on paper towels. Heat the oil in a deep-fryer or a large pan to 180°C/350°F.

Skewer the sweetbreads with a fork and dip in the batter. Fry until golden in the hot oil, then drain on paper towels and serve on a bed of lettuce leaves.

Breaded Calf Brain

All regions

Preparation time:		15 minutes
Soaking time:		4 hours
Cooking time:		10 minutes
Serves:		4

14 oz	calf brain	400 g
*	salt	*
1 tbsp	vinegar	1 tbsp
*	freshly ground black pepper	*
2	eggs	2
1 tbsp	milk	1 tbsp
½ cup/2 oz	cornflour (corn starch)	50 g
1½ cups/3½ oz	dry breadcrumbs	100 g
6-8 tbsp	clarified butter or oil	6–8 tbsp
4	lemon quarters	4

Soak the brain for several hours in icy water, turning it a nice light colour. Bring plenty of salted water to a boil in a pan, add the vinegar and then remove the pan from the heat. Poach the brain for 2–3 minutes then take out of the pan and drain.

Cut the brain into about 1-cm (½-inch) thick slices, and season with salt and pepper. Whisk the eggs in a deep plate with the milk and a little salt. Put the cornflour (corn starch) and breadcrumbs on separate plates. One slice at a time, dredge the brain in the flour, then in the egg, and finally in the breadcrumbs.

Heat the clarified butter or oil in a large frying pan or skillet over a medium heat. Fry the breaded brain slices on both sides for a few minutes until golden brown. Drain on paper towels. Arrange the brain slices on warmed plates and place 1 lemon quarter on each plate.

Filet Mignon

All regions

Preparation time:		10 minutes
Cooking time:		1 hour
Serves:		4

4 × 1¾ lbs	centre-cut tenderloin (filet mignon) steaks	4 × 800 g
1–2 tsp	oil	1–2 tsp
4 tbsp	butter	4 tbsp
1	garlic clove	1
1	sprig of thyme	1
1	strip of unwaxed lemon zest	1
*	salt	*
*	freshly ground black pepper	*

Preheat the oven to 100°C/200°F/Gas Mark ¼. Put a shelf on the middle oven rail and put a drip tray under it. Flatten the steaks a little with the heel of your hand. Heat the oil in a frying pan or skillet and sear the steaks on all sides over a medium heat. Transfer the steaks to the oven and cook for 50–60 minutes until medium rare.

Melt the butter in a frying pan or skillet over a low heat. Peel and slice the garlic. Add the garlic, thyme, and lemon zest to the melted butter, let infuse for 3–4 minutes, then remove and discard.

Turn the steaks in the butter and season with salt and pepper.

Steak au Poivre

All regions

Preparation time:		15 minutes
Cooking time:		50 minutes
Serves:		4

1 tbsp	oil	1 tbsp
4 × 7oz	rib-eye steaks	4 × 200g
½–1 tbsp	coloured peppercorns	½–1 tbsp
*	salt	*
3 tbsp	port	3 tbsp
5 tbsp	red wine	5 tbsp
1⅔ cup/14 fl oz	veal stock	400 ml
1 tsp	cornflour (corn starch)	1 tsp
1 tbsp	cold butter	1 tbsp
*	Green Beans (p. 296)	*
*	Mixed Vegetables (p. 295), to serve	*
*	Parsley Potatoes (p. 260), to serve	*

Preheat the oven to 100°C/200°F/Gas Mark ¼. Put a shelf on the middle of the oven and place a drip tray under it. Heat the oil in a frying pan or skillet over a medium heat. Season the steaks with the peppercorns and sear on both sides and around the edges. Transfer directly onto the oven shelf and cook, about 50 minutes, until medium rare. Season with salt.

Deglaze the caramelised juices in the frying pan or skillet with the port and red wine and simmer to reduce. Add the stock and simmer again to reduce to 250 ml (1 cup/8 fl oz). Dissolve the cornflour (corn starch) completely in a little cold water and gradually mix it into the lightly simmering stock to lightly thicken. Mix in the cold butter and season the sauce with salt.

Spoon the sauce onto the plates and place the steaks on top. Accompany with Green Beans (p. 296), Mixed Vegetables (p. 295), and Parsley Potatoes (p. 260).

Swabian-Style Beef Tenderloin with Fried Onion Rings

Baden-Württemberg

Preparation time:		10 minutes
Cooking time:		30 minutes
Serves:		4

For the beef tenderloin:		
3	onions	3
2 tbsp	oil	2 tbsp
1 tsp	icing (confectioners') sugar	1 tsp
1 tbsp	tomato pureé (paste)	1 tbsp
⅔ cup/5 fl oz	dry red wine	150 ml
3½ cups/27 fl oz	chicken stock	800 ml
1	bay leaf	1
½ tsp	juniper berries	½ tsp
1	garlic clove, sliced	1
2 tsp	cornflour (corn starch)	2 tsp
*	salt	*
*	freshly ground black pepper	*
4	slices beef fillet (tenderloin)	4

For the fried onion rings:		
2	onions	2
¾ cup/7 fl oz	oil, for deep-frying	200 ml
⅔ cup/2¾ oz	cornflour (corn starch)	70 g
1 tsp	sweet paprika	1 tsp

For the beef tenderloin: Peel and finely chop the onions. Heat 1 tablespoon of oil in a frying pan or skillet and lightly fry the finely chopped onions. Sprinkle with the sugar and lightly caramelise. Stir in the tomato pureé (paste) and cook briefly. Deglaze the pan with the wine and simmer until almost completely reduced.

Add 750 ml (3 cups/25 fl oz) of the stock. Put the bay leaf, juniper berries and garlic in a spice bag, close, and add to the sauce. Infuse the spices in the sauce at a gentle simmer for 20 minutes, then remove and discard. Dissolve the cornflour (corn starch) completely in a little cold water and gradually mix it into the simmering sauce to lightly thicken. Season with salt and pepper.

Heat the remaining oil in a frying pan or skillet and sear the steaks on both sides over a medium heat. Season with salt and pepper, add to the sauce and simmer for a few minutes. Deglaze the caramelised juices in the frying pan or skillet with the rest of the stock and stir into the sauce.

For the fried onion rings: Heat the oil to 170°C/350°F. Peel and slice the onions into rings. Mix the cornflour (corn starch) with the paprika, dredge the onion rings, and shake off the excess. Deep-fry the onion rings in the hot oil until golden brown. Take them out of the pan with a slotted spoon or skimmer and drain on paper towels.

Place the steaks with the sauce on warmed plates and scatter over the onion rings.

Loin of Beef

All regions

North Rhine-Westphalia

Preparation time:		10 minutes
Cooking time:		2 hours
Serves:		4

1–2 tbsp	oil	1–2 tbsp
2 lb 8 oz	beef strip loin, trimmed	1.2 kg
2–3 tbsp	Beurre Noisette (p. 112)	2–3 tbsp
*	salt	*
*	Remoulade (p. 114), to serve	*

Preheat the oven to 100°C/200°F/Gas Mark ¼. Put a shelf on the middle oven rail and put a drip tray under it.

Heat the oil in a frying pan or skillet and sear the meat on all sides over a medium heat. Transfer directly onto the oven shelf and cook for about 2 hours until medium rare.

Warm the Beurre Noisette (p. 112) in a frying pan or skillet. Turn the meat in the Beurre Noisette and season with salt. Serve with Remoulade (p. 114).

Düsseldorf-Style Beef Tenderloin with Mustard Crust

North Rhine-Westphalia

Preparation time:		10 minutes
Cooking time:		10 minutes
Serves:		4

4 oz	onions	120 g
3 oz	hot mustard	80 g
2 tbsp	toasted breadcrumbs	2 tbsp
4 × 5 oz	slices beef fillet (tenderloin)	4 × 150 g
*	salt	*
*	freshly ground black pepper	*
½ cup/ 2¼ oz	plain (all-purpose) flour	60 g
3 tbsp	oil	3 tbsp
*	Pan-Fried Potatoes (p. 265), to serve	*

For the mustard crust: Peel, finely chop and blanch the onions for about 3 minutes. Drain in a sieve, plunge into iced water and squeeze well with your hands. Mix the onions with the mustard and breadcrumbs.

Flatten the tenderloin slices a little with the heel of your hand and season with salt and pepper. Coat one side with the onion and mustard mixture and sprinkle with flour.

Heat the oil in a frying pan or skillet and sear the slices on the crust-side over a medium heat until golden brown. Turn and cook on the other side for 3 minutes. Take the pan off the heat and finish cooking the meat for a few minutes in the residual heat.

Cut the meat into pieces and serve on warmed plates. Accompany with Pan-Fried Potatoes (p. 265).

Beef Tenderloin

Preparation time:		5 minutes
Cooking time:		1½–1¼ hours
Serves:		4

1 tbsp	oil	1 tbsp
1 lb 2 oz	beef fillet (tenderloin)	500 g
2 oz	Beurre Noisette (p. 112)	50 g
1 sprig	tarragon	1 sprig
*	salt	*
*	Mixed Beans (p. 294), to serve	*

Preheat the oven to 100°C/200°F/Gas Mark ¼. Put a shelf on the middle rail of the oven and place a drip tray under it.

Heat the oil in a frying pan or skillet and sear the meat on all sides over a medium heat. Transfer directly onto the oven shelf and cook for 1½–1¼ hours, depending on the thickness, until medium rare.

Heat the Beurre Noisette (p. 112) with the tarragon in a frying pan or skillet over a medium heat and season with salt. Before serving, turn the meat in the Beurre Noisette, then cut into slices and arrange on warmed plates. The meat can be accompanied with Mixed Beans (p. 294).

Pot Roast (Rinderschmorbraten)

Preparation time:		20 minutes
Cooking time:		3 hours 30 minutes
Serves:		4

2	onions	2
3½ oz	celeriac	100 g
1	small carrot	1
2–3 tbsp	oil	2–3 tbsp
3 lb 4 oz	beef shoulder (top blade) roast	1.5 kg
1 tbsp	icing (confectioners') sugar	1 tbsp
1 tbsp	tomato pureé (paste)	1 tbsp
5 tbsp	brandy	5 tbsp
1½ cups/12 fl oz	heavy red wine	350 ml
4½ cups/34 fl oz	chicken stock	1 litre
½ tsp	allspice berries	½ tsp
½ tsp	peppercorns	½ tsp
1	bay leaf	1
5	juniper berries	5
1	garlic clove	1
1	strip of unwaxed lemon zest	1
1	strip of unwaxed orange zest	1
1 tbsp	cornflour (corn starch)	1 tbsp
*	salt	*
1–2 tbsp	cold butter	1–2 tbsp
*	Dumplings (p. 268), to serve	*
*	Brussels Sprouts (p. 302), to serve	*

Peel and cut the onions, celeriac and carrot into 1-cm (½-inch) dice. Heat 1–2 tablespoons oil in a casserole (Dutch oven) and sear the meat on all sides over a medium heat, then take off the heat. Sprinkle the sugar into the pan and lightly caramelise, then stir in the tomato pureé (paste) and cook briefly. Deglaze the pan with the brandy and one-third of the wine and reduce to thicken. Add the remaining wine a little at a time, reducing each time.

Add the diced vegetables, stock and meat, cover with the lid, leaving a small gap, and braise for 3 hours 30 minutes. Turn the meat over from time to time. After about 2 hours 30 minutes of the cooking time, add the allspice, peppercorns, bay leaf and juniper berries. 30 minutes before the end of the cooking time, add the garlic and lemon and orange zests and infuse.

Take the cooked meat out of the pan and set aside in a warm place. Filter the sauce through a sieve, pressing lightly on the vegetables. Return the sauce to the pan and simmer to reduce by half. Dissolve the cornflour (corn starch) in a little cold water. Stir into the simmering sauce to lightly thicken. Season with salt and mix in the cold butter.

Cut the meat into slices and serve on warmed plates with the sauce. This dish can be accompanied with Dumplings (p. 268) and Brussels Sprouts (p. 302).

Beef with Onion Sauce

Westphalia

Preparation time:	20 minutes
Cooking time:	3 hours
Serves:	4

For the meat:

2 lb 4 oz	braising steak	1 kg
*	salt	*
3	onions	3
7 oz	celeriac	200 g
1	carrot	1
1	small leek	1
2–3	parsley stems	2–3
½ tsp	peppercorns	½ tsp
3	juniper berries	3
1	bay leaf	1
*	freshly ground black pepper	*

For the onion sauce:

9 oz	onions	250 g
2 tbsp	butter	2 tbsp
⅓ cup/1½ oz	plain (all-purpose) flour	40 g
3 cups/ 25 fl oz	reserved meat cooking liquid	750 ml
1 tsp	hot mustard	1 tsp
1 tbsp	white wine vinegar	1 tbsp
*	salt	*
*	freshly ground black pepper	*
*	granulated sugar	*
*	Boiled Potatoes (p. 260), to serve	*
*	Green Bean Salad (p. 55), to serve	*

For the meat: Bring 2.5 litres (10½ cups/84 fl oz) water to a boil in a large pan and add the meat, ensuring it is completely covered. Season with 1 teaspoon salt and steep, rather than simmer over a low heat for 2½–3 hours until the meat is tender. Skim regularly.

Halve one unpeeled onion. Peel the remaining onions, celeriac and carrot, and trim and wash the leek. Wash and shake dry the parsley. Cut the vegetables into large chunks and add with the parsley to the pan with the meat after 1 hour of cooking. Then 30 minutes before the end, add the peppercorns, juniper berries and bay leaf to the stock. Finally, take the meat out of the pan and cut across the grain into finger-width slices. Season the stock with salt and pepper, and measure out 750 ml (3 cups/25 fl oz) for the sauce.

For the onion sauce: Peel and finely chop the onions. Sauté with the butter in a pan over a low heat for a few minutes until translucent and turning golden. Stir in the flour and cook briefly for a few minutes to make a roux. Remove the pan from the heat and let cool, taking care that the flour doesn't turn dark.

Stir the hot stock, a little at a time, into the cold roux. Return the pan to the heat, stirring constantly, and simmer for a few minutes. Remove from the heat again, stir in the mustard and season with the vinegar, salt, pepper and a little sugar for a touch of sweetness.

Arrange the meat slices on warmed plates and pour over the onion sauce. Accompany with Boiled Potatoes (p. 260) and Green Bean Salad (p. 55).

Beef Goulash

All regions

Preparation time:	20 minutes
Cooking time:	4 hours
Serves:	4

2 lb 4 oz	beef shin (shank or chuck)	1 kg
2 lb 4 oz	onions	1 kg
2 tbsp	oil	2 tbsp
1 tbsp	tomato pureé (paste)	1 tbsp
4¼ cups/34 fl oz	chicken stock	1 litre
2	cloves garlic	2
1 tsp	cumin seeds	1 tsp
1 tsp	dried marjoram	1 tsp
½–1 tsp	grated unwaxed lemon zest	½–1 tsp
½ tbsp	sweet paprika	½ tbsp
*	salt	*
*	cayenne pepper	*

Trim the fat and large tendons from the beef, then cut the meat into 3-cm (1½-inch) cubes. Peel, halve and cut the onions crosswise into strips.

Heat the oil in a large casserole (dutch oven). Sear the meat on all sides over a medium heat and take out of the pan. Sauté the onions in the oil and meat fat until they turn translucent. Stir in the tomato pureé (paste) and cook briefly.

Return the meat to the pan and add the stock. The meat should be just covered. Cover with the lid, leaving a small gap, and braise the goulash for 4 hours over a low heat without letting it boil. After 2 hours 30 minutes, remove the lid.

Peel and finely chop the garlic, together with the cumin seeds, marjoram and lemon zest. Dissolve the paprika in a little cold water. At the end of the cooking time, stir in the paprika, garlic and spices. Infuse for 5–10 minutes, then season the goulash with salt and cayenne pepper.

Beef Roulade

All regions

Preparation time:		30 minutes
Cooking time:		2 hours 30 minutes
Serves:		4

3	onions	3
3½ oz	Pickled Cucumbers (p. 29)	100 g
3½ oz	smoked back bacon	100 g
4 × 4 oz	slices lean round steak	4 × 120 g
*	salt	*
*	freshly ground black pepper	*
4 tsp	hot mustard	4 tsp
1	carrot	1
4 oz	celeriac	120 g
2 tbsp	oil	2 tbsp
1 tsp	icing (confectioners') sugar	1 tsp
1 tbsp	tomato pureé (paste)	1 tbsp
⅔ cup/5 fl oz	heavy red wine	150 ml
2 cups/17 fl oz	chicken stock	500 ml
1	small bay leaf	1
½	garlic clove	½
1	strip unwaxed lemon zest	1
1 tsp	cornflour (corn starch)	1 tsp
¼–¾ oz	cold butter	10–20 g
*	Mashed Potato (p. 261), to serve	*

Peel, halve and slice two onions. Drain the Pickled Cucumbers (p. 29) and cut into slices or quarter lengthwise. Cut the bacon into slices. Pat the cutlets dry and lay side-by-side on the work surface. Season with salt and pepper and spread with mustard. Cover the cutlets with bacon, onions and Pickled Cucumbers. Roll up the cutlets tightly from the shorter end, pat the edges inward and secure with metal or bamboo skewers.

Peel and cut the remaining onions, the carrot, and celeriac into 5mm (¼ inch) dice. Heat the oil in a roasting pan and sear the roulades well on all sides. Take out of the pan. Sprinkle in the sugar into the pan and cook briefly to lightly caramelise, then stir in the tomato pureé (paste). Deglaze with the wine and simmer until completely reduced. Then add the diced vegetables and the stock.

Return the roulades to the pan, cover, and braise in the sauce for about 2 hours 30 minutes. About 20 minutes before the end, add the bay leaf. Finally, peel and slice the garlic and add with the lemon zest to the sauce, let infuse for a few minutes, then remove and discard. Take out the roulades and set aside. Remove the skewers.

Filter the sauce through a sieve into a pan, lightly pressing on the vegetables. The sauce can be thickened by stirring in 1 teaspoon cornflour (corn starch) dissolved in a little water. Add in the cold butter and season the sauce with salt and pepper.

When it is ready to serve, reheat the roulades in the sauce, and serve with the sauce on warmed plates. Accompany with Mashed Potato (p. 261).

Franconian-Style Pot Roast

Bavaria

Preparation time:		2 minutes
Marinating time:		4 days
Cooking time:		2 hours 30 minutes
Serves:		4

1	large onion	1
1	leek	1
1	carrot	1
3½ oz	celeriac	100 g
2 cups/17 fl oz	wine vinegar	500 ml
1 tsp	allspice berries	1 tsp
1 tsp	peppercorns	1 tsp
1 tsp	juniper berries	1 tsp
2	bay leaves	2
4	cloves	4
3¼ lbs	beef shoulder	1.5 kg
	(top blade roast)	
1–2 tbsp	oil	1–2 tbsp
1¼–1½ oz	packet gingerbread	30–40-g
*	salt	*
*	freshly ground black pepper	*
*	cinnamon, to season	*
*	Bread Dumplings (p. 286), to serve	*
*	Red Cabbage (p. 308), to serve	*

Trim, peel and dice the vegetables. Combine the vinegar with 1 litre (4¼ cups/34 fl oz) water in a pan, bring to a boil, then turn off the heat. Add the vegetables and whole spices and let cool. Add the meat, making sure it's completely covered by the water and cover with a lid, and marinate in the refrigerator for 3–4 days, turning the meat over from time to time.

When ready to cook, take the meat out of the marinade and pat dry with paper towels. Heat the oil in a roasting pan and brown the meat on all sides. Add the vegetables from the marinade and sauté. Add enough of the marinade to just cover the meat, then cover the pan and braise over a low heat for about 2 hours 30 minutes.

Take out the meat and set aside. Filter the sauce through a sieve, pressing lightly on the vegetables. Crumble the gingerbread and stir into the sauce. Season with salt and pepper, and cinnamon if you like.

Cut the meat into slices and serve on warmed plates with the sauce. Accompany with Bread Dumplings (p. 286) and Red Cabbage (p. 308).

Braised Beef Cheeks

Bavaria

Preparation time:		30 minutes
Cooking time:		3 hours 30 minutes
Serves:		4

2	onions	2
3½ oz	celeriac	100 g
1	small carrot	1
4 × 12 oz	beef cheeks	4 × 350 g
1 tsp	oil	1 tsp
4½ cups/34 fl oz	chicken stock	1 litre
1 tbsp	icing (confectioners') sugar	1 tbsp
1–2 tbsp	tomato pureé (paste)	1–2 tbsp
1½ cups/12 fl oz	heavy red wine	350 ml
1 tsp	cornflour (corn starch)	1 tsp
½ tsp	allspice berries	½ tsp
½ tsp	juniper berries	½ tsp
1 tsp	peppercorns	1 tsp
1	bay leaf	1
1	garlic clove	1
½ tsp	chopped dark chocolate	½ tsp
1½ oz	cold butter	40 g
1	strip unwaxed lemon zest	1
1	strip unwaxed orange zest	1
1 tbsp	cider vinegar	1 tbsp
*	salt	*
*	freshly ground black pepper	*
4	rashers (slices) bacon	4
*	Mashed Potato (p. 261), to serve	*

Trim, peel, and cut the onions, celeriac, and carrot into about 1 cm (½ inch) dice. Roll up the beef cheeks and secure the rolls with string. Heat the oil in a frying pan or skillet and sear the cheeks on all sides over a medium heat. Take out the cheeks, deglaze the pan with about 100 ml (½ cup/3½ fl oz stock), and set aside for the sauce.

Put the sugar into a casserole (Dutch oven) over a medium heat and lightly caramelise. Sauté the onions, celeriac and carrot, about 5 minutes. Add the tomato pureé (paste) and cook briefly. Deglaze three times with a third of the wine, slowly reducing each time. Add the remaining stock and bring to a simmer.

Dissolve the cornflour (corn starch) completely in a little cold water, stir into the simmering sauce, then bring to a boil and reduce the heat. Add the cheeks and the set aside cooking liquid, and cover with the lid, leaving a small gap. Simmer the cheeks for 3 hours 30 minutes until tender. About 45 minutes before the end of the cooking time, add the juniper and allspice berries, peppercorns, bay leaf and garlic.

Take out the cheeks and filter the sauce through a sieve into a pan, pressing lightly on the vegetables. Lightly reduce the sauce, then incorporate the chocolate and butter. Add the zest strips, briefly infuse, and season the sauce with vinegar. Remove the zest strips and season the sauce with salt and pepper. Remove the string and keep the cheeks warm in the sauce.

Fry the bacon in a dry frying pan until crispy. Cut the cheeks into slices and arrange with the sauce on plates. Top with bacon. Serve with Mashed Potatoes (p. 261).

Beer-Braised Beef (Bierfleisch)

Bavaria

Preparation time:		20 minutes
Cooking time:		3 hours–3 hours 30 minutes
Serves:		4

2 lbs 4 oz	braising steak	1 kg
2	large onions	2
3 tbsp	oil	3 tbsp
1 tbsp	tomato pureé (paste)	1 tbsp
⅔ cup/5 fl oz	brown ale	150 ml
4¼ cups/34 fl oz	chicken stock	1 litre
2	cloves garlic	2
1 tsp	cumin seeds	1 tsp
1 tsp	dried marjoram	1 tsp
*	salt	*
½–1 tsp	grated unwaxed lemon zest	½–1 tsp
1	floury potato	1
½–1 tsp	paprika	½–1 tsp
*	mild chilli powder	*
4	rashers (slices) bacon	4
5 oz	chanterelle mushrooms	150 g
1 tbsp	butter	1 tbsp
1 tbsp	finely chopped parsley	1 tbsp
*	tagliatelle, to serve	*

Cut the meat into 3 cm (1 inch) cubes. Peel and finely chop the onions. Heat 2 tablespoons oil in a casserole (dutch oven), sear half of the meat at a time, and set aside.

Sauté the onions in the oil and fat released from the meat until they turn translucent. Stir in the tomato pureé (paste) and cook briefly. Deglaze the pan with the beer and reduce a little. Return the meat to the pan and add enough stock to just cover. Cover with the lid, leaving a small gap, and braise for 3 hours–3 hours 30 minutes until tender. Remove the lid after 2 hours.

For the goulash seasoning: Peel the garlic and finely chop together with the cumin seeds and marjoram. Mix with a pinch of salt and crush with the back of a knife, then mix with the lemon zest.

Towards the end of the cooking time, peel the potato. and finely grate into the goulash seasoning mixture. Dissolve the paprika completely in a little water with 1 teaspoon oil and mix into the beef with the goulash seasoning. Let infuse for 5–10 minutes, then adjust the seasoning with salt and a pinch of chilli powder.

Heat the remaining oil in a frying pan or skillet and fry the bacon on both sides over a low heat until crispy. Drain on paper towels.

Clean, wipe dry and lightly chop the mushrooms. Heat the butter in a frying pan or skillet and sauté the mushrooms over a low heat. Season with salt and stir in the parsley.

Serve the beef in warmed deep plates, garnished with the bacon and mushrooms and sprinkle with parsley. Accompany with tagliatelle.

Veal & Beef

Ox Tongue Ragout

Lower Saxony

Preparation time:		30 minutes
Cooking time:		4 hours
Serves:		4–6

For the tongue:		
12¾–17 cups	chicken stock	3–4 litres
1	onion	1
1	bay leaf	1
2	cloves	2
3 lb 8 oz	beef tongue	1.6 kg
1 tsp	peppercorns	1 tsp

For the sauce:		
2	onions	2
2 tsp	icing (confectioners') sugar	2 tsp
1 tbsp	tomato pureé (paste)	1 tbsp
1 cup/8 fl oz	red wine	250 ml
3 tbsp	Madeira wine	3 tbsp
1 tbsp	cornflour (corn starch)	1 tbsp
2 tbsp	cold butter	2 tbsp
2	cloves garlic	2
2 strips	unwaxed lemon zest	2 strips
11 oz	button mushrooms	300 g
*	salt	*
*	freshly ground black pepper	*

For the tongue: Bring the stock to a boil in a large pan. Peel the onion and attach the bay leaf by studding with the cloves. Wash the tongue, put into the boiling stock, add the peppercorns and studded onion, and simmer for 3 hours 30 minutes until soft.

Filter the stock through a sieve into a pan. Measure out 1.2 litres (5 cups/40 fl oz) stock. Refresh the tongue in iced water, peel, remove any gristle and let marinate in cold, lightly salted water.

For the sauce: Peel and finely chop the onions. Sprinkle the sugar into a dry frying pan or skillet and lightly caramelise. Stir in the onion and sauté over a low heat until glazed.

Stir in the tomato pureé (paste) and cook lightly, until a brown layer forms on the bottom of the pan. Deglaze the pan with the red wine, reduce to a syrupy consistency, then deglaze again with the Madeira, simmer to reduce a little, and add the reserved stock. Simmer until reduced by about a third.

Dissolve the cornflour (corn starch) completely in a little cold water, stir into the sauce to lightly thicken and gently simmer for a few minutes. Mix in the butter. Add the garlic and lemon zest, let infuse for a few minutes, then remove and discard.

Clean, wipe dry and cut the mushrooms into thick slices. Cut the tongue into 5 mm (½ inch) thick slices and then into about 4 cm (2 inch) squares.

Stir the tongue and mushrooms into the sauce and let stand for a few minutes without boiling. Season the sauce with salt and pepper. The ragout can be used as a filling for vol-au-vents.

Oxtail Ragout

Baden-Württemberg

Preparation time:		40 minutes
Cooking time:		3 hours 30 minutes
Serves:		4

2	onions	2
1	carrot	1
4 oz	celeriac	120 g
3 tbsp	oil	3 tbsp
5 lbs 8 oz	oxtail pieces	2.5 kg
1 tbsp	icing (confectioners') sugar	1 tbsp
1 tbsp	tomato pureé (paste)	1 tbsp
⅓ cup/2¼ fl oz	Madeira wine	80 ml
1 cup/8 fl oz	port	250 ml
2 cups/17 fl oz	heavy red wine	500 ml
5 cups/40 fl oz	chicken stock	1.2 litres
3	juniper berries	3
5	coriander seeds	5
5	peppercorns	5
1	bay leaf	1
1	garlic clove, halved	1
1	sprig rosemary	1
1	strip unwaxed lemon zest	1
1½ tbsp	cold butter	1½ tbsp
*	salt	*
*	freshly ground black pepper	*
*	Stewed Leeks and Mushrooms (p. 297),to serve	*

Peel and cut the onions, carrot, and celeriac into 1–2-cm (½–¾-inch) dice. Heat 2 tablespoons oil in a large casserole (Dutch oven). Sear the oxtail in batches over a medium heat and take out of the pan.

Sprinkle the sugar into the pan and lightly caramelise. Stir in the tomato pureé (paste) and cook briefly. Deglaze the pan with the Madeira, port and a third of the red wine and simmer to reduce to a syrupy consistency. Add the remaining wine a little at a time, reducing at a simmer each time.

Heat the remaining oil in a frying pan or skillet and sauté the diced vegetables over a medium heat. Add the vegetables to the casserole (dutch oven). Return the meat to the pan and add enough stock to cover the contents with liquid. Cover with a lid, leaving a small gap, and braise the meat over a low heat until tender, about 3 hours 30 minutes. Then 30 minutes before the end, add the juniper berries, coriander seeds, peppercorns and bay leaf.

Take the oxtail pieces out of the pan and let cool. Remove the meat from the bones. Filter the sauce through a sieve into a pan, pressing firmly on the vegetables.

Simmer the sauce until reduced by half. Add the garlic, rosemary and lemon zest, let infuse for a few minutes, then remove and discard. Stir in the cold butter in small pieces and melt in the sauce. Put the oxtail meat into the pan and reheat. Season the ragout with salt and pepper. Serve the oxtail ragout on plates. Accompany with Stewed Leeks and Mushrooms (p. 297).

Veal & Beef

Meat Patties (Burgers)

Berlin and Northern Germany

Preparation time:		10 minutes
Cooking time:		10 minutes
Serves:		4

3 oz	white bread	80 g
½ cup/ 3 fl oz	milk	100 ml
½	onion	½
1 tbsp	oil	1 tbsp
9 oz	minced (ground) beef	250 g
9 oz	minced (ground) pork	250 g
2	eggs	2
2 tsp	hot mustard	2
1 tbsp	finely chopped parsley	1 tbsp
1	pinch dried marjoram	1
*	freshly grated nutmeg	*
*	salt	*
*	freshly ground black pepper	*
*	oil, for frying	*
*	Mashed Potatoes (p. 261), to serve	*
*	Kohlrabi (p. 292), to serve	*

Cut the bread into cubes and soak in the milk. Peel and finely chop the onion. Heat the oil in a frying pan or skillet and sauté the onion over a low heat until translucent.

Combine the minced (ground) beef and pork in a bowl with the soaked bread, eggs, sautéed onion, mustard, parsley, a pinch of marjoram and a little nutmeg then mix well with your hands. Season with salt and pepper.

Wet your hands and shape the mixture into 4 equal patties. Heat a little oil in a frying pan or skillet with oil and fry the patties over a medium heat until golden brown. Drain on paper towels.

Serve the patties with mustard, Mashed Potatoes (p. 259), and Kohlrabi (p. 292).

Königsberg-Style Meatballs with Caper Sauce

East Prussia

Preparation time:		25 minutes
Cooking time:		15 minutes
Serves:		4

For the meatballs:		
11 oz	minced (ground) veal	300 g
7 oz	minced (ground) beef	200 g
2¼ oz	white bread	60 g
½ cup/3½ fl oz	milk	100 ml
4	anchovy fillets	4
1	onion	1
1 tbsp	finely chopped parsley	1 tbsp
*	salt	*
*	freshly ground black pepper	*
3 cups/25 fl oz	meat stock	750 ml
1	bay leaf	1
2	peppercorns	2

For the sauce:		
2 tbsp	butter	2 tbsp
1 tbsp	plain (all-purpose) flour	1 tbsp
6 tbsp	single (light) cream	6 tbsp
1–2 tbsp	lemon juice	1–2 tbsp
*	salt	*
*	freshly ground black pepper	*
2–3 tbsp	capers	2–3 tbsp
*	boiled rice, to serve, optional	*

For the meatballs: Mix the two types of minced (ground) meat together in a bowl. Cut the bread into cubes. Heat the milk and soak the bread in the milk. Wash, pat dry, and finely chop the anchovies. Peel and finely chop the onion. Squeeze the bread and add to the meat with the anchovies, onion, and parsley. Knead until smooth. Season the mixture with salt and pepper, and shape into 16 equal meatballs.

Bring the stock to a boil in a pan with the bay leaf and peppercorns. Add the meatballs and simmer for about 10 minutes until cooked. Use a slotted spoon or skimmer to transfer the meatballs from the pan to a bowl and set aside in a warm place. Filter the stock through a sieve into the pan.

For the sauce: Melt the butter in a pan and cook the flour. Deglaze the pan with the stock and whisk briskly. Bring to a boil for a few minutes. Add the cream and season with lemon juice, salt and pepper.

Add the meatballs and capers to the sauce and let infuse for a few minutes. Serve the meatballs with boiled rice.

Veal & Beef

_____

Pork

_____

Bavarian-Style Roast Pork

Bavaria

3	large white onions	3
1	carrot	1
5 oz	celeriac	150 g
1–2 tbsp	oil	1–2 tbsp
3 lbs 4 oz	pork neck, skin removed	1.5 kg
1 lb 5 oz	small waxy potatoes	600 g
1 tsp	icing (confectioners') sugar	1 tsp
1 tbsp	tomato purée (paste)	1 tbsp
1 cup/7 fl oz	light red wine	200 ml
4½ cups/34 fl oz	chicken stock	1 litre
1	small bay leaf	1
2	cloves garlic, halved	2
½–1 tsp	dried marjoram	½–1 tsp
1	pinch ground cumin	1
1	strip unwaxed lemon peel	1
*	salt	*
*	freshly ground black pepper	*

Preparation time: 25 minutes
Cooking time: 3 hours
Serves: 4

Preheat the oven to 160°C/325F/Gas Mark 3. Peel and cut the onions, carrots and celeriac into 1.5–2 cm (¾–1 inch) chunks. Heat the oil in a frying pan or skillet and brown the meat on all sides. Take out and set aside. Sauté the vegetables in the oil and meat fat.

Peel, wash and halve or quarter the potatoes. Put the sugar into a roasting pan over a medium heat and lightly caramelise. Stir in the tomato purée (paste) and cook briefly. Deglaze the pan with the wine and simmer until thick and reduced. Add the vegetables, potatoes and stock. Put the pork into the pan, place on the middle shelf of the oven and roast for about 3 hours, turning from time to time.

Take the pork out of the pan and set aside in a warm place. Filter the sauce through a sieve into a pan. Put the vegetables into another pan and set aside. Skim the sauce if necessary, add the bay leaf and simmer to reduce a little.

Add the garlic, marjoram, a pinch of cumin and lemon zest to the sauce and let infuse for 5–10 minutes. Pour the sauce through a sieve over the vegetables, heat to a simmer and adjust the seasoning with salt and pepper.

Cut the pork into slices. Arrange on warmed plates with the braised vegetables and sauce.

Breaded Pork Schnitzel

All regions

2	eggs	2
1	pinch unwaxed lemon zest	1
*	freshly grated nutmeg	*
1 tbsp	double (heavy) cream	1 tbsp
¾ cup/3 oz	plain (all-purpose) flour	80 g
2¾ cups/7 oz	white breadcrumbs	200 g
8 × 2¼ oz	very thin pork cutlets	8 × 60 g
*	salt	*
*	freshly ground black pepper	*
⅔ cup/5 fl oz	oil	150 ml
2 oz	Beurre Noisette (p. 112)	50 g
*	lemon wedges	*

Preparation time: 10 minutes
Cooking time: 10 minutes
Serves: 4

Crack the eggs into a deep plate and beat. Add a pinch each of lemon zest, nutmeg and the cream and mix well. Put the flour and breadcrumbs into separate deep plates. Season the cutlets with salt and pepper. Dredge the cutlets one at a time in the flour and tap to remove the excess. Then dip in the egg and cream mixture and finally dredge in the breadcrumbs, pressing very lightly.

Heat the oil and Beurre Noisette (p. 112) in a deep frying pan or skillet and fry the breaded cutlets over a medium heat, first on one side, until golden brown, then turn over and fry on the other side. Add more oil if necessary. Lightly shake the pan, letting the oil cover the schnitzels. You can also spoon hot fat over the schnitzels. Fry until golden brown. Drain the schnitzels on paper towels. Arrange the schnitzels on warmed plates and garnish with lemon wedges.

Pork Chops

All regions

Preparation time:		5 minutes
Cooking time:		45 minutes
Serves:		4

4 × 9 oz	pork chops	4 × 250 g
1 tsp	oil	1 tsp
*	salt	*
*	freshly ground black pepper	*
*	herb butter, to serve, optional	*

Preheat the oven to 100°C/200°F/Gas Mark ¼. Put a shelf on the middle oven rail and put a drip tray under it. Wash and pat dry the chops. Heat the oil in a frying pan or skillet and brown the chops on both sides and around the edges over a medium heat. Transfer to the oven shelf and cook for 30–45 minutes, depending on their thickness.

Season with salt and pepper and serve. Cover the chops with thin slices of Herb Butter, and flash under the grill, if you like.

Marinated Pork Steaks (Schwenkbraten)

Saarland

Preparation time:		5 minutes
Marinating time:		12 hours
Cooking time:		10 minutes
Serves:		4

2	onions	2
2	cloves garlic	2
6 tbsp	oil	6 tbsp
1 tsp	sweet paprika	1 tsp
1 tsp	dried thyme	1 tsp
1 tsp	dried oregano	1 tsp
*	freshly ground black pepper	*
4 × 9 oz	thick pork shoulder steaks	4 × 250 g
*	salt	*
*	Potato Salad (p. 62), to serve	*
*	Tomato Salad (p. 65), to serve	*
*	Bread, to serve	*
*	Baked Potatoes (p. 258), to serve	*
*	cold beer, to serve	*

To make this recipe, you will need a hanging grill over a fire pit.

Peel and cut the onions into thin rings. Peel and finely chop the garlic. Mix the onions and garlic with the oil and season with the paprika, thyme, oregano and pepper. Add the meat with the marinade and leave in the refrigerator overnight.

Burn charcoal to glowing embers in a firepit beneath a hanging grill or a Schwenker (Saarland-style suspended grill). Take the steaks out of the marinade, season with salt, and grill on both sides, keeping juicy. Don't hang the grill too close to the embers.

Accompany with Potato Salad (p. 62), Tomato Salad (p. 55), bread, Baked Potatoes (p. 258) and cold beer.

Pork Schnitzel with Mushroom Sauce (Jägerschnitzel)

All regions

Preparation time:		10 minutes
Cooking time:		15 minutes
Serves:		4

4 oz	white mushrooms	100 g
4 oz	chestnut mushrooms	100 g
4 oz	porcini mushrooms	100 g
1	onion	1
3 tsp	oil	3 tsp
8 × 2¾ oz	thin pork cutlets	8 × 70 g
½ cup/3½ fl oz	chicken stock	100 ml
6 tbsp	single (light) cream	6 tbsp
1 tsp	plain (all-purpose) flour	1 tsp
1 tbsp	cold butter	1 tbsp
*	salt	*
*	freshly ground black pepper	*
1	pinch ground cumin	1
1–2 tsp	finely chopped parsley	1–2 tsp
*	Spätzle (p. 288)	*
*	Pan-Fried Potatoes (p. 265)	*

Clean, wipe dry and cut the mushrooms into 5 mm (¼ inch) thick slices. Peel and finely chop the onion.

Heat 1 teaspoon oil in a large, deep frying pan or skillet over a medium heat and fry the cutlets on both sides for 30–60 seconds then set aside.

Heat the rest of the oil in the frying pan or skillet, fry the mushrooms in batches over a medium heat for a few minutes and set aside. Sauté the onion in the frying pan or skillet for a few minutes.

Deglaze the pan with the stock. Add the cream, quickly bring to a boil then simmer for a few minutes. Dissolve the plain (all-purpose) flour completely in a little cold water and stir into the gently simmering sauce to lightly thicken. Stir in the butter and season with salt, pepper and a pinch of ground cumin. Add the meat and mushrooms to the sauce and briefly heat through. Sprinkle with parsley before serving. Accompany with Spätzle (p. 288) and Pan-Fried Potatoes (p. 265).

Pork Schnitzel with Tomato Sauce (Zigeunerschnitzel)

All regions

Preparation time:		15 minutes
Cooking time:		20 minutes
Serves:		4

1	red bell pepper	1
1	green bell pepper	1
1	onion	1
1 tbsp	oil	1 tbsp
8 × 2¾ oz	pork cutlets	8 × 70 g
1¼ cup/7 oz	tomato purée (paste)	200 g
½ cup/3 oz	ketchup	80 g
½ cup/3½ fl oz	chicken stock	100 ml
1 tsp	sweet paprika	1 tsp
½ tsp	hot paprika	½ tsp
*	salt	*
*	freshly ground black pepper	*

Halve the bell peppers lengthwise, seed, wash and slice into thin strips. Peel, halve and slice the onion crosswise into thin strips.

Heat half the oil in a large frying pan or skillet over a medium heat, and fry the cutlets, a few at a time, on both sides until light golden. Set aside.

Add the remaining oil and lightly sauté the onion. Add the bell pepper strips and sauté for a few minutes with the onion. Add the tomato purée (paste), ketchup and stock and braise the peppers, at boiling point, for 15–20 minutes. Stir in the paprika and season with salt and pepper. Return the schnitzels to the pan and cover with a little sauce. Simmer for 5 minutes.

Pork Tenderloin

All regions

Preparation time:		20 minutes
Cooking time:		45 minutes
Serves:		4

12	bacon rashers (slices)	12
3 oz	finely minced (ground) veal	80 g
2 tbsp	single (light) cream	2 tbsp
2 tsp	sherry	2 tsp
1 tbsp	thyme leaves	1 tbsp
2–3 tbsp	finely chopped parsley	2–3 tbsp
2 × 11 oz	centre-cut pork tenderloins	2 × 300 g
1 tbsp	oil	1 tbsp
*	Sweetheart Cabbage (p. 303)	*

Preheat the oven to 100°C/200°F/Gas Mark ¼. Put a shelf on the middle oven rail and put a drip tray under it.

Lay 6 rashers (slices) of bacon side-by-side, slightly overlapping, on a sheet of clingfilm (plastic wrap). Do the same again with the remaining slices. Mix the minced (ground) veal with the cream and sherry, spread in an even layer over the bacon and sprinkle with thyme and parsley. Trim the tenderloins of any fat, lay each tenderloin over the bacon and use the clingfilm (plastic wrap) to roll it up, then discard the clingfilm (plastic wrap).

Heat the oil in a frying pan or skillet over a medium heat. Place the tenderloins in the pan seam-side down, and turn gradually to sear on all sides. Transfer the meat directly on to the oven shelf and cook for 45 minutes, depending on the thickness of the tenderloins, until medium rare. Cut the tenderloins into slices and serve on top of Sweetheart Cabbage (p. 303).

Köthen-Style Roast Pork Neck with Potatoes and Pears

Saxony-Anhalt

Preparation time:		20 minutes
Marinating time:		12 hours
Cooking time:		2 hours 30 minutes
Serves:		4

2 lbs 4 oz	pork neck, boneless	1 kg
2	bay leaves	2
1 tsp	peppercorns	1 tsp
½ tsp	allspice berries	½ tsp
*	salt	*
1 lb 2 oz	onions	500 g
2 lbs 4 oz	waxy potatoes	1 kg
2 lbs 4 oz	firm pears	1 kg
½ tsp	cumin seeds	½ tsp
1 tbsp	sugar	1 tbsp
1	pinch ground cloves	1

Combine the pork neck with the bay leaves, peppercorns and allspice berries in a pan of salted water and gently simmer for about 30 minutes. Marinate the meat overnight in the cooking liquid.

The following day, peel and quarter the onions and potatoes. Peel, quarter and core the pears.

Preheat the oven to 160°C/325F/Gas Mark 3. Take the meat out of the marinade, place in the middle of a roasting pan and spread the onions around. Set aside the marinade. Arrange the potatoes on one side of the pan, next to the meat, and season with salt and cumin seeds. Arrange the pears on the other side of the meat and season with sugar and a pinch of ground cloves.

Filter the marinade through a sieve and pour into the roasting pan to a depth of 2 cm (1 inch). Cover the pan with a lid, put on the middle shelf of the oven and cook the meat until tender, about 2 hours.

Cut the meat into slices, arrange on warmed plates with the potatoes, onions, and pears next to it, then drizzle over a little of the cooking liquid from the pan.

Pork Roast with Crackling

Southern Germany

Preparation time:		30 minutes
Cooking time:		3 hours 30 minutes
Serves:		4

4¼ cups/34 fl oz	chicken stock	1 litre
2 lbs 8 oz	pork belly, skin on	1.2 kg
3	onions	3
1	carrot	1
4 oz	celeriac	120 g
1 tsp	icing (confectioners') sugar	1 tsp
1 tbsp	tomato purée (paste)	1 tbsp
⅔ cup/5 fl oz	red wine	150 ml
1	bay leaf	1
2	cloves garlic, sliced	2
1 strip	unwaxed lemon zest	1 strip
½–1 tsp	dried marjoram	½–1 tsp
½ tsp	cumin seeds	½ tsp
*	salt	*
*	freshly ground black pepper	*
*	Potato Dumplings (p.268)	*

Preheat the oven to 130°C/250°F/Gas Mark ½. Put half of the stock into a roasting pan then put in the pork, skin-side down. Put the pan on the middle shelf of the oven and cook for 1 hour.

Peel the onions, trim and peel the carrots and celeriac, and cut everything into 1.5 cm (¾ inch) dice.

Take the pork out of the oven and use a sharp knife to score the skin at 1 cm (½ inch) intervals against the grain. Raise the oven temperature to 160°C/325°F/Gas Mark 3. Transfer the stock from the pan to a container and set aside.

Wipe the pan dry with paper towels, add the sugar and caramelise over a low heat. Add the vegetables and sauté, then stir in the tomato purée (paste) and cook briefly. Add all of the stock. In a separate pan, reduce the wine to one two thirds then add to the roasting pan.

Put the pork, skin-side up, into the sauce, put the pan on the lowest shelf of the oven and roast for 2 hours. Raise the oven temperature as high as possible. Take the pork out of the oven, transfer to a baking sheet, rub the skin with salt and roast on the lowest shelf of the oven for about 20–30 minutes to crisp the skin.

Strain the sauce through a sieve into a clean pan, return the vegetables to the roasting pan and set aside. Skim the sauce if necessary, add the bay leaf, and simmer to reduce a little.

Add the garlic, lemon zest, marjoram and cumin seeds to the sauce and let infuse for 5–10 minutes. Pour the sauce through a sieve over the vegetables, heat to a simmer, and adjust the seasoning with salt and pepper. Take the pork out of the oven and cut into slices. Arrange the meat on warmed plates with the braised vegetables and sauce. Accompany with Potato Dumplings (p. 268).

Pork Medallions with Creamy Mushroom Sauce

All regions

Preparation time:		10 minutes
Cooking time:		25 minutes
Serves:		4

1 lb 2 oz	pork tenderloin	500 g
½	onion	½
5 oz	button (white) mushrooms	150 g
1–2 tbsp	oil	1–2 tbsp
1 tsp	icing (confectioners') sugar	1 tsp
¼ cup/2 fl oz	white wine	50 ml
1¼ cups/ 10 fl oz	chicken stock	300 ml
⅔ cup/5 fl oz	single (light) cream	150 g
1 tbsp	plain (all-purpose) flour	1 tbsp
1 tsp	Dijon mustard	1 tsp
*	salt	*
*	pinch ground cumin	*
½ tsp	grated unwaxed lemon zest	½ tsp
1 tsp	finely chopped parsley	1 tsp
*	tagliatelle, to serve	*
*	Spätzle (p. 288), to serve	*
*	Potato Purée (p. 261), to serve	*
*	Mixed Vegetables (p. 295), to serve	*

Cut the tenderloin into 8 medallions and flatten each one with the heel of your hand. Peel and finely chop the onion. Clean, wipe dry and cut the mushrooms into 5 mm (½ inch) thick slices.

Heat the oil in a frying pan or skillet over a medium heat and brown the medallions on both sides for about 2 minutes. Set aside.

Add the onion to the frying pan or skillet, sprinkle with a little sugar, and sauté for a few minutes. Deglaze the pan with the wine, simmer to reduce and add the stock. Simmer gently for another 10 minutes then add the cream and bring back to a simmer.

Dissolve the plain (all-purpose) flour completely in a little cold water, add to the sauce and simmer to thicken. Add the mustard, stir in the mushroom slices and heat to a simmer. Season with salt, a pinch of cumin, the lemon zest and parsley.

Add the browned medallions and their juices to the mushroom sauce and simmer until medium rare. Arrange the medallions on warmed plates and add the sauce. Accompany with tagliatelle, Spätzle (p. 288), Potato Purée (p. 261), and Mixed Vegetables (p. 295).

Roasted Pork Shoulder (Schäufele)

Southern Germany

1⅔ cups/14 fl oz	chicken stock	400 ml
4	slices pork shoulder (butt), skin-on, bone-in	4
1	carrot	1
5 oz	celeriac	150 g
1 lb 5 oz	small waxy potatoes	600 g
3	large onions	3
1 tbsp	oil	1 tbsp
*	salt	*
1	clove garlic, sliced	1
1 tsp	dried marjoram	1 tsp
½ tsp	cumin seeds	½ tsp
1 strip	unwaxed lemon peel	1 strip
*	freshly ground black pepper	*
*	Coleslaw (p. 58), to serve	*

Preheat the oven to 130°C/250°F/Gas Mark ½. Put the stock into a roasting pan and add the meat, skin-side down. Cook the meat on the middle shelf inside the oven for about 1 hour. Raise the oven temperature to 160°C/325°F/Gas Mark 3. Take the pork out of the oven and use a sharp knife to score the skin at 1 cm (½ inch) against the grain.

Trim and peel the carrot and celeriac. Peel the potatoes, peel the onions and cut all the vegetables into 1–2 cm (½–1 inch) chunks. Lightly colour the onions, celeriac, and carrots in a pan with the oil and add to the stock with the potatoes. Put the pork, skin-side up, on top of the vegetables, put the roasting pan on the middle shelf of the oven and cook for another 1 hour 30 minutes–2 hours.

Then raise the oven temperature to 220°C/425°F/Gas Mark 7 or turn on the oven fan. Take the pork out of the oven, transfer to a baking sheet, rub the skin with salt. Put on the lowest shelf of the oven and roast for about 20–30 minutes to crisp the skin.

Add the garlic, marjoram, cumin seeds and lemon zest to the sauce, infuse for 5–10 minutes then remove and discard. Season the sauce with salt and pepper.

Arrange the meat on warmed plates with the braised vegetables and sauce. Accompany with Coleslaw (p. 58).

Cordon Bleu

Thuringia

4 × 6 oz	pork cutlets ·	4 × 180 g
4	slices Emmental cheese	4
4 × 1¼ oz	slices cooked ham	4 × 30 g
*	salt	*
*	freshly ground black pepper	*
2	eggs	2
1 tbsp	double (heavy) cream	1 tbsp
1	pinch unwaxed lemon zest	1
1	dash lemon juice	1
1	pinch cayenne pepper	1
1	pinch freshly grated nutmeg	1
⅔ cup/3 oz	plain (all-purpose) flour	80 g
2¾ cups/7 oz	white breadcrumbs	200 g
½ cup/3½ fl oz	oil	100 ml
4	unwaxed lemon wedges	4
*	Cucumber Salad (p. 56), to serve	*
*	Potato Salad (p. 62), to serve	*

Lightly pound the cutlets to flatten them, then cut a pocket into each.

Fill each pocket with 1 slice of cheese and 1 slice of ham, then season with salt and pepper.

Use a fork to beat the eggs in a deep plate and add the cream, a pinch of lemon zest and a dash of juice, and a pinch each of cayenne pepper and nutmeg. Put the flour and breadcrumbs into separate deep plates. Dredge the stuffed cutlets in the flour, dip in the beaten egg and dredge in the breadcrumbs.

Heat plenty of oil in a frying pan or skillet over a medium heat. Fry the stuffed cutlets on both sides until golden brown for about 3 minutes. Drain on paper towels. Adjust the seasoning with salt and serve with lemon wedges. Accompany with Cucumber Salad (p. 56) and Potato Salad (p. 62).

Rolled Pork Belly Roast

All regions

Preparation time: 10 minutes
Cooking time: 2 hours 30 minutes
Serves: 4

9 oz	finely minced (ground) veal	250 g
2 tbsp	single (light) cream	2 tbsp
1 tbsp	fennel seeds	1 tbsp
1	small clove garlic, grated	1
½–1 tsp	unwaxed lemon zest	½–1 tsp
1	dash lemon juice	1
2 tbsp	finely chopped rosemary	2 tbsp
2¾ lbs	boneless pork belly, skin on	1 kg
*	salt	*
*	freshly ground black pepper	*
*	Mixed beans (p. 294), to serve	*
*	Bavarian Coleslaw (p. 60), to serve	*
*	Bread Dumplings (p. 286), to serve	*

Preheat the oven to 160°C/325°F/Gas Mark 3. Put a shelf on the middle oven shelf and put a drip tray under it. Mix the minced (ground) veal with the cream until smooth and season with the garlic, lemon zest and juice and rosemary.

Season the meat side of the pork belly with salt and pepper then spread with the minced veal mixture. Starting at the longer edge and with the skin-side outward, roll up the pork and tie with string.

Put the rolled pork directly onto the oven shelf and roast for 2 hours. Then raise the oven temperature to 240°C/475°F/Gas Mark 9 and roast the meat for a furhter 25–30 minutes to crisp the skin. Turn the meat from time to time. Brush with heavily salted water in the last 10 minutes. If you prefer to use the grill to crisp the skin, shorten the cooking time by 10 minutes.

Remove the string and cut the rolled pork into slices. The roast can be served with Mixed Beans (p. 294), Bavarian Coleslaw (p. 60) and Bread Dumplings (p. 286).

Salt-Crusted Pork Roast

All regions

Preparation time: 5 minutes
Cooking time: 2 hours 15 minutes
Serves: 4–6

2 lbs 8 oz	pork belly	1.2 kg
1¼ cups/11 oz	salt	300 g
*	Bavarian Coleslaw (p. 60), to serve	*
*	mustard, to serve	*

Preheat the oven to 180°C/350°F/Gas Mark 4. Lay the pork, skin-side up, on a baking sheet. Cover the skin with a 5–10 mm (¼–½ inch) thick layer of salt, put the baking sheet on the third-lowest shelf of the oven and roast for 2 hours. Take the pork out of the oven and remove the salt crust.

If you have an electric fan oven, raise the oven temperature to 230°C/450°F/Gas Mark 8, place the pork on the baking sheet inside the lowest third of the oven and roast for 10–15 minutes to crisp the skin. If you have a conventional oven, raise the temperature as the high as it will go and place the pork on the middle shelf of the oven.

Cut the pork into slices. Arrange the slices on warmed plates and serve with Bavarian Coleslaw (p. 60) and mustard.

Corned Pork Shoulder

All regions

Preparation time:		30 minutes
Cooking time:		4 hours
Serves:		4

3	onions	3
2	bay leaves	2
3	cloves	3
17–21¼ cups	chicken stock	4–5 litres
3 lbs 4 oz	corned pork shoulder, skin-on	1.5 kg
1 tsp	icing (confectioners') sugar	1 tsp
1 tbsp	tomato purée (paste)	1 tbsp
1 cup/8 fl oz	heavy red wine	250 ml
1	carrot	1
4 oz	celeriac	120 g
1 tbsp	oil	1 tbsp
2	cloves garlic, halved	2
1	strip unwaxed lemon zest	1
½–1 tsp	dried marjoram	½–1 tsp
½ tsp	cumin seeds	½ tsp
*	salt	*
*	freshly ground black pepper	*

Peel 1 onion and attach a bay leaf to it by studding with the cloves. Bring the stock to a boil in a large pan, add the meat and studded onion and gently simmer for 2 hours.

Take the meat out of the pan and use a sharp knife to score the skin at 1 cm (½ inch) intervals against the grain. Measure out 800 ml (3¼ cups/27 fl oz) stock for the sauce and set aside.

Preheat the oven to 160°C/325°F/Gas Mark 3. Lightly caramelise the sugar in a roasting pan over a low heat. Stir in the tomato purée (paste) and cook briefly. Deglaze the pan three times with a third of the wine, slowly reducing until syrupy each time.

Peel and cut the remaining onions, carrot and celeriac into 1.5 cm (¾ inch) chunks. Heat the oil in a frying pan or skillet and sauté the diced vegetables over a medium heat. Add the set-aside stock and the vegetables to the roasting pan. Put the meat, skin-side up, into the pan, put on the lowest shelf of the oven and cook for 1 hour 30 minutes.

Raise the oven temperature to 220°C/425°F/Gas Mark 7. Take the pork out of the oven, transfer to a baking sheet and put on the lowest shelf of the oven. Roast for 20–30 minutes to crisp the skin.

Strain the sauce through a sieve into a small pan, return the vegetables to the roasting pan and set aside. Skim the sauce if necessary, add the remaining bay leaf and simmer to reduce a little.

Add the garlic, lemon zest, marjoram and cumin seeds to the sauce and infuse for 5–10 minutes. Pour the sauce through a sieve over the vegetables, heat to a simmer and adjust the seasoning with salt and pepper. Cut the meat into slices and arrange on warmed plates and serve with the braised vegetables and sauce.

Mecklenburg-Style Pork Belly with Apples and Prunes

Mecklenburg-Western Pomerania

Preparation time:		40 minutes
Cooking time:		1 hour 30 minutes
Serves:		4

3½ oz	prunes	100 g
2 lbs 8 oz	pork belly, bone-in	1.2 kg
*	salt	*
*	freshly ground black pepper	*
1	pinch dried marjoram	1
2 tbsp	raisins	2 tbsp
2	slices toasted bread	2
2	apples	2
1 tbsp	lemon juice	1 tbsp
1 tsp	granulated sugar	1 tsp
2 tbsp	oil	2 tbsp
1	onion	1
1	leek	1
1	carrot	1
1	celery stalk	1
2	bay leaves	2
3	peppercorns	3
2	allspice berries	2
½ tsp	mustard seeds	½
*	Red Cabbage (p. 308), to serve	*
*	Boiled Potatoes (p. 260), to serve	*

Soak the prunes in cold water for several hours to soften. Use a sharp knife to score the pork belly skin with a criss-cross pattern but without cutting through the skin. Cut a pocket into the pork. Season the rib side with salt, pepper, and a pinch of marjoram. Heat the oven to 200°C/400°F/Gas Mark 6.

Wash the raisins in a sieve with hot water and drain. Remove the crust from the toast and cut into cubes. Drain and halve the prunes. Peel, quarter, core and dice the apple. Sprinkle 1 tablespoon of diced apple with the lemon juice and set aside with about 4 prunes for the sauce.

Mix the remaining prunes and apple with the raisins and bread in a bowl and season with a little salt, pepper, marjoram and the sugar. Fill the pocket in the pork with the mix, and close with a bamboo skewer or tie with string.

Heat the oil in a roasting pan. Put the pork, skin-side up, into the pan, brown briefly, then put in the oven and continue to brown for about 10 minutes.

In the meantime, peel and finely chop the onion. Trim and wash the vegetables, peel, and cut into chunks. Spread the vegetables around the pork in the roasting pan and cook for 10 more minutes. Pour 500 ml (2 cups/17 fl oz) hot water around the pork. Add the bay, peppercorns, allspice berries and mustard seeds. Lower the oven to 180°C/350°F/Gas Mark 4. Cook the pork for another 1 hour 30 minutes, adding hot water from time to time.

Take the pork out of the pan and set aside in a warm place. If necessary, skim the fat from the liquid, then filter through a sieve, lightly pressing on the vegetables.

Add the set-aside prunes and diced apple, bring to a boil and reduce the heat. If necessary, stir in plain (all-purpose) flour to thicken the sauce. Adjust the seasoning. Cut the pork into slices and arrange on plates with the sauce. Accompany with Red Cabbage (p. 308) and Boiled Potatoes (p. 260).

Suckling Pig Loin

All regions

Preparation time:		20 minutes
Cooking time:		1 hour 35 minutes
Serves:		4

1⅔ cups/14 fl oz	chicken stock	400 ml
2 lbs 4 oz	suckling pig loin, bone-in, skin on	1 kg
1–2 tsp	cumin seeds	1–2 tsp
1	clove garlic	1
4 tbsp	butter	4 tbsp
1 tbsp	salt	1 tbsp
1 tsp	grated unwaxed lemon zest	1 tsp
2 tbsp	finely chopped parsley	2 tbsp
*	Sautéed Parsnips (p. 300), to serve	*

Preheat the oven to 160°C/325°F/Gas Mark 3. Bring the stock to a simmer in a deep frying pan or skillet. Put the meat, skin-side down, into the stock and gently simmer for 20–30 minutes to soften the skin. Take out the meat and score the skin. Transfer the stock to a roasting pan, adding a little more stock if necessary. Put the meat, skin-side up, into the pan, put on the lowest shelf of the oven, and cook for 45 minutes. Raise the oven temperature to 220–230°C/425-450°F/Gas Mark 7-8 and roast for a further 20 minutes to crisp the skin.

Toast the cumin seeds in a dry frying pan or skillet until they begin to release their aroma. Peel and slice the garlic. Finely grind the cumin seeds and garlic in a mortar, add to the frying pan or skillet with the butter and melt over a low heat. Mix the salt with the lemon zest and season the butter with the mixture. Stir in the parsley. Drizzle the suckling pig loin with the melted butter mixture and cut into slices. Serve with Sautéed Parsnips (p. 300).

Bavarian-Style Ham Hocks (Schweinshaxe)

Bavaria

Preparation time:		10 minutes
Cooking time:		2 hours 30 minutes
Serves:		4

1	onion	1
1	bay leaf	1
3	cloves	3
*	salt	*
1 tsp	peppercorns	1 tsp
1 tsp	cumin seeds	1 tsp
2 × 3 lbs 4 oz	ham hocks	2 × 1.5 kg
*	Bavarian Coleslaw (p. 60), to serve	*

Peel the onion and attach the bay leaf to it by studding with the cloves. Bring plenty of salted water to a boil in a large pan and add the studded onion, peppercorns, and cumin. Add the ham hocks to the pan, making sure they are completely covered by the water then cover with a lid. Gently simmer for 1 hour 30 minutes.

Preheat the oven to 220°C/425°F/Gas Mark 7. Put a shelf on the middle oven shelf and put a drip tray under it. Transfer the ham hocks directly onto the oven shelf and roast for 1 hour to crisp the skin.

When it is ready to serve, take the ham hocks out of the oven and run a serrated knife along the bone. Twist the bone to release and remove, then cut the meat into portions and serve with the mustard. Accompany with Bavarian Coleslaw (p. 60).

Suckling Pig Shoulder Roast

All regions

*	salt	*
3 lbs 4 oz	suckling pig shoulder, skin-on	1.5 kg
1	large onion	1
1	small carrot	1
3 oz	celeriac	80 g
1–2 tsp	icing (confectioners') sugar	1–2 tsp
⅔ cup/5 fl oz	heavy red wine	150 ml
1¼ cups/10 fl oz	chicken stock	300 ml
1	pinch ground cumin	1
1	pinch dried marjoram	1
½	clove garlic, sliced	½
1	strip unwaxed lemon peel	1

Preparation time: 25 minutes
Cooking time: 2 hours
Serves: 4

Bring plenty of salted water to a boil in a pan and gently cook the meat for 10–15 minutes. Take out the meat and pat dry with paper towels. Use a sharp knife to lightly score the skin.

Peel and cut the onion into thin rings. Peel and slice the carrot. Peel and cut the celeriac into 1–1.5 cm (¼–½ inch) chunks.

Preheat the oven to 160°C/325°F/Gas Mark 3. Lightly caramelise the icing (confectioners') sugar in a roasting pan over a low heat. Add the onion, carrot and celeriac and sauté until glazed. Deglaze the pan with the wine and simmer until reduced by two-thirds. Add the stock, put the meat into the roasting pan, put on the middle shelf of the oven and cook, for about 1 hour 30 minutes.

At the end of the cooking time, raise the oven temperature to 220°C/425°F/Gas Mark 8 (or the highest possible heat). Season the skin with salt and cook the meat for a further 30 minutes to crisp the skin.

Season the cooking liquid with salt and a pinch of both cumin and marjoram. Add the garlic and lemon zest, let infuse for a few minutes, then remove and discard. Strain the sauce through a sieve and serve the roast suckling pig and sauce separately.

Fried Suckling Pig Hocks

Bavaria

1	onion	1
1	bay leaf	1
3	cloves	3
3 × 1 lb 6 oz	salted suckling pig hocks	3 × 650 g
1½ cups/3½ oz	plain (all-purpose) flour	100 g
1 cup/3½ oz	white breadcrumbs	100 g
2	eggs	2
*	pinch freshly grated nutmeg	*
*	clarified butter, for frying	*
*	salt	*
*	Carrot and Apple Slaw (p. 58)	*

Preparation time: 20 minutes
Cooking time: 3 hours
Serves: 4

Peel the onion and attach the bay leaf to it by studding with the cloves. Put the hocks in a large pan and cover with water. Add the studded onion to the pan, bring to a boil and gently simmer the hocks for 2 hours 30 minutes–3 hours until tender.

When the hocks are cool enough to handle, strain the cooking liquid through a fine sieve and set aside. Remove the bones and fat from the hocks and shred the meat.

Put the flour and breadcrumbs separately into deep plates. Beat the eggs in another deep plate and season with a pinch of nutmeg. Dredge the hock pieces first in flour, then dip in the beaten egg and dredge in the breadcrumbs.

Heat enough clarified butter in a deep frying pan or skillet to reach a depth of 1 cm (½ inch). Fry the hock pieces on all sides over a medium heat until golden brown. Drain on paper towels, lightly season with salt and keep warm. The ham hocks can be accompanied with Carrot and Apple Slaw (p. 58).

Cured and Smoked Pork Loin with Sauerkraut

Berlin

Preparation time:	15 minutes
Cooking time:	50 minutes
Serves:	4

For the meat:		
2 lbs 8 oz	cured and smoked pork loin	1.2 kg
1⅔ cups/14 fl oz	vegetable stock	400 ml
1	bay leaf	1

For the sauerkraut:		
1	large onion	1
1 tbsp	oil	1 tbsp
5⅓ cups/1¾ lbs	sauerkraut	800 g
½ cup/3½ fl oz	dry white wine	100 ml
1⅔ cups/14 fl oz	vegetable stock	400 ml
1	thick rasher smoked back bacon	1
5	peppercorns	5
2	juniper berries, lightly crushed	2
1	bay leaf	1
2 tbsp	apple purée	2 tbsp
1 tbsp	butter	1 tbsp
*	salt	*
*	freshly ground black pepper	*
1	pinch sugar	1

Preheat the oven to 160°C/325°F/Gas Mark 3. Put the meat, stock and bay leaf in a roasting pan, cover with a lid, and cook in the oven for about 40 minutes.

For the sauerkraut: Peel and finely chop the onion. Heat the oil in a pan and sauté the onion over moderate heat. Add the sauerkraut and continue to sauté briefly. Deglaze the pan with the wine and simmer until almost completely reduced.

Add the stock and the bacon. Braise over a low heat for about 45 minutes. In the meantime, put the peppercorns, juniper berries and bay leaf into a spice bag and close. After cooking for 30 minutes of the cooking time, add the apple purée and the spice bag to the pan.

At the end of the cooking time remove the spice bag. Mix in the butter and season the sauerkraut with salt and pepper and a pinch of sugar.

Arrange the sauerkraut on warmed plates. Cut the meat into slices and place on top of the sauerkraut.

Boiled Ham Hock (Eisbein)

Berlin and Brandenburg

Preparation time:	5 minutes
Cooking time:	3 hours
Serves:	4

1	onion	1
1	bay leaf	1
2	cloves	2
2 × 3 lbs 4 oz	salted ham hocks	2 × 1.5 kg
1 tsp	peppercorns	1 tsp
3	juniper berries, lightly crushed	3
*	Boiled Potatoes (p. 260), to serve	*
*	Sauerkraut (p. 310), to serve	*
*	Mashed Peas (p. 306), to serve	*

Peel the onion and attach the bay leaf to it by studding with the cloves. Wash the ham hocks and put in a large pan and completely cover with water. Bring to a boil with the studded onion and gently simmer the hocks for 2 hours–2 hours 30 minutes.

Add the peppercorns and juniper berries to the pan and cook the meat for a further 30 minutes, until tender and can be easily removed from the bone.

Remove the skin and bones from the hocks and slice the meat against the grain. Accompany with Boiled Potatoes (p. 260), Sauerkraut (p. 310) and Mashed Peas (p. 306).

Meatloaf
(Falscher Hase)

Berlin and Brandenburg

Preparation time:		25 minutes
Cooking time:		40 minutes
Serves:		4

3 oz	toast	80 g
½	onion	½
3 tbsp	milk	3 tbsp
5	eggs	5
2 tsp	hot mustard	2 tsp
1	clove garlic, finely chopped	1
2	pinches dried marjoram	2
½	unwaxed lemon, zested	½
7 oz	minced (ground) veal	200 g
5 oz	minced (ground) pork	150 g
5 oz	minced (ground) beef	150 g
1 tbsp	finely chopped parsley	1 tbsp
*	salt	*
*	freshly ground black pepper	*
*	hot paprika	*
*	oil, for greasing	*
½ cup/4 fl oz	chicken stock	125 ml
1	clove garlic, sliced	1
1 tbsp	cold butter	1 tbsp
*	Boiled Potatoes (p. 260), to serve	*
*	Mixed Vegetables (p. 295), to serve	*

Cut the toast into small cubes and put into a bowl. Peel and finely chop the onion. Combine with 100 ml (scant ½ cup/3½ fl oz) water in a frying pan or skillet and sauté for a few minutes, boiling off all the water, until soft.

Combine the milk and 2 eggs in a measuring jug. Mix in the mustard, garlic, a pinch of marjoram and the lemon zest. Mix the milk and egg mixture with the bread and soak for 5 minutes.

Mix the three types of minced (ground) meat with the softened bread and mix in the finely chopped onion and parsley. Season well with salt, pepper and paprika.

Preheat the oven to 140°C/275°F/Gas Mark 1. Hard-boil the remaining 3 eggs for 10 minutes, then refresh in iced water and peel.

Grease a roasting pan with oil. Put the minced meat mixture into the pan and shape with wet hands into a long and narrow rectangle. Make a shallow trough in the middle of the meat, running the length of the rectangle, insert the boiled eggs, encase in the meat, then shape into a loaf.

Put the roasting pan on the lowest shelf of the oven and bake for about 25 minutes. Raise the oven temperature to 160°C/325°F/Gas Mark 3 and cook for a further 10–15 minutes. In the meantime, as soon as you see brown caramelised juices building up around the meatloaf, deglaze the pan with the stock and add the garlic. Finally, season the resulting gravy with a pinch of marjoram and, if necessary, salt and pepper. Add the butter.

Cut the meatloaf into slices, arrange on warmed plates and add the gravy. Accompany with Boiled Potatoes (p. 260) and Mixed Vegetables (p. 295).

Peppered Pork Stew
(Schweinepfeffer)

Hesse

Preparation time:		20 minutes
Cooking time:		2 hours
Serves:		4

5 oz	celeriac	150 g
1	carrot	1
2	onions	2
2 lbs 4 oz	pork shoulder, boneless and skin removed	1 kg
2 tsp	icing (confectioners') sugar	2 tsp
1 tbsp	tomato purée (paste)	1 tbsp
3 tbsp	brandy	3 tbsp
1 cup/8 fl oz	red wine	250 ml
3 cups/25 fl oz	chicken stock	750 ml
1	bay leaf	1
½ tsp	peppercorns	½ tsp
2	juniper berries, lightly crushed	2
5	allspice berries	5
2	cloves garlic, sliced	2
1	strip unwaxed lemon zest	1
5 tbsp	red wine vinegar	5 tbsp
3½ oz	black pudding (blood sausage)	100 g
¼ oz	dark chocolate	10 g
*	salt	*
*	freshly ground black pepper	*
2 tbsp	butter	2 tbsp

Peel and cut the celeriac, carrot and onions into 1 cm (½ inch) dice. Remove any nerves from the meat and cut into 2–3-cm (1–1½ inch) chunks.

Sprinkle half of the sugar into a large pan and lightly caramelise. Stir in the tomato purée (paste) and lightly brown, then deglaze the pan with the brandy and wine and reduce until syrupy. Add the vegetables, meat and stock then braise over a low heat for about 2 hours until the meat is tender. After 1 hour 30 minutes of the cooking time, add the bay leaf, peppercorns, juniper and allspice berries.

Take the braised meat out of the pan. Strain the remaining sauce through a sieve, pressing lightly on the vegetables. Add the garlic and lemon zest to the sauce, let infuse for a few minutes, then remove and discard.

Lightly caramelise the remaining sugar in a frying pan or skillet over a medium heat, deglaze the pan with the vinegar, and reduce by half. Chop up the black pudding (blood sausage), stir into the sauce, and remove from the heat. Season with the chocolate, salt, pepper, and vinegar reduction. Finally, add the butter and stir until melted. Return the meat to the sauce and heat through.

Pork

Pan-Fried Blood and Liver Sausages with Mashed Potatoes

All regions

Preparation time:		15 minutes
Cooking time:		40 minutes
Serves:		4

2 lbs 4 oz	floury potatoes	1 kg
*	salt	*
1 cup/8 fl oz	hot milk	250 ml
*	freshly grated nutmeg	*
4 × 5 oz	black pudding	4 × 150 g
4 × 5 oz	fresh liver sausages	4 × 150 g
*	Mashed Potatoes (p. 261), to serve	*
*	Sauerkraut (p. 310), to serve	*

Wash but do not peel the potatoes and boil until tender in plenty of salted water. Drain the potatoes, peel while as hot as possible, and put into a bowl. Coarsely mash with a potato masher leaving small chunk of potato. Gradually mix in the hot milk. Season with salt and nutmeg.

Remove the skin from the black puddings (blood sausages) and liver sausages. Put 2 large frying pans or skillets over a medium heat and fry each kind of sausage separately, stirring constantly, until they fall apart.

Serve on warmed plates with Mashed Potatoes (p. 261) and Sauerkraut (p. 310).

Ham in a Bread Crust with Chive Sauce

All regions

Preparation time:		15 minutes
Cooking time:		2 hours 45 minutes
Serves:		8

For the ham:		
1	onion	1
1	bay leaf	1
3	cloves	3
4 lbs 8 oz	lightly salted ham	2 kg
3 lbs 4 oz	raw bread dough	1.5 kg
*	flour, for dusting	*

For the sauce:		
1 cup/7 oz	crème fraîche	200 g
1 cup/7 fl oz	sour cream	200 ml
1 tsp	hot mustard	1 tsp
1–2 tbsp	lemon juice	1–2 tbsp
3 tbsp	finely chopped chives	3 tbsp
*	salt	*
1	pinch sugar	1
1	pinch hot paprika	1
*	green salad, to serve	*

For the ham: Peel the onion and attach the bay leaf to it by studding with the cloves. Put the ham with the studded onion in a large pan, and completely cover with water, and simmer for about 1 hour 30 minutes. Let the ham cool in its cooking liquid.

Preheat the oven to 180°C/350°F/Gas Mark 4. Roll out the dough on a floured work counter to the thickness of a finger. Take the ham out of the cooking liquid, pat dry and encase in the dough. Lay the encased ham, seam-side down, on a baking sheet lined with baking (parchment) paper. Put on the lowest shelf of the oven and bake for 1 hour 15 minutes until the bread forms a good crust. Brush the dough with water 2 or 3 times during the last 15 minutes.

For the sauce: Mix the crème fraîche with the sour cream, mustard and lemon juice. Stir in the chives and season with salt and a pinch each of sugar and paprika.

Cut the ham into slices and arrange on plates with the sauce. Accompany with a dressed green salad.

Palatinate-Style Stuffed Pork Stomach

Palatinate

Preparation time:		30 minutes
Cooking time:		3 hours
Serves:		6–8

1 lb 5 oz	potatoes	600 g
1 lb 5 oz	carrots	600 g
*	salt	*
1	onion	1
1 tbsp	oil	1 tbsp
2 lbs 4 oz	pork (neck and shoulder)	1 kg
11 oz	bratwurst sausage meat	300 g
2 tbsp	finely chopped parsley	2 tbsp
2	pinches freshly grated nutmeg	2
1 tsp	dried marjoram	1 tsp
½ tsp	ground coriander seeds	½ tsp
½ tsp	dried thyme	½ tsp
*	freshly ground black pepper	*
1	medium pork stomach	1
*	Sauerkraut (p. 310), to serve	*
*	Mashed Potatoes (p. 261), to serve	*

Peel and wash the potatoes, and trim and peel the carrots. Cut the potatoes and carrots into 1-cm (½-inch) dice and blanch in boiling salted water, about 3 minutes. Drain in a sieve, plunge in iced water, and let drain.

Peel and finely chop the onion. Heat the oil in a frying pan or skillet and sauté the onion over a low heat.

Cut the pork into cubes and mix with the potatoes, carrots, onion, sausage meat and parsley. Season well with 2 pinches of nutmeg, the marjoram, coriander seeds, thyme, about 2 teaspoons salt and a little pepper. Mix thoroughly.

Wash the stomach thoroughly under running water and pat dry with paper towels. Close two of the three stomach openings securely with string. Stuff the stomach loosely with the meat and potato mixture through the third opening. (Overfilling will cause it to burst when cooked.) Tie the opening securely.

Bring plenty of salted water to a boil in a pan, then reduce the heat. Simmer the stomach in the hot water for 2–3 hours until cooked. Do not boil. Take the stomach out of the pan, let drain. Then cut into slices and serve. Accompany with Sauerkraut (p. 310) and Mashed Potatoes (p. 261).

Homemade Thuringian-Style Bratwurst

Thuringia

Preparation time:		30 minutes
Cooking time:		10–15 minutes
Makes:		about 30

16 feet 6 inches	sausage casing	5 metres
3 lbs 4 oz	pork belly	1.5 kg
3 lbs 4 oz	pork neck, boneless	1.5 kg
5	cloves garlic	5
1 tbsp	dried marjoram	1 tbsp
1 level tsp	ground cumin	1 level tsp
5 tsp	salt	5 tsp
*	freshly ground black pepper	*

Soften the sausage casing in lukewarm water. Cut the pork meat into about 3 cm (1 inch) cubes and chill for 15 minutes in the freezer.

Peel and finely chop the garlic. Mix the meat with the garlic, marjoram, cumin, and season with salt and pepper. Pass through a mincer using a coarse plate. Transfer to a food processor with a mixing blade and mix for about 15 minutes, until the mixture binds.

Screw a sausage stuffer funnel attachment to the mincer, slide the casing over the funnel and knot the end. Feed the sausage meat into the mincer and gradually feed it into the casing. Twist the casing to form individual sausages every 15 cm (5½ inches). Use a knife to separate the sausages. Lightly score the sausages diagonally with a knife tip, to prevent from bursting. Grill or fry the sausages for around 10–15 minutes, depending on thickness.

Lamb & Game

Lamb Chops

All regions

2 × 8-rib	racks of lamb, fat removed	2 × 8-rib
1 tbsp	oil	1 tbsp
4 tbsp	olive oil	4 tbsp
2	cloves garlic, sliced	2
2	strips unwaxed lemon zest	2
1	sprig rosemary	1
*	salt	*
*	freshly ground black pepper	*
*	Mixed Beans (p. 292), to serve	*

Preparation time:	10 minutes
Cooking time:	25 minutes
Serves:	4

Preheat the oven to 120°C/250°F/Gas Mark ½. Put a shelf on the middle rail of the oven and put a drip tray under it. Use a small knife to carefully scrape the ends of the ribs (French trim), then wash the racks and pat dry with paper towels.

Heat the oil in a large frying pan or skillet over a medium heat and brown the racks on all sides. Transfer directly onto the oven shelf and roast for 20–25 minutes until medium-rare.

Meanwhile, lightly warm the olive oil in a large frying pan or skillet with the garlic, lemon zest and rosemary. Turn the racks in the olive oil, coat well then season with salt and pepper.

Immediately before serving, cut the racks into individual chops. Arrange the lamb chops on warmed plates. Accompany with Mixed Beans (p. 292).

Roasted Leg of Lamb (Heidschnuckenbraten)

Lower Saxony

Marinating time:	2 days
Preparation time:	25 minutes
Cooking time:	2 hours 30 minutes
Serves:	6–8

1 × 4 lbs 8-oz	leg of lamb, bone in	1 × 2.2-kg
1¼ cups/11 oz	plain yoghurt	300 g
2	onions	2
2 oz	celeriac	50 g
½	small carrot	½
2 tbsp	oil	2 tbsp
1 tsp	icing (confectioners') sugar	1 tsp
½–1 tbsp	tomato purée (paste)	½–1 tbsp
1½ cups/12 fl oz	chicken stock	350 ml
5	allspice berries	5
1	clove garlic, sliced	1
1	bay leaf	1
1	strip unwaxed lemon zest	1
1	sprig thyme	1
1	pinch granulated sugar	1
*	salt	*
*	freshly ground black pepper	*
*	cornflour (corn starch)	*

Coat the meat on all sides with yoghurt, put into a freezer bag and marinate in the refrigerator for 1–2 days.

When ready to cook, preheat the oven to 120°C/250°F/Gas Mark ½. Peel and dice the onions, celeriac and carrot. Wipe the yoghurt off the meat with paper towels. Heat the oil in a large frying pan or skillet, brown the meat on all sides and set aside.

Sprinkle the icing (confectioners') sugar into the frying pan or skillet, lightly caramelise and then sauté the vegetables. Add the tomato purée (paste) and cook briefly. Deglaze the pan with a little stock, then transfer the contents of the frying pan or skillet to a roasting pan. Add the remaining stock and the meat, put the pan on the lowest shelf of the oven and roast until medium-rare, about 2 hours 30 minutes. Baste the meat regularly with the liquid in the pan.

Take the meat out of the roasting pan and set aside in a warm place. Strain the sauce through a sieve into a clean pan, pressing lightly on the vegetables. Heat the sauce, add the allspice berries, garlic, bay leaf, lemon zest and thyme and simmer gently for a few minutes. Strain the sauce again and adjust the seasoning with a pinch of sugar, salt and pepper. The sauce can be thickened if necessary with a little cornflour (corn starch). Keep warm.

Pour the sauce onto warmed plates. Cut the meat into thin slices and arrange over the sauce.

Braised Shoulder of Lamb

All regions

Preparation time:		20 minutes
Cooking time:		2 hours 30 minutes
Serves:		4

2	onions	2
5 oz	celeriac	150 g
2	small carrots	2
2 lbs 8 oz	lamb shoulder, boneless	1.3 kg
*	salt	*
*	freshly ground black pepper	*
4 tbsp	oil	4 tbsp
1–2 tsp	icing (confectioners') sugar	1–2 tsp
1¼ cups/10 fl oz	red wine	300 ml
1 tbsp	tomato purée (paste)	1 tbsp
2 cups/17 fl oz	chicken stock	500 ml
1	bay leaf	1
2	slices garlic	2
1	sprig rosemary	1
1	strip unwaxed lemon zest	1
*	cayenne pepper	*

Peel the onions, celeriac and carrots. Cut the onions into wedges and the celeriac and carrots into batons 1 cm (½ inch) thick and 3 cm (1 inch) long. Season the meat with salt and pepper and brown in a roasting pan with 2 tablespoons oil. Take out the meat and pour off the oil and fat.

Sprinkle the sugar into the roasting pan and lightly caramelise over a low heat, then deglaze the pan with a third of the wine. Stir in the tomato purée (paste) and simmer to reduce. Add the remaining wine, half at a time, simmering to reduce each time. Add the stock, vegetables and meat and braise for about 2 hours 30 minutes, basting the meat regularly.

Take the meat out of the pan and lightly reduce the sauce if necessary. Add the bay leaf, garlic, rosemary and lemon zest and let infuse for a few minutes, then remove and discard. Season with salt and cayenne pepper.

Cut the meat into slices, arrange on warmed plates, then drizzle over a little sauce.

Roast Leg of Lamb

Lower Saxony

Preparation time:		30 minutes
Cooking time:		3 hours 30 minutes
Serves:		4

2	onions	2
5 oz	celeriac	150 g
1	carrot	1
½	fennel bulb	½
3 tbsp	oil	3 tbsp
1 × 3 lbs 4-oz	leg of lamb, boneless	1 × 1.5-kg
2 tsp	icing (confectioners') sugar	2 tsp
1 tbsp	tomato purée (paste)	1 tbsp
1¼ cups/10 fl oz	heavy red wine	300 ml
4¼ cups/34 fl oz	chicken stock	1 litre
1	fresh bay leaf	1
2 tsp	plain (all-purpose) flour	2 tsp
1	clove garlic, halved	1
1	sprig rosemary	1
1	strip unwaxed lemon zest	1
*	salt	*
*	freshly ground black pepper	*

Preheat the oven to 130°C/230°F/Gas Mark ½. Peel, halve and cut the onions into wedges. Peel and cut the celeriac and carrot into batons 1 cm (½ inch) thick and 3 cm (1 inch) long. Trim, wash and halve the fennel lengthwise, and cut crosswise into 1-cm (½-inch) thick pieces.

Heat 2 tablespoons oil in a casserole (Dutch oven) and sear the meat over a medium heat. Take out the meat and pour off the oil and fat.

Sprinkle the sugar into the pan and lightly caramelise over a low heat. Stir in the tomato purée (paste) and cook briefly. Deglaze the pan three times with a third of the wine, simmering to reduce each time.

Sauté the vegetables in the remaining oil in a frying pan or skillet, then add to the casserole with the stock. Add the lamb, put the casserole on the middle shelf inside the oven and braise until medium rare, about 3 hours 30 minutes, basting the meat regularly.

Take the meat out of the pan and set aside in a warm place. Strain the sauce through a sieve into a pan and set aside the vegetables. Add the bay leaf to the sauce, put the pan over a low heat, and simmer to reduce the sauce by a third. Dissolve the flour in a little cold water, stir into the sauce and simmer for 1–2 minutes.

Add the garlic, rosemary and lemon zest to the sauce and let infuse for a few minutes, then remove together with the bay leaf and discard. Season the sauce with salt and pepper. Cut the meat into slices and arrange on warmed plates with the sauce and vegetables.

Lamb Tenderloin with a Herb Crust

All regions

Preparation time:		30 minutes
Cooking time:		10 minutes
Serves:		4

4	tomatoes	4
1	onion	1
2	yellow or red bell peppers	2
4 oz	soft butter	120 g
½	clove garlic, chopped	½
1–2 tbsp	finely chopped parsley	1–2 tbsp
1 tsp	finely chopped thyme	1 tsp
1 tsp	hot mustard	1 tsp
*	salt	*
*	freshly ground black pepper	*
3 tbsp	dry breadcrumbs	3 tbsp
1 tbsp	oil	1 tbsp
1 lb 2 oz	lamb tenderloin	500 g
1 tbsp	olive oil	1 tbsp
1	clove garlic	1
3 tbsp	chicken stock	3 tbsp
1 tsp	finely chopped tarragon	1 tsp

Remove the stems from the tomatoes, cut a cross into the base and blanch for 20 seconds in boiling water. Plunge the tomatoes into iced water, then peel, quarter, seed and quarter again. Peel and finely chop the onion. Halve the bell peppers lengthwise, seed, wash and cut into 1-cm (½-inch) strips.

Whip the butter in a bowl, until fluffy. Stir in the chopped garlic, herbs and mustard and season with salt and pepper. Finally, stir the breadcrumbs into the herb crust mixture.

Turn on the oven grill. Heat the oil in a frying pan or skillet and brown the meat over a low heat for about 5 minutes. Season with salt and pepper and transfer to a baking sheet. Spread the crust mixture over the tenderloin, then put the baking sheet on the lowest shelf of the oven and grill for 4–5 minutes until golden brown.

Wipe the frying pan or skillet clean with paper towels. Heat the olive oil in the pan and sauté the onion, peppers and unpeeled garlic clove over a low heat until glazed. Remove and discard the garlic clove, add the stock and simmer for 2 minutes. Add the tomatoes and season the vegetables with salt, pepper and tarragon.

Arrange the vegetables on warmed plates. Cut the tenderloin into thick slices and arrange on top.

Braised Lamb Shank

All regions

Preparation time:		30 minutes
Cooking time:		3 hours 30 minutes
Serves:		4

1	large onion	1
1	carrot	1
4 oz	celeriac	120 g
½	fennel bulb	½
½	thin leek	½
3 tbsp	oil	3 tbsp
4 × 11–12-oz	lamb shanks	4 × 300–350-g
1 tbsp	icing (confectioners') sugar	1 tbsp
1 tbsp	tomato purée (paste)	1 tbsp
½ cup/3½ fl oz	port	100 ml
1 cup/8 fl oz	heavy red wine	250 ml
1⅔ cup/14 fl oz	chicken stock	400 ml
1	bay leaf	1
2 tsp	plain (all-purpose) flour	2 tsp
1	clove garlic, halved	1
1	strip unwaxed lemon zest	1
1	sprig thyme	1
*	salt	*
*	freshly ground black pepper	*

Peel the onion, carrot and celeriac. Trim and wash the fennel and leek. Cut the vegetables into 1-cm (½-inch) dice. Preheat the oven to 140°C/275°F/Gas Mark 1. Heat 2 tablespoons oil in a casserole (dutch oven) and sear the meat on all sides over a medium heat. Take out the meat and pour off the oil and fat.

Sprinkle the sugar into the pan and lightly caramelise over a low heat. Stir in the tomato purée (paste) and cook briefly. Deglaze the pan three times, first with the port, then half of the wine and finally with the remaining wine, simmering to reduce each time.

Sauté the onion, carrot, celeriac and fennel in a frying pan or skillet with the rest of the oil, then add to the casserole (dutch oven) with the stock and the meat. Cover with a lid and put on the middle shelf inside the oven and braise for about 3 hours 30 minutes, turning the meat several times. About 20 minutes before the end of the cooking time, add the bay leaf and leek.

Take the meat out of the pan and strain the sauce through a sieve into a clean pan. Set aside the meat and vegetables. Put the pan over a low heat and simmer to lightly reduce the sauce. Dissolve the flour completely in a little cold water, stir into the sauce and simmer for 1–2 minutes.

Remove the pan from the heat, add the garlic, lemon zest and thyme, let infuse for a few minutes, then remove and discard. Season the sauce with salt and pepper. Heat the vegetables and meat gently in the sauce, then serve on warmed plates. The shanks can be deboned and cut into slices.

Rhön-Style Ground Lamb with Cabbage

Rhön Mountains and Hesse

Preparation time:		15 minutes
Cooking time:		20 minutes
Serves:		4

2	onions	2
2	cloves garlic	2
½	small savoy cabbage	½
½	bunch thyme	½
2 tbsp	oil	2 tbsp
1 lb 5 oz	minced (ground) lamb	600 g
*	salt	*
*	freshly ground black pepper	*
1 cup/8 fl oz	meat stock	250 ml
1 tbsp	cumin seeds	1 tbsp
1 cup/8 oz	sour cream	250 g
*	Pan-Fried Potatoes (p. 265), to serve	*

Peel and finely chop the onions and garlic. Trim, wash and halve the cabbage. Remove the hard stem and cut the cabbage halves crosswise into about 2-cm (¾-inch) strips. Wash, shake dry and pluck the thyme.

Heat the oil in a frying pan or skillet and brown the meat until golden brown. Add the onions and garlic and briefly sauté with the meat. Add the cabbage and sauté a little longer. Season with salt and pepper.

Add the stock, cumin seeds and half of the thyme leaves and mix well with the meat. Let simmer for about 20 minutes.

Stir in the sour cream, bring to a boil and then lower the heat. Adjust the seasoning with salt and pepper and stir in the remaining thyme leaves. Accompany with Pan-Fried Potatoes (p. 265).

Braised Leg of Hare

All regions

Preparation time:		25 minutes
Cooking time:		4 hours
Serves:		4

For the meat:		
4 × 12-oz	hare legs	4 × 350-g
2–3 tbsp	oil	2–3 tbsp
2 tsp	icing (confectioners') sugar	2 tsp
1 tsp	tomato purée (paste)	1 tsp
5 tbsp	port	5 tbsp
1 cup/8 fl oz	heavy red wine	250 ml
1	onion	1
1	carrot	1
4 oz	celeriac	120 g
1 cup/8 fl oz	chicken stock	250 ml

For the sauce:		
1	bay leaf	1
½ tsp	peppercorns	½ tsp
5	allspice berries	5
5	juniper berries, crushed	5
1 tsp	plain (all-purpose) flour	1 tsp
1	cinnamon stick shard	1
1	star anise	1
1	strip unwaxed lemon zest	1
1	strip unwaxed orange zest	1
1	sprig thyme	1
2 tbsp	cold butter	2 tbsp
*	salt	*
*	freshly ground black pepper	*
*	aged balsamic vinegar	*
*	Spätzle (p. 288), to serve	*
*	Potato Purée (p. 261), to serve	*

For the meat: Wash and pat dry the hare legs. Heat 1–2 tablespoons oil in a large, shallow pan. Brown the meat on all sides over a low heat and set aside. Sprinkle the sugar into the pan and lightly caramelise. Stir in the tomato purée (paste) and cook briefly. Deglaze the pan three times, first with the port, then half of the wine and finally the remaining wine, simmering to reduce each time.

Peel and cut the onion, carrot and celeriac into 1.5-cm (¾-inch) chunks. Heat the remaining oil in a frying pan or skillet and sauté the vegetables over a medium heat.

Add the vegetables to the wine reduction in the pan and add the stock. Lay the legs over the vegetables, making sure they're covered by the stock. Cover with the lid, leaving a small gap, and gently simmer until the meat comes away easily from the bone, about 3 hours 30 minutes–4 hours. Take out the meat and set aside.

For the sauce: Add the bay leaf, peppercorns, allspice and juniper berries to the cooking liquid in the pan. Simmer to reduce a little, then strain the sauce through a sieve into a clean pan, pressing lightly on the vegetables.

Dissolve the flour in a little cold water, stir into the sauce and simmer for 2 minutes. Add the cinnamon, star anise, citrus zests and thyme. Let infuse in the sauce for a few minutes, then remove and discard. Add the butter and season with salt, pepper and vinegar.

Return the meat to the sauce and heat through. Serve with Spätzle (p. 288) or Potato Purée (p. 261).

Braised Hare (Hasenpfeffer)

All regions

Preparation time:		30 minutes
Cooking time:		2 hours
Serves:		4

5 oz	celeriac	150 g
1	carrot	1
2	onions	2
2 tbsp	oil	2 tbsp
2 lbs 4 oz	hare leg meat	1 kg
2 tsp	icing (confectioners') sugar	2 tsp
1 tbsp	tomato purée (paste)	1 tbsp
2 tbsp	brandy	2 tbsp
1¼ cups/10 fl oz	red wine	300 ml
3 cups/25 fl oz	chicken stock	750 ml
1	bay leaf	1
½ tsp	peppercorns	½ tsp
5	juniper berries, lightly crushed	5
5	allspice berries	5
½ tsp	coriander seeds	½ tsp
1	clove garlic, halved	1
5 tbsp	red wine vinegar	5 tbsp
12	prunes	12
¼ oz	dark chocolate	10 g
1 tbsp	redcurrant jelly	1 tbsp
*	salt	*
*	freshly ground black pepper	*
2 tbsp	butter	2 tbsp
*	Spätzle (p. 288), to serve	*
*	Mashed Potatoes (p. 261), to serve	*

Peel and cut the celeriac, carrot and onions into 1-cm (½-inch) dice. Sauté in a frying pan or skillet with the oil over a medium heat for 2–3 minutes.

Remove any tendons from the meat, then wash and pat dry with paper towels. Cut into 3-cm (1-inch) chunks. Sprinkle 1 teaspoon sugar into a large pan and lightly caramelise. Stir in the tomato purée (paste) and lightly brown, then deglaze the pan with the brandy and wine and reduce until thick. Add the vegetables, meat and stock and braise the meat over a low heat for 1 hour 30 minutes–2 hours until tender. After 1 hour of the cooking time, add the bay leaf, peppercorns, juniper and allspice berries and coriander seeds.

Take the braised meat out of the pan. Strain the sauce through a sieve, pressing lightly on the vegetables. Add the garlic, let infuse for a few minutes, then remove and discard.

Lightly caramelise the remaining sugar in a frying pan or skillet over a medium heat, deglaze the pan with the vinegar and reduce by half.

Stir the prunes into the sauce, season with the chocolate, redcurrant jelly, salt, pepper and the vinegar reduction. Add the butter and let it melt into the sauce. Return the meat to the sauce and heat through. Serve with Spätzle (p. 288), or Mashed Potatoes (p. 261).

Hare Ragout

All regions

Marinating time:		12 hours
Preparation time:		30 minutes
Cooking time:		50 minutes
Serves:		4

1 tsp	peppercorns	1 tsp
3	allspice berries	3
2	juniper berries	2
1	bay leaf	1
1	clove garlic	1
1	carrot	1
1	onion	1
3½ oz	celeriac	100 g
2 tbsp	raisins	2 tbsp
2 tbsp	port	2 tbsp
4 × 7-oz	hare legs	4 × 200-g
2 cups/17 fl oz	red wine	500 ml
2 tbsp	red wine vinegar	2 tbsp
*	salt	*
*	freshly ground black pepper	*
2 tbsp	olive oil	2 tbsp
1 tsp	tomato purée (paste)	1 tsp
1	sprig rosemary	1
1	strip unwaxed orange zest	1
1 tsp	cornflour (corn starch)	1 tsp
1 tsp	dark chocolate couverture	1 tsp
*	tagliatelle, to serve	*

Put the peppercorns, allspice and juniper berries, bay leaf and unpeeled garlic clove into a spice bag and close. Peel and finely dice the vegetables. Soak the raisins in the port.

Debone the legs and cut the meat into 2-cm (1-inch) cubes. Cut the bones at the joint. Combine the meat, bones, vegetables, spice bag, wine and vinegar in a container and marinate overnight in the refrigerator.

When ready to cook, put the meat into a sieve to drain then pat dry with paper towels. Season with salt and pepper. Brown the meat with the oil in a casserole (Dutch oven), then add the vegetables and bones. Stir in the tomato purée (paste) and cook briefly, then deglaze the pan with the marinade, and braise the meat over a low heat for 50 minutes. After 30 minutesof the cooking time add the spice bag and then the rosemary and orange zest shortly before the end of the cooking time. Add the raisins and port.

Take the meat and vegetables out of the roasting pan and set aside in a warm place. Remove the bones, spices, orange zest and rosemary and discard. Strain the sauce through a sieve into a pan and set aside the meat and vegetables. Dissolve the cornflour (corn starch) completely in a little cold water, bring the sauce to a boil and stir in the cornflour (corn starch). Gently simmer for 2 minutes, then add the chocolate. Return the meat and vegetables to the sauce and heat through. Season with salt and pepper. Accompany with tagliatelle.

Hare in a Pot (Dippehas)

Hesse, Rhineland and Saarland

Preparation time:		20 minutes
Cooking time:		1 hour 30 minutes
Serves:		4

3 lbs 8 oz	hare pieces (e.g. legs, loin)	1.75 kg
12 oz	fresh pork belly	350 g
3–4	onions	3–4
2	cloves garlic	2
*	salt	*
*	freshly ground black pepper	*
*	flour, for dredging	*
2 cups/17 fl oz	red wine	500 ml
2	bay leaves	2
3	cloves	3
5	juniper berries, lightly crushed	5
1½ cups/3½ oz	dark rye bread, grated	100 g
1 tbsp	blackcurrant jelly	1 tbsp
*	Potato Dumplings (p. 268), to serve	*

Wash and pat dry the hare pieces. Finely dice the fatty part of the pork belly and fry until crispy in a dry roasting pan over a low heat, then drain on paper towels. Cut the rest of the pork belly into bite-size pieces. Peel the onions and garlic, and chop the onions as finely as possible.

Preheat the oven to 200°C/400°F/Gas Mark 6. Season the hare pieces with salt and pepper, dredge in the flour and tap to remove the excess. Brown the hare pieces in batches in the melted fat left in the roasting pan. Set aside. Put the pork belly pieces, onions and whole garlic cloves into the roasting pan over a low to medium heat and brown. Deglaze the pan with the wine. Put the bay leaves, cloves and juniper berries into a spice bag and add with the hare and grated bread to the sauce. Bring to a boil, then cover with a lid and put the pan on the middle shelf of the oven and braise for 1 hour–1 hour 30 minutes.

Take the hare and pork belly pieces out of the roasting pan and set aside in a warm place. Remove and discard the spices. Stir the blackcurrant jelly into the sauce. Bring the sauce to a boil while stirring, reduce the heat and season with salt and pepper. Strain through a sieve if necessary. Return the meat to the sauce and scatter over the crispy pork belly cubes. Accompany with Potato Dumplings (p. 268).

Leg of Rabbit in Red Wine Sauce

All regions

Preparation time:		30 minutes
Cooking time:		1 hour 30 minutes
Serves:		4

14 oz	shallots	400 g
2	carrots	2
2	celery stalks	2
2–3 tbsp	oil	2–3 tbsp
4 × 11 oz–12 oz	rabbit legs	4 × 300–350g
1 tsp	icing (confectioners') sugar	1 tsp
1 tbsp	tomato purée (paste)	1 tbsp
¼ cup/2¼ fl oz	port	70 ml
⅔ cup/5 fl oz	heavy red wine	150 ml
⅔ cup/5 fl oz	chicken stock	500 ml
1	bay leaf	1
1	cinnamon stick shard	1
5	juniper berries	5
½ tsp	allspice berries	½ tsp
1 tsp	peppercorns	1 tsp
1 tsp	cornflour (corn starch)	1 tsp
1	clove garlic	1
2	sprigs thyme	2
¼ oz	cold butter	10 g
*	salt	*
*	freshly ground black pepper	*

Peel and halve the shallots. Trim, peel and halve the carrots lengthwise, then cut diagonally into 5 cm (2 inch) lengths. Trim, wash and cut the celery diagonally into 5 cm (2 inch) lengths. Heat 1 tablespoon oil in a frying pan or skillet and sauté the vegetables for 2–3 minutes. Wash and pat dry the rabbit legs.

Heat the rest of the oil in a casserole (dutch oven), lightly brown the meat on all sides over a low heat and set aside. Sprinkle the sugar into the pan and lightly caramelise. Stir in the tomato purée (paste) and cook briefly. Deglaze the pan three times, first with the port, then half of the wine and finally with the remaining wine, simmering to reduce each time.

Add the stock, vegetables and meat to the pan and cover with the lid, leaving a small gap. Let simmer for about 1 hour 30 minutes until the meat is tender. In the meantime, put the bay leaf, cinnamon, juniper and allspice berries and peppercorns into a spice bag and close. After about 1 hour of the cooking time, add the bag to the pan and infuse in the sauce.

Strain the sauce through a sieve into a clean pan. Take the meat and vegetables out of the pan and set aside in a warm place. Remove the spice bag and discard. Simmer the sauce to reduce by half. Dissolve the cornflour (corn starch) completely in a little cold water, stir into the sauce and simmer for 2 minutes.

Peel and halve the garlic clove. Add the garlic and thyme to the sauce, let infuse for a few minutes then remove and discard. Stir in the butter and season the sauce with salt and pepper. Return the meat and vegetables to the sauce and heat through.

Serve the rabbit legs on warmed plates with the vegetables and sauce.

Lamb & Game

Pan-Fried Rabbit Tenderloin

All regions

Preparation time:		5 minutes
Cooking time:		10 minutes
Serves:		4

1 tbsp	oil	1 tbsp
4	rabbit tenderloins	4
2 tbsp	butter	2 tbsp
1	clove garlic, sliced	1
3 tbsp	chicken stock	3 tbsp
1	strip unwaxed lemon zest	1
1	strip unwaxed orange zest	1
*	root vegetables, to serve	*

Heat the oil in a frying pan or skillet and sear the tenderloins on all sides over a medium heat. Melt the butter in another frying pan or skillet, add the garlic, stock, lemon and orange zest and let infuse for a few minutes. Turn the meat in the seasoned butter and coat well.

Cut the meat into medallions and serve drizzled with the butter. Accompany with root vegetables.

Shoulder of Roe Venison

All regions

Preparation time:		30 minutes
Cooking time:		2 hours 30 minutes
Serves:		4

3	onions	3
1	small carrot, trimmed	1
4 oz	celeriac, trimmed	120 g
1	roe venison shoulder, boneless	1
1–2 tbsp	oil	1–2 tbsp
2 tsp	icing (confectioners') sugar	2 tsp
1 tbsp	tomato purée (paste)	1 tbsp
1¼ cups/10 fl oz	chicken stock	300 ml
1¼ cups/10 fl oz	heavy red wine	300 ml
1	bay leaf	1
5	juniper berries	5
1 tsp	allspice berries	1 tsp
1 tsp	peppercorns	1 tsp
1 tsp	plain (all-purpose) flour	1 tsp
1	clove garlic	1
1	sprig thyme	1
2 tsp	dried white mushrooms	2 tsp
1½ oz	cold butter	40 g
*	salt	*
*	freshly ground black pepper	*
*	Spätzle (p. 288), to serve	*

Trim, peel and cut the onions, carrot and celeriac into 1-cm (½-inch) dice. Wash the meat and pat dry with paper towels. Remove any fat and tendons. Truss the meat with string.

Heat the oil in a casserole (dutch oven) and sear the meat on all sides over a medium heat. Set aside. Sprinkle the sugar into the pan and lightly caramelise. Add the vegetables and sauté for a few minutes. Stir in the tomato purée (paste) and cook briefly. Add the stock.

Put the wine into another pan and reduce by two-thirds, then add to the casserole (dutch oven) with the meat. Cover with the lid, leaving a small gap. Let simmer for about 2 hours 30 minutes, turning the meat several times.

Take the meat out of the pan and set aside in a warm place. Strain the sauce through a sieve into a clean pan, pressing well on the vegetables. Add the bay leaf, juniper and allspice berries, and peppercorns to the sauce and reduce a little. Thicken the sauce with the plain (all-purpose) flour and simmer for 2 minutes. Peel and halve the garlic clove. Add it with the thyme and dried mushrooms to the sauce and simmer for a few minutes. Strain through a sieve, then stir in the butter and season the sauce with salt and pepper. Accompany with Spätzle (p. 288).

Slow-Roasted
Saddle of Roe Venison

Baden-Württemberg

Preparation time:		45 minutes
Cooking time:		2 hours 30 minutes
Serves:		4

3 lbs 4 oz	saddle of roe venison, bone-in	1.5 kg
2	onions	2
1	carrot	1
5 oz	celeriac	150 g
1 tsp	icing (confectioners') sugar	1 tsp
1 tbsp	tomato purée (paste)	1 tbsp
3 tbsp	port	3 tbsp
1¼ cups/10 fl oz	heavy red wine	300 ml
8 cups/68 fl oz	chicken stock	2 litres
2 tbsp	plain (all-purpose) flour	2 tbsp
½ tsp	peppercorns	½ tsp
½ tsp	allspice berries	½ tsp
1 tsp	juniper berries, lightly crushed	1 tsp
1	bay leaf	1
1	cinnamon stick shard	1
1	strip unwaxed orange zest	1
½ tsp	chopped dark chocolate	½ tsp
1–2 tsp	lingonberry compote	1–2 tsp
4 tbsp	single (light) cream	4 tbsp
*	salt	*
*	freshly ground black pepper	*
1 tbsp	cold butter	1 tbsp
½ tsp	oil	½ tsp
¾ oz	Beurre Noisette (p. 112)	20 g
*	Spätzle (p. 288), to serve	*
*	Carrots and Peas (p. 294), to serve	*

Preheat the oven to 220°C/425°F/Gas Mark 7. Use a knife to detach the meat from the bone and remove tendons.

Chop the bones into small pieces, put in a roasting pan and brown in the oven for 30 minutes. Take the pan out of the oven and pour off the fat.

Peel and cut the onions, carrot and celeriac into 2 cm (1 inch) dice. Sprinkle the sugar into a pan and lightly caramelise over a medium heat. Add the diced vegetables and sauté. Add the tomato purée (paste) and cook briefly. Deglaze the pan with the port and 100 ml (½ cup/3 fl oz) red wine and simmer until reduced to a syrup. Add the remaining wine, half at a time, reducing until syrupy each time. Then add all the browned bones and stock to the pan, cover with a sheet of greaseproof (wax) paper and steep, rather than simmer, over a low heat for 2 hours.

Strain the sauce through a sieve into a pan and reduce by a third. Dissolve the flour completely in a little cold water, add to the sauce and simmer to thicken.

Add the peppercorns, allspice and juniper berries, bay leaf, cinnamon and zest to the sauce, infuse for a few minutes, then strain. Add the chocolate, lingonberry and cream and season. Stir in the butter.

Preheat the oven to 100°C/200°F/Gas Mark ¼. Put a shelf on the middle rail of the oven and put a drip tray under it. Heat a pan over a medium heat and brush with the oil. Brown the meat and roast for 30–40 minutes until medium-rare.

Heat the Beurre Noisette (p. 112) in a pan and season with salt and pepper. Add the meat, turning to coat well. Cut the meat into medallions, serve with the sauce, Spätzle (p. 288) and Carrots and Peas (p. 294).

Roe Venison Escalope
with Morel Sauce

All regions

Soaking time:		1 hour
Preparation time:		10 minutes
Cooking time:		20 minutes
Serves:		4

	For the sauce:	
20	small dried morels	20
2 cups/15 fl oz	chicken stock	450 ml
2	shallots	2
1 tsp	Beurre Noisette (p. 112)	1 tsp
1 tbsp	plain (all-purpose) flour	1 tbsp
⅓ cup/2⅓ fl oz	single (light) cream	80 ml
1	clove garlic, sliced	1
1	bay leaf	1
1	dash sherry	1
*	salt	*

	For the meat:	
½ tsp	peppercorns	½ tsp
½ tsp	allspice berries	½ tsp
3	juniper berries	3
4–5 tbsp	Beurre Noisette (p. 112)	4–5 tbsp
1	bay leaf	1
1	clove garlic, sliced	1
*	salt	*
*	freshly ground black pepper	*
1 lb 5 oz	roe venison leg or rump	600 g
*	Celeriac Mash (p. 312), to serve	*

For the sauce: Put the diced morels into a bowl, cover with the stock and soak for about 1 hour. Once soaked, tip the morels into a sieve to drain. Collect the soaking water and strain through fine filter paper.

Peel and finely chop the shallots. Heat the Beurre Noisette (p. 112) in a pan, sauté the shallots over a medium heat and deglaze the pan with the morel soaking water. Dissolve the flour completely in a little cold water and gradually mix it into the simmering sauce until it thickens. Let simmer for a further 2–3 minutes.

Stir in the cream. Add the garlic and bay leaf, let infuse for a few minutes, then remove and discard. Season with sherry and salt, add the morels and keep warm.

For the meat: Toast the peppercorns, allspice and juniper berries in a dry frying pan or skillet until they release their aromas. Stir in 3–4 tablespoons Beurre Noisette (p. 112). Add the bay leaf and garlic and let infuse for a few minutes. Season with salt and pepper.

Cut the meat into thin slices. Pour the remaining Beurre Noisette into a griddle pan and briefly fry the escalopes on both sides over a medium heat. Set aside in a warm place.

Pour the morel sauce onto warmed plates and arrange the escalopes on top. Serve with Celeriac Mash (p. 312).

Roe Venison Ragout

All regions

Preparation time:		45 minutes
Cooking time:		1 hour 30 minutes
Serves:		4

5 oz	celeriac	150 g
1	carrot	1
2	medium onions	2
2 tbsp	oil	2 tbsp
2 lbs 4 oz	roe venison shoulder	1 kg
2 tsp	icing (confectioners') sugar	2 tsp
1 tbsp	tomato purée (paste)	1 tbsp
2 tbsp	brandy	2 tbsp
1¼ cups/10 fl oz	red wine	300 ml
3 cups/25 fl oz	chicken stock	750 ml
1	bay leaf	1
½ tsp	peppercorns	½ tsp
5	juniper berries, lightly crushed	5
5	allspice berries	5
½ tsp	coriander seeds	½ tsp
1	clove garlic, halved	1
1 tbsp	mild vinegar	1 tbsp
¼ oz	dark chocolate	10 g
1 tbsp	redcurrant jelly	1 tbsp
*	salt	*
*	freshly ground black pepper	*
3 tbsp	butter	3 tbsp
*	single (light) cream, optional	*
3 oz	small white mushrooms	80 g
3 oz	seedless grapes	80 g
2 tbsp	walnuts	2 tbsp
2 oz	Black Forest ham	50 g

Peel and cut the celeriac, carrot and onions into 1 cm (½ inch) dice. Sauté in a frying pan or skillet with some of the oil for 2–3 minutes.

Remove any tendons from the meat and cut into 3–4 cm (1–1½ inch) cubes. Heat the remaining oil in a wide pan and brown the meat on all sides, one batch at a time, over a medium heat. Sprinkle the sugar into the pan and lightly caramelise. Add the tomato purée (paste), lightly brown and deglaze the pan with the brandy and a third of the red wine. Reduce until syrupy. Add the remaining wine, half at a time, simmering to reduce each time.

Add the vegetables, meat and stock and braise the meat for 1 hour 30 minutes over a low heat until tender. After 1 hour of cooking, add the bay leaf, peppercorns, juniper and allspice berries and coriander seeds.

Take the meat out of the pan. Strain the sauce through a sieve, pressing lightly on the vegetables. Add the garlic to the sauce, let infuse for a few minutes, then remove and discard. Season the sauce with vinegar, chocolate, redcurrant jelly, salt and pepper, then add 2 tablespoons butter and let melt. Return the meat to the sauce and heat through. Adjust the consistency by adding cream.

Clean, wipe dry and sauté the mushrooms in the remaining butter. Season with salt and pepper. Wash and pat dry the grapes. Add to the sauce with the walnuts and briefly heat through. Cut the ham into 5–10 mm (¼–½ inch) wide strips. Serve the ragout garnished with the ham.

Venison Ragout

All regions

Preparation time:		20 minutes
Cooking time:		2 hours 30 minutes
Serves:		4

2 lbs 4 oz	venison shoulder	1 kg
2	onions	2
½	small carrot	½
4 oz	celeriac	120 g
2 tbsp	oil	2 tbsp
1 tsp	icing (confectioners') sugar	1 tsp
1 tbsp	tomato purée (paste)	1 tbsp
⅓ cup/5 fl oz	red wine	150 ml
scant 1 cup/7 fl oz	chicken stock	200 ml
1	bay leaf	1
1 tbsp	juniper berries	1 tbsp
1 tbsp	coriander seeds	1 tbsp
1 tbsp	peppercorns	1 tbsp
1	square dark chocolate	1
1 tbsp	lingonberries (from a jar)	1 tbsp
*	Potato Dumplings (p. 268), to serve	*
*	Savoy Cabbage (p. 308), to serve	*

Remove any tough tendons from the meat and cut into 2-cm (¾-inch) cubes. Peel the onions, trim and peel the carrot and celeriac, and cut everything into about 1-cm (½-inch) dice.

Heat the oil in a large pan and sear the meat on all sides over a medium heat. Set aside. Sauté the vegetables in the fat released by the meat, then sprinkle with the sugar and lightly caramelise. Add the tomato purée (paste) and cook briefly. Deglaze the pan with the wine and let reduce. Add the stock and gently simmer the meat for about 2 hours 30 minutes. After 2 hours of the cooking time, add the bay leaf, juniper and allspice berries, coriander seeds, peppercorns, chocolate and lingonberries.

Serve the ragout on warmed plates and garnish with more lingonberries if desired. Accompany with Potato Dumplings (p. 268) and Savoy Cabbage (p. 308).

Lamb & Game

Loin of Venison

All regions

Preparation time:		20 minutes
Cooking time:		45 minutes
Serves:		4

For the meat:		
1 lb 2 oz	venison loin	500 g
3 tbsp	Beurre Noisette (p. 112)	3 tbsp
*	salt	*
*	freshly ground black pepper	*

For the sauce:		
1 cup/7 fl oz	Brown Sauce (p. 122)	200 ml
1	bay leaf	1
½ tsp	juniper berries, crushed	½ tsp
½ tsp	allspice berries, crushed	½ tsp
½ tsp	peppercorns	½ tsp
1	cinnamon stick shard	1
1	clove	1
¼ tsp	grated dark chocolate	¼ tsp
1 tsp	lingonberry compote	1 tsp
1 tsp	icing (confectioners') sugar	1 tsp
1	dash port	1
⅓ cup/2¾ fl oz	heavy red wine	80 ml
1 tsp	cornflour (corn starch)	1 tsp
1 tbsp	cold butter	1 tsp
*	salt	*
*	Black Salsify (p. 302), to serve	*

For the meat: Preheat the oven to 100°C/200°F/Gas Mark ¼. Put a shelf on the middle rail of the oven and put a drip tray under it. Cut the loin into 4 equal steaks and flatten each one with the heel of your hand.

Heat 1–2 teaspoons Beurre Noisette (p. 112) in a griddle pan and sear the steaks on all side over a medium heat. Transfer the steaks directly onto the oven shelf and cook until medium-rare, about 45 minutes. Heat the remaining Beurre Noisette in a frying pan or skillet and season with salt and pepper. Turn the steaks in the Beurre Noisette and coat well, then set aside in a warm place.

For the sauce: Combine the Brown Sauce (p. 122) in a pan with the bay leaf, juniper and allspice berries, peppercorns, cinnamon and the clove and simmer for a few minutes. Stir the chocolate and lingonberry compote into the sauce and let infuse for a few minutes.

Lightly caramelise the icing (confectioners') sugar in a frying pan or skillet over a medium heat and lightly caramelize. Deglaze the pan with the port and red wine, simmer to reduce by about two-thirds and stir the reduction into the sauce. Dissolve the cornflour (corn starch) completely in a little cold water and stir into the simmering sauce to lightly thicken. Simmer the sauce for a further 1–2 minutes, then strain through a sieve, stir in the cold butter and season with salt.

Arrange the steaks on warmed plates and drizzle with the sauce. Serve with Black Salsify (p. 302).

Venison Tenderloin with Creamy Juniper Sauce

Lower Saxony

Preparation time:		30 minutes
Cooking time:		30 minutes
Serves:		4

4	rashers (slices) bacon, optional	4
1 tsp	oil	1 tsp
3	shallots	3
1½ oz	carrots	40 g
3 oz	celeriac	80 g
2 tbsp	Beurre Noisette (p. 112)	2 tbsp
1⅔ cups/14 fl oz	game stock	400 ml
1 lb 2 oz	venison tenderloin	500 g
2 tsp	icing (confectioners') sugar	2 tsp
1 tbsp	tomato purée (paste)	1 tbsp
3 tbsp	port	3 tbsp
⅔ cup/8 fl oz	heavy red wine	150 ml
1 tbsp	dried white mushrooms	1 tbsp
1 tsp	crumbled gingerbread	1 tsp
⅔ cup/5 fl oz	single (light) cream	150 ml
1 tbsp	plain (all-purpose) flour	1 tbsp
1 tbsp	juniper berries	1 tbsp
3–4	cinnamon stick shards	3–4
1 tsp	marzipan	1 tsp
1	strip unwaxed orange zest	1
2	garlic slices	2
¼ tsp	instant coffee	¼ tsp
*	salt	*
*	freshly ground black pepper	*

Cut the bacon into 1 cm (½ inch) strips if using. Heat the oil in a frying pan or skillet and fry the bacon strips on both sides until crispy. Drain on paper towels.

Peel the shallots. Trim and peel the carrots and celeriac. Cut into 5 mm (¼ inch) dice. Heat 1 tablespoon Beurre Noisette (p. 112) in a frying pan or skillet and sauté the vegetables for a few minutes over a medium heat. Deglaze with 100 ml (scant ½ cup/3½ fl oz) stock and simmer until reduced.

Cut the venison into 5–10 mm (¼-½ inch) strips. Heat the rest of the Beurre Noisette in a frying pan or skillet and quickly brown the meat, one batch at a time. Set aside. Deglaze the pan with 100 ml (scant ½ cup/3½ fl oz) stock.

Put the sugar into a pan over a medium heat and lightly caramelise. Stir in the tomato purée (paste) and cook briefly. Deglaze the pan with the port and red wine and reduce by two-thirds. Pour in the rest of the stock together with the meat juices from the pan.

Add the dried mushrooms and gingerbread to the pan and reduce the sauce by a third. Add the cream. Dissolve the flour completely in a little cold water. Stir into the sauce to thicken, and simmer for 1–2 minutes.

Lightly crush the juniper berries and heat in a dry frying pan or skillet over a medium heat until they begin to turn shiny. Stir the berries and the cinnamon into the sauce. Cut the marzipan into small pieces and add to the sauce. Add the zest, garlic and coffee and stir. Let infuse for a few minutes.

Strain the sauce through a sieve into a clean pan. Add the braised vegetables and meat, season with salt and pepper and heat through, but do not cook.

Serve the venison with the vegetables and sauce in warmed deep plates. Sprinkle over the bacon strips.

Lamb & Game

Wild Boar Roast

All regions

Preparation time:		30 minutes
Cooking time:		2 hours 30 minutes
Serves:		4

3	onions	3
1	carrot	1
5 oz	celeriac	150 g
4 tbsp	oil	4 tbsp
2 tsp	icing (confectioners') sugar	2 tsp
1 tbsp	tomato purée (paste)	1 tbsp
⅓ cup/2½ fl oz	port	80 ml
1 cup/8 fl oz	heavy red wine	250 ml
3 cups/25 fl oz	chicken stock	750 ml
3 lbs 4 oz	wild boar shoulder	1.5 kg
1 tbsp	juniper berries	1 tbsp
1 tsp	allspice berries	1 tsp
1 tsp	fennel seeds	1 tsp
1 tsp	peppercorns	1 tsp
2	bay leaves	2
*	cinnamon stick shards	*
2 tbsp	dried white mushrooms	2 tbsp
1	clove garlic, sliced	1
½ tsp	grated dark chocolate	½ tsp
1	sprig rosemary	1
*	salt	*
4	rashers (slices) bacon	4
*	seasonal vegetables, to serve	*
*	Potato Purée (p. 261), to serve	*

Preheat the oven to 150°C/300°F/Gas Mark 2. Peel the onions and trim and peel the carrot and celeriac. Cut everything into 1.5 cm (¾ inch) dice. Heat 1 tablespoon oil in a roasting pan and sauté the vegetables for 2–3 minutes. Sprinkle over the sugar and caramelise, then stir in the tomato purée (paste) and cook briefly. Add the port and a third of the red wine and reduce, at a simmer, to thicken. Add the remaining wine, half at a time, reducing each time, then add the stock.

Heat 2 tablespoons oil in a frying pan or skillet and brown the meat on all sides. Add the meat to the sauce and cover the roasting pan with a lid. Put the pan on the middle shelf inside the oven and braise the meat until tender for about 2 hours 30 minutes.

Toast the juniper and allspice berries, fennel seeds and peppercorns in a dry non-stick frying pan or skillet over a low heat. About 30 minutes before the end of the cooking time, add to the sauce with the bay leaves, cinnamon, mushrooms and garlic and let infuse. At the end of the cooking time, stir in the chocolate, add the rosemary and simmer for a few minutes.

Take the meat out of the roasting pan and set aside in a warm place. Strain the sauce through a sieve into a clean pan, pressing lightly on the vegetables. Season lightly with salt if necessary.

Cut the bacon slices into about 3-cm (1½-inch) strips, fry in a frying pan or skillet with the remaining oil, and drain on paper towels. Cut the meat into slices. Arrange the meat on warmed plates with the sauce and scatter over with the bacon strips. This dish can be served with blanched red cabbage leaves tossed in butter, and with Potato Purée (p. 261).

Wild Boar Goulash

All regions

Preparation time:		20 minutes
Cooking time:		3 hours
Serves:		4

2 lbs 4 oz	wild boar shoulder	1 kg
1 lb 12 oz	onions	800 g
2 tbsp	oil	2 tbsp
1 tsp	tomato purée	1 tsp
3 cups/25 fl oz	chicken stock	750 ml
5	juniper berries, crushed	5
5	allspice berries	5
½ tsp	peppercorns	½ tsp
1	bay leaf	1
1	clove garlic	1
1	sprig thyme	1
1	strip unwaxed lemon zest	1
1	strip unwaxed orange zest	1
*	salt	*
1	pinch cayenne pepper	1
*	Bread Dumplings (p. 286)	*
*	Red Cabbage (p. 308)	*

Wash and pat dry the meat. Remove any tendons and cut into 3–4-cm (1½–1¼-inch) cubes). Peel, halve and cut the onions into strips.

Heat the oil in a large casserole (Dutch oven) and brown the meat in two batches, on all sides, over a medium heat. Set aside. Add the onions to the pan and sauté until translucent. Stir in the tomato purée (paste) and cook briefly. Add the meat and stock, and gently simmer for 3 hours.

Put the juniper and allspice berries and peppercorns in a spice bag and add to the goulash with the bay leaf about 15 minutes before the end of the cooking time. At the end of the cooking time, peel and halve the garlic, then add to the goulash along with the thyme and lemon and orange zests. Infuse for 5 minutes, then remove together with the spice bag and bay leaf and discard. Season the goulash with salt and a pinch of cayenne pepper. Serve with Bread Dumplings (p. 286) and Red Cabbage (p. 308).

Lamb & Game

Baked Potatoes

Preparation time:		5 minutes
Cooking time:		1 hour
Serves:		4

8 × 3½ oz	all-purpose potatoes	8 × 100 g
1 tbsp	coarse sea salt	1 tbsp
1 tsp	cumin seeds	1 tsp
*	Bell Pepper Dip with Herbs (p. 118)	*

Preheat the oven to 200°C/400°F/Gas Mark 6. Thoroughly wash the unpeeled potatoes and wrap individually in aluminium foil with a little salt and cumin. Put the potatoes on a baking sheet, put on the middle shelf of the oven, and bake for 50 minutes–1 hour.

Unwrap the potatoes, make a lengthwise or crosswise cut in each, and fill with Bell Pepper Dip with Herbs (p. 118).

Potatoes in Béchamel Sauce

Preparation time:		20 minutes
Cooking time:		40 minutes
Serves:		4

2¼ lbs	all-purpose potatoes	1 kg
*	salt	*
2	shallots	2
1½ oz	butter	40 g
1½ oz	ham, diced	40 g
2 tbsp	plain (all-purpose) flour	2 tbsp
½ cup/4 fl oz	vegetable stock	125 ml
1 cup/8 fl oz	single (light) cream	250 ml
*	freshly ground white pepper	*
*	freshly grated nutmeg	*
1 tbsp	finely chopped parsley	1 tbsp

Boil the potatoes, in their skins, in salted water. Let cool a little, then peel and cut into slices or large chunks.

Peel and finely chop the shallots. Heat the butter in a large frying pan or skillet and sauté the shallots until translucent. Stir in the ham.

Add the flour and stir over the heat until light golden. Add the stock and whisk briskly with the flour. Gradually mix in the cream, making sure no lumps form in the sauce. Bring the sauce to a boil while stirring constantly.

Lower the heat and simmer to reduce lightly, stirring from time to time. Season with salt, pepper and nutmeg. Add the potatoes and mix well. Sprinkle with parsley and serve.

Parsley Potatoes

All regions

2¼ lbs	waxy potatoes	1 kg
*	salt	*
1	bunch parsley	1
¾–1¼ oz	butter	20–30 g

Preparation time: 5 minutes
Cooking time: 20 minutes
Serves: 4

Peel and wash the potatoes, put into a pan and cover with water. Make sure the potatoes are of uniform size so that they cook evenly. Bring to a boil and add 1 heaped teaspoon salt. Boil the potatoes for 15–20 minutes until cooked. Drain and leave to steam while gently shaking.

Wash, shake dry, pluck, and finely chop the parsley. Melt the butter, toss the boiled potatoes in the butter and sprinkle with parsley.

Boiled Potatoes

All regions

2¼ lbs	small waxy potatoes	1 kg
*	salt	*
1 tsp	cumin seeds	1 tsp
½ tsp	peppercorns	½ tsp

Preparation time: 5 minutes
Cooking time: 30 minutes
Serves: 4

Scrub the potatoes thoroughly under running water, and put into a pan with plenty of salted water, the cumin and peppercorns. Boil until tender.

Drain in a colander and, depending on the use they're to be given, peel as hot as possible. If using new potatoes, leave unpeeled.

Potato Purée

All regions

Preparation time:		10 minutes
Cooking time:		25 minutes
Serves:		4

2¼ lbs	floury potatoes	1 kg
*	salt	*
½ tsp	cumin seeds	½ tsp
1 cup/8 fl oz	milk	250 ml
1 tbsp	butter	1 tbsp
2 tbsp	Beurre Noisette (p. 112)	2 tbsp
*	freshly grated nutmeg	*

Wash the potatoes and boil until tender in plenty of salted water with the cumin. Drain the potatoes, peel while they're as hot as possible, and press through a ricer.

Heat the milk and, using a wooden spoon, stir into the mashed potatoes, to a fine purée. Incorporate the butter and Beurre Noisette (p. 112). Season with salt and nutmeg.

Variations:

Potato and Lemon Purée: Stir the grated zest of 1 unwaxed lemon into the finished Potato Purée.

Potato and Spinach Purée: Sort, wash and drain 100 g (1⅓ cups/3½ oz) baby spinach leaves, removing any larger stems. Stir the spinach into the finished Potato Purée.

Potato and Apple Purée: Peel, quarter, core and cut 1 apple into small dice. Stir the diced apple and 2 tablespoons apple purée into the finished Potato Purée.

Potato and Pear Purée: Peel, quarter, core then chop 2 ripe pears into small dice. Stir the diced pears into the finished Potato Purée.

Potato and Celeriac Purée: Purée 300 g (11 oz) boiled celeriac and stir into the finished Potato Purée.

Potato and Leek Purée: Purée 400 g (14 oz) boiled leeks and stir into the finished Potato Purée.

Potato and Wild Garlic Purée: Wash, shake dry and cut 50 g (2 oz) wild garlic into strips. Stir the wild garlic strips into the finished Potato Purée.

Potato and Chicory (endive) Purée: Boil 2 teaspoons mustard seeds in salted water until soft, drain in a sieve, and rinse in cold water. Cut 100 g (3½ oz) bacon into small cubes, fry in a frying pan or skillet until crispy in 1–2 tablespoons oil, and drain on paper towels. Wash, shake dry and cut 2 chicory (endive) leaves into thin strips. Stir the mustard seeds, bacon cubes and chicory into the finished Potato Purée.

Mashed Potatoes

All regions

Preparation time:		10 minutes
Cooking time:		25 minutes
Serves:		4

2¼ lbs	floury potatoes	1 kg
2 cups/17 fl oz	vegetable stock	500 ml
1	bay leaf	1
1 scant cup/7 fl oz	milk	200 ml
2 tbsp	Beurre Noisette (p. 112)	2 tbsp
½	grated unwaxed lemon zest	2 tsp
*	freshly grated nutmeg	*

Peel, wash, and cut the potatoes into about 1 cm (½ inch) dice. Cook in the stock with the bay leaf until soft. Drain well in a sieve and discard the bay leaf.

Heat the milk. Coarsely mash the potatoes with a potato masher, and stir in the milk and Beurre Noisette (p. 112). Season with lemon zest and nutmeg.

Sour Potatoes

Bavaria

Preparation time:		20 minutes
Cooking time:		20 minutes
Serves:		4

3½ oz	leek	100 g
1	carrot	1
5 oz	celeriac	150 g
1¾ lbs	small waxy potatoes	800 g
1 tsp	icing (confectioners') sugar	1 tsp
½ cup/4 fl oz	white wine	120 ml
2–3 tbsp	white wine vinegar	2–3 tbsp
1⅔ cup/14 fl oz	vegetable stock	400 ml
5	allspice berries	5
1	bay leaf	1
½	clove garlic	½
5 tbsp	cream	5 tbsp
*	salt	*
*	freshly ground black pepper	*
*	freshly grated nutmeg	*
1 tbsp	cold butter	1 tbsp
4	Pickled Cucumbers (p. 29)	4
1 tbsp	finely chopped parsley	1 tbsp

Trim, wash and cut the leek into 1–2 cm (½–1 inch) wide strips. Trim, wash and cut the carrot, on the diagonal, into 5 mm (½ inch) thick slices. Peel, wash and cut the celeriac, first into 5 mm (½ inch) slices, and then into about 2 cm (1 inch) chunks. Quarter the potatoes lengthwise.

Lightly caramelise the icing (confectioners') sugar in a pan over a medium heat, deglaze the pan with the wine and vinegar, and simmer the liquid until reduced by two-thirds. Add the potatoes, celeriac and carrot. Pour in the stock and gently simmer for 20 minutes until the vegetables are just tender. After 15 minutes of cooking, add the leek, allspice, bay leaf and garlic.

As soon as the vegetables are cooked, strain the stock through a sieve into a measuring jug, remove and discard the whole spices, and return the vegetables to the pan. Add the cream and a few potato pieces to the stock and purée with a stick (immersion) blender until smooth and creamy. Add the sauce to the vegetables in the pan.

Season the vegetables with salt, pepper and nutmeg, and adjust the seasoning with a few drops of vinegar if necessary. Add the butter. Halve the Pickled Cucumbers (p. 29) and mix, with the parsley, into the potatoes and vegetables.

Potato Wedges with Rosemary

All regions

Preparation time:		10 minutes
Cooking time:		45 minutes
Serves:		4

2¼ lbs	waxy new potatoes	1 kg
3–4	small sprigs rosemary	3–4
2–3 tbsp	olive oil	2–3 tbsp
1–2 tsp	sea salt	1–2 tsp
*	freshly ground black pepper	*
2–3	cloves garlic, crushed	2–3

Preheat the oven to 180°C/350°F/Gas Mark 4. Thoroughly wash the potatoes and wipe dry. Cut into wedges.

Wash, shake dry, and strip the rosemary leaves. Finely chop the leaves, mix with the olive oil and season with salt and pepper.

Mix the potato wedges with the seasoned oil and spread out over a baking sheet. Sprinkle with the crushed garlic, put the baking sheet on the middle shelf of the oven, and bake for about 45 minutes.

Potatoes & Dumplings

Bouillon Potatoes

Preparation time:		15 minutes
Cooking time:		15 minutes
Serves:		4

1 lb 2 oz	small waxy potatoes	500 g
2	carrots	2
6 oz	celeriac	175 g
1	leek	1
½	onion	½
1	small bay leaf	1
1	clove	1
1½ cups/12 fl oz	meat stock	350 ml
1	strip unwaxed lemon zest	1
*	salt	*
*	ground cumin	*
1 tbsp	finely chopped parsley	1 tbsp

Peel, wash and dice the potatoes. Trim, peel and dice the carrots and celeriac. Trim, wash and cut the leek into rings. Peel the onion and attach the bay leaf to it by studding with the clove.

Combine the stock, potatoes, carrots, celeriac, leek and studded onion in a pan and simmer for 12–15 minutes until tender.

Add the lemon zest, infuse for a few minutes, then remove together with the onion and discard. Season the potatoes with salt and a pinch of cumin. Serve sprinkled with parsley.

Crispy Potato Cubes

Preparation time:		10 minutes
Cooking time:		20 minutes
Serves:		4

1 lb 10½ oz	waxy potatoes	750 g
3–4 tbsp	olive oil	3–4 tbsp
1 tbsp	butter	1 tbsp
*	salt	*
*	freshly ground black pepper	*
2	onions, optional	2
1	clove garlic, optional	1

Peel, wash and cut the potatoes into about 1 cm (½ inch) dice. Thoroughly wipe dry with paper towels or a dish towel.

Heat the oil in a frying pan or skillet and fry the diced potatoes over medium heat for 15–20 minutes until golden brown.

Take them out of the pan with a slotted spoon and drain on paper towels.

Pour off the fat, heat the butter in the frying pan or skillet, and toss the potato cubes in the butter. Season with salt and pepper.

If desired, 2 peeled and diced onions and/or 1 crushed garlic clove can be cooked with the potato cubes in the last 5 minutes.

Pan-Fried Potatoes

All regions

Preparation time:		15 minutes
Cooking time:		40 minutes
Serves:		4

2¼ lbs	waxy potatoes	1 kg
1 tbsp	oil	1 tbsp
1	onion	1
*	salt	*
½–1 tsp	dried marjoram	½–1 tsp
¼–½ tsp	ground cumin	¼–½ tsp
*	freshly ground black pepper	*
1 tbsp	finely chopped parsley	1 tbsp
1 tbsp	butter	1 tbsp

Wash the potatoes then boil in a pan with salted water for 15–20 minutes.

Peel the potatoes and cut into thick slices. Heat the oil in a frying pan or skillet, lay the potato slices side by side in the oil and fry slowly over a medium heat.

Turn the potatoes when they begin to brown. Peel and cut the onion into strips and add to the pan Fry with the potatoes, tossing from time to time.

Season the potatoes with salt, marjoram, cumin and pepper. Add the parsley and melt the butter in the frying pan or skillet, tossing the potatoes thoroughly.

Potato Cakes

All regions

Preparation time:		30 minutes
Cooking time:		40 minutes
Makes:		about 12

1 lb 7 oz	floury potatoes	650 g
*	salt	*
2	egg yolks	2
1 tbsp	plain (all-purpose) flour	1 tbsp
*	freshly grated nutmeg	*
3½ oz	ham	100 g
1	onion	1
3 tbsp	oil	3 tbsp
1 tbsp	crème fraîche	1 tbsp
*	dried marjoram	*
1 tbsp	finely chopped parsley	1 tbsp
*	flour, for dusting	*

Wash the potatoes and boil until tender in plenty of salted water. Drain the potatoes, peel as hot as possible and press through a ricer.

Briskly stir the egg yolk into the potatoes and incorporate the flour until smooth. Season with salt and nutmeg.

Finely dice the ham. Peel and finely chop the onion. Heat 1 tablespoon oil in a frying pan or skillet and sauté the onion until translucent. Mix the onion, ham, crème fraîche, a pinch of marjoram and the parsley with the potato mixture.

Transfer to a floured work counter and shape into 4 cm (1½ inch) thick rolls, cut into 1–2 cm (½–1 inch) thick discs, and shape into small cakes with your hands. Heat the remaining oil in a frying pan or skillet and fry the cakes on both sides over medium heat until golden brown. Drain on paper towels.

Potato Fingers (Bubespitzle)

Preparation time:		30 minutes
Cooling time:		30 minutes
Cooking time:		40 minutes
Serves:		4

1 lb 5 oz	floury potatoes	600 g
*	salt	*
1 tsp	cumin seeds	1 tsp
2 tbsp	Beurre Noisette (p. 112)	2 tbsp
2	egg yolks	2
1 cup/4 oz	plain (all-purpose) flour	120 g
*	freshly grated nutmeg	*
1–2 tbsp	oil	1–2 tbsp
*	freshly ground black pepper	*
2 tbsp	butter	2 tbsp

Wash the potatoes and boil until tender in plenty of salted water with the cumin. Drain the potatoes, let steam, peel as hot as possible, and press through a ricer. Spread out the potato and let cool, about 30 minutes.

Mix the potato with the Beurre Noisette (p. 112) and egg yolks. Sift the plain flour over the potato mixture and knead to a smooth dough. Season with salt and nutmeg.

Divide the dough into thirds, and shape each piece on a floured work counter into 1.5 cm (¾ inch) diameter rolls. Cut the rolls into 3 cm (1½ inch) long pieces, and shape with floured hands into rolls about 7 cm (3 inches) in length, with pointed ends.

Bring salted water to a boil in a pan. Put the potato fingers into the water and simmer for a few minutes, until they float to the surface. Bring the water back to a boil, remove the potato fingers with a slotted spoon, plunge into iced water and drain on paper towels.

Heat the oil in a frying pan or skillet and fry the potato fingers, on all sides, over a medium heat until golden brown. Season with salt and pepper, add the butter to the pan and turn the potato fingers to coat well.

Potato Croquettes

Preparation time:		30 minutes
Cooking time:		45 minutes
Makes:		about 20

1 lb 7 oz	floury potatoes	650 g
*	salt	*
2	egg yolks	2
1 tbsp	cornflour (corn starch)	1 tbsp
*	freshly grated nutmeg	*
*	flour, for dusting	*
2	eggs	2
1 cup/3½ oz	plain (all-purpose) flour	100 g
1½ cups/3½ oz	white breadcrumbs	100 g
*	fat or oil, for deep-frying	*

Wash the potatoes and boil until tender in plenty of salted water. Drain the potatoes, peel as hot as possible and press through a ricer.

Briskly stir the egg yolks into the potatoes and incorporate the cornflour (corn starch) until smooth. Season the mixture with salt and nutmeg, transfer to a piping (pastry) bag, and attach a 1.5 cm (¾ inch) diameter plain tip. Pipe the mixture into lines of uniform thickness over a lightly floured work counter.

Beat the eggs in a deep plate. Put the flour and breadcrumbs into separate deep plates. Cut the lines of croquette mixture into 4 cm (1½ inch) lengths. Dredge the croquettes in the flour, then dip them in the beaten egg, and finally dredge in the breadcrumbs.

Heat the fat or oil in a large pan or deep-fryer to 170°C/325°F. Fry the croquettes in batches for a few minutes until golden brown. Take them out with a slotted spoon and drain on paper towels.

Potato Dumplings

Preparation time:		25 minutes
Cooking time:		25 minutes
Serves:		4

⅔ cup/5 fl oz	milk	150 ml
*	salt	*
1¼ oz	farina	35 g
*	freshly grated nutmeg	*
2½ lb	floury potatoes	1.2 kg

Bring the milk to a boil in a pan with 1 heaped teaspoon salt and sprinkle in the farina while stirring constantly. Continue to stir and cook the mixture to a paste, about 5 minutes, then cover with a lid and set aside in a warm place. Season with nutmeg.

Peel and finely grate the potatoes into a bowl. Then wrap the grated potatoes in a sturdy dish towel or a muslin (cheesecloth) and squeeze tightly until no more liquid comes out.

Collect the liquid and let stand for a few minutes until the potato starch settles at the bottom of the container. Drain off the water, leaving only the starch. Loosen the grated potatoes and mix with the starch and the hot farina paste.

Wet your hands and shape the mixture into 8 small, round dumplings. Bring plenty of salted water to a boil in a large pan, reduce the heat and cook the dumplings in gently simmering water, about 20 minutes.

Thuringian-Style Potato Dumplings

Preparation time:		25 minutes
Cooking time:		40 minutes
Serves:		4

3¼ lbs	floury potatoes	1.5 kg
*	salt	*
1	bread roll	1
1–2 tbsp	butter	1–2 tbsp
1 tsp	Knödelhilfe (sodium sulfite antioxidant)	1 tsp

Peel and wash the potatoes. Finely grate about two-thirds of the potatoes into a bowl. Line a sieve with a sturdy dish towel, add the grated potatoes and press firmly, collecting the liquid in a container.

Chop the remaining potatoes into small pieces, put into a pan with about 350 ml (1½ cups/12 fl oz) water to only just cover, add half a teaspoon of salt, cover with a lid, and cook until tender, about 20 minutes.

Cut the bread roll into 1 cm (½ inch) cubes. Melt the butter in a frying pan or skillet and make croutons by frying the bread until golden brown.

Crush the cooked potatoes and cooking liquid to a thin, lump-free mash. Loosen the grated raw potatoes, season with 1 teaspoon salt and mix with the Knödelhilfe. This will stop the raw potatoes from discolouring. Carefully drain off the potato water, leaving only the starch at the bottom of the container and add to the grated potatoes.

Bring the potato mash to a boil while stirring constantly, until bubbles start to appear. Use a wooden spoon to mix the hot mash briskly with the grated potatoes. When cool enough to handle, wet your hands and shape the mixture into about 8 round dumplings. Press 3–4 croutons into the centre of each dumpling. Bring plenty of salted water to a boil in a large pan and cook the dumplings over very low heat for 15–20 minutes.

Half and Half Potato Dumplings

Preparation time:		30 minutes
Cooking time:		50 minutes
Makes:		6

1½	slices bread	1½
1–2 tbsp	butter	1–2 tbsp
1 tsp	finely chopped parsley	1 tsp
2¼ lbs	floury potatoes	1 kg
*	salt	*
½ tsp	cumin seeds	½ tsp
2	egg yolks	2
1 heaped tbsp	cornflour (corn starch)	1 heaped tbsp

Cut the bread into small cubes. Melt the butter in a frying pan or skillet and make croutons by frying the cubes over a medium heat until golden brown. Drain on paper towels and mix with the parsley in a bowl.

For the dumplings: Wash 300 g (11 oz) potatoes and boil until tender in plenty of salted water with the cumin. Drain them, peel as hot as possible, and press through a ricer.

Meanwhile, wash, peel, and finely grate the remaining potatoes. Roll up the grated potatoes in a dish towel and squeeze tightly to release the residual water. Collect the potato water in a container and let stand for 10 minutes so that the starch settles on the bottom. Carefully drain off the water and mix the starch with the grated potatoes in a bowl.

Add the mashed potatoes, egg yolks and cornflour (cornstarch), season with salt, and mix until smooth.

Wet your hands and shape the mixture into 6 round dumplings, press to flatten slightly, press croutons into the centres, then roll until smooth and round.

Bring salted water to a boil in a pan, reduce the heat, and steep the dumplings rather than simmering for 20 minutes. (If the mixture is too soft, the dumplings will flake. To prevent this, dissolve the cornflour (cornstarch) completely in a little cold water and add to the cooking water.)

Potato Dumplings with Parsley

Preparation time:		20 minutes
Cooking time:		50 minutes
Makes:		8

2	slices bread	2
1–2 tbsp	butter	1–2 tbsp
1 tsp	finely chopped parsley	1 tsp
2¼ lbs	floury potatoes	1 kg
*	salt	*
1 tsp	cumin seeds	1 tsp
1 cup/3½ oz	plain (all-purpose) flour	100 g
2	egg yolks	2
3 tbsp	Beurre Noisette (p. 112)	3 tbsp
*	freshly grated nutmeg	*

Cut the bread into small cubes. Make croutons by frying the bread cubes in the butter over a medium heat until golden brown. Drain on paper towels and mix with the parsley in a bowl.

Wash the potatoes and boil until tender in plenty of salted water with the cumin. Drain the potatoes, peel as hot as possible and press through a ricer.

Mix the mashed potatoes with the flour, egg yolks, Beurre Noisette, salt and a little nutmeg until smooth.

Wet your hands and shape the mixture into 8 round dumplings, press to flatten slightly, press croutons into the centres, then shape into smooth, round dumplings. Bring salted water to a boil in a pan, reduce the heat and simmer the dumplings for 20 minutes until cooked. Take the dumplings out of the water with a slotted spoon.

Rolled Dumplings with Bacon and Breadcrumbs

Central Germany

Preparation time:		30 minutes
Resting time:		12 hours
Cooking time:		20 minutes
Serves:		4

1 lb 5 oz	floury potatoes	600 g
*	salt	*
1⅓ cups/5 oz	plain (all-purpose) flour	150 g
4	egg yolks	4
4 tbsp	Beurre Noisette (p. 112)	4 tbsp
*	freshly ground black pepper	*
*	freshly grated nutmeg	*
⅓ cup/1 oz	white breadcrumbs	30 g
3 tbsp	butter	3 tbsp
2¼ oz	bacon	60 g
1 tbsp	oil	1 tbsp
1 tbsp	finely chopped parsley	1 tbsp
*	flour, for dusting	*

The day before cooking, wash the potatoes and boil in a pan with salted water until soft. Drain, let steam briefly, peel, and press through a potato ricer. Let rest in the refrigerator overnight.

Mix the mashed potatoes with the flour, egg yolks, Beurre Noisette (p. 112), salt, pepper, and a little nutmeg, and knead until smooth.

Toast the breadcrumbs in the butter until golden brown. Cut the bacon into small cubes, fry in a frying pan or skillet with the oil until golden brown, and drain on paper towels. Mix the breadcrumbs with the parsley and bacon.

Roll out the dough on a floured work counter into a 40 x 15 cm (16 x 6 inch) rectangle. Cut the rectangle into four uniform 10 x 15 cm (4 x 6 inch) strips, and lay on a dish towel. Spread the bacon and breadcrumb mixture over the dough strips, roll up in the dish towel, and tie the ends with string. Gently simmer the dumplings in a pan wrapped in the cloth with salted water for 20 minutes.

Sausage-Stuffed Dumplings with a Creamy Bacon Sauce

Hesse

Preparation time:		30 minutes
Cooking time:		20 minutes
Serves:		4

For the dumplings:		
2¼ lbs	floury potatoes	1 kg
2	eggs	2
3½ oz	potato starch	100 g
½ tsp	dried marjoram	½ tsp
*	salt	*
5 oz	Ahle Wurst (air-dried Dauerwurst sausage)	150 g

For the sauce:		
5 oz	smoked back bacon joint	150 g
9 oz	onions	250 g
1 cup/9 fl oz	sour cream	250 ml
½ cup/4 fl oz	milk	125 ml
*	salt	*
*	freshly ground white pepper	*

For the dumplings: Peel and finely grate the potatoes. Mix with the eggs, potato starch, marjoram and a little salt, and knead into a smooth, firm dough.

Cut the sausage into 1.5 cm (¾ inch) cubes. Wet your hands and shape the dough into 12–16 round dumplings and press 1–2 sausage cubes into the centres of each.

Bring plenty of salted water to a boil in a large pan. Add the dumplings, reduce the heat and simmer very gently for 15–20 minutes.

For the sauce: Cut the bacon into small cubes and fry in a dry frying pan or skillet over low heat until crispy. Take out about 2 tablespoons of bacon cubes and drain on paper towels.

Peel and cut the onions into short strips, and add to the bacon remaining in the frying pan or skillet. Sauté the onions over a low heat. Stir in the sour cream and milk. Bring the sauce to a boil briefly then reduce the heat. Season with salt and pepper.

Carefully lift the dumplings out of the water, drain briefly, and arrange with the sauce on plates. Sprinkle the rest of the bacon on the top.

Potatoes & Dumplings

Meat-Stuffed Potato Dumplings (Gefillde Klees)

Saarland and Rhineland-Palatinate

Preparation time:		1 hour
Cooking time:		55 minutes
Serves:		4

For the dumplings:		
5½ lbs	floury potatoes	2.5 kg
*	salt	*
14 oz	leeks	400 g
11 oz	smoked bacon	300 g
2	large onions	2
2	day-old bread rolls	2
1 tbsp	oil	1 tbsp
14 oz	minced meat	400 g
2	egg yolks	2

For the sauce:		
2	onions	2
9 oz	smoked back bacon	250 g
1 tbsp	butter	1 tbsp
4 tbsp	sour cream	4 tbsp
1 level tsp	cornflour (corn starch)	1 level tsp
1 scant cup/7 fl oz	single (light) cream	200 ml
*	salt	*
*	freshly ground black pepper	*

For the dumplings: Wash 500 g (1 lb 2 oz) potatoes and boil until soft in salted water. Peel and mash finely.

Peel, wash and finely grate the raw potatoes. Wrap the grated potatoes in a thin and sturdy dish towel and squeeze well until no more liquid comes out. Collect the potato water in a container and let stand until the starch settles on the bottom. Drain off the water, leaving only the starch. Spread the grated potato over a work counter and season with salt. Spread the freshly mashed potato over the grated potato, add the potato starch, and knead everything into a firm and smooth dough.

Trim, wash and cut the leeks into 5 mm (¼ inch) strips. Cut the bacon into very fine dice. Peel and dice the onions. Cut the bread into 5 mm (¼ inch) cubes.

Heat the oil in a large frying pan or skillet and lightly fry the bacon, onions and leeks. Add the minced meat and cook briefly. Add the bread and braise everything, stirring often. Transfer the mixture to a bowl, let cool a little, incorporate the egg yolks then cool to lukewarm. Divide the mixture into 8, and shape into round dumplings.

Wet your hands and shape into dumplings, flatten a little, then put one ground meat dumpling on top of each and encase in the dough. Wet your hands and shape into round dumplings. Gently simmer in salted water, 25 minutes.

For the sauce: Peel and finely dice the onions. Cut the bacon into very small cubes. Lightly fry the bacon and onions in the butter for a few minutes in a pan over a low heat. Mix the sour cream with the cornflour (cornstarch), and stir with the cream into the bacon and onion mixture. Bring to a boil, reduce the heat and season. Serve the dumplings on heated plates, with the sauce.

Potato Pancakes

All regions

Preparation time:		10 minutes
Cooking time:		20 minutes
Makes:		8–10

1 lb 2 oz	floury potatoes	500 g
2	egg yolks	2
*	salt	*
*	freshly ground black pepper	*
*	freshly grated nutmeg	*
2 tbsp	oil	2 tbsp
*	Apple Puree (p. 362), optional	*

Peel, wash and finely grate the raw potatoes. Use your hands to squeeze the strips well. Mix the egg yolks with the potatoes and season the mixture with salt, pepper and a little nutmeg.

Heat a little oil in a frying pan or skillet. Use a spoon to put some of the potato mixture into the pan and then to flatten into a 6–7 cm (2½ inch) diameter pancake. Fry the undersides until golden brown, about 2 minutes, then turn over and fry the other side, about 2 minutes. Drain the potato pancake on paper towels. Repeat the process with the rest of the mixture. This dish can be served with with Apple Purée (p. 362).

Variations:

Potato Pancakes with Bacon and Pears: Dice 100 g (3½ oz) bacon as finely as possible, fry in a frying pan or skillet over a low heat with 1–2 teaspoons oil until crispy, and drain on paper towels. Peel, quarter and core 1 pear and dice as finely as possible. Mix the pear and bacon into the potato mixture and finish as described above.

Potato Pancakes with Leek: Finely dice 100 g (3½ oz) leeks (preferably the light green part) and mix into the potato mixture. Finish as described above.

Potato Rösti

Southern Germany

Preparation time:		10 minutes
Cooking time:		25 minutes
Serves:		4

11 oz	waxy potatoes	300 g
*	salt	*
*	cumin seeds	*
*	freshly ground black pepper	*
*	freshly grated nutmeg	*
1–2 tbsp	oil	1–2 tbsp

Wash the potatoes and cook in plenty of salted water with a pinch of cumin, about 15 minutes. The drain and let steam. Peel, wash and coarsley grate the raw potatoes. while still hot. Season with salt, pepper and nutmeg.

Heat 1 tablespoon of oil in a frying pan or skillet. Add the potato strips, spread out to a uniform 5 mm (¼ inch) thickness, and lightly press. Fry the rösti on one side over medium heat until golden brown, about 4 minutes. To turn, slide the rösti out of the pan onto a plate. Then place the upturned pan over the rösti and flip both pan and plate over at the same time. Add a little oil and fry the other side until golden brown, about 4 minutes. Drain the rösti on paper towels.

Variations:

Vegetable Rösti: Trim, wash and peel if necessary, a choice of 100 g (3½ oz) leek, 1 small carrot, 100 g (3½ oz) fennel, 100 g (3½ oz) celeriac, or 100 g (3½ oz) courgette (zucchini), and shred into thin strips. Mix the vegetable and potato strips together. Season and fry as described above.

Rösti with Raw Potatoes: Peel and wash 500 g (1 lb 2 oz) waxy potatoes, and use a grater to shred into thin strips. Season with salt, pepper and nutmeg, and let stand for a few minutes to infuse. Then transfer the strips to a sieve and squeeze well with your hands. Fry the rösti as described above.

Potato Pancakes with Bacon and Herbs

Bergisches and Rhineland

Preparation time:		20 minutes
Cooking time:		25 minutes
Serves:		4

2¼ lbs	waxy potatoes	1 kg
4 oz	smoked back bacon joint	120 g
2	onions	2
3 tbsp	oil	3 tbsp
*	salt	*
1 cup/4 oz	plain (all-purpose) flour	120 g
4	eggs	4
1 scant cup/7 fl oz	milk	200 ml
*	freshly ground white pepper	*
*	freshly grated nutmeg	*
1 tsp	dried marjoram	1 tsp
½	bunch parsley	½
½	bunch chives	½
4 tbsp	clarified butter	4 tbsp

Peel and wash the potatoes and cut or shred into thin strips. Put the potato strips into a sieve, rinse under cold water, and let drain. Pat dry with paper towels. Cut the bacon into very small cubes. Peel and finely chop the onions.

Heat the oil in a large frying pan or skillet and fry the bacon over a low to medium heat until crispy. Add the onions and sauté. Add the potato strips to the onion and bacon mixture and fry together, about 8 minutes, carefully turning over from time to time. Season the potato mixture with salt, then transfer to paper towels to drain.

Combine the flour, eggs and milk in a bowl and mix together with a hand mixer. Season with salt, pepper, a pinch of nutmeg and the marjoram. Wash and shake dry the parsley and chives. Finely chop the parsley leaves, and cut the chives into thin rings. Stir the herbs into the batter.

Preheat the oven to 100°C/210°F/Gas Mark ¼. Heat 1 tablespoon clarified butter in a frying pan or skillet. Put a quarter of the potato mixture into the frying pan or skillet, cover with a quarter of the batter, stir briefly and fry on one side until golden brown, about 4 minutes.

Carefully turn over, fry the other side, about 2 minutes, and slide the pancake onto a plate. Keep the pancake warm in the oven. Make three more pancakes with the rest of the mixture. The pancakes can be served with a green salad.

Potato Strudel

Southern Germany

Preparation time:		45 minutes
Cooking time:		30 minutes
Serves:		6

2¼ cups/9 oz	plain (all-purpose) flour	250 g
*	salt	*
3 tbsp	oil	3 tbsp

For the filling:		
1 lb 2 oz	floury potatoes	500 g
*	salt	*
½ cup/4 fl oz	hot milk	125 ml
150 g	smoked back bacon	50 g
1	onion	1
1 tsp	finely chopped parsley	1 tsp
4 tbsp	butter	4 tbsp
3	egg yolks	3
*	freshly ground black pepper	*
*	dried marjoram	*
*	grated nutmeg	*
*	ground cumin	*

Mix the flour with a pinch of salt, then add 125 ml (½ cup/ 4 fl oz) lukewarm water and 2 tablespoons oil and knead to a smooth dough. Roll into a ball, brush with the rest of the oil, put into a warmed metal bowl and rest for 30 minutes.

For the filling: Boil the potatoes in salted water for 20 minutes, then peel and set aside one large potato. Press the remaining potatoes through a potato ricer and mix with the milk until smooth.

Cut the bacon into cubes and fry in a frying pan or skillet until translucent. Peel and finely chop the onion, add to the bacon, and sauté. Mix the bacon, onion and parsley with the mashed potatoes. Preheat the oven to 180°C/350°F/Gas Mark 4.

Dice the set-aside potato and fry in a pan with 2 tbsp butter until golden brown. Mix the potato cubes and 2 egg yolks into the mashed potatoes and season well with salt, pepper and a pinch each of marjoram, nutmeg and cumin.

Roll out the dough as thinly as possible on a floured cloth. Melt the remaining butter, brush over the dough and spread with the filling. Use the cloth to roll the strudel and transfer to a greased baking tin (pan). Whisk the remaining egg yolk with a little water and brush over the strudel. Put the baking tin (pan) on the middle shelf of the oven and bake for 25–30 minutes, until golden.

Potato Pancakes with Apple and Pear Purée and Westphalian Ham

Westphalia

Preparation time:		20 minutes
Cooking time:		35 minutes
Makes:		8–10

For the pancakes:		
1 lb 2 oz	floury potatoes	500 g
2	egg yolks	2
*	salt	*
*	freshly grated nutmeg	*
*	oil, for frying	*
12	slices Westphalian ham	12

For the purée:		
2	tart apples	2
2	ripe, firm pears	2
1½ oz	sugar	40 g
4 tsp	calvados	4 tsp
¼ cup/2 fl oz	white wine	60 ml
1	clove	1
½	vanilla bean, scraped	½
1	shard of cinnamon stick	1
1 pinch	unwaxed orange zest	pinch
1–2 tsp	butter	1–2 tsp

For the pancakes: Peel, wash and finely grate the potatoes. Use your hands to squeeze out part of the potato water. Stir in the egg yolks and season the mixture with salt and nutmeg.

Heat the oil in a frying pan or skillet. Put some potato mixture into the frying pan or skillet and use a tablespoon to spread the mixture to make a 6–7 cm (2½ inch) diameter pancake. Fry the pancakes one at a time on both sides for 4–5 minutes over low heat until golden brown. Drain on paper towels and set aside in a warm place.

For the purée: Wash, halve, and core one apple and one pear, and cut one apple and pear half into small wedges. Peel the other halves, and peel, quarter and core the remaining apple and pear, and cut all the flesh into 1 cm (½ inch) dice.

Put the diced fruit into a pan, add the sugar, and stir over a low heat. Add the calvados and wine, clove, vanilla bean and cinnamon, cover, and let simmer for about 20 minutes. Then remove the whole spices and use a stick (immersion) blender to purée the stewed fruit and cooking liquid. Add the orange zest.

Lightly fry the pear and apple wedges in a frying pan or skillet with the butter over a medium heat.

Arrange the potato pancakes with 3 slices ham on heated plates. Arrange the apple and pear wedges on one side, and serve with the apple and pear purée.

Potato Gratin

All regions

Preparation time:		20 minutes
Cooking time:		20 minutes
Serves:		4

1 tbsp	butter, for greasing	1 tbsp
1⅔ cup/14 fl oz	double (heavy) cream	400 ml
1	clove garlic, halved	1
1	strip unwaxed lemon zest	1
1	sprig thyme	1
*	salt	*
*	freshly ground black pepper	*
*	freshly grated nutmeg	*
2¼ lbs	floury potatoes	1 kg
1 cup/3½ oz	grated alpine cheese	100 g

Preheat the oven to 180°C/350°F/Gas Mark 4. Grease a casserole (Dutch oven) with butter. Bring the cream to a boil in a pan and remove from the heat.

Add the garlic, lemon zest and thyme to the cream, infuse for a few minutes, then remove and discard. Season the cream with salt, pepper and nutmeg.

Peel, wash, and cut the potatoes into 2 mm (⅛ inch) thick slices.

Lay the potato slices inside the casserole dish, slightly overlapping in layers, and pour over the cream. Put the dish on the middle shelf of the oven and bake until golden, about 40 minutes.

Sprinkle the gratin with grated alpine cheese before baking, if you like.

Roast Potatoes with Pork Patties (Hackus und Knieste)

Northern Germany and Lower Saxony

Preparation time:		15 minutes
Cooking time:		1 hour
Serves:		4

2¼ lbs	all-purpose potatoes	1 kg
5 tbsp	oil	5 tbsp
*	salt	*
1–2 tbsp	cumin seeds	1–2 tbsp
11 oz	sour pickles	300 g
2	onions	2
1¾ lb	very fresh minced pork	800 g
*	freshly ground black pepper	*

Preheat the oven to 200°C/400°F/Gas Mark 6. Thoroughly wash the potatoes, brushing if necessary, then wipe dry and halve. Brush a baking tin (pan) with 4 tablespoons oil, put the potatoes inside, cut-side down, and brush the outsides with oil. Sprinkle with salt and cumin, position the baking tin on the middle shelf inside the oven and roast for 50–60 minutes. Baste regularly with oil from the pan.

Peel and finely dice the pickles. Peel and finely chop the onions. Season the minced pork well with salt and pepper, and shape into 4 uniform patties.

Arrange a patty on each plate, make a small mound of onions and pickles next to it, and serve with the potatoes.

Potato Loaf with Smoked Pork Sausage (Potthucke)

Sauerland and Siergerland

Preparation time:	15 minutes
Cooling time:	12 hours
Cooking time:	1 hour 10 minutes
Serves:	4

2¼ lbs	floury potatoes	1 kg
3	eggs	3
1 scant cup/7 fl oz	single (light) cream	200 ml
3 tsp	salt	3 tsp
1 cup/4 oz	plain (all-purpose) flour	120 g
*	butter, for greasing	*
7 oz	smoked Mettenden sausages	200 g
*	clarified butter, for frying	*

Preheat the oven to 200°C/400°F/Gas Mark 6. Peel, wash and finely grate the potatoes into a bowl. Mix the eggs with the cream and season with salt. Stir in the flour.

Grease a loaf tin (pan) with soft butter, fill with half the grated potatoes, cover with the sausages and fill the tin (pan) with the remaining potatoes. Put the tin on the second shelf from the top of the oven and bake for 50–60 minutes until golden. Let cool a little, unmould and cool overnight in the refrigerator.

The next day, cut the potato loaf into roughly 1.5 cm (¾ inch) slices. Heat a frying pan or skillet over medium heat, add 1–2 tablespoons clarified butter, and fry the slices, on both sides, until golden brown.

Potato Loaf (Kastenpickert)

North Rhine-Westphalia, Osnabrücker Land and Lower Saxony

Preparation time:	30 minutes
Rising time:	1 hour
Cooking time:	1 hour 15 minutes

1 lb 5 oz	floury potatoes	600 g
2	eggs	2
4½ cups/1 lb 2 oz	plain (all-purpose) flour	500 g
¾ oz	packet dried yeast	7 g
5 tbsp	milk	5 tbsp
1 level tbsp	salt	1 level tbsp
1 tsp	sugar	1 tsp
2 oz	raisins	50 g
*	butter, for greasing	*
2 oz	butter, for frying	50 g
*	marmalade, optional	*
*	liverwurst, optional	*

Peel, wash, and finely grate the potatoes.

Combine the potatoes, eggs, flour, yeast, milk, salt and sugar in a mixing bowl and work for a few minutes, either in a food processor or with a hand mixer, to a smooth dough. Finally, work in the raisins.

Grease a 30 cm (1 foot) long loaf tin (pan) with butter and fill to just above halfway with the dough. Cover with a dish towel and let rise, at room temperature, for about an hour.

Preheat the oven to 180°C/350°F/Gas Mark 4. As soon as the dough has risen to the rim of the tin, put it on the middle shelf of the oven and bake until golden, about 1 hour 15 minutes. Let it cool a little inside the tin, then unmould onto a rack and let cool completely, preferably overnight.

Cut the loaf into 1–1.5 cm (½–¾ inch) thick slices and fry in a frying pan or skillet with the butter, on both sides, over medium heat, until golden brown. The slices can be spread with marmalade or a good serving of liverwurst.

Potato and Leek Casserole

All regions

Preparation time:	20 minutes
Cooking time:	45 minutes
Serves:	4

2¼ lbs	potatoes	1 kg
9 oz	cooked ham	250 g
2	leeks	2
2 tbsp	oil	2 tbsp
4	eggs	4
1¼ cups/10 fl oz	milk	300 ml
*	freshly grated nutmeg	*
*	salt	*
*	freshly ground black pepper	*
1 cup/3½ oz	grated gouda cheese	100 g

Preheat the oven to 190°C/375°F/Gas Mark 5. Peel and thinly slice the potatoes. Cut the ham into very small cubes.

Halve and thoroughly wash the leeks. Cut crosswise into thin strips. Heat the oil in a frying pan or skillet and sauté the leeks until translucent.

Arrange the potato slices in layers in a greased ovenproof dish. Scatter with the ham. Cover with the leeks.

Whisk the eggs with the milk and season with nutmeg, salt and pepper. Pour over the potatoes.

Put the ovenproof dish on the middle shelf of the oven and bake for 35 minutes. Sprinkle with the cheese and grill for 10 more minutes.

Potato Casserole with Sausage and Bacon (Döbbekuchen)

Rhineland-Palatinate, Rhine-Westphalia, Hesse and Saarland

Preparation time:	20 minutes
Cooking time:	1 hour
Serves:	4

1	day-old bread roll	1
2	Mettenden sausages	2
2¼ lbs	all-purpose potatoes	1 kg
2	eggs	2
*	salt	*
*	freshly ground black pepper	*
*	freshly grated nutmeg	*
*	sweet paprika	*
*	dried lovage	*
5 oz	smoked back bacon	150 g
2 tbsp	Beurre Noisette (p. 112)	2 tbsp
*	green salad, to serve, optional	*

Preheat the oven to 220°C/425°F/Gas Mark 7. Soak the bread in water to soften, then squeeze and cut into small pieces. Thinly slice the sausages. Peel, wash and coarsely grate the potatoes.

Mix the potatoes with the eggs, sausage slices and bread, and season well with salt, pepper, nutmeg and a pinch of paprika and lovage.

Finely dice the bacon. Heat the Beurre Noisette (p. 112) in an ovenproof dish and fry the bacon over medium heat. Spread the potato mixture over the bacon, transfer to the middle shelf of the oven and bake until crispy, about 1 hour. The casserole can be served with a green salad.

Potatoes and Dumplings with a Creamy Bacon Sauce

Saarland

Preparation time:		20 minutes
Cooking time:		15 minutes
Serves:		4

3½ cups/14 oz	plain (all-purpose) flour	400 g
3½ oz	low-fat Quark	100 g
½ cup/3 ½ fl oz	sparkling mineral water	100 ml
2	eggs	2
*	salt	*
*	freshly ground black pepper	*
*	freshly grated nutmeg	*
1 lb 10½ oz	waxy potatoes	750 g
7 oz	smoked back bacon	200 g
1 tbsp	butter	1 tbsp
1¼ cups/10 fl oz	single (light) cream	300 ml
1 tbsp	finely chopped parsley	1 tbsp

Mix the flour with the Quark, mineral water and eggs, seasoned with salt, pepper and nutmeg, to a thick dough. Then use a wooden spoon or food processor to beat briskly for a few minutes.

Peel and cut the potatoes into small wedges or 1 cm (½ inch) thick batons, and boil for 5 minutes in a pan with salted water. Dip a tablespoon in the hot cooking water and use it to scoop out dumplings from the dough. Add to the boiling water with the potatoes. Boil with the potatoes until cooked, about 10 more minutes.

Meanwhile, dice the bacon, melt a little in a pan with the butter and add the cream. Season with salt and pepper.

Take the potatoes and dumplings out of the water with a skimmer, arrange in deep plates and cover with the bacon sauce. Sprinkle with parsley.

Potato and Bacon Waffles

Palatinate and Saarland

Preparation time:		15 minutes
Cooking time:		20 minutes
Serves:		4

1¾ lbs	floury potatoes	800 g
1	large carrot	1
1	onion	1
1	thin leek	1
3	small eggs	3
1 cup/4 oz	plain (all-purpose) flour	120 g
*	salt	*
*	freshly ground black pepper	*
*	freshly grated nutmeg	*
4 oz	smoked side bacon	120 g
1 tbsp	oil	1 tbsp
*	root vegetables, to serve	*
*	Apple Purée (p. 362), to serve	*

Peel and grate the potatoes, carrot and onion as finely as possible into a bowl.

Trim, halve lengthwise, and wash the leek, then cut crossways into thin strips. Mix with the eggs and flour into the grated vegetables. Season with salt, pepper, and nutmeg. Finely dice the bacon.

Preheat a waffle maker (preferably for heart-shaped waffles) on the medium setting, brush with oil, and spread out about a quarter of the diced bacon in the waffle maker. Fill with a quarter of the batter, close the lid, and cook for a few minutes until golden brown and crispy.

Repeat the process to use up the rest of the bacon and batter, regularly brushing the waffle maker with oil. Accompany with root vegetables and Apple Purée.

Black Pudding with Bacon, Apple and Potatoes (Himmel un Ääd)

Rhineland, Westphalia, Lower Saxony, Silesia

Preparation time:		30 minutes
Cooking time:		40 minutes
Serves:		4

2¼ lbs	floury potatoes	1 kg
*	salt	*
½ tsp	cumin seeds	½ tsp
1 cup/7–8 fl oz	milk	200–250 ml
1 tbsp	butter	1 tbsp
2 tbsp	Beurre Noisette (p. 112)	2 tbsp
*	freshly grated nutmeg	*
2¼ lbs	tart apples (e.g. Boskoop)	1 kg
1 pinch	unwaxed lemon zest	1 pinch
2	onions	2
7 oz	bacon	200 g
2–3 tbsp	oil	2–3 tbsp
1 lb 2 oz	black pudding	500 g
*	cornflour (corn starch)	*

Wash the potatoes and boil until tender in salted water with the cumin. Drain, peel while still hot, and mash with a potato masher. Heat the milk and gradually pour into the mashed potatoes while stirring with a wooden spoon. Add the butter and Beurre Noisette (p. 112), and season the mashed potatoes with salt and nutmeg.

Peel, quarter and core the apples, then cut into 5–10 mm (¼–½ inch) dice. Combine the diced apples with 200 ml (scant 1 cup/7 fl oz) water in a wide and deep frying pan, skillet or pan, cover with a lid and braise over a medium heat for 3–5 minutes. Remove the lid and let the liquid evaporate. The diced apples should be soft but not crumbly. Mix the diced apples, with the lemon zest, into the mashed potatoes.

Peel and cut the onions into rings. Cut the bacon into strips. Heat 1 tablespoon oil in a frying pan or skillet and gently fry the bacon. Add the onions and lightly fry.

Cut the black pudding into 1 cm (½ inch) thick slices, dredge in the flour, and fry on both sides in a non-stick pan with the remaining oil.

Serve the apple mashed potato on heated plates with black pudding slices arranged next to it, garnished with fried bacon cubes and onion rings.

Cheese Spätzle with Fried Onions

Swabia and Allgäu

Preparation time:		10 minutes
Cooking time:		30 minutes
Serves:		4

For the fried onions:		
2	onions	2
2 tbsp	butter	2 tbsp
*	sugar	*

For the cheese spätzle:		
3½ oz	Allgäuer emmental cheese	100 g
3½ oz	Allgäuer bergkäse cheese	100 g
2 oz	weisslacker cheese	50 g
3½ cups/14 oz	plain (all-purpose) flour	400 g
8	eggs	8
1 tbsp	oil	1 tbsp
*	salt	*
*	freshly grated nutmeg	*
1	bay leaf	1
⅓ cup/2½ fl oz	vegetable broth	75 ml
1	small bunch chives	1

For the fried onions: Peel and cut the onions into strips. Heat the butter in a frying pan or skillet and fry the onions, with a pinch of sugar over a low heat until a uniform brown colour.

For the cheese spätzle: Finely grate the emmental and bergkäse, and finely dice the weisslacker. Combine the flour, eggs, oil, 1 tablespoon salt, and a little nutmeg in a bowl and use a hand mixer with a dough hook to knead for 3–5 minutes, until bubbles appear in the resulting dough.

Bring salted water to a boil, with the bay leaf, in a large pan. Immerse the spätzle maker briefly into the boiling water, fill with the dough and slide the box from side to side, dropping the dumplings into the boiling water. Bring to a boil briefly, turn off the heat and use a slotted spoon or skimmer to take the dumplings and bay leaf out of the pan. Put the dumplings into a heated deep frying pan or skillet.

Add the cheese and broth, and reheat the spätzle over a low heat. Remove and discard the bay leaf.

Wash, shake dry and finely chop the chives. Serve the spätzle on heated plates with the fried onions and sprinkle with the chives.

Pancake Scrapings (Kratzede)

Baden-Württemberg and Markgräflerland

Preparation time:		25 minutes
Resting time:		20 minutes
Cooking time:		10 minutes
Serves:		4

1¾ cups/7 oz	plain (all-purpose) flour	200 g
½ tsp	baking powder	½ tsp
1 cup/8 fl oz	milk	250 ml
3	eggs, separated	3
2¼ oz	Beurre Noisette (p. 112)	60 g
*	salt	*
*	freshly grated nutmeg	
1 tbsp	oil	1 tbsp
*	asparagus, to serve	*

Sift the flour, with the baking powder, into a bowl and mix with the milk until smooth. Stir the egg yolks into the batter. Warm the Beurre Noisette (p. 112) and stir in two-thirds. Season with salt and nutmeg and rest for 20 minutes.

Beat the egg whites to soft peaks with a pinch of salt, and fold into the batter. Preheat the grill (broiler) to its highest setting.

Place a large non-stick frying pan or skillet over medium heat. Brush with a little oil. Fill to a depth of 1–2 cm (½–1 inch) with the batter and fry until the underside is golden brown. Put the frying pan or skillet in the lowest third of the oven under the grill (broiler) and cook for a few minutes until light golden.

Slide the pancake onto a chopping board and use two forks to tear it into small pieces. Repeat the process with the remaining batter. Finally, put all of the pancake scrapings into a large frying pan or skillet and briefly reheat with the remaining Beurre Noisette. Serve with asparagus.

Spätzle with Smoked Bacon and Sauerkraut

Swabia and Allgäu

Preparation time:		25 minutes
Cooking time:		45 minutes
Serves:		4

For the sauerkraut:

1	onion	1
1 tsp	oil	1 tsp
2⅔ cups/14 oz	sauerkraut (from a can)	400 g
¼ cup/1¾ fl oz	dry white wine	50 ml
scant 1 cup/7 fl oz	vegetable stock	200 ml
1	piece smoked pork skin	1
5	peppercorns	5
2	juniper berries, lightly crushed	2
1	bay leaf	1
2 tbsp	Apple Purée (p. 362)	2 tbsp
1 tsp	cumin seeds	1 tsp
1 tbsp	butter	1 tbsp
*	sugar	*
*	salt	*

For the spätzle:

3½ cups/14 oz	plain (all-purpose) flour	400 g
8	eggs	8
*	salt	*
1 tbsp	oil	1 tbsp
5 oz	smoked back bacon	150 g
2 tbsp	butter	2 tbsp

For the sauerkraut: Peel and finely chop the onion. Heat the oil in a pan and sauté the onion over moderate heat. Add the sauerkraut and sauté briefly. Deglaze the pan with the wine and simmer until almost completely reduced.

Add the stock and the pork skin. Braise over a low heat for about 45 minutes. Meanwhile, put the peppercorns, juniper berries and bay leaf into a spice bag and close. After cooking for 30 minutes, add the apple purée and the spice bag to the pan.

At the end of the cooking time, remove the spice bag. Mix in the butter and season the sauerkraut with sugar. Adjust the seasoning with salt if necessary.

For the spätzle: Work the flour with the eggs, 1 teaspoon salt, and oil, using a hand mixer with a dough hook, and knead for 3–5 minutes until bubbles start to form in the dough. Alternatively, stir the dough with a wooden spoon.

Bring plenty of salted water to a boil in a large pan. Immerse the spätzle maker briefly in the boiling water, fill with the dough and slide the box from side to side, dropping the dumplings into the boiling water. When the dumplings float to the surface, bring to a boil briefly then turn off the heat. Use a slotted spoon to take the dumplings out of the water and set aside.

Dice the bacon and fry lightly in a large and deep frying pan or skillet with the butter. Add the dumplings and fry lightly. Finally, add the sauerkraut and heat through briefly.

Swabian-Style Sauerkraut Rolls

Swabia and Allgäu

For the pasta:		
2½ cups/10 oz	plain (all-purpose) flour	275 g
¾ cup/4 oz	semolina	120 g
4	eggs	4
3 tbsp	olive oil	3 tbsp
*	salt	*

For the sauerkraut:		
5⅓ cups/1¾ lb	sauerkraut	800 g
3½ oz	smoked back bacon	100 g
1	large onion	1
1 tsp	oil	1 tsp
½ cup/3½ fl oz	dry white wine	100 ml
1¼ cups/10 fl oz	chicken stock	300 ml
5	peppercorns	5
2	juniper berries, lightly crushed	2
1	bay leaf	1
2 tbsp	Apple Purée (p. 362)	2 tbsp
1 tbsp	butter	1 tbsp
*	sugar	*
*	salt	*
4½ cups/34 fl oz	chicken stock (broth)	1 litre
2 tbsp	Beurre Noisette (p. 112)	2 tbsp
*	green salad, to serve	*

Preparation time: 50 minutes
Cooking time: 35 minutes
Serves: 4

For the pasta: Mix the flour, semolina, eggs, olive oil and a pinch of salt and knead into a smooth dough. Cover the dough with clingfilm (plastic wrap) and rest in the refrigerator for about 30 minutes.

For the sauerkraut: Wash the sauerkraut briefly under cold water and squeeze out the water. Finely dice the bacon. Peel and finely chop the onion.

Heat the oil in a pan and sauté the bacon and onion over moderate heat until translucent. Add the sauerkraut and sauté briefly. Deglaze the pan with the wine and simmer until almost completely reduced.

Add the stock and braise over a low heat for about 30 minutes. Meanwhile, put the peppercorns, juniper berries and bay leaf into a spice bag and close. After cooking for 15 minutes, add the purée and the spice bag to the pan.

At the end of the cooking time, remove the spice bag. Incorporate the butter and season the sauerkraut with sugar. Adjust the seasoning with salt if necessary. The liquid should have evaporated completely, otherwise drain in a sieve. Leave it to cool slightly.

Preheat the oven to 180°C/350°F/Gas Mark 4. Halve the pasta dough and use a rolling pin to roll out each half into a 16–18 cm (6–7 inches) wide rectangular sheet. Dust with a little flour. Spread the sauerkraut over each sheet, leaving an uncovered space around the edges. Roll up the dough from the long side, lay the rolls on their seam side, and cut into 4.5–5 cm (1¾–2 inch) pieces.

Arrange the sauerkraut rolls, seam-side up, next to each other in an ovenproof dish or roasting tin (pan). Add the stock, covering the rolls well. Cover with a lid or aluminium foil, and cook in the oven for about 35 minutes. Finally, brush with Beurre Noisette. Serve with green salad.

Swabian-Style Ravioli (Schwäbische Maultaschen)

Baden-Württemberg

For the pasta:		
1¾ cups/7 oz	plain (all-purpose) flour	200 g
⅔ cup/3½ oz	semolina	100 g
3	eggs	3
2–3 tbsp	olive oil	2–3 tbsp
*	salt	*

For the filling:		
2 oz	bread	50 g
¼ cup/1¾ fl oz	milk	50 ml
1	small onion	1
3 oz	smoked side bacon	80 g
9 oz	spinach	250 g
7 oz	minced veal	200 g
5 oz	Bratwurst sausagemeat	150 g
1	large egg	1
1	small egg, beaten	1
1 tbsp	hot mustard	1 tbsp
*	salt	*
*	freshly ground black pepper	*
1	pinch unwaxed lemon zest	1
1 tbsp	finely chopped parsley	1 tbsp
*	flour, for dusting	*

Preparation time: 50 minutes
Cooking time: 10 minutes
Serves: 4

For the pasta: Mix the flour, semolina, eggs, olive oil and a pinch of salt and knead into a smooth dough. Cover the dough with clingfilm (plastic wrap) and rest in the refrigerator, about 30 minutes.

For the filling: Finely dice the bread. Soak the bread in a bowl with the milk. Peel and finely chop the onion. Finely dice the bacon and fry in a dry frying pan or skillet over medium heat until the fat is crispy. Once the bacon has released some of its fat, add the onion and sauté until transparent, stirring from time to time.

Select the best spinach leaves, then wash, drain and remove the larger stems. Blanch in boiling salted water for 2 minutes. Drain off the water, plunge into iced water, then drain. Squeeze the leaves well, then finely chop.

Add the veal and sausagemeat to the bread in the bowl. Whisk the large egg and add to the bowl with the mustard, bacon and onion mixture, and spinach, and mix thoroughly. Season with salt, pepper, zest, and the parsley.

Divide the pasta dough into manageable-sized portions and use a rolling pin to roll out each portion into a 10–12 cm (4–4¾ inches) wide band. Dust with a little flour. Immediately cover each band with clingfilm. Fill a piping (pastry) bag fitted with a plain tip about 1.5 cm (¾ inch) in diameter with the filling mixture.

Brush each pasta band with the beaten egg. Pipe the filling in a long line over the bottom third of each pasta band. Roll up the filling-covered bands along their lengths. Use the handle of a wooden spoon to press down on the pasta roll at 3 cm (1¼ inch) intervals. Cut through the flattened parts of the pasta roll to separate into individual Maultaschen, and press down on the ends of each. Gently simmer the pasta in salted water or vegetable stock for 5–8 minutes. Lift out with a slotted spoon and serve.

Bread Dumplings

Southern Germany

Preparation time:		35 minutes
Cooking time:		20 minutes
Makes:		8

11 oz	day-old sesame buns	300 g
1 cup/8 fl oz	milk	250 ml
3	eggs	3
*	salt	*
*	freshly ground black pepper	*
*	freshly grated nutmeg	*
1 tbsp	finely chopped parsley	1 tbsp

Cut the bread into very thin slices. Bring the milk to a boil in a pan then take off the heat. Beat the eggs, stir into the milk, and season with salt, pepper and a pinch of nutmeg. Pour the milk over the bread in a bowl, add the parsley, and knead with your hands to a compact mixture. Cover the bowl and rest for 20 minutes.

Wet your hands and shape the mixture into 8 round dumplings. Bring plenty of salted water to a boil in a large pan and gently simmer the dumplings for 15–20 minutes.

Variations:

Bacon Dumplings: Add cubes of fried bacon (drained of fat) and sautéed finely chopped onion to the dumpling mixture.

Herb Dumplings: Add 3–5 tablespoons freshly cut herbs to the dumpling mixture.

Pasta with Ham, Spinach and Mushrooms in Cream Sauce

All regions

Preparation time:		10 minutes
Cooking time:		20 minutes
Serves:		4

1	onion	1
1–2 tbsp	olive oil	1–2 tbsp
1 cup/8 fl oz	chicken stock	250 ml
1	small bay leaf	1
½ cup/3½ fl oz	cream	100 ml
1 tbsp	butter	1 tbsp
1 tbsp	Beurre Noisette (p. 112)	1 tbsp
3½ oz	cooked ham	100 g
3½ oz	spinach	100 g
3½ oz	small white mushrooms	100 g
*	salt	*
4 cups/14 oz	macaroni	400 g
1–2 tsp	peppercorns, crushed	1–2 tsp
*	freshly grated nutmeg	*
1 tbsp	finely chopped chives	1 tbsp

Peel and finely chop the onion. Heat 1 tablespoon oil in a pan and sauté the onion over a low heat, until translucent. Add the stock and bay leaf and simmer gently for about 10 minutes. Remove and discard the bay leaf, and stir in the cream. Mix in the butter and Beurre Noisette (p. 112).

Cut the ham into 5–10 mm (¼–½ inch) strips. Select the best spinach leaves, then wash, drain and remove the larger stems. Blanch in boiling salted water for 2 minutes. Drain off the water in a sieve, plunge into iced water, then drain. Squeeze the leaves well with your hands, then tear into pieces.

Clean, wipe dry and quarter the mushrooms. Heat some olive oil in a frying pan or skillet, sauté the mushrooms for a few minutes and season with salt.

Boil the macaroni in a pan with plenty of salted water until al dente, following the instructions on the packet, stirring from time to time. Pour into a colander to drain. Return the pasta to the pan.

Add the cream sauce to the pasta and heat through. Stir in the ham, spinach, mushrooms and crushed peppercorns, and adjust the seasoning with salt and nutmeg. Serve the pasta on heated bowls and sprinkle with finely chopped chives.

Spätzle

Swabia

Preparation time:		10 minutes
Cooking time:		10 minutes
Serves:		4

3½ cups/14 oz	plain (all-purpose) flour	400 g
8	eggs	8
*	salt	*
1 tbsp	oil	1 tbsp
1–2 tbsp	melted butter	1–2 tbsp
*	freshly ground black pepper	*
*	freshly grated nutmeg	*

Work the flour with the eggs, 1 teaspoon salt and the oil to a dough in a food processor, or in a bowl using a hand mixer with a dough hook. Continue to knead for 3–5 more minutes, until bubbles appear in the dough.

Bring plenty of salted water to a boil in a large pan and dip the spätzle maker briefly into the hot water. Fill with the dough and slide the box from side to side, dropping the dumplings into the boiling water.

When the dumplings float to the surface, bring to a boil briefly, then turn off the heat. Use a slotted spoon to transfer the dumplings from the water to a frying pan or skillet over medium heat with the butter, and turn to coat well. Season with salt, pepper and nutmeg.

Pearl Barley with Bacon

All regions

Preparation time:		20 minutes
Cooking time:		45 minutes
Serves:		4

3½ oz	pearl barley	100 g
2¾ cups/22 fl oz	vegetable stock	650 ml
1	small bay leaf	1
3 oz	smoked side bacon	80 g
1 tbsp	oil	1 tbsp
1	small carrot	1
3 oz	celeriac	80 g
2¾ oz	leek	70 g
2 tsp	capers	2 tsp
1	clove garlic, halved	1
1	strip unwaxed lemon zest	1
1 tbsp	butter	1 tbsp
*	salt	*
*	freshly ground black pepper	*
1 tbsp	finely chopped chives	1 tbsp

Put the barley in a sieve, wash under cold running water, and let drain. Combine the barley with 500 ml (generous 2 cups/17 fl oz) stock in a pan, bring to a boil and simmer for about 10 minutes. Add the bay leaf, take the pan off the heat, cover with a lid, and leave to swell for 35 minutes. Pour the barley into a sieve to drain. Remove and discard the bay leaf.

Finely dice the bacon. Heat the oil in a frying pan or skillet and fry the bacon until crispy. Drain on paper towels.

Trim and peel the carrot and celeriac. Trim and wash the leek. Dice the vegetables as finely as possible.

Combine the diced vegetables with the remaining stock in a large pan and cook at a gentle simmer for 4 minutes. Add the barley, bacon, capers, halved garlic and lemon zest, and heat through. Mix in the butter and season with salt and pepper. Remove and discard the garlic and lemon zest. Stir in the chives shortly before serving.

Vegetables

Kohlrabi

All regions

Preparation time:	10 minutes
Cooking time:	15 minutes
Serves:	4

4	small kohlrabi	4
1¼ cups/10 fl oz	vegetable stock	300 ml
3 oz	single (light) cream	80 g
2 tbsp	butter	2 tbsp
1 tbsp	Beurre Noisette (p. 112)	1 tbsp
*	salt	*
1	pinch freshly grated nutmeg	1
1 tsp	cornflour (corn starch)	1 tsp
1 tbsp	finely chopped parsley	1 tbsp

Use a sharp knife to thinly peel the kohlrabi, removing any woody parts, then quarter and cut into 3–4-mm (¼-inch) -thick slices or small wedges. Combine with the stock in a wide but shallow pan, cover with a lid and gently simmer until tender, about 12 minutes.

Use a slotted spoon to remove from the pan and set aside. Blend in the cream, butter and Beurre Noisette (p. 112) with a stick (immersion) blender. Season with salt and a pinch of nutmeg. Dissolve the cornflour (corn starch) completely in a little cold water, add to the sauce and briefly bring to the boil. Add the kohlrabi to the sauce and sprinkle with the parsley.

Broccoli with Almond Butter

All regions

Preparation time:	10 minutes
Cooking time:	5 minutes
Serves:	4

½ cup/2 oz	sliced almonds	50 g
4 tbsp	butter	4 tbsp
1	large broccoli	1
3 tbsp	vegetable stock	3 tbsp
*	freshly grated nutmeg	*
*	salt	*
*	freshly ground pepper	*

Toast the almonds in a dry frying pan or skillet over a medium heat, then set aside. Let the frying pan or skillet cool slightly, then melt the butter and mix in the almonds.

Trim and wash the broccoli and cut into individual florets. Peel and slice the stems. Blanch the florets and stems in salted water for 4–5 minutes until just tender, plunge into iced water and drain.

Combine the broccoli with the stock in a frying pan or skillet, heat through and season with salt, pepper and nutmeg. Drizzle with the almond butter to serve.

Vegetables

Carrots and Peas

All regions

Preparation time:		10 minutes
Cooking time:		10 minutes
Serves:		4

1 lb 5 oz	carrots	600 g
2½ tbsp	butter	2½ tbsp
14 oz	frozen peas	400 g
½ cup/3½ fl oz	vegetable stock	100 ml
*	salt	*
*	freshly ground pepper	*
*	sugar	*
*	few sprigs flat-leaf parsley	*

Trim and peel the carrots, and cut into small dice. Melt the butter in a pan over a medium heat. Sauté the carrots while stirring constantly. Add the peas and cook briefly. Add the stock, bring to a boil and reduce the heat. Cover with a lid and simmer for 8–10 minutes.

Wash, shake dry and pluck the parsley then finely chop the leaves.

Season the vegetables with salt, pepper and a pinch of sugar. Sprinkle with parsley and serve.

Mixed Beans

All regions

Preparation time:		5 minutes
Cooking time:		10 minutes
Serves:		4

11 oz	canned butter beans	300 g
11 oz	canned kidney beans	300 g
7 oz	runner beans	200 g
1–2	sprigs savory	1–2
¼ cup/2 fl oz	vegetable stock	60 ml
1	slice garlic	1
1	strip unwaxed lemon zest	1
2 tbsp	butter	2 tbsp
1 tbsp	finely chopped dill	1 tbsp
*	salt	*
*	freshly ground pepper	*

Put the butter beans and kidney beans into a sieve, rinse under cold running water and let drain.

Trim and wash the runner beans, then cut diagonally into 1–2 cm (½–1 inch) lengths. Cook in boiling salted water for 5–8 minutes with the savory until tender. Pour into a sieve then plunge into iced water and let drain.

Put the stock into a small pan with the three types of beans, garlic, and lemon zest and heat through. Add the butter and melt. Season with salt and pepper. Finally, add the dill and remove and discard the garlic and lemon zest.

Broad (Fava) Beans with Bacon

Westphalia

Preparation time:		20 minutes
Cooking time:		15 minutes
Serves:		4

4 lbs 8 oz	fresh broad (fava) beans	2.2 kg
1 lb 2 oz	waxy potatoes	500 g
4 oz	smoked side bacon	120 g
1	onion	1
1 tsp	clarified butter	1 tsp
1 cup/8 fl oz	chicken stock	250 ml
2	sprigs thyme	2
*	salt	*
*	freshly ground pepper	*
*	freshly grated nutmeg	*

Shell the beans and blanch in salted water for a few minutes until just tender. Pour off the cooking water, plunge in iced water and let drain.

Wash, peel and cut the potatoes into 1 cm (½ inch) dice. Cut the bacon into cubes. Peel and finely chop the onion.

Lightly fry the onion and bacon for a few minutes in a large and deep frying pan or skillet, with the clarified butter, over medium heat. Add the potatoes, stock and thyme. Cover with a lid, leaving a small gap, and simmer the potatoes until just tender, about 15 minutes. Finally, mix in the beans and heat through briefly. Add the butter and season with salt, pepper and nutmeg. Remove and discard the thyme.

Mixed Vegetables

All regions

Preparation time:		15 minutes
Cooking time:		10 minutes
Serves:		4

7 oz	broccoli	200 g
7 oz	green asparagus	200 g
2	celery stalks	2
2	carrots	2
⅓ cup/2.5 fl oz	vegetable stock	80 ml
1	clove garlic	1
1	strip unwaxed lemon zest	1
1–2 tbsp	finely chopped parsley	1–2 tbsp
1 tbsp	butter	1 tbsp
*	salt	*
*	freshly ground pepper	*
*	freshly grated nutmeg	*

Trim and wash the broccoli, and cut into individual florets. Peel and slice the stems. Blanch in boiling salted water for a few minutes until tender but firm to the bite, then pour off the water, plunge in iced water and let drain.

Peel the bottom third of the asparagus spears and cut off the woody ends. Cut diagonally into 5–6 cm (2–2¼ inch) lengths. Trim, wash and cut the celery on the diagonal into 1.5-cm (¾-inch) lengths. Trim, peel and quarter the carrots lengthwise, then cut into 5–6 cm (2–2¼ inch) lengths.

Combine the carrots, asparagus and celery with the stock in a deep frying pan or skillet, cover with a lid, leaving a small gap, and braise for 6–7 minutes until tender but firm to the bite. Peel and slice the garlic. Add to the broccoli, lemon zest and parsley and heat through. Add the butter and season the vegetables with salt, pepper and nutmeg.

Green Beans

All regions

Preparation time:		5 minutes
Cooking time:		20 minutes
Serves:		4

1 lb 8 oz	green beans	750 g
3–4	sprigs savory	3–4
1	onion	1
1½ oz	butter	40 g
*	salt	*
*	freshly ground pepper	*

Trim and wash the beans and let drain. Cut into pieces if desired. Bring 2 litres (8½ cups/68 fl oz) salted water to a boil and cook the beans for 8–12 minutes.

Wash, pat dry, pluck and finely chop the savory. Peel and dice the onion.

Melt the butter in a pan and sauté the onion until translucent. Add the savory. Plunge the cooked beans into iced water and let drain. Add to the onions. Season with salt and pepper and mix.

Cauliflower with Breadcrumbs

All regions

Preparation time:		15 minutes
Cooking time:		20 minutes
Serves:		4

4 tbsp	white breadcrumbs	4 tbsp
8 tbsp	butter	8 tbsp
1 lb 8½ oz	cauliflower	700 g
¼ cup/2 fl oz	vegetable stock	60 ml
*	salt	*
*	freshly ground pepper	*
	freshly grated nutmeg	*

Fry the breadcrumbs with half of the butter in a frying pan or skillet over a low heat until golden brown. Season with salt and pepper.

Wash the cauliflower and cut into small florets. Cook in boiling salted water for 6–8 minutes until just tender. Pour into a sieve, plunge into iced water then drain. Put the cauliflower into a deep frying pan or skillet with the stock and heat through again. Add the remaining butter and season with salt and a pinch of nutmeg. When serving, scatter over with the fried breadcrumbs.

Braised Cucumbers

Preparation time:		10 minutes
Cooking time:		15 minutes
Serves:		4

1 lb 2 oz	firm cucumbers	500 g
⅓ cup /2½ fl oz	vegetable stock	70 ml
*	salt	*
*	freshly ground pepper	*
3 tbsp	cold butter	3 tbsp
1 tbsp	finely chopped dill	1 tbsp

Preheat the oven to 180°C/350°F/Gas Mark 4. Peel, halve lengthwise and seed the cucumbers, then cut into 5-mm (¼-inch)-thick slices. Put into a baking pan and add the stock. Season with salt and pepper, put the pan on the middle shelf of the oven and cook for 10 minutes. Turn over and braise for 5 more minutes.

Take the cucumbers out of the oven, pour the braising liquid into a small pan and blend in the butter with a stick (immersion) blender. Add the braised cucumbers and dill to the sauce and adjust the seasoning if necessary.

Stewed Leeks and Mushrooms

Preparation time:		15 minutes
Cooking time:		10 minutes
Serves:		4

2	thin leeks	2
7 oz	small white mushrooms	200 g
1 tbsp	oil	1 tbsp
⅓ cup/2½ fl oz	dry white wine	80 ml
⅔ cup 5 fl oz	vegetable stock	150 ml
1	clove garlic	1
1	strip unwaxed lemon zest	1
4 tbsp	cream	4 tbsp
2 tbsp	butter	2 tbsp
*	freshly ground pepper	*
*	salt	*
1 tbsp	finely chopped parsley	1 tbsp

Trim the leek, removing the dark green outer leaves. Cut the leek lengthwise, then wash and cut into 1–2-cm (½–¾-inch)-wide strips. Clean, wipe dry and slice the mushrooms.

Heat the oil in a pan and sauté the leeks for 2 minutes over a medium heat. Deglaze the pan with the wine and simmer until almost completely reduced.

Add the stock and gently simmer for about 6 minutes. Add the mushrooms. Peel and halve the garlic clove, then add to the vegetables with the lemon zest. Infuse for a few minutes then remove and discard.

Season with salt and pepper. Add the cream. Stir in the butter and let melt, then sprinkle with parsley.

Lentils

Baden-Württemberg

Preparation time:		10 minutes
Cooking time:		50 minutes
Serves:		4

5 oz	small green lentils	150 g
½	onion	½
1 tbsp	oil	1 tbsp
1¼ oz	carrot	30 g
2¼ oz	celeriac	60 g
2¼ oz	leek	60 g
1 tbsp	tomato purée (paste)	1 tbsp
⅓ cup/2½ fl oz	heavy red wine	80 ml
2 cups/17 fl oz	chicken stock	500 ml
1	bay leaf	1
1	strip unwaxed lemon zest	1
2	slices garlic	2
¼ oz	cold butter	10 g
¼ oz	Beurre Noisette (p. 112)	10 g
*	salt	*
*	dried marjoram	*
*	sugar	*
½–1 tbsp	red wine vinegar	½–1 tbsp

Soak the lentils in water for 2 hours, then pour into a sieve to drain. Peel and finely chop the onion.

Heat the oil in a pan and sauté the onion, carrot and celeriac over a low heat. Stir in the tomato purée (paste) and cook briefly. Add the lentils, deglaze the pan with the wine and simmer to reduce a little. Add the vegetables and stock and steep rather than simmer for 45–50 more minutes. Add the bay leaf after 15 minutes of cooking. Towards the end of the cooking time, add the diced leek together with the lemon zest and garlic and let infuse for a few minutes. Finally, remove and discard the zest and garlic. Mix the cold butter into the lentils and season with salt, a pinch of marjoram, sugar and the vinegar.

Pickled Beetroots (Beets)

All regions

Preparation time:		15 minutes
Cooking time:		1 hour 30 minutes
Makes:		2 (1 litre) jars

2½ lbs	medium beetroots (beets)	1.2 kg
1	onion	1
2	small bay leaves	2
1 tsp	cumin seeds	1 tsp
2	cloves garlic, sliced	2
1	pinch cumin seeds	1
1	pinch fennel seeds	1
2	strips unwaxed orange zest	2
10½ cups/ 84 fl oz	white wine vinegar	2.5 litres
3 oz	sugar	85 g
*	salt	*

Wash the beetroots (beets) and boil in salted water until tender, for about 1 hour. Drain in a sieve, plunge into iced water, then drain. Peel, halve and cut into wedges. Peel and cut the onion into small wedges.

Preheat the oven to 200°C/400°F/Gas Mark 6. Put a deep tray on the lowest oven shelf, fill with water to a depth of about 2 cm (1 inch) and cover the bottom of the tray with two paper towels. Fill the jars evenly with the beetroots (beets) and onion wedges together with the spices in layers, pressing firmly.

Combine 600 ml (2½ cups/20 fl oz) water with the vinegar, sugar and 20 g (¾ oz) salt, then bring to a boil and fill the jars. They should be completely covered with liquid. Seal the jars tightly and place them in the tray with space between them. Cook in the oven for 20 minutes, then leave inside the closed oven to cool.

The beetroots (beets) will keep in a cool room for about 6 months.

Sautéed Parsnips (Parsley Roots)

Bavaria

Preparation time:		5 minutes
Cooking time:		15 minutes
Serves:		4

1 lb 9 oz	(parsnip) parsley roots	750 g
⅓ cup/2½ fl oz	vegetable stock	80 ml
1 tbsp	finely chopped parsley	1 tbsp
1 tbsp	cold butter	1 tbsp
1 tbsp	Beurre Noisette (p. 112)	1 tbsp
*	salt	*
*	freshly ground pepper	*
*	freshly grated nutmeg	*

Peel the parsnip (parsley roots) and halve lengthways. Cut the thick top parts into wedges.

Put the stock in a pan, add the parsnip (parsley roots), cover with a lid, leaving a small gap, and braise at boiling point for 12–15 minutes, until tender. Add a little water if necessary. Finally, stir in the cold butter and Beurre Noisette (p. 112) and season with salt, pepper and nutmeg.

Pumpkin and Pearl Barley

All regions

Preparation time:		10 minutes
Cooking time:		40 minutes
Serves:		4

1	onion	1
1	bay leaf	1
3	cloves	3
2¾ oz	pearl barley	75 g
5 oz	Pickled Pumpkin (p. 28)	150 g
1	small piece butter	1
*	salt	*
*	freshly ground pepper	*
½–1 tsp	unwaxed orange zest	½–1 tsp
1 tbsp	pumpkin pickling liquid (p. 28)	1 tbsp
1 tbsp	chives, finely chopped	1 tbsp

Peel the onion and attach the bay leaf by studding with the cloves. Boil the barley in salted water with the studded onion for 30–40 minutes until soft. Drain in a sieve and discard the onion. Rinse the barley under cold running water.

Dice the Pickled Pumpkin (p. 28).

Mix the barley with the pumpkin in a small pan and heat through. Stir in the butter and season with salt, pepper, the orange zest and pickling liquid. Adjust the seasoning if needed and stir in the chives before serving.

Black Salsify

All regions

Preparation time:		15 minutes
Cooking time:		15 minutes
Serves:		4

1¾ lbs	black salsify	800 g
1¼ oz	butter	30 g
⅔ cup/5 fl oz	veal stock	150 ml
*	salt	*
*	freshly ground pepper	*
*	freshly grated nutmeg	*
½ tsp	coriander seeds, crushed	½ tsp
1 tbsp	chervil, finely chopped	1 tbsp

Thoroughly wash the salsify, peel and cut into about 2-cm (¾-inch) chunks.

Sauté the salsify in melted butter. Add the stock and season with salt, pepper, nutmeg and coriander seeds. Cover with a lid and cook over low heat for 12–15 minutes. Sprinkle with chervil.

Brussels Sprouts

All regions

Preparation time:		15 minutes
Cooking time:		15 minutes
Serves:		4

2¼ lbs	Brussels sprouts	1 kg
1	onion	1
4¼ oz	smoked back bacon	125 g
1 tsp	oil	1 tsp
½ cup/3½ fl oz	cream	100 ml
½ tsp	cornflour (corn starch)	½ tsp
*	salt	*
*	freshly ground pepper	*
*	freshly grated nutmeg	*

Clean the Brussels sprouts, remove the outer leaves and trim off a little of the stem, making a crosswise incision in each.

Blanch the Brussels sprouts in boiling salted water, plunge into iced water then drain.

Peel and finely chop the onion. Finely dice the bacon.

Heat the oil in a deep frying pan or skillet over a medium heat and lightly fry the onions and bacon for a few minutes.

Add the Brussels sprouts and heat through. Dissolve the cornflour (corn starch) completely in the cream, add to the Brussels sprouts and simmer lightly for 1–2 minutes. Season with salt, pepper and nutmeg.

Vegetables

Sweetheart Cabbage

Baden-Württemberg

Preparation time:		5 minutes
Cooking time:		15 minutes
Serves:		4

1	head sweetheart cabbage	1
⅔ cup/5 fl oz	chicken stock	150 ml
⅓ cup/2¼ fl oz	apple juice	70 ml
1	pinch unwaxed lemon zest	1
1 tbsp	parsley, finely chopped	1 tbsp
1 tbsp	Beurre Noisette (p. 112)	1 tbsp
*	salt	*
*	freshly ground pepper	*

Trim the cabbage, remove the outer leaves and cut out the stem. Cut the cabbage into diamond shapes, then wash and let drain.

Put the cabbage into a large pan and add the stock. Cover with a lid and braise for 10–15 minutes, stirring often.

Add the apple juice and simmer to reduce a little. Add the lemon zest, parsley, Beurre Noisette (p. 112) and season with salt and pepper.

Spinach

All regions

Preparation time:		10 minutes
Cooking time:		5 minutes
Serves:		4

1 lb 2 oz	spinach	500 g
1	shallot	1
1 tbsp	butter	1 tbsp
3 tbsp	vegetable stock	3 tbsp
*	salt	*
*	freshly ground pepper	*
*	freshly grated nutmeg	*
1	pinch unwaxed lemon zest	1

Select the best spinach leaves, then wash, let drain and remove the larger stems. Peel and finely chop the shallot.

Heat the butter in a frying pan or skillet and sauté the shallot over low heat until translucent. Add the stock, then add the spinach and wilt. Season with salt, pepper, nutmeg and lemon zest.

Creamed Rapini (Broccoli Rabe)

Rhineland

Preparation time:		10 minutes
Cooking time:		5 minutes
Serves:		4

1 lb 2 oz	rapini (broccoli rabe)	500 g
2	shallots	2
1	clove garlic	1
1¼ oz	butter	30 g
1 cup/7 fl oz	single (light) cream	200 ml
*	freshly ground pepper	*
*	freshly grated nutmeg	*
*	salt	*

Select the best greens, wash and cut into roughly 3-cm (¼ inch) lengths (the leaves can also be used).

Peel and dice the shallots and garlic and sauté in a pan with the butter until translucent. Add the wet greens and briefly sauté. Add the cream and season with salt, pepper and nutmeg. Let simmer for 4–5 minutes.

Creamed Spinach with Fried Egg

All regions

Preparation time:		25 minutes
Cooking time:		20 minutes
Serves:		4

2	floury potatoes	2
1¾ lbs	spinach	800 g
1 cup/8 fl oz	single (light) cream	250 ml
4 tbsp	butter	4 tbsp
*	freshly ground pepper	*
*	freshly grated nutmeg	*
4	eggs	4
*	salt	*

Peel, wash, and cut the potatoes into 5-mm (¼-inch) dice. Boil the potatoes in salted water for 10–15 minutes until tender, then drain in a sieve.

Select the best spinach leaves, then wash, let drain and remove the larger stems. Blanch the leaves in salted water for about 3 minutes. Drain in a sieve and plunge into iced water. Let the spinach drain, then squeeze out the excess water with your hands. Very roughly chop the leaves.

Heat the cream in a pan. Put in a blender (or use a stick (immersion) blender) with the potatoes, spinach and half of the butter, and purée. Return the mixture to the pan and warm over low heat. Adjust the seasoning with salt, pepper and nutmeg.

Heat the remaining butter in a large frying pan or skillet. Crack the eggs and slide, side by side, into the frying pan or skillet. Let stand until the white sets, leaving the yolks shiny. Season the egg white with salt and pepper. Serve with the potatoes.

Mashed Peas

Berlin and Hunsrück

Preparation time:		10 minutes
Cooking time:		40 minutes
Serves:		4

7 fl oz	floury potatoes	200 g
1 lbs 8½ oz	frozen peas	750 g
⅔ cup/5 fl oz	vegetable stock	150 ml
3 tbsp	butter	3 tbsp
2 tbsp	single (light) cream	2 tbsp
*	salt	*
*	freshly grated nutmeg	*
4–6	mint leaves	4–6

Wash and boil the potatoes in salted water until tender, then drain, let steam and peel.

Braise the peas in the stock, then drain and put into a bowl. Add the butter and cream and season with salt and nutmeg then blend with a stick (immersion) blender. Press the potatoes through a potato ricer and add to the mixture. Wash and pat dry the mint leaves, finely chop and stir into the mashed peas.

Yellow Pea Purée

Berlin and Rhineland-Palatinate

Preparation time:		10 minutes
Cooking time:		45 minutes
Serves:		4

1	onion	1
9 oz	yellow split peas	250 g
1¼ oz	carrot	30 g
1¼ oz	celeriac	30 g
1 tbsp	butter	1 tbsp
*	salt	*
*	freshly ground pepper	*
1	pinch marjoram, optional	1

Peel and finely chop the onion. Cover the peas with water and bring to a boil. Add the onion and diced vegetables and boil for about 45 minutes.

Drain in a sieve then purée with a stick (immersion) blender. Add the butter and season with salt and pepper and add marjoram if desired.

Teltow Turnips

Preparation time:		15 minutes
Cooking time:		15 minutes
Serves:		4

1¾ lbs	Teltow turnips (with greens)	800 g
1¾ oz	butter	60 g
1 tbsp	sugar	1 tbsp
*	freshly ground pepper	*
*	salt	*
1 cup/8 fl oz	meat stock	250 ml

Remove the leaves from the turnips, leaving only the small young ones. Peel and wash the turnips.

Heat the butter in a casserole (dutch oven), add the turnips and season with sugar, salt and pepper. Glaze for a few minutes while carefully stirring with a wooden spoon. Add the stock, cover with a lid and simmer for 10–15 minutes until cooked.

Take off the lid and, if necessary, reduce the liquid a little. Shake the pan to coat the vegetables with the reduced sauce.

Root Vegetable Purée

All regions

Preparation time:		10 minutes
Cooking time:		20 minutes
Serves:		4

11 oz	carrots	300 g
3	large onions	3
11 oz	celeriac	300 g
1½ cups/ 12 fl oz	vegetable stock	350 ml
6 tbsp	single (light) cream	6 tbsp
*	salt	*
1	pinch freshly grated nutmeg	1
3 tbsp	butter	3 tbsp
1 tbsp	Beurre Noisette (p. 112)	1 tbsp

Trim, peel and cut the carrots, onions and celeriac into 2 cm (1 inch) dice. Combine the diced vegetables with the stock in a pan, cover with a lid and braise over a low heat for 20 minutes, until the vegetables are very soft and the cooking liquid has almost completely evaporated.

Pour the vegetables into a sieve and let drain. Combine with the cream in a food processor, or use a stick (immersion) blender and finely purée. Season well with salt and a pinch of nutmeg. Finally, mix in the butter and Beurre Noisette (p. 112).

Savoy Cabbage

All regions

Preparation time:		10 minutes
Cooking time:		15 minutes
Serves:		4

2¼ lbs	savoy cabbage	1 kg
1	onion	1
1½ oz	butter	40 g
*	salt	*
*	freshly grated nutmeg	*
*	freshly ground pepper	*
½ cup/4 fl oz	vegetable stock	125 ml

Trim the cabbage, removing the outer leaves. Cut the cabbage into eighths and cut out the stem. Wash, let drain and cut the cabbage into thin strips. Peel the onion and finely chop. Melt butter in a pan and briefly sauté the onion. Add the cabbage and sauté. Add the stock, cover with a lid and cook for about 15 minutes. Season with salt, pepper and nutmeg.

Red Cabbage

All regions

Preparation time:		15 minutes
Cooking time:		1 hour 30 minutes
Serves:		4

1¾ lbs	red cabbage	800 g
1 tbsp	icing (confectioners') sugar	1 tbsp
½ cup/3½ fl oz	port	100 ml
1 cup/7 fl oz	heavy red wine	200 ml
½ cup/4 fl oz	vegetable stock	125 ml
1	bay leaf	1
5	allspice berries	5
½ tsp	peppercorns	½ tsp
1	shard of a cinnamon stick	1
2–3 tbsp	Apple Purée (p. 362)	2–3 tbsp
1	strip unwaxed orange peel	1
¾ oz	cold butter	20 g
*	sugar	*
*	salt	*
1 tbsp	mild vinegar	1 tbsp

Trim the cabbage, remove the outer leaves and cut out the stem. Use a grater to shred the cabbage into coarse strips. Lightly caramelise the sugar in a pan, deglaze with the port and red wine and simmer to reduce by two-thirds. Add the cabbage and stock and cover with a lid. Reduce the heat to low and steep rather than simmer for about 1 hour 30 minutes, stirring often.

Add the bay leaf after 1 hour. Put the allspice, peppercorns and cinnamon into a spice bag, close and add to the cabbage.

At the end of the Cooking time: stir the Apple Purée (p. 362) into the cabbage. Add the orange zest, let infuse for a few minutes, remove and discard. Remove the bay leaf and spice bag and add the butter. Adjust the seasoning with salt, sugar and vinegar.

Creamed Savoy Cabbage

All regions

2¼ lbs	savoy cabbage	1 kg
⅓ cup/2¾ fl oz	vegetable stock	80 ml
½ cup/4 fl oz	single (light) cream	120 ml
*	salt	*
*	cayenne pepper	*
*	freshly grated nutmeg	*
*	creamed or grated fresh horseradish	*

Preparation time: 15 minutes
Cooking time: 10 minutes
Serves: 4

Trim the cabbage, remove the outer leaves, cut out the trunk and separate into individual leaves. Remove the ribs and wash the leaves.

Boil the cabbage in salted water for about 10 minutes. Pour into a sieve, plunge into iced water and drain. Press to remove excess water. Cut the leaves into roughly 2 cm (1 inch) pieces.

Heat the cabbage with the stock and cream in a pan and season with salt, cayenne pepper and nutmeg. If desired, stir in 2–3 tablespoons creamed horseradish from a jar, or grate fresh horseradish over the top, to serve.

Sauerkraut

All regions

Preparation time: 10 minutes
Cooking time: 45 minutes
Serves: 4

1	large onion	1
1 tbsp	oil	1 tbsp
1¾ lbs	sauerkraut	800 g
½ cup/3½ fl oz	dry white wine	100 ml
1⅔ cups/14 fl oz	vegetable stock	400 ml
1	thick slice smoked side bacon	1
5	peppercorns	5
2	juniper berries, lightly crushed	2
1	bay leaf	1
2 tbsp	apple purée	2 tbsp
1 tbsp	butter	1 tbsp
1	pinch sugar	1

Peel and finely chop the onion. Heat the oil in a pan and sauté the onion over a low heat, until translucent. Add the sauerkraut and sauté briefly. Deglaze the pan with the wine and simmer until almost completely reduced.

Add the stock and the bacon. Braise over low heat for about 45 minutes. In the meantime, put the peppercorns, juniper berries and bay leaf into a spice bag and close. After cooking for 30 minutes, add the apple purée and the spice bag to the pan.

At the end of the cooking time, remove the spice bag and bacon. Mix in the butter and season the sauerkraut with a pinch of sugar. Adjust the seasoning with salt if desired.

Bavarian-Style Cabbage

Bavaria

Preparation time:		15 minutes
Cooking time:		30 minutes
Serves:		4

½	small white cabbage	½
1	onion	1
1 tbsp	oil	1 tbsp
1	dash apple juice	1
1 cup/7 fl oz	vegetable stock	200 ml
*	salt	*
1	pinch ground cumin	1
1 tbsp	finely chopped parsley	1 tbsp
1 tbsp	butter	1 tbsp
1	dash cider vinegar	1
3½ oz	smoked side bacon	100 g

Clean the cabbage, remove the outer leaves and cut out the stem. Cut the cabbage into diamond shapes.

Peel and finely chop the onion. Heat the oil in a pan and sauté the onion over a medium heat until translucent. Add the cabbage and braise lightly. Deglaze the pan with the apple juice. Add the stock and cook the vegetables for 20–30 minutes until tender.

Season with salt and a pinch of cumin, then stir in the parsley and butter and adjust the seasoning with the cider vinegar. If desired, cut 100 g (3½ oz) of smoked side bacon into small cubes and fry in a frying pan or skillet over a medium heat with 1 tablespoon oil. Take out the bacon, drain on paper towels, and mix with the cooked cabbage.

Celeriac Mash

All regions

Preparation time:		10 minutes
Cooking time:		20 minutes
Serves:		4

12 oz	celeriac	350 g
½ cup/ 3½ fl oz	single (light) cream	100 ml
2 oz	Beurre Noisette (p. 112)	50 g
*	freshly ground pepper	*
*	freshly grated nutmeg	*
*	salt	*

Trim, peel and cut the celeriac into small dice. Heat the cream in a pan, add the diced celeriac, cover with a lid and braise until tender, about 20 minutes.

Use a slotted spoon to take out the celeriac, transfer to a food processor and purée, adding as much cooking liquid as necessary for consistency. Add the Beurre Noisette (p. 112). Season with salt, pepper and a little nutmeg.

Cauliflower Gratin

All regions

Preparation time:		15 minutes
Cooking time:		25 minutes
Serves:		4

1	large head cauliflower	1
12 oz	cooked ham joint	350 g
2 tbsp	butter	2 tbsp
1½ oz	plain (all-purpose) flour	40 g
1 cup/7 fl oz	cold vegetable stock	200 ml
1 cup/7 fl oz	cold milk	200 ml
3 tbsp	cream	3 tbsp
3 oz	grated Emmental cheese	80 g
*	salt	*
*	freshly ground pepper	*
*	freshly grated nutmeg	*
*	dressed lettuce, to serve	*
*	bread, to serve	*

Preheat the oven to 220°C/425°F/Gas Mark 7. Trim the cauliflower, cut into individual florets and wash. Boil for 3–4 minutes in salted water until just cooked, then pour into a sieve to drain.

Dice the ham. Grease an ovenproof dish and spread out the cauliflower and ham inside it.

Melt the butter in a large pan and toast the flour while stirring constantly. Stir in the butter and milk. Gently simmer for 10 minutes, stirring often. Remove the pan from the heat, add in the cream and cheese and season with salt, pepper and nutmeg.

Spread the sauce evenly over the cauliflower, put the dish inside the lowest third of the oven and cook for 10–15 minutes until golden brown. Accompany with dressed butterhead lettuce and bread.

White Asparagus with Butter and Ham

All regions

Preparation time:		10 minutes
Cooking time:		10 minutes
Serves:		4

*	salt	*
1 tbsp	sugar	1 tbsp
4½ lbs	white asparagus	2 kg
5–7 oz	butter	150–200 g
7 oz	Black Forest ham	200 g
*	Pancake Scrapings (p. 282), to serve	*
*	Boiled Potatoes (p. 260), to serve	*

Peel the asparagus spears and cut off the woody ends. Bring 2 litres (8½ cups/68 fl oz) water to a boil in a wide pan. Add 1–2 tablespoons of salt and the sugar. Cook the asparagus for 15–20 minutes, depending on thickness. Take the asparagus out of the cooking water and drain briefly.

Melt the butter in another pan. Arrange the asparagus and ham on plates. Drizzle with the butter and serve with Pancake Scrapings (p. 282), or Boiled Potatoes (p. 260), if you like.

Stuffed Bell Peppers

All regions

4	red bell peppers	4
1	onion	1
1 tbsp	oil	1 tbsp
9 oz	minced beef	250 g
9 oz	minced pork	250 g
1–2 tbsp	tomato purée (paste)	1–2 tbsp
4¼ oz	long-grain rice	125 g
¾ cup/6 fl oz	chicken stock	175 ml
*	paprika	*
*	salt	*
*	freshly ground pepper	*

Preparation time:		20 minutes
Cooking time:		40 minutes
Serves:		4

Cut the tops of the peppers off and set aside to use as caps. Leave the stems on. Seed and wash the peppers. Peel and dice the onion.

Heat the oil in a frying pan or skillet and sauté the onion until translucent. Add the minced meat and fry until it's crumbly and lightly coloured.

Stir in the tomato purée (paste) and rice and cook lightly. Add 100 ml (½ cup/3½ fl oz) stock and season with salt, pepper and paprika.

Pour the remaining stock into a casserole dish. Stuff the peppers with the mince. Preheat the oven to 180°C/350°F/Gas Mark 4.

Stand the peppers side by side in the dish and cover with the caps. Put the dish on the middle shelf of the oven and braise until tender, about 40 minutes.

Ham-Wrapped Endives

All regions

Preparation time:		10 minutes
Cooking time:		30 minutes
Serves:		4

4	Belgian endives	4
8	slices ham	8
1¼ oz	butter	30 g
1½ oz	all-purpose flour	40 g
1 cup/7 fl oz	cold vegetable stock	200 ml
1 cup/7 fl oz	cold milk	200 ml
3 tbsp	cream	3 tbsp
3 oz	grated emmental or gouda cheese	80 g
*	salt	*
*	freshly ground pepper	*
*	freshly grated nutmeg	*

Trim the endives, removing any wilted outer leaves if necessary, then halve lengthwise, wash and let drain. Cut out each of the stems but keep the leaves attached.

Wrap each endive half with a slice of ham. Arrange the endive halves, rounded-side up, side by side in a large ovenproof dish. Preheat the oven to 180°C/350°F/Gas Mark 4.

Melt the butter in a large pan and toast the flour while stirring constantly. Stir in the butter and milk. Gently simmer the sauce for 10 minutes, stirring often. Remove the pan from the heat, add in the cream and cheese and season with salt, pepper and nutmeg.

Spread the sauce evenly over the endives, put the dish inside the lowest third of the oven to cook until golden brown, about 20 minutes.

Cold Savoy Cabbage Rolls

Southern Germany

Preparation time:		20 minutes
Cooling time:		1 hour
Serves:		4

9 oz	cooked ham joint	250 g
7 oz	finely minced veal	200 g
1 tsp	brandy	1 tsp
4	sheets gelatine	4
2 tbsp	veal stock (from a jar)	2 tbsp
1 cup/7 fl oz	double (heavy) cream	200 ml
16	large savoy cabbage leaves	16
8	slices cooked ham	8
*	freshly ground pepper	*
*	salt	*
*	dressed lettuce, to serve	*

Put the ham and the minced veal through a mincer. Add the brandy, season with salt and pepper and blend to a smooth paste in a food processor.

Soften the gelatine in cold water, squeeze well and add to the hot stock. Carefully stir into the stuffing mixture then whip the cream to soft peaks and stir in.

Briefly blanch the cabbage leaves in salted water, then plunge into iced water. Lay side by side over a cloth and let drain.

Trim the ribs until flat, then lay one slice of ham over 8 leaves. Cover with another leaf and spread with the stuffing. Fold the edges over the stuffing and roll up lengthwise. Cover the rolls with clingfilm (plastic wrap) to prevent from opening. Let stand in the refrigerator for about 1 hour.

Cut the rolls into slices and serve on plates accompanied with dressed lettuce leaves.

Cabbage Rolls

Berlin and Brandenburg

Preparation time:		25 minutes
Cooking time:		45 minutes
Serves:		4

½	small white cabbage	½
2 oz	toasted bread	50 g
½ cup/3½ fl oz	milk	100 ml
2	onions	2
7 oz	minced veal	200 g
7 oz	minced pork	200 g
1	egg	1
1 tsp	hot mustard	1 tsp
*	salt	*
½	unwaxed lemon, zested	½
*	freshly ground pepper	*
*	dried marjoram	*
*	freshly grated nutmeg	*
1 tbsp	finely chopped parsley	1 tbsp
1 tbsp	Beurre Noisette (p. 112)	1 tbsp
3 oz	celeriac	80 g
½	carrot	½
1 tsp	icing (confectioners') sugar	1 tsp
1 tbsp	tomato purée (paste)	1 tbsp
⅔ cup/5 fl oz	red wine	150 ml
1 cup/8 fl oz	chicken stock	250 ml

Remove the outer leaves from the cabbage and cut out the hard stem. Bring plenty of water to a boil in a large pan, enough to cover the whole cabbage. Pierce deep into the cavity with a meat fork and immerse the cabbage for 1–2 minutes in the boiling water, until the outermost leaf become supple. Take the cabbage out of the water and detach the leaf. Repeat the process until you have a total of 4 leaves.

Pat the leaves dry and halve, cutting out the thick ribs. Lay each leaf, slightly overlapping, over a dish cloth, cover with another cloth and roll flat with a rolling pin.

Remove the crust from the bread, cut into cubes and soak in the milk. Peel and finely chop 1 onion and blanch for 2 minutes. Combine the minced veal and pork with the soaked bread, onion, egg, mustard and lemon zest and mix well. Season with salt, pepper, marjoram, a pinch of nutmeg and the parsley.

Put a quarter of the stuffing on each cabbage leaf. Fold the longer sides over the filling and roll up from the narrower side. Tie with string to secure. Heat 2 table-spoons of Beurre Noisette (p. 112) in a frying pan or skillet and lightly fry the rolls on all sides.

Peel the remaining onion and trim and peel the celeriac and carrot. Cut the vegetables into 5 mm (¼ inch) dice. Put the icing (confectioners') sugar into a roasting pan over a medium heat and lightly caramelise. Add the vegetables and sauté. Stir in the tomato purée (paste) and cook briefly. Deglaze with a third of the wine and reduce until syrupy. Add the remaining wine, half at a time, reducing each time. Add the stock and cabbage rolls, half-cover with a lid and gently simmer for about 45 minutes. Arrange the rolls with the sauce on plates and serve.

Vegetable Casserole

All regions

Preparation time:		20 minutes
Cooking time:		1 hour
Serves:		4

1	onion	1
1	red bell pepper	1
3–4 tbsp	vegetable stock	3–4 tbsp
3½ oz	broccoli	100 g
1	courgette (zucchini)	1
1 lb 2 oz	all-purpose potatoes	500 g
2 tbsp	butter	2 tbsp
1½ oz	plain (all-purpose) flour	40 g
1 cup/7 fl oz	cold vegetable stock	200 ml
1 cup/7 fl oz	cold milk	200 ml
5 oz	grated emmental cheese	150 g
1 tsp	mixed dried herbs	1 tsp
1	clove garlic, finely grated	1
½ tsp	grated unwaxed lemon zest	½ tsp
*	freshly ground pepper	*
*	freshly grated nutmeg	*
*	salt	*

Peel the onion and cut into about 1.5-cm (¾-inch)-thick slices. Halve, trim, seed and wash the pepper. Cut into about 2-cm- (1-inch-) wide pieces.

Combine the onion, pepper and stock in a small pan. Cover with greaseproof (wax) paper and simmer for 5 minutes.

Wash and cut the broccoli into small florets. Boil until tender but firm to the bite in salted water, then plunge into iced water, then drain.

Peel, wash and cut the courgette (zucchini) into 5-mm (¼-inch) rounds. Peel, wash, and cut the potatoes into very thin slices. Preheat the oven to 180°C/350°F/Gas Mark 4.

Melt the butter in a pan over a low heat, stir in the flour and lightly toast for a few minutes while stirring constantly. Gradually add the stock and milk and continue stirring constantly. Gently simmer the sauce for 10 minutes, stirring often.

Mix the sauce with the onion and pepper mixture, broccoli, courgette (zucchini) and potatoes. Mix in half of the cheese. Add the mixed herbs, garlic and lemon zest then season with salt, pepper and a little nutmeg.

Grease a casserole dish and fill with the mixture and sprinkle the remaining cheese over the top. Put the dish on the middle shelf of the oven and bake for 45–50 minutes until golden brown.

Kale with Pinkel, Kassler and Mettenden

Lower Saxony and Bremen

Preparation time:		25 minutes
Cooking time:		1 hour 30 minutes
Serves:		4

3¼ lbs	kale	1.5 kg
2	onions	2
2 tbsp	lard or goose fat	2 tbsp
1–2 tsp	sugar	1–2 tsp
2 cups/17 fl oz	chicken or vegetable stock	500 ml
2 tbsp	rolled oats	2 tbsp
9 oz	smoked bacon joint	250 g
4	slices Kassler (smoked pork)	4
4	Mettenden sausages	4
4	Pinkel (groats) sausages	4
*	freshly ground pepper	*
*	salt	*
*	Boiled Potatoes (p. 260), to serve	*
3½ oz	mustard (medium-strength)	100 g

Trim the kale, select the best leaves, cut off the stems and cut out the large ribs. Thoroughly wash the leaves and let drain. Blanch the leaves in boiling salted water for 2 minutes, then plunge into iced water and squeeze out the water. Cut the leaves into small pieces.

Peel and dice the onions. Heat the fat in a large pan and sauté the onions. Add the sugar and kale and sauté for a few minutes. Add enough stock to allow the kale to float a little, cover with a lid and gently simmer for 1 hour.

Stir in the oats and season with salt and pepper. Then add the bacon, Kassler, Mettenden and Pinkel sausages, replace the lid leaving a small gap, and continue to simmer until the meat is cooked, about 30 minutes. Take out the bacon, cut into slices and return to the pan.

Serve the kale with the sausages and meat in heated plates, accompanied with Boiled Potatoes (p. 260) and mustard.

Vegetables

Fried Potatoes with Sausages and Eggs (Kartoffelgröstl)

Southern Germany

Preparation time:		30 minutes
Cooking time:		40 minutes
Serves:		4

1 lb 2 oz	waxy potatoes	500 g
1	onion	1
3½ oz	runner green beans	100 g
1–2 tbsp	Beurre Noisette (p. 112)	1–2 tbsp
*	salt	*
*	freshly ground pepper	*
¼ tsp	ground cumin	¼ tsp
½ tbsp	dried marjoram	½ tbsp
½ tsp	oil	½ tsp
10	pan-fried Nuremberg sausages	10
1 tbsp	finely chopped parsley	1 tbsp
4	eggs	4

Thoroughly wash the unpeeled potatoes and boil until tender in salted water. Drain, let steam and peel the potatoes while as hot as possible. Let cool, then cut into slices.

Peel the onion and cut into 1–1.5 cm (½–¾ inch) slices. Trim, wash and cut the beans diagonally into 1–1.5-cm (½–¾ inch) lengths. Cook in boiling salted water for 4–5 minutes until almost tender. Pour into a sieve, plunge into iced water then drain.

Heat 1 tablespoon Beurre Noisette (p. 112) in a frying pan or skillet, fry the onions until golden brown and set aside. Fry the potatoes in batches in the same frying pan or skillet. Season with cumin, marjoram, salt and pepper. Return the onion to the pan and add the beans. Mix well.

Heat the oil in another frying pan or skillet and fry the sausages on all sides. Drain on paper towels and halve crosswise on the diagonal (if using boiled beef, cut into 2-cm (1–inch) chunks, add to the potatoes in the frying pan or skillet and heat through). Mix the sausages with the potatoes. Season everything with salt and stir in the parsley. Add a little more Beurre Noisette, if desired.

Fry the eggs sunny-side up in the frying pan or skillet and serve over the pan-fried meat and potatoes.

Stuffed Cucumbers with Tomato Sauce

All regions

Preparation time:		30 minutes
Cooking time:		30 minutes
Serves:		4

For the stuffing:		
4 oz	toasted bread	120 g
1	small onion	1
5 oz	smoked back bacon	150 g
3	eggs	3
½ cup/4 fl oz	milk	120 ml
1 tbsp	hot mustard	1 tbsp
2	cloves garlic, finely chopped	2
1	unwaxed lemon, zested	1
*	sweet paprika	*
11 oz	minced veal	300 g
8 oz	minced pork	225 g
8 oz	minced beef	225 g
½–1 tbsp	finely chopped dill	½–1 tbsp
½–1 tbsp	finely chopped parsley	½–1 tbsp
*	salt	*

For the cucumbers and sauce:		
5 oz	chicken stock	150 g
11 oz	tinned chopped tomatoes	300 g
½	clove garlic, finely chopped	½
½ tbsp	dried oregano	½ tbsp
*	sugar	*
4	firm cucumbers	4
*	salt	*
*	freshly ground pepper	*
*	Boiled Potatoes (p. 260), to serve	*

For the stuffing: Cut the bread into cubes and put into a bowl. Peel and finely chop the onion. Combine with 100 ml (½ cup/3½ fl oz) of water in a frying pan or skillet and sauté for a few minutes, boiling off all the water until soft. Cut the bacon into small cubes and fry in a frying pan or skillet over a medium heat until crispy. Drain in a sieve.

Combine the eggs with the milk in a bowl. Add the mustard, garlic and lemon zest, season with a little salt and paprika, and blend with a stick (immersion) blender. Mix the milk and egg mixture with the bread and soak for 5 minutes. Mix the three types of minced meat with the softened bread and mix in the onion, dill and parsley. Preheat the oven to 220°C/425°F/Gas Mark 7.

For the cucumbers and sauce: Combine the stock with the tomatoes and garlic in a pan and bring to a boil. Season with oregano, salt, pepper and a pinch of sugar, mix thoroughly using a stick (immersion) blender, and transfer to a deep baking pan or large ovenproof dish.

Peel and halve the cucumbers lengthwise. Use a spoon to scoop out the seeds. Fill the cucumber halves with the stuffing and lay in the sauce. Cover the pan with aluminium foil, put on the middle shelf inside the oven and bake for about 30 minutes. Remove the foil after 20 minutes. Serve the stuffed cucumbers on plates with the sauce and Boiled Potatoes (p. 260).

Lentils with Spätzle

Baden-Württemberg

Soaking time:	2 hours
Preparation time:	20 minutes
Cooking time:	25 minutes
Serves:	4

For the lentils:

5 oz	brown or small green lentils	150 g
½	onion	½
1¼ oz	carrot	30 g
1¼ oz	celeriac	30 g
1¼ oz	leek	30 g
1 tbsp	oil	1 tbsp
2 tsp	tomato purée (paste)	2 tsp
⅓ cup/2 ½ fl oz	red wine	80 ml
2 cups/17 fl oz	chicken stock	500 ml
1	bay leaf	1
*	Cayenne pepper	*
½–1 tbsp	red wine vinegar	½–1 tbsp
*	salt	*

For the spätzle:

14 oz	plain (all-purpose) flour	400 g
8	eggs	8
1 tbsp	oil	1 tbsp
1 tbsp	clarified butter	1 tbsp
*	salt	*
*	freshly ground pepper	*
*	small Vienna sausages, optional	*

For the lentils: Soak the lentils in water for 2 hours, then let drain. Cut the vegetables into small dice, and peel and finely chop the onion.

Sauté the onion, carrot, and celeriac in a pan with oil over low heat until translucent. Stir in the tomato purée (paste), cook a little, then add the soaked lentils. Deglaze the pan with the wine and simmer to reduce a little. Add the stock and steep rather than simmer for 20–25 minutes.

Add the bay leaf after 15 minutes and reduce at the end of the cooking time. Finally, add the leek and season with salt, a pinch of cayenne powder and vinegar.

For the spätzle: Work the flour with the eggs, 1 teaspoon salt and oil, using a food processor or hand mixer with a dough hook, and knead for 3–5 minutes until bubbles start to form in the dough. Alternatively, stir the dough with a wooden spoon.

Bring plenty of salted water to a boil in a large pan. Immerse the spätzle maker briefly into the boiling water, fill with the dough and slide the box from side to side, dropping the dumplings into the boiling water. When the dumplings float to the surface, bring to a boil briefly, then turn off the heat. Use a slotted spoon to take the dumplings out of the water, let drain, lightly sauté in the clarified butter and season with salt and pepper.

Serve the lentils with the dumplings on plates. They can be accompanied with small Vienna sausages, if you like.

Celeriac Schnitzel

All regions

Preparation time:	15 minutes
Cooling time:	1 hour
Cooking time:	15 minutes
Serves:	4

4¼ oz	unsalted butter, softened	125 g
1–2 tsp	hot mustard	1–2 tsp
1 tbsp	rosemary finely chopped	1 tbsp
1 tbsp	parsley, finely chopped	1 tbsp
1 tbsp	grated hard cheese	1 tbsp
1	clove garlic, finely grated	1
1¼ oz	white breadcrumbs	30 g
*	oil, for greasing	*
1	small celeriac	1
*	salt	*
*	freshly ground pepper	*

Whip the butter until fluffy. Mix in the mustard, rosemary, parsley, cheese, garlic and breadcrumbs and season with salt and pepper. Use greaseproof (wax) paper to roll up the mixture into a cylinder of about 3-cm (1¼-inches) in diameter and refrigerate for 30 minutes–1 hour.

Turn on the oven grill. Grease a baking sheet with oil. Cut 4 x 1.5 cm (¾ inch) slices from the celeriac. Peel the celeriac slices and cook in salted water for 10–15 minutes, until almost tender. Drain on paper towels, then lay the slices side by side on the baking sheet.

Cut the cold butter mixture into thin slices and cover the celeriac with several overlapped slices. Place the baking sheet on the middle shelf of the oven and grill until golden brown, about 4 minutes.

Vegetables

Bread Dumplings in a Creamy Mushroom Sauce

Bavaria

Preparation time:		10 minutes
Cooking time:		30 minutes
Serves:		4

2 cups/17 fl oz	vegetable stock	500 ml
3 tbsp	dried white mushrooms	3 tbsp
1	onion	1
½	carrot	½
2 oz	celeriac	50 g
1 cup/7 fl oz	single (light) cream	200 ml
1–2 tbsp	cornflour (cornstarch)	1–2 tbsp
4½ tbsp	cold butter	4½ tbsp
1 lb 5 oz	fresh mushrooms	600 g
1–2 tbsp	oil	1–2 tbsp
*	ground cumin	*
1	pinch unwaxed lemon zest	1
1 tbsp	chopped parsley	1 tbsp
*	salt	*
*	freshly ground pepper	*
8	Bread Dumplings (p. 286)	8

Heat the stock, add the dried mushrooms and gently simmer for 20 minutes. Drain the mushrooms in a sieve and collect the stock. Let the mushrooms cool a little and finely chop. Trim, peel and cut the onion, carrot, and celeriac into 3 mm (¼ inch) dice. Simmer in the mushroom-infused stock for 3–4 minutes, drain in a sieve and collect the stock.

Add the cream to the stock and bring to a simmer. Dissolve the cornflour (corn starch) completely in a little cold water, stir into the sauce and simmer for 2 minutes. Use a stick (immersion) blender to mix in 4 tablespoons of butter. Add the finely chopped mushrooms and diced vegetables to the sauce and season with salt.

Clean the fresh mushrooms, if necessary wipe dry, and cut into pieces. Heat the oil in a frying pan or skillet and sauté the mushrooms in batches over a medium heat for about 3 minutes. Season with a pinch of cumin, the lemon zest and salt and pepper. Add the remaining butter and stir in the parsley.

Mix the sautéed mushrooms with the cream sauce and adjust the seasoning if you like. Pour the sauce onto warmed plates and arrange the dumplings on top.

Chicken-Stuffed Mushrooms

All regions

Preparation time:		20 minutes
Cooking time:		15 minutes
Serves:		4

8	medium white mushrooms	8
*	salt	*
*	freshly ground pepper	*
½	onion	½
8 oz	spinach	200 g
5¼ oz	skinless chicken breast	150 g
1 tbsp	olive oil	1 tbsp
*	salt	*
*	freshly ground pepper	*
1	small clove garlic	1
2 tbsp	minced parsley, basil, chervil	2 tbsp
*	freshly grated nutmeg	*
2 tbsp	warm Beurre Noisette (p. 112)	2 tbsp
4	slices Emmental cheese	4

Clean and wipe the mushrooms dry. Cut off the stems and mince. Set aside the caps. Mince the onion. Select the best spinach leaves, then wash and let drain. Wash, pat dry, and cut the meat into 1 cm (½ inch) chunks.

Briefly fry the meat on all sides in a skillet with 1 tablespoon oil over medium heat. Season with salt and pepper and set aside. Sweat the onion and mushroom stems in the skillet with the meat juices, adding a little more oil if necessary. Add the spinach and garlic and sweat, until the leaves wilt. Add the meat and herbs, and season with nutmeg.

Preheat the oven to 160°C/320°F/Gas Mark 3. Brush the mushroom caps all over with olive oil, and season the underside with salt and pepper. Lightly fry the rounded side of the caps in a dry skillet over medium heat. Stuff the caps with the warm spinach and chicken mixture, arrange in a baking pan, and bake in the oven for 7–8 minutes.

Take the mushrooms out of the oven and turn on the broiler. Halve the cheese slices and lay, slightly overlapped, over the mushrooms. Put the mushrooms on the middle shelf inside the oven and grill for 3–4 minutes, then serve.

Vegetables

Sautéed Mushrooms

All regions

Preparation time:		5 minutes
Cooking time:		10 minutes
Serves:		4

14 oz	porcini mushrooms	400 g
1–2 tsp	oil	1–2 tsp
*	salt	*
*	freshly ground pepper	*
1 tbsp	butter	1 tbsp
1 tbsp	parsley, finely chopped	1 tbsp
*	fresh herbs, to serve	*
*	bacon, diced and fried, optional	*

Wipe the porcini clean. Wipe off any dirt from the caps or stems. Cut off any spongy parts from larger porcini mushrooms.

Cut the clean mushrooms into about 5-mm (¼-inch)-thick slices. Divide the oil into two large frying pan or skillets and heat. Spread the mushroom slices out inside both frying pan or skillets and sauté for about 2 minutes.

Season with salt and pepper. Stir in the butter and sprinkle with the parsley. The mushrooms can also be served with herbs and diced and fried bacon.

Mixed Vegetables with Crayfish

Leipzig and Saxony

Preparation time:		15 minutes
Cooking time:		1 hour
Serves:		4

12	live crayfish	12
½ tsp	cumin seeds	½ tsp
2¼ oz	butter	60 g
1¼ oz	dried black morel mushrooms	30 g
½	small head cauliflower	½
1	kohlrabi	1
11 oz	white asparagus	300 g
11 oz	small carrots	300 g
*	salt	*
*	sugar	*
11 oz	frozen peas	300 g
½ cup/3½ fl oz	vegetable stock	100 ml
*	freshly ground pepper	*
*	freshly grated nutmeg	*

Preheat the oven to 120°C/250°F/Gas Mark ½. Cook the crayfish with the cumin in boiling salted water for 1–2 minutes. Transfer to a sieve and refresh in iced water. Separate the tails and claws from the bodies. Peel the tail meat. Make a cut along the back of the crayfish body and remove the entrails. Crack the claws and take out the meat. Set aside all of the meat in the refrigerator.

Thoroughly wash the carcasses and let drain. Transfer to a baking pan and roast in the oven for 30–40 minutes, then crumble.

Melt 50 g (1¼ oz) butter in a frying pan or skillet, add 2 tablespoons crumbled crayfish carcasses and let infuse for 15 minutes over a low heat. Filter the crayfish butter through a sieve.

Put the mushrooms into 500 ml (2 cups/17 fl oz) water in a pan and bring to a boil. Let swell for 5 minutes, then drain in a sieve. Trim the cauliflower, cut into individual florets, and wash. Trim, peel and cut the kohlrabi into 1-cm (½-inch)-thick batons. Peel the asparagus spears and cut off the woody ends. Cut into 5 cm (2 inch) lengths. Trim, peel and cut the carrot into thin batons.

Heat plenty of water in a pan and season well with salt and sugar. Blanch the asparagus, carrots, cauliflower, kohlrabi and peas, separately, in the water until tender but firm to the bite, then remove with a skimmer, plunge into iced water, and let drain.

Heat the vegetables with the rest of the butter in a large pan with the stock over a medium heat and season with salt, pepper and nutmeg. Warm the crayfish meat in the crayfish butter in a pan over low heat. Serve with the vegetables in warmed plates.

Desserts

Strawberry Cream Cheese Dessert

All regions

Preparation time:		20 minutes
Resting time:		4 hours
Serves:		4

1¾ cups/7 oz	strawberries, halved	200 g
⅔ cup/4¼ oz	Quark	125 g
½ cup/3¼ oz	caster (superfine) sugar	90 g
6 tbsp	lemon juice	6 tbsp
½	vanilla bean, seeds scraped	½
2	egg whites	2
*	salt	*
1 cup/8 fl oz	double (heavy) cream	250 ml

Trim and halve the strawberries. Put into a mixing bowl and purée with a stick (immersion) blender. Press through a sieve into a bowl (it should make about 130 g/4½ oz strawberry purée).

Mix the Quark in a bowl with 2–3 tablespoons sugar, the lemon juice, vanilla seeds and strawberry purée.

Beat the egg whites with a pinch of salt and a third of the remaining sugar until creamy, then gradually add the remaining sugar and beat to stiff peaks. Whip the cream to soft peaks. Loosely mix the beaten egg whites with the whipped cream, then fold into the Quark mixture.

Put a sieve over a bowl and line with a dish cloth. Put the cream cheese mixture into the sieve, cover with the overhanging sides of the cloth and refrigerate. Let drain for 3–4 hours. Fill a bowl with the strawberry cream cheese or divide into individual portions and serve immediately.

Rhubarb and Cream Cheese Dessert

Lower Saxony

Preparation time:		30 minutes
Resting time:		1 hour 30 minutes
Serves:		4

1 lb 2 oz	young rhubarb	500 g
⅔ cup/4¼ oz	caster (superfine) sugar	120 g
1	vanilla bean, seeds scraped	1
⅔ cup/5 oz	whole-milk yoghurt	150 g
½	unwaxed lemon	½
1¼ cups/9 oz	Quark	250 g
½ cup/4 fl oz	double (heavy) cream	125 ml
4	sprigs lemon balm	4

Wash, peel and cut the rhubarb into about 2 cm (¾ inch) lengths. Put into a bowl, sprinkle with 80 g (scant ½ cup/2¾ oz) of sugar and let rest for about 1 hour 30 minutes.

Stir the vanilla seeds into the yoghurt together with the lemon zest, juice and remaining sugar.

Transfer the rhubarb with its juice and the vanilla bean to a pan, heat and simmer for a few minutes. The rhubarb should be soft but still whole. Put into a sieve and collect the juice. Discard the vanilla bean.

Put the Quark into a bowl and mix with the yoghurt and rhubarb juice to a soft and smooth cream. Whip the cream to stiff peaks and fold into the Quark cream.

Divide the cream cheese between four bowls, cover with the rhubarb pieces and garnish with the lemon balm.

Bavarian Cream

Bavaria

Preparation time:		10 minutes
Chilling time:		2 hours
Serves:		4

2	sheets gelatine	2
1¼ cups/10 fl oz	double (heavy) cream	300 ml
3	egg yolks	3
½ cup/2 oz	icing (confectioners') sugar	50 g
2	vanilla beans, seeds scraped	2
1 tbsp	kirsch	1 tbsp

Soften the gelatine sheets in cold water. Put the cream into a mixing bowl and whip to soft peaks with a hand mixer. Combine the egg yolks with the sugar and vanilla seeds in a bowl and whisk until light and fluffy.

Heat the kirsch in a small pan and remove from the heat. Squeeze the gelatine well, add to the kirsch and stir to dissolve, then mix into the egg mixture. Use a whisk to mix a third of the whipped cream into the egg mixture and fold in the remaining cream.

Fill individual moulds about 120 ml (½ cup/4 fl oz) capacity with the Bavarian Cream, cover and let set in the refrigerator for about 2 hours.

When serving, the moulds can be dipped to below the rim in hot water for 7–8 seconds before turning out onto dessert plates.

'Berlin Air'

Berlin

Preparation time:		25 minutes
Chilling time:		2 hours
Serves:		4

2¼ cups/9 oz	strawberries	250 g
⅔ cup/3 oz	raspberries	80 g
½ cup/3 oz	blueberries	80 g
1 tbsp	icing (confectioners') sugar	1 tbsp
4 tsp	orange liqueur	4 tsp
1½	sheets gelatine	1½
3	eggs	3
2 tbsp	white wine	2 tbsp
⅓ cup/2¾ oz	caster (superfine) sugar	70 g
4 tbsp	lemon juice	4 tbsp
*	salt	*

Wash, trim and clean the strawberries. Set aside 80 g (3 oz) small strawberries. Put the remainder in a mixing bowl and purée with a stick (immersion) blender. Press through a sieve. Select the best raspberries and blueberries, then wash and carefully pat them dry.

Mix the set-aside strawberries with the raspberries and blueberries and set aside about 2 tablespoons mixed berries for the garnish. Mix the rest of the berries with the strawberry purée and add the icing (confectioners') sugar and orange liqueur.

Soften the gelatine sheets in cold water. Separate the eggs. Combine the wine with 45 g (¼ cup/1¾ oz) sugar, the lemon juice and egg yolks in a pan and bring to a boil while stirring constantly. Squeeze the gelatine well and stir into the hot mixture.

Beat the egg whites, with the rest of the sugar and a pinch of salt, to soft peaks. Take some of the beaten egg white and mix into the egg mixture. Then add this mixture to the beaten egg whites and fold gently.

Divide the marinated berries into dessert glasses, cover with the egg cream. Chill in the refrigerator for 2 hours, then serve.

Riesling Jelly

Rhineland-Palatinate

Preparation time:		25 minutes
Marinating time:		30 minutes
Chilling time:		3 hours
Serves:		4

1 lb 2 oz	white grapes	500 g
3 tbsp	grappa	3 tbsp
4 tbsp	icing (confectioners') sugar	4 tbsp
6	sheets gelatine	6
1½ cups/13 fl oz	riesling wine	375 ml
1 cup/7 oz	double (heavy) cream	200 ml

Wash the grapes, remove the stems, peel, halve and seed. Mix the grapes with the grappa and sugar, cover and marinate for 30 minutes.

Soften the gelatine sheets in cold water. Heat the wine, squeeze the gelatine well, then dissolve in the wine.

Put the grapes into a mould, fill with the wine gelatine mixture and let set in the refrigerator for at least 3 hours.

Run a knife tip around the inside edge of the mould to loosen the jelly, dip the mould quickly in hot water and turn out the jelly. Whip the cream to soft peaks, then serve with the jelly.

German-Style Zabaglione (Weinschaumcreme)

All regions

Preparation time:		20 minutes
Cooking time:		15 minutes
Serves:		4

5	egg yolks	5
¼ cup/2 oz	caster (superfine) sugar	50 g
1 cup/7 fl oz	sweet white wine	200 ml
1 tbsp	lemon juice	1 tbsp
1 tbsp	honey	1 tbsp
1	pinch ground allspice	1
7 oz	small seedless white grapes	200 g
1 tbsp	icing (confectioners') sugar	1 tbsp
⅓ cup/2½ fl oz	port	80 ml
2 tbsp	cold butter	2 tbsp
1	pinch grated nutmeg	1
1 tbsp	grappa	1 tbsp

Mix the egg yolks with the sugar, wine, lemon juice, honey and allspice in a bowl. Place over a bain-marie and whisk to a thick and airy cream, while ensuring that the temperature does not exceed 80°C/175°F.

Remove the stems from the grapes, wash and let drain. Lightly caramelise the icing (confectioners') sugar in a frying pan or skillet and deglaze with the port to dissolve the caramel.

Add the grapes, shake to coat well and briefly heat. Remove the frying pan or skillet from the heat and stir in the butter in small pieces. Flavour with nutmeg and grappa.

Divide the grapes into dessert glasses, then fill with the airy cream mixture (sabayon). Serve immediately.

Buttermilk Mousse

All regions

Preparation time:		30 minutes
Chilling time:		3 hours
Serves:		4

⅓ cup/1¼ oz	icing (confectioners') sugar	30 g
1 cup/8 fl oz	buttermilk	250 ml
1 tbsp	lemon juice	1 tbsp
½ tbsp	unwaxed lemon zest	½ tbsp
½ tbsp	unwaxed orange zest	½ tbsp
3½	sheets gelatine	3½
½ cup/4 fl oz	double (heavy) cream	120 ml
1	egg white	1
2 tbsp	caster (superfine) sugar	2 tbsp
2¼ cups/9 oz	strawberries	250 g
*	mint leaves, to garnish	*

Sift the icing (confectioners') sugar and mix in a bowl with the buttermilk, lemon juice, lemon and orange zest. Soften 3 gelatine sheets in cold water. Put 5 tablespoons of buttermilk mixture into a small pan and heat lightly. Squeeze the gelatine and dissolve in the warm mixture, then stir the contents of the pan into the rest of the buttermilk mixture.

Whip the cream to soft peaks and set aside in the refrigerator. Beat the egg white with 1 heaped tablespoon of sugar to stiff peaks. Loosely fold the beaten egg white into the whipped cream and briefly refrigerate. Put the bowl with the buttermilk mixture over iced water and stir until it begins to set slightly, then fold in the beaten egg white and whipped cream mixture.

For a marbling effect, soften the remaining gelatine in cold water. Wash and trim 150 g (5 oz) of strawberries and combine with 1 tablespoon of sugar in a mixing bowl. Purée with a stick (immersion) blender, press through a sieve and weigh out 60 g (2¼ oz). Set aside the remaining purée in the refrigerator. Lightly heat 30 g (1¼ oz) strawberry purée in a pan, then squeeze the gelatine and dissolve. Stir the strawberry gelatine mixture into the remaining 30 g (1¼ oz) of strawberry purée in a bowl.

Put the bowl with the strawberry purée over iced water and stir until the mixture begins to set slightly. Drizzle the purée over the buttermilk mousse. Move the handle of a wooden spoon through both mixtures several times to create a marbling effect. Carefully fill dessert glasses with the mousse, then cover and let set in the refrigerator for 2–3 hours.

Wash, trim, and cut the leftover strawberries crosswise into fourths or eighths. Mix the strawberry pieces with the set-aside strawberry purée and pour over the mousse in the glasses. Garnish with mint leaves and serve.

Raspberry and Buttermilk Mousse (Errötendes Mädchen)

Schleswig-Holstein

Preparation time:		30 minutes
Chilling time:		1 hour
Serves:		4

3	sheets gelatine	3
1 cup/7 fl oz	buttermilk	200 ml
½ cup/2 oz	icing (confectioners') sugar	50 g
*	salt	*
2 tbsp	lime juice	2 tbsp
½ tbsp	unwaxed lime zest	½ tbsp
1 cup/7 fl oz	double (heavy) cream	200 ml
⅓ cup/2¼ oz	caster (superfine) sugar	60 g
2 cups/9 oz	raspberries	250 g
1 tbsp	lemon juice	1 tbsp
½ cup/2¼ oz	berries (e.g. blueberries)	60 g
*	mint leaves, to garnish	*

Soften the gelatine sheets in cold water. Mix the buttermilk with the icing (confectioners') sugar and a pinch of salt in a bowl.

Squeeze the gelatine and heat with the lime juice and zest in a pan until dissolved. Stir in the buttermilk and let the mixture cool until it starts to set.

Whip the cream to soft peaks with 2 tablespoons of sugar and fold into the buttermilk.

Sort and wash the raspberries. Combine with the lemon juice and 2 tablespoons of sugar in a mixing bowl and purée with a stick (immersion) blender. Press the purée through a sieve into a bowl.

Mix 130 g (1 cup/4½ oz) of raspberry purée with the buttermilk. Take out a third of the mixture and mix with the rest of the purée.

Pour the darker mixture into dessert glasses, then pour the lighter mixture over the top to form two layers. Let set in the refrigerator for about 1 hour. Garnish the buttermilk mousse with the assorted berries and mint leaves, and serve.

Guelph Pudding (Welfenspeise)

Lower Saxony

Preparation time:		15 minutes
Cooking time:		10 minutes
Chilling time:		1 hour
Serves:		4

For the vanilla cream:

2 tbsp	cornflour (cornstarch)	2 tbsp
⅔ cup/5 fl oz	milk	150 ml
½	vanilla bean	½
½ cup/3½ fl oz	double (heavy) cream	100 ml
3½ tbsp	caster (superfine) sugar	3 ½ tbsp
2	egg whites	2
*	salt	*

For the German-style zabaglione:

1 tbsp	cornflour (cornstarch)	1 tbsp
½ cup/4 fl oz	dry white wine	125 ml
1 tbsp	lemon juice	1 tbsp
2	egg yolks	2
2 tbsp	caster (superfine) sugar	2 tbsp
2 tbsp	chopped pistachio nuts	2 tbsp
*	mint leaves, to garnish	*

For the vanilla cream: Dissolve the cornflour (cornstarch) completely in a little milk. Split the vanilla bean lengthwise and scrape out the seeds. Combine the remaining milk and cream in a pan with 1–2 teaspoons of sugar, the vanilla bean and seeds over a medium heat. Gradually stir the dissolved cornflour (cornstarch) into the simmering milk. Bring to a boil and remove from the heat.

Beat the egg whites with the rest of the sugar and a pinch of salt into soft peaks. Fold the beaten egg whites into the hot vanilla cream and pour into dessert glasses.

For the German-style zabaglione: Mix a heaped tablespoon of cornflour (cornstarch) with the wine, then combine in a metal bowl with the lemon juice, egg yolks and sugar. Put the bowl over a bain-marie and whisk or beat with a hand mixer until almost boiling. Then pour over the vanilla cream in the glasses and refrigerate to set for about 1 hour. Garnish with the chopped pistachios and mint leaves, or with pieces of fruit if desired, and serve.

Lemon Cream with Raspberries

All regions

Preparation time:		20 minutes
Chilling time:		2 hours 30 minutes
Serves:		6

1 scant cup/7 fl oz	milk	200 ml
1⅔ cups/14 fl oz	double (heavy) cream	400 ml
1⅓ cups/5 oz	caster (superfine) sugar	150 g
4	sheets gelatine	4
1 tbsp	grated unwaxed lemon zest	1 tbsp
2	lemons, juiced	2
⅔ cup/3 oz	small raspberries	80 g
*	mint leaves, to garnish	*

Combine the milk with 200 ml (scant 1 cup/7 fl oz) cream and the sugar in a pan, bring to a boil, then remove from the heat. Soften the gelatine sheets in cold water, squeeze and stir into the hot cream mixture. Mix in the lemon zest and let cool at room temperature. Strain through a sieve into a bowl.

Whip the rest of the cream to soft peaks. Stir the lemon juice into the cream mixture, put the bowl over ice or cold water and stir until the cream starts to set. Fold in the whipped cream, then fill individual, about 150 ml (⅔ cup/5 fl oz capacity) moulds and refrigerate for at least 2 hours.

Sort, carefully wash and pat dry the raspberries. Run a knife around the inside of the moulds, dip to below the rim in hot water and turn out the lemon creams onto dessert plates. Garnish with raspberries and mint leaves.

Desserts

Westphalian-Style Vanilla Pudding

Westphalia and Münster

Preparation time:	10 minutes
Cooking time:	5 minutes
Chilling time:	1 hour
Serves:	4

1 packet	instant custard (pudding)	1 packet
3 tbsp	caster (superfine) sugar	3 tbsp
2 cups/17 fl oz	milk	500 ml
3½ oz	dark couverture chocolate	100 g
1¼ cups/10 fl oz	double (heavy) cream	300 ml
2 tbsp	wheat schnapps or rum	2 tbsp
*	wafer rolls, to serve	*

Dissolve the custard (pudding) powder and sugar in a little milk. Bring the remaining milk to a boil in a pan, whisk in the dissolved powder and briefly simmer. Transfer to a bowl, cover with greaseproof (wax) paper and let cool.

Finely chop the couverture chocolate and set aside 1 tablespoon for garnish. Whip the cream to stiff peaks.

Stir the pudding until smooth, then mix in the chocolate and schnapps and fold in the whipped cream. Serve the pudding in dessert glasses sprinkled with chopped chocolate. The pudding can be served with wafer rolls, if you like.

Red Berry Pudding (Rote Grütze)

Schleswig-Holstein

Preparation time:	15 minutes
Cooking time:	5 minutes
Resting time:	30 minutes
Serves:	4

2 tbsp	cornflour (corn starch)	2 tbsp
⅔ cup/5 fl oz	blackcurrant juice	150 ml
½ cup/3½ fl oz	cherry juice	100 ml
2 tbsp	caster (superfine) sugar	2 tbsp
½	vanilla bean	½
1	cinnamon stick	1
3 tbsp	crème de cassis	3 tbsp
3⅓ cups/1 lb 2 oz	assorted berries	500 g
*	Vanilla Sauce (p. 359), to serve	*

Dissolve the cornflour (cornstarch) in 3 tablespoons of blackcurrant juice. Combine the remaining blackcurrant juice with the cherry juice and sugar in a pan and bring to a boil. Stir in the dissolved cornflour (cornstarch) and gently simmer for 2 minutes.

Remove the pan from the heat. Scrape the seeds from the vanilla bean and add them together with the bean and the cinnamon to the juice mixture. Stir in the crème de cassis. Let infuse for 10 minutes.

Sort and wash the berries. Wash, trim and cut the strawberries crosswise into quarters or eighths. Strain the juice mixture through a sieve into a bowl. Add the berries and let steep for about 20 minutes.

Serve the pudding with Vanilla Sauce (p. 359).

Gooseberry Pudding

Mecklenburg-Western Pomerania

Preparation time:	5 minutes
Cooking time:	10 minutes
Chilling time:	4 hours
Serves:	4

1 lb 2 oz	gooseberries	500 g
1 cup/7 oz	caster (superfine) sugar	200 g
1	small piece unwaxed lemon zest	1
⅔ cup/3½ oz	sago (tapioca) pearls	100 g
1 scant cup/7 fl oz	double (heavy) cream	200 ml
1 tbsp	vanilla sugar	1 tbsp

Top and tail the gooseberries, then wash the berries. Combine 1 litre (4¼ cups/34 fl oz) water with the sugar and lemon zest and bring to a boil. Add the berries and continue to boil until they split open.

Press the fruit through a sieve or purée in a food mill. Mix the purée with the sago in a pan and bring to a boil. Continue to boil while stirring constantly until a thick cream forms.

Fill four chilled and rinsed moulds with the fruit mixture and set aside for a few hours in the refrigerator. Mix the cream with the vanilla sugar. Turn out the puddings onto plates and pour over with the cream.

Chocolate Pudding

All regions

Preparation time:	5 minutes
Cooking time:	10 minutes
Chilling time:	2 hours
Serves:	4

2¾ cups/23 fl oz	milk	700 ml
⅓ cup/2¼ oz	caster (superfine) sugar	60 g
*	salt	*
½ cup/2¼ oz	cornflour (cornstarch)	55 g
2 tbsp	cocoa powder	2 tbsp
2	egg yolks	2
1 tbsp	sugar, for sprinkling	1 tbsp
*	lemon balm leaves, optional	*
*	white chocolate curls, optional	*
*	physalis, optional	*
*	single (light) cream, optional	*

Combine 500 ml (2 cups/17 fl oz) of milk, the sugar and a pinch of salt in a pan and bring to a boil.

Dissolve the cornflour (cornstarch) and cocoa powder in the remaining milk and add, together with the egg yolks, stirring constantly with a whisk, into the boiling milk and then let simmer a little.

Fill four individual moulds with the pudding mixture, sprinkle with sugar, let cool and refrigerate for 2 hours.

When serving, turn the puddings out onto dessert plates. Serve with phyalis, fruit sauce, or cream, if you like.

Vanilla Pudding

All regions

Preparation time:		10 minutes
Chilling time:		2 hours
Serves:		4

3½ cups/27 fl oz	milk	800 ml
3 tbsp	cornflour (cornstarch)	3 tbsp
1	vanilla bean	1
scant ½ cup/3 oz	caster (superfine) sugar	80 g
3	eggs	3

Put the milk into a pan. Take out 5 tablespoons milk and dissolve the cornflour (cornstarch). Split the vanilla bean, add to the milk with the sugar and bring to a boil. Simmer for 10 minutes.

Separate the eggs. Remove the vanilla bean from the pan, discard and stir in the dissolved cornflour (cornstarch).

Whisk in the egg yolks one at a time, then remove the pan from the heat.

Beat the egg whites to stiff peaks, then carefully stir into the vanilla milk with a whisk. Let cool, then put in serving dishes.

Apple and Pumpernickel Trifle (Verschleiertes Bauernmädchen)

Friesland and Holstein

Preparation time:		25 minutes
Chilling time:		1 hour
Serves:		4

4	tart apples (e.g. Bramley)	4
3 tbsp	brown sugar	3 tbsp
1	cinnamon stick	1
1 tbsp	lemon juice	1 tbsp
4 tbsp	orange juice	4 tbsp
4 tbsp	apple juice	4 tbsp
2 tsp	calvados	2 tsp
½	vanilla bean	½
3 oz	pumpernickel bread	80g
½ tbsp	ground cinnamon	½ tbsp
5 tsp	caster (superfine) sugar	5 tsp
1	pinch unwaxed orange zest	1
1 cup/7 fl oz	double (heavy) cream	200 ml
4 tbsp	strawberry purée	4 tbsp
4 tbsp	raspberries	4 tbsp
*	mint leaves, to garnish	*

Peel, quarter, and core the apples, then cut into 5 mm (¼ inch) dice.

Lightly caramelise the brown sugar in a pan over a medium heat. Add the diced apple, cinnamon stick, the lemon, orange and apple juice, calvados and seeds from the vanilla bean and stew for 10–12 minutes until the apple is soft and the liquid has evaporated. Remove the pan from the heat and let the stewed apple cool.

Grind the pumpernickel to fine crumbs in a food processor. Mix with the ground cinnamon, sugar and orange zest.

Whip the cream to stiff peaks. Divide half of the stewed apple into dessert glasses, cover with a little whipped cream and sprinkle with breadcrumbs. Repeat the process, finishing off with cream and breadcrumbs. Add 1 tablespoon strawberry purée to each glass and garnish with berries and mint leaves. Chill for 1 hour, then serve.

Desserts

Semolina Pudding

All regions

Preparation time:		25 minutes
Cooking time:		5 minutes
Chilling time:		2 hours
Serves:		4

2	egg yolks	2
4 tbsp	caster (superfine) sugar	4 tbsp
3	sheets gelatine	3
½	vanilla bean	½
4 tsp	milk	4 tsp
1	pinch unwaxed lemon zest	1
1	pinch unwaxed orange zest	1
¼ cup/1½ oz	semolina or farina	40 g
1 tbsp	rum	1 tbsp
1 tbsp	orange liqueur	1 tbsp
1	egg white	1
*	salt	*
1 cup/7 fl oz	double (heavy) cream	200 ml
*	white chocolate curls, optional	*
*	lemon balm leaves, optional	*

Beat the egg yolks with 1 tablespoon of sugar in a bowl until thick and pale. Soften the gelatine sheets in cold water.

Split the vanilla bean. Combine the milk with 2 tablespoons of sugar, the lemon and orange zest and split vanilla bean in a pan and bring to a boil. Gradually stir the semolina into the mixture. Cook over a low heat while stirring constantly for 3–5 minutes to make a paste. Remove the pan from the heat and remove and discard the vanilla bean halves.

Gradually stir the semolina paste into the egg yolks. Squeeze the gelatine well and dissolve in the warm mixture. Mix in the rum and orange liqueur and let the mixture cool at room temperature.

Beat the egg white with a pinch of salt and the remaining sugar to soft peaks. Whip the cream to soft peaks. Loosely mix the beaten egg whites with the whipped cream then fold into the semolina mixture.

Fill individual moulds about 120 ml (½ cup/4 fl oz) capacity with the semolina mixture, cover and refrigerate for 2 hours.

When serving, dip the moulds to below the rim in hot water for 7–8 seconds before turning out the semolina puddings onto dessert plates. The pudding can be served with white chocolate curls and garnished with lemon balm leaves.

Deep-Fried Semolina Dumplings

Southern Germany

Preparation time:		30 minutes
Cooking time:		20 minutes
Serves:		4

1 cup/8 fl oz	milk	250 ml
2 tbsp	caster (superfine) sugar	2 tbsp
*	salt	*
½	vanilla bean	½
½ cup/2½ oz	semolina	75 g
1 tbsp	unwaxed lemon zest	1 tbsp
1 tbsp	unwaxed orange zest	1 tbsp
½ tbsp	ground cinnamon	½ tbsp
2	eggs	2
*	oil, for deep-frying	*
½ cup/2 oz	plain (all-purpose) flour	50 g
¾ cup/2 oz	white breadcrumbs	50 g
*	Rhubarb Compote (p. 362)	*
¾ cup/2 oz	white breadcrumbs	50 g
*	icing (confectioners') sugar	*
*	lemon balm, optional	*

Combine the milk with the sugar, a pinch of salt and the seeds from half a vanilla bean in a pan and bring to a boil. Use a whisk to stir in the semolina, then simmer while stirring constantly for about 2 minutes, to make into a thick paste. Remove the pan from the heat and transfer the semolina paste to a bowl. Mix in the lemon and orange zest and cinnamon and finish with 1 egg. Cover with clingfilm (plastic wrap) and let cool.

Fill a pan with oil to a depth of 4–5 cm (1½–2 inches) and heat to about 170°C/350°F. Use two wet tablespoons to shape the paste into quenelles. Beat the remaining egg in a deep plate and put the flour and breadcrumbs into separate deep plates. Dredge the dumplings first in the flour, then dip in the egg and finally coat with breadcrumbs. Fry in the hot oil on all sides for 3–4 minutes until golden brown, then drain on paper towels.

Put Rhubarb Compote (p. 362) on warmed plates and arrange the deep-fried dumplings over it. Dust with a little icing (confectioners') sugar and serve. Garnish with lemon balm if desired.

Farina Slices

All regions

Preparation time:		15 minutes
Chilling time:		2 hours
Cooking time:		10 minutes
Serves:		4

4¼ cups/34 fl oz	milk	1 litre
*	salt	*
⅓ cup/5 oz	caster (superfine) sugar	130 g
1	strip unwaxed lemon zest	1
1¾ cups/7 oz	farina	200 g
4	eggs	4
1½ cups/3½ oz	white breadcrumbs	100 g
2 tbsp	milk	2 tbsp
½ tbsp	ground cinnamon	½ tbsp
*	clarified butter, for frying	*

Combine the milk with a pinch of salt, 50 g sugar and lemon zest and bring to a boil. Use a whisk to gradually stir in the farina. Beat 2 eggs and stir into the hot paste. Immediately spread the paste out to a thickness of 1.5 cm (¾ inch) in a baking tin (pan) and let cool.

Put the breadcrumbs into a deep plate. Beat the remaining eggs with the milk in a deep plate. Mix the rest of the sugar and the cinnamon in a small bowl.

Cut the farina paste with a knife into about 8 x 4 cm (3 x 1½ inch) rectangles. First dredge the slices in the beaten egg and then coat in the breadcrumbs. Heat clarified butter in a large frying pan or skillet and fry the slices one at a time on both sides until golden brown. Arrange on a warmed plate and sprinkle with the cinnamon sugar. Keep warm until it's time to serve.

Baked Semolina Pudding

Saxony-Anhalt

Preparation time:		20 minutes
Cooking time:		20 minutes
Serves:		4

3 cups/25 fl oz	milk	750 ml
⅔ cup/3½ oz	semolina	100 g
*	salt	*
¼ cup/2 oz	butter	50 g
1	strip unwaxed lemon zest	1
6	eggs	6
¼ cup/2 oz	caster (superfine) sugar	50 g
*	butter, for greasing	*
*	sugar, for coating	*
*	fruit compote, to serve	*

Bring the milk to a boil in a pan and gradually stir in the semolina. Add a pinch of salt, the butter and lemon zest and let thicken over a medium heat for about 15 minutes. Chill the semolina paste.

Separate the eggs. Beat the egg whites, with a pinch of salt, to stiff peaks, gradually adding the sugar. Mix the egg yolks and add into the semolina paste. Fold in the egg whites to make a smooth batter.

Fill a baking pan or wide pan with water and put into the oven. Preheat the oven to 250°C/480°F/Gas Mark 9.

Grease four 8 cm (3 inch) diameter ramekins with butter and sprinkle with sugar. Fill with the batter and smooth the surface. Put the ramekins into the water bath and bake for about 20 minutes. Serve the puddings with fruit compote.

Desserts

Rice Pudding

All regions

Preparation time:		5 minutes
Cooking time:		30 minutes
Serves:		4

1	vanilla bean	1
2¾ cups/23 fl oz	milk	700 ml
⅔ cup/4½ oz	short-grain pudding rice	130 g
*	salt	*
2 tbsp	caster (superfine) sugar	2 tbsp
1	pinch unwaxed lemon zest	1
1	pinch unwaxed orange zest	1
¼ tbsp	ground cinnamon	¼ tbsp
*	berries or fruit compote	*

Split the vanilla bean lengthwise and scrape out the seeds with a knife tip. Combine the milk with the rice in a pan and add the vanilla seeds and bean, a pinch of salt and the sugar.

Slowly bring to a boil then reduce the heat to low and very gently simmer for 25–30 minutes, stirring from time to time. Before serving, remove the vanilla bean and stir in the zests and cinnamon. Accompany with berries, fruit compote or fruit sauce.

Frankfurt-Style Pudding

Frankfurt am Main and Hesse

Preparation time:		30 minutes
Cooking time:		25 minutes
Serves:		4

3 oz	toasted bread	80 g
6 tbsp	red wine	6 tbsp
3 tbsp	sliced almonds	3 tbsp
2	eggs	2
⅓ cup/2¾ oz	soft butter	70 g
*	ground cinnamon	*
1	pinch ground cloves	1
1 tbsp	freshly ground coffee	1 tbsp
¼ cup/¾ oz	candied orange peel	20 g
1 tbsp	orange liqueur	1 tbsp
1½ oz	dark chocolate	40 g
1	pinch vanilla seeds	1
*	salt	*
⅓ cup/2¼ oz	caster (superfine) sugar	60 g
*	butter, for greasing	*
*	sugar, for coating	*
*	icing (confectioners') sugar	*

Cut the bread into cubes and drizzle with the wine. Toast the almonds in a dry non-stick frying pan or skillet. Preheat the oven to 190°C/375°F/Gas Mark 5.

Separate the eggs. Beat the butter and egg yolks until creamy then mix in a pinch of cinnamon with the ground cloves and coffee. Drizzle the orange peel with the liqueur and finely chop. Finely chop the chocolate. Add the bread, toasted almonds, orange peel, chocolate and vanilla seeds to the egg mixture and mix thoroughly.

Beat the egg whites, with a pinch of salt, to soft peaks, gradually adding the sugar. Fold the beaten egg whites into the egg and butter mixture.

Grease 4 x 110 ml (scant ½ cup/3½ fl oz) soufflé moulds with butter and sprinkle with sugar. Fill the moulds with the batter and place, side by side, in a baking dish lined with paper towels. Fill the dish with hot water to a depth of 1–2 cm (½–¾ inch). Put the pan on the lowest shelf of the oven and bake for about 25 minutes.

Turn the puddings out of the moulds and dust with icing (confectioners') sugar.

Lübeck-Style Trifle

Schleswig-Holstein

Preparation time:		15 minutes
Cooking time:		15 minutes
Chilling time:		2 hours
Serves:		6

2 cups/17 fl oz	milk	500 ml
1	vanilla bean, split	1
½ cup/3½ oz	caster (superfine) sugar	100 g
½ cup/ 2¼ oz	instant vanilla (custard) pudding powder	60 g
3	egg yolks	3
1⅔ cups/9 oz	assorted wild berries	250 g
2 tbsp	raspberry brandy	2 tbsp
1 cup/8 fl oz	double (heavy) cream	250 ml
5 oz	sponge cake	150 g
2 tbsp	raspberry preserve	2 tbsp
3 tbsp	semi-dry sherry	3 tbsp
8	small amaretti cookies	8

Combine the milk with the split vanilla bean in a pan and infuse over a medium heat for about 15 minutes. Take out the bean and use a knife tip to scrape the seeds into the milk.

Mix 80 g (3 oz) sugar with the custard (pudding) powder and egg yolks in a bowl. Bring the milk to a boil, and use a wooden spoon to stir in the egg mixture. Stir until thickened. Sprinkle the custard with a little sugar and cool.

Wash and dry the berries. Set aside a few pretty berries for the garnish. Marinate the remaining berries in the remaining sugar mixed with the raspberry brandy.

Whip the cream to stiff peaks and fold a third into the cooled custard, until smooth.

Spread the sponge or ladyfingers with raspberry preserve, cut into squares, and cover the bottom of a glass bowl with half of them. Soak with half of the sherry, cover with half of the marinated berries and then with half of the custard. Repeat, then chill in the refrigerator.

Before serving, decorate with the remaining whipped cream and garnish with the berries and amaretti cookies.

Baked Rice Pudding with Apples

All regions

Preparation time:		20 minutes
Cooking time:		1 hour 40 minutes
Serves:		4

¾ cup/6 oz	short-grain pudding rice	180 g
4¼ cups/34 fl oz	milk	1 litre
⅔ cup/4 oz	caster (superfine) sugar	120 g
*	salt	*
*	butter, for greasing	*
2	tart apples	2
1 tbsp	lemon juice	1 tbsp
⅓ cup/3 oz	soft butter	80 g
1	pinch unwaxed orange zest	1
3	pinches unwaxed lemon zest	3
5	eggs	5
*	icing (confectioners') sugar	*

Combine the rice with the milk, 40 g (¼ cup/1½ oz) sugar and a pinch of salt in a pan, bring to a boil and simmer gently for 20–25 minutes until soft, stirring often. Remove the pan from the heat to cool.

Preheat the oven to 180°C/350°F/Gas Mark 4. Grease a 30 x 20 cm (11½ x 8½ inch) baking dish with butter. Peel, quarter and core the apples. Cut the flesh into 5-mm (¼-inch) dice and put into a bowl. Drizzle with lemon juice.

Beat the butter with the orange and lemon zest until creamy. Separate the eggs and gradually stir the egg yolks into the butter. Beat 3 egg whites with a pinch of salt and 50 g (2 oz) of sugar to soft peaks. Mix the rice with the butter mixture. Fold in the beaten egg whites and diced apple and fill the baking dish. Put the dish on the lowest shelf of the oven and bake for about 1 hour 15 minutes, covering with aluminium foil for the last 15 minutes.

Beat the remaining egg whites with a pinch of salt and the leftover sugar to soft peaks, then spoon into the baking dish. Dust with icing (confectioners') sugar and bake for 7–8 more minutes until golden brown. Take out of the oven and dust again with icing (confectioners') sugar.

Apple Pancakes

All regions

Preparation time:		20 minutes
Cooking time:		20 minutes
Serves:		4

2	eggs	2
1⅓ cups/5 oz	plain (all-purpose) flour	150 g
1 cup/8 fl oz	milk	250 ml
½ tbsp	unwaxed lemon zest	½ tbsp
1	pinch ground cinnamon	1
½	vanilla bean	½
1 tbsp	rum	1 tbsp
2 tbsp	caster (superfine) sugar	2 tbsp
*	salt	*
2	tart dessert apples	2
¼ oz	Beurre Noisette (p. 112)	10 g
*	icing (confectioners') sugar	*
*	hazelnut or vanilla ice cream	*

Preheat the oven to 200°C/400°F/Gas Mark 6. Separate the eggs. Mix the flour with the milk until smooth, then mix in the egg yolks, lemon zest, cinnamon, seeds from the vanilla bean and rum.

Beat the egg whites with the sugar and a pinch of salt to soft peaks. Stir a third of the beaten egg whites into the batter then fold in the rest.

Peel, quarter, core and cut the apples into small wedges.

Lightly heat the Beurre Noisette (p. 112) in 2 x 20 cm (7¾ inches) diameter, ovenproof frying pans or skillets over a medium heat and pour half of the batter into each one. Distribute half of the apple wedges evenly over the batter and cook until the underside is cooked but has no colour.

Put the frying pans or skillets, one at a time, on the lowest shelf of the oven and bake until the top is cooked but not coloured, about 10 minutes. Take the pans out of the oven and turn on the oven grill (broiler). Dust the pancakes with icing (confectioners') sugar and put the frying pans or skillets, one at a time, on the lowest shelf again and caramelise for 2–3 minutes until golden brown. Cut the pancakes into pieces and arrange on plates. They can be dusted again with icing (confectioners') sugar and served with hazelnut or vanilla ice cream.

Apple Fritters

Southern Germany

Preparation time:		15 minutes
Cooking time:		15 minutes
Makes:		about 18

¾ cup/16 fl oz	milk	170 ml
3 tbsp	butter	3 tbsp
*	salt	*
1 cup/3½ oz	plain (all-purpose) flour	100 g
3	eggs	3
1⅔ cups/14 fl oz	vegetable oil	400 ml
scant ½ cup/3 oz	caster (superfine) sugar	80 g
½–1 tbsp	ground cinnamon	½–1 tbsp
3	tart apples	3

Combine 70 ml (⅓ cup/2½ fl oz) milk with 70 ml (⅓ cup/ 2½ fl oz) water, the butter and a pinch of salt in a small pan and bring to a boil. Add the sifted flour while stirring constantly with a wooden spoon and continue to stir until the resulting paste comes away from the bottom of the pan, about 1 minute. Transfer to a bowl, gradually mix in the eggs and the remaining milk to form a thick batter.

Heat the fat or oil in a pan or deep-fryer to 180°C/350°F. The fat is hot enough when small bubbles form around the handle of a wooden spoon when dipped into it.

Mix the caster (superfine) sugar with the cinnamon. Peel and core the apples. Cut the apples into about 1 cm (½ inch) thick slices. Coat the slices in the batter, drain off the excess and fry for a few minutes until golden brown. Use a slotted spoon to take out the fritters, drain briefly on paper towels and coat in the cinnamon sugar.

Apple Dumplings

All regions

Preparation time:		15 minutes
Cooking time:		25 minutes
Serves:		4

11 oz	frozen puff pastry sheets	300 g
4	medium dessert apples	4
2 tbsp	caster (superfine) sugar	2 tbsp
¼–½ tbsp	ground cinnamon	¼–½ tbsp
2 tbsp	soft butter	2 tbsp
2–3 tbsp	raisins	2–3 tbsp
*	flour, for dusting	*
1	egg yolk	1
1–2 tbsp	double (heavy) cream	1–2 tbsp
*	Vanilla Sauce (p. 359), to serve	*

Lay the puff pastry sheets side by side and let thaw. Preheat the oven to 200°C/400°F/Gas Mark 6.

Peel and core the apples. Mix the sugar and cinnamon together, mix with the soft butter and raisins and fill the apple cavities with the mixture.

Lay the pastry sheets on top of each other, roll out to a thickness of about 3 mm (⅛ inch), and cut into four about 20 cm (7¾ inch) squares. Put one apple at the centre of each square, bring the corners of the pastry up over the apple, and press lightly together. Stand the apples on a baking sheet lined with greaseproof (wax) paper.

Cut small discs out of the remaining pastry. Mix the egg yolk with the cream, brush over the discs and attach where the pastry corners meet. Brush the egg and cream mixture all over the pastry.

Put the baking sheet on the middle shelf of the oven and bake for 20–25 minutes until golden brown. Serve hot. Accompany with Vanilla Sauce (p. 359).

'Drunken Maidens' (Versoffene Jungfern)

Bavaria

Preparation time:		10 minutes
Cooking time:		20 minutes
Serves:		4

For the sauce:		
2–3 tbsp	icing (confectioners') sugar	2–3 tbsp
1¼ cups/3 fl oz	dry white wine	300 ml
2 cups/17 fl oz	apple juice	500 ml
2	star anise	2
2	shards cinnamon stick	2
1 tbsp	green cardamom pods	1 tbsp
2	cloves	2
1	vanilla bean, split	1
1	strip unwaxed lemon zest	1
1	strip unwaxed orange zest	1
2–3 tbsp	cornflour (cornstarch)	2–3 tbsp

For the dumplings:		
scant ½ cup/3½ oz	soft butter	100 g
1	vanilla bean, split	1
1	unwaxed lemon, zested	1
scant ½ cup/3 oz	caster (superfine) sugar	80 g
4	eggs	4
1⅓ cup/5 oz	plain (all-purpose) flour	150 g
2 tbsp	cornflour (cornstarch)	2 tbsp
½ tbsp	baking powder	½ tbsp
*	salt	*
*	oil, for deep-frying	*
*	icing (confectioners') sugar	*

For the sauce: Sprinkle the icing (confectioners') sugar into a pan and lightly caramelise over a medium heat. Deglaze the pan with the wine and add the apple juice. Add the star anise, cinnamon, cardamom, cloves, vanilla bean and lemon and orange zest. Dissolve the cornflour (cornstarch) completely in a little cold water and gradually mix it into the simmering liquid to thicken lightly. Gently simmer for a few minutes and strain the sauce through a sieve.

For the dumplings: Beat the butter with the seeds from the vanilla bean, lemon zest and half of the sugar until pale and fluffy. Separate the eggs and mix the egg yolks into the butter mixture. Sift the flour with the cornflour (cornstarch) and baking powder into a bowl. Beat the egg whites with the remaining sugar and a pinch of salt to soft peaks and stir with the flour mixture into the beaten butter.

Pour oil into a deep frying pan or skillet to a depth of 4–5 cm (1¾–2 inches) and heat to 165–170°C/325°F. Use two wet tablespoons to shape the dumpling mixture into quenelles, dipping the spoons in warm water between dumplings, and fry in batches on all sides until golden brown. Use a slotted spoon to take the dumplings out of the pan, and drain on paper towels. Coat with the sauce, sprinkling with icing (confectioners') sugar, if you like.

Elderflower Fritters

Southern Germany

Preparation time:		20 minutes
Cooking time:		10 minutes
Serves:		4

1¾ cups/7 oz	plain (all-purpose flour)	200 g
1¼ cups/10½ fl oz	white wine or beer	300 ml
2	eggs	2
4 tbsp	Beurre Noisette (p. 112)	4 tbsp
1	pinch vanilla seeds	1
1	pinch ground cinnamon	1
*	salt	*
2¾ oz	caster (superfine) sugar	70 g
*	oil, for deep-frying	*
12	elderflower heads	12

Mix the flour with the wine or beer in a bowl to a smooth batter. Separate the eggs. Mix the egg yolks, Beurre Noisette (p. 112), vanilla seeds and a pinch of cinnamon into the batter.

Beat the egg whites with a pinch of salt and 20 g (¾ oz) sugar to stiff peaks, then fold into the batter.

Heat the oil in a wide pan or deep-fryer to 180°C/350°F/Gas Mark 4. The oil is hot enough when small bubbles form around the handle of a wooden spoon when dipped into it.

Mix the remaining sugar with ½ teaspoon of ground cinnamon. Select the elderflower heads, dip one at a time into the batter, drain off the excess and fry until golden brown. Drain on paper towels and dip immediately afterwards in the cinnamon sugar.

Popovers

Baden-Württemberg

Preparation time:		10 minutes
Cooking time:		30 minutes
Serves:		4

*	butter, for greasing	*
1¼ cups/4¾ oz	plain (all-purpose) flour	140 g
1 cup/8 fl oz	milk	250 ml
2	eggs	2
1 tbsp	caster (superfine) sugar	1 tbsp
¼ tsp	vanilla bean paste	¼ tsp
*	salt	*
*	icing (confectioners') sugar	*
*	fruit compote, to serve	*
*	Vanilla Sauce (p. 359), to serve	*

Preheat the oven to 200°C/400°F/Gas Mark 6. Brush four moulds of a muffin (popover) tin (pan) with butter. Alternatively, use four 125 ml (½ cup/4 fl oz) capacity oven-safe cups.

Mix the flour with 100 ml (½ cup/3½ fl oz) milk, the eggs, sugar vanilla and a pinch of salt to a smooth paste. Heat the remaining milk to just under boiling and stir into the paste.

Pour the batter into the moulds; the cavities should only be half filled at most. Put the muffin tin on a baking sheet, place in the lowest third of the oven and bake for about 30 minutes. They should be at least double in volume and turn golden brown and a little crispy. Take out of the oven, let rest and serve hot or lukewarm.

Dust the popovers with icing (confectioners') sugar and serve accompanied, if desired, with compote or Vanilla Sauce (p. 359).

Shredded Pancake (Kaiserschmarren)

Bavaria

Preparation time:		10 minutes
Cooking time:		10 minutes
Serves:		4

1 cup/4 oz	plain (all-purpose) flour	120 g
1 cup/8 fl oz	milk	250 ml
4	eggs	4
1	vanilla bean, split	1
1 pinch	unwaxed lemon zest	1 pinch
1 tbsp	rum	1 tbsp
*	salt	*
⅓ cup/2¼ oz	caster (superfine) sugar	60 g
4 tbsp	butter	4 tbsp
3 tbsp	Rum-Soaked Raisins (p. 362)	3 tbsp
*	Apple Purée (p. 362), to serve	*
*	Plum Compote (p. 366), to serve	*

Mix the flour with the milk until smooth. Separate the eggs. Stir the egg yolks, seeds from the vanilla bean, lemon zest, rum and a pinch of salt into the batter. Beat the egg whites with half of the sugar and a pinch of salt to firm peaks and fold into the batter.

Heat 1 tablespoon butter in each of two 24–26-cm (9¼–10-inch) diameter ovenproof frying pans or skillets. Pour the batter into the pans and cook over a low heat until the underside is light golden. Sprinkle with the Rum-soaked Raisins (p. 362) and make sure they sink into the batter. Remove the frying pans or skillets from the heat, and put the pans, one after the other, on the lowest shelf of the grill (broiler) and cook for 3 minutes until golden brown.

Use two forks to shred the pancakes into bite-size pieces. Add the remaining butter and sugar, return the frying pans or skillets to the stove and cook a little more while stirring constantly.

Serve the shredded pancakes on warmed plates. They go well with Apple Purée (p. 362), or Plum Compote (p. 366).

Apple Strudel

Southern Germany

Preparation time:		20 minutes
Cooking time:		25 minutes
Serves:		4

4	dessert apples	4
⅓ cup/1¼ oz	sliced almonds	35 g
⅓ cup/1¼ oz	caster (superfine) sugar	30 g
¼ tbsp	ground cinnamon	¼ tbsp
1¼ oz	Rum-Soaked Raisins (p. 360)	30 g
½	lemon, juiced	½
2 oz	sponge cake crumbs	50 g
2	sheets strudel or	2
	filo (phyllo) pastry	
*	flour, for dusting	*
2 tbsp	melted butter	2 tbsp
*	Vanilla Sauce (p. 359), to serve	*
*	whipped cream, to serve	*

Peel and core the apples and slice with a mandoline. Alternatively, peel, quarter and core the apples. Cut the quarters into 5–10 mm (¼–½ inch) dice.

Lightly toast the almonds in a dry frying pan or skillet, stirring constantly. Let cool. Mix the sugar with the cinnamon, then add, together with the Rum-Soaked Raisins (p. 360), lemon juice, sponge cake crumbs and almonds, to the apples and mix.

Preheat the oven to 200°C/400F/Gas Mark 6. Line a baking sheet with greaseproof (wax) paper. Lay one pastry sheet on a floured work counter and lightly brush with the melted butter. Lay another sheet over it and brush with melted butter.

Make a thick line of apple filling along the length of one side of the pastry. Leave a 5 cm (2 inch) wide space free of filling at both ends of the sheet and fold over the filling. Slide the strudel onto a cloth and use it to roll up the strudel, pressing in the ends. Lay the strudel, seam-side down, on the baking sheet. Brush with the leftover melted butter, put the baking sheet on the lowest shelf of the oven, and bake for 20–25 minutes until golden brown. Serve with Vanilla Sauce (p. 359), or whipped cream.

Quark and Rhubarb Strudel

Bavaria

Preparation time:		30 minutes
Cooking time:		30 minutes
Serves:		8–10

¼ cup/2¼ oz	soft butter	60 g
scant ½ cup/3 oz	caster (superfine) sugar	80 g
2	eggs, at room temperature	2
1	vanilla bean, split	1
1	unwaxed lemon, zested	1
*	salt	*
2½ cups/7 oz	Quark, at room temperature	500 g
½ cup/4 fl oz	double (heavy) cream	125 ml
½ cup/4 fl oz	sour cream	125 ml
1 tbsp	ground almonds	1
12 oz	strudel or filo (phyllo) pastry	350 g
*	flour, for dusting	*
¼ cup/2 oz	melted butter	50 g
7 oz	Rhubarb Compote (p. 364), drained	200 g
*	butter, for greasing	*
2 tbsp	caster (superfine) sugar	2 tbsp
½ cup/4 fl oz	milk	125 ml

Beat the soft butter with 3 tablespoons of sugar in a bowl until pale and fluffy. Mix in the eggs one at a time. Stir the seeds from the vanilla bean, lemon zest, a pinch of salt, the remaining sugar and the Quark into the butter. Whip the cream to soft peaks, mix with the sour cream and fold into the Quark mixture. Lightly toast the ground almonds in a dry pan and mix in.

Preheat the oven to 200°C/400°F/Gas Mark 6. Dust the pastry sheet with flour, lay over a floured dish cloth (about 40 x 40 cm/15½ x 15½ inch), and roll out lightly with a rolling pin. Spread the pastry over the backs of your hands and carefully stretch to a paper-thin rectangle, divide in two then brush with the melted butter.

Spread half of the Quark mixture in a 10–15 cm (4–6 inch) wide band along the length of the pastry. Leave a 5 cm (2 inch) wide space free of filling at both shorter ends of the pastry and fold inward over the filling. Spread half of the drained rhubarb over the filling. Slide the strudel back onto the cloth and use it to roll up the strudel. Lay the strudel, seam-side down, in a baking tin (pan) greased with butter. Repeat the operation to make a second strudel. Brush the strudels with the remaining melted butter and sprinkle with the sugar.

Place the strudels on the middle shelf of the oven and bake for 10–15 minutes. Then add the milk to the baking tin (pan) and bake for 25–30 more minutes. Take the baking tin (pan) out of the oven and leave the strudels inside to cool, about 15 minutes. Cut into portions and serve.

Quark and Sour Cream Strudel (Millirahmstrudel)

Bavaria

Preparation time:		35 minutes
Cooking time:		45 minutes
Serves:		8–10

For the strudel:		
½ cup/4 oz	butter	120 g
scant ½ cup/1½ oz	icing (confectioners') sugar	40 g
1	unwaxed lemon, zested	1
½	unwaxed orange, zested	½
1 tbsp	vanilla sugar	1 tbsp
2	eggs	2
2 cups/14 oz	Quark, at room temperature	400 g
1¼ cups/10 fl oz	sour cream	300 ml
¼ cup/2 oz	caster (superfine) sugar	50 g
*	salt	*
¼ cup/1 oz	plain (all-purpose) flour	25 g
2 oz	Rum-Soaked Raisins (p. 362)	50 g
4	sheets strudel or filo (phyllo) pastry	4
*	flour, for dusting	*
¼ cup/2 oz	melted butter	50 g
*	butter, for greasing	*

For the egg milk:		
1 cup/8 fl oz	milk	250 ml
¼ cup/2¼ oz	crème fraîche	60 g
2	eggs	2
3 tbsp	caster (superfine) sugar	3 tbsp
1	vanilla bean, split	1

For the strudel: Beat the butter with the icing (confectioners') sugar, lemon and orange zests and vanilla sugar in a bowl. Separate the eggs and mix the egg yolks into the butter mixture. Gradually mix in the Quark and sour cream.

Beat the egg whites with a third of the sugar and a pinch of salt to make soft peaks, gradually adding the remaining sugar. Sift the flour into the butter mixture and carefully mix together with the raisins. Fold in the beaten egg whites.

Preheat the oven to 180°C/350°F/Gas Mark 4. Lay the strudel pastry sheets over a floured dish cloth, about 40 x 40 cm/15 x 15 inches, and roll each one out lightly with a rolling pin. One at a time, spread the pastry sheets over the back of your hands and carefully stretch to a paper-thin rectangle, then immediately brush with the butter.

Spread a quarter of the filling in a thick line along the length of each sheet. Leave a 5 cm (2 inch) wide space free of filling at both shorter ends of the pastry and fold inward. Slide the strudel back onto the cloth and use it to roll up the strudel. Lay the strudels, seam-side down, in a baking tin (pan) or ovenproof dish (25 x 30 cm/10 x 12 inches) greased with butter. Brush the strudels with butter, and bake for 15 minutes.

For the egg milk: Combine the milk, crème fraîche, eggs, sugar and vanilla seeds in a bowl. Mix together using a stick (immersion) blender and strain through a sieve. Then add to the baking tin (pan) and bake the strudels for 30 more minutes.

Take out the strudels and let cool a little. Cut into pieces and serve, dusted with icing (confectioners') sugar.

Desserts

French Toast (Arme Ritter)

All regions

Preparation time:		10 minutes
Cooking time:		5 minutes
Serves:		4

½	loaf day-old sweet yeast bread	½
3½ oz	Plum Compote (p. 366)	100 g
¾ cup/5 oz	caster (superfine) sugar	150 g
¼–½ tbsp	ground cinnamon	¼–½ tbsp
1	pinch ground cloves	1
1	pinch ground cardamom	1
3	eggs	3
⅔ cup/5 fl oz	milk	150 ml
½	vanilla bean, split	½
*	clarified butter, for frying	*

Cut the bread into about 5 mm (¼ inch) thick slices. Spread half of the slices well with Plum Compote. Cover with the remaining slices.

Mix the sugar with cinnamon, cloves and cardamom in a deep plate.

Whisk the eggs with the milk and seeds from the vanilla bean. Heat the clarified butter in a frying pan or skillet. Dip the sandwiches briefly in the egg milk, then fry on both sides in the hot clarified butter over a low heat until golden brown. Drain on paper towels, then coat in the spiced sugar while still hot. Arrange on plates or in a serving dish.

Bread Pudding (Scheiterhaufen)

Altbayern

Preparation time:		25 minutes
Cooking time:		55 minutes
Serves:		4

For the pudding:

2 tbsp	raisins	2 tbsp
1–2 tbsp	rum	1–2 tbsp
1	apple	1
1	pear	1
1 tbsp	butter	1 tbsp
2 tbsp	caster (superfine) sugar	2 tbsp
2–3 tbsp	apple juice	2–3 tbsp
2–3	milk buns or brioche	2–3
*	butter, for greasing	*
2 tbsp	toasted sliced almonds	2 tbsp
*	icing (confectioners') sugar	*
*	fruit compote, to serve	*

For the egg milk:

1	egg	1
½ cup/4 fl oz	milk	125 ml
½ cup/4 fl oz	double (heavy) cream	125 ml
5	egg yolks	5
3 tbsp	sugar	3 tbsp
1 tbsp	rum	1 tbsp
½	vanilla bean, split	½

For the beaten egg whites:

5	egg whites	5
¾ cup/5 oz	caster (superfine) sugar	150 g
*	salt	*

For the pudding: Mix the raisins with the rum in a small bowl. Peel, quarter, core and cut the apples and pears into 3–4 mm (¼ inch) thick slices. Heat the butter in a frying pan or skillet and lightly braise the apple and pear slices on both sides over a medium heat with the sugar and apple juice for 2 minutes. Preheat the oven to 170°C/350°F/Gas Mark 4.

For the egg milk: Whisk the egg with the milk, cream, egg yolks, sugar, rum and seeds from the vanilla bean.

For the beaten egg whites: Beat the egg whites with the sugar and a pinch of salt to soft peaks.

Cut the buns into 5 mm (¼ inch) thick slices. Grease a large ovenproof dish or four 200 ml (scant 1 cup/7 fl oz) capacity ramekins with butter. Line the dish or ramekins with half of the bread slices, then cover with the apple and pear mixture. Cover with a layer of raisins and almonds and with the remaining bread slices. Gradually pour over the egg milk. Put the dish on the middle shelf of the oven and bake for 35 minutes (if using ramekins, 15 minutes will be enough).

Take out of the oven, spread with the beaten egg whites and use a spatula to form peaks. Put the pudding back into the oven and bake for 20 more minutes until golden brown.

Take out of the oven and dust liberally with icing (confectioners') sugar. Arrange on pudding plates with the compote of your choice.

Apricot Dumplings

Southern Germany

Preparation time:		35 minutes
Chilling time:		12 hours
Cooking time:		15 minutes
Serves:		4

For the dumplings:

1 lb 2 oz	floury potatoes	500 g
½ cup/2 oz	cornflour (cornstarch)	50 g
½ cup/2 oz	plain (all-purpose) flour	50 g
⅓ cup/2 oz	semolina	50 g
1	egg	1
4 tbsp	melted Beurre Noisette (p. 112)	4 tbsp
1	unwaxed lemon, zested	1
½	vanilla bean, split	½
*	salt	*
12	small apricots	12
12	sugar cubes	12
*	apricot schnapps	*

For the cooking liquid:

2 tbsp	salt	2 tbsp
½ cup/3 oz	caster (superfine) sugar	80 g
1	vanilla bean, split	1
½ stick	cinnamon	½ stick
2	strips unwaxed lemon zest	2
2	strips unwaxed orange zest	2

For the cinnamon breadcrumbs:

scant 1 cup/3 oz	white breadcrumbs	80 g
⅓ cup/3 oz	butter	80 g
2 tbsp	caster (superfine) sugar	2 tbsp
½ tbsp	ground cinnamon	½ tbsp
*	icing (confectioners') sugar	*

For the dumplings: Boil the potatoes in salted water until tender, drain, peel while still hot and press through a potato ricer. Spread the mashed potato out over a large plate or tray, let steam, cover and let cool for several hours, or overnight in the refrigerator.

Mix the cooled mashed potato with the cornflour (cornstarch), flour, semolina, egg, Beurre Noisette (p. 112), lemon zest, seeds from the vanilla bean and a pinch of salt then knead to a smooth dough.

Wash the apricots, cut halfway open and remove the stone (pit). In place of the pit, put 1 sugar cube into each and sprinkle with a few drops of apricot schnapps.

Divide the dough into 12 equal portions and press flat. Place 1 apricot on each portion and wrap in the dough. Wet your hands and turn the dumplings until smooth.

For the cooking liquid: Combine 3 litres (12½ cups) of water with the salt and sugar in a pan and bring to a boil. Add the vanilla bean, cinnamon and zests. Add the dumplings to the liquid and simmer very gently for about 15 minutes.

Meanwhile, prepare the cinnamon breadcrumbs: Fry the breadcrumbs with the butter in a frying pan or skillet over a low heat until golden brown. Mix the breadcrumbs with the sugar and cinnamon and transfer to a plate.

Use a slotted spoon to take the dumplings out of the pan, drain on paper towels, roll in the cinnamon breadcrumbs, and dust with icing (confectioners') sugar.

Bread and Butter Pudding with Cherries (Kirschenmichel)

Southern Germany

Preparation time:		25 minutes
Cooking time:		45 minutes
Serves:		4

6 cups/2¼ lbs	cherries	1 kg
3 tbsp	kirsch	3 tbsp
6	stale buns	6
1 cup/8 fl oz	milk	250 ml
½ cup/2 oz	chopped almonds	50 g
½ cup/3½ oz	soft butter	100 g
scant ½ cup/3 oz	caster (superfine) sugar	80 g
1	pinch vanilla sugar	1
1	unwaxed lemon, zested	1
3	eggs	3
*	salt	*
½ tbsp	ground cinnamon	½ tbsp
*	butter, for greasing	*
*	dry breadcrumbs, for coating	*
*	icing (confectioners') sugar	*

Wash and pit the cherries. Combine with the kirsch in a bowl, cover and marinate for 15 minutes.

Cut the buns into slices or cubes. Lightly warm the milk and pour over the bread. Soak for 10 minutes. Lightly toast the almonds in a dry pan.

Mix the butter with half of the sugar, the vanilla sugar and lemon zest until creamy. Separate the eggs. Mix in the egg yolk into the butter, then add in the bread and almonds.

Preheat the oven to 180°C/350°F/Gas Mark 4. Beat the egg whites with a pinch of salt to stiff peaks, gradually adding the remaining sugar. Fold the beaten egg whites into the pudding mixture. Mix the cherries and cinnamon.

Grease an ovenproof dish and coat with breadcrumbs. Fill with the pudding mixture, smooth the surface, then put the dish on the middle shelf inside the oven and bake for about 45 minutes. Before serving, dust liberally with icing (confectioners') sugar.

Desserts

Steamed Sweet Dumplings (Dampfnudeln)

Southern Germany

Preparation time:		25 minutes
Rising time:		1 hour 20 minutes
Cooking time:		35 minutes
Serves:		6

2 cups/17 fl oz	milk	500 ml
1 oz	fresh yeast	25 g
2 oz	caster (superfine) sugar	50 g
4½ cups/1 lb 2 oz	plain (all-purpose) flour	500 g
2	eggs	2
*	salt	*
⅓ cups/3 oz	butter, softened	80 g
*	flour, for dusting	*
3 tbsp	butter	3 tbsp
1 oz	clarified butter	30 g
*	Vanilla Sauce (p. 359), to serve	*

Heat half of the milk until lukewarm. Dissolve the yeast in the milk and add 2 teaspoons sugar. Put the flour into a bowl and make a well in the centre. Pour in the milk and yeast and mix with a little of the flour. Cover the starter and rest in a warm place for 15 minutes.

Whisk the eggs and add to the starter with a pinch of salt, 5 teaspoons of sugar and the softened butter. Mix with the flour. Put the dough into a food mixer or use a hand mixer with a dough hook to knead until it becomes shiny and elastic and comes away easily from the sides of the bowl. Cover and let rise in a warm place for about 45 minutes until it doubles in volume.

Turn the dough out onto a lightly floured work counter and vigorously knead the dough with your hands. Roll into 4–5 cm (2 inch) diameter cylinders. Cut the rolls into about 5 cm (2 inch) wide pieces and roll each piece into a smooth ball.

Preheat the oven to 180°C/350°F/Gas Mark 4. In a large, deep, ovenproof pan about 30 cm (1 foot) in diameter, heat the remaining milk with the rest of the sugar, then add the butter and clarified butter and melt. Remove the pan from the heat. Put the dough balls, seam-side down, into the lukewarm milk, cover with a lid and rest for 20 minutes. Put the pan on the stove and cook on a medium heat for 10 minutes.

Put in the oven for about 35 minutes. Don't remove the lid during this time as the dumplings may collapse. If the crust formed on the bottom still has a very light colour, put the pan back on the stove and continue to cook until the dumplings turn golden. Serve the dumplings while still warm, with Vanilla Sauce (p. 359).

Sweet Buns (Buchteln)

Saxony, Bavaria, Baden-Württemberg and Palatinate

Preparation time:		20 minutes
Rising time:		55 minutes
Baking time:		20 minutes
Serves:		4–6

¾ cup/6 fl oz	milk	180 ml
8 tsp	fresh yeast	8 tsp
4 cups/1 lb	plain (all-purpose) flour	450 g
⅓ cup/2¾ oz	caster (superfine) sugar	75 g
3	egg yolks	3
1 tbsp	almond liqueur (e.g. amaretto)	1 tbsp
1 tbsp	rum	1 tbsp
*	salt	*
1	vanilla bean, split	1
1 tbsp	unwaxed lemon zest	1 tbsp
1 tbsp	unwaxed orange zest	1 tbsp
⅓ cup/2¾ oz	butter, softened	75 g
*	flour, for dusting	*
*	butter, for greasing	*
¼ cup/2¼ oz	melted butter, for brushing	60 g
*	icing (confectioners') sugar	*
*	Elderberry Compote (p. 364)	*

Heat the milk until lukewarm. Crumble the yeast and dissolve in the milk. Combine the yeast and milk mixture with the flour, sugar, egg yolks, almond liqueur, rum, a pinch of salt, the seeds from the vanilla bean and orange and lemon zests then knead together. Add the soft butter and knead for a few more minutes to a smooth dough. Put the dough into a bowl, cover with clingfilm (plastic wrap), and leave to rise in a warm place, about 30 minutes.

Briefly knead the dough again, dust with a little flour and roll into a thick cylinder. Cut the cylinder into discs of even thickness and shape each into a ball. Grease a baking tin (pan) or ovenproof dish about 20 x 30-cm (8 x 12 inches) with butter, put in the balls, cover, and prove in a warm place for 25 minutes.

Preheat the oven to 180°C/350°F/Gas Mark 4. Carefully brush the buns with melted butter, put the baking tin (pan) on the lowest shelf of the oven and bake until golden brown, about 20 minutes.

Take the tin (pan) out of the oven and leave the buns in the pan to cool. Dust the buns with icing (confectioners') sugar and serve with Elderberry and Pear Compote (p. 364).

Sweet Dumplings with Pear Soup

Saxony-Anhalt

Preparation time:		20 minutes
Cooking time:		25 minutes
Serves:		4

2	eggs	2
2 cups/17 fl oz	milk	500 ml
*	salt	*
5 tbsp	sugar	5 tbsp
2¼ cups/9 oz	plain (all-purpose) flour	250 g
4	pears	4

Mix the eggs with 150 ml (⅔ cup/5 fl oz) of milk, a pinch of salt and 1½ tablespoons sugar in a bowl. Mix in the flour and beat the mixture with a wooden spoon or in a food mixer for a few minutes to a smooth dough. Set aside. Bring salted water to a boil in a wide pan.

Peel, quarter and core the pears, then cut into about 1.5 cm (¾ inch) dice. Combine with 200 ml (1 cup/7 fl oz) water and 2 tablespoons sugar in a pan and simmer for 5–15 minutes, depending on the ripeness of the pears, until soft.

Use two wet tablespoons to shape the dough into dumplings, put into the boiling water and simmer for a few minutes until the dumplings float to the surface. Use a skimmer to take the dumplings out of the water and add to the pears.

Remove the pan from the heat and add the remaining milk. The soup mustn't continue to cook after the milk is added. Adjust the sweetness of the soup with the remaining sugar.

Saxon-Style Pancakes

Saxony

Preparation time:		30 minutes
Cooking time:		40 minutes
Serves:		4

1 lb 2oz	floury potatoes	500 g
1¾ cups/13 oz	Quark	375 g
1⅓ cups/5 oz	plain (all-purpose) flour	150 g
¾ cup/5½ oz	caster (superfine) sugar	165 g
2	eggs	2
*	salt	*
½ tbsp	unwaxed lemon zest	½ tbsp
½ tbsp	unwaxed orange zest	½ tbsp
2 oz	Rum-Soaked Raisins (p. 362)	50 g
*	flour, for dusting	*
4 tbsp	oil	4 tbsp
½–1 tbsp	ground cinnamon	½–1 tbsp

Wash the potatoes and boil in salted water in a pan until tender. Drain, let steam briefly and peel. Then press through a potato ricer into a bowl and leave to cool. Add the Quark, flour, 65 g (⅓ cup/2½ oz) sugar, the eggs, a pinch of salt and the zests and work into a smooth dough. Add the raisins.

Use your hands to roll the dough on a floured work counter into a 6 cm (2¼ inches) thick cylinder and cut into about 1.5 cm (¾ inch) thick disks. Dredge the discs in flour.

Heat the oil in a non-stick frying pan or skillet and fry the pancakes on both sides until golden brown. Mix the remaining sugar with the cinnamon. Drain the pancakes on paper towels and dip in the cinnamon sugar.

Desserts

Quark Casserole

All regions

Preparation time:		25 minutes
Cooking time:		1 hour
Serves:		4

⅓ cup/2 oz	raisins	50 g
2 tbsp	apple juice (or rum)	2 tbsp
scant ½ cup/2 oz	sliced almonds	50 g
1 lb 2 oz	apples	500 g
1 tbsp	vanilla sugar	1 tbsp
½	lemon, juiced	½
*	butter, for greasing	*
¼ cup/2 oz	soft butter	50 g
½ cup/3½ oz	sugar	100 g
4	eggs, separated	4
½	unwaxed lemon, zested	½
2½ cups/1 lb 2 oz	low-fat Quark	500 g
⅓ cup/2 oz	semolina	50 g
*	salt	*

Soak the raisins in the apple juice to soften. Toast the almonds in a dry frying pan or skillet until golden brown. Peel, quarter and core the apples, then cut into roughly 5 mm (¼ inch) thick slices. Sprinkle with 1 teaspoon vanilla sugar, drizzle with the lemon juice and mix. Brush a large casserole dish with butter and spread the apples out in it.

Preheat the oven to 175°C/350°F/Gas Mark 4. Beat the butter with 50 g (¼ cup/2 oz) of sugar, the egg yolks, remaining vanilla sugar and lemon zest until fluffy. Mix in the Quark, semolina, almonds and raisins. Beat the egg whites with the remaining sugar and a pinch of salt to soft peaks and fold into the Quark mixture.

Put the casserole dish in the lowest third of the oven and bake until golden brown, about 1 hour.

Dumplings with Plum Compote (Germknödeln)

Bavaria

Preparation time:		20 minutes
Rising time:		45 minutes
Cooking time:		8 minutes
Serves:		8

½ cup/3½ fl oz	milk	100 ml
4 tsp	fresh yeast	4 tsp
1 tbsp	caster (superfine) sugar	1 tbsp
2¼ cups/9 oz	plain (all-purpose) flour	250 g
1	egg	1
*	salt	*
5 tsp	butter, softened	5 tsp
*	flour, for dusting	*
⅓ cup/3½ oz	Plum Compote (p. 382)	100 g
½ cup/4¼ oz	butter, melted	125 g
4 tbsp	poppy seeds	4 tbsp
4 tbsp	icing (confectioners') sugar	4 tbsp

Heat the milk until lukewarm. Dissolve the yeast in the milk and add 1 teaspoon of sugar. Put the flour into a bowl and make a well in the centre. Pour in the milk and yeast and mix with a little of the flour. Cover the starter and rest in a warm place for 15 minutes.

Whisk the egg and add to the starter with a pinch of salt, the remaining sugar and the soft butter. Mix with the flour. Put the dough into a food mixer or use a hand mixer with a dough hook to knead until it becomes shiny and elastic and comes away easily from the sides of the bowl. Cover and leave to rise in a warm place, about 30 minutes.

Meanwhile, fill two wide pans with salted water and heat to a simmer.

Roll out the dough on a floured work counter to about 1 cm (½ inch) cylinders and cut into 8 uniform pieces. Flatten the pieces a little, put Plum Compote in the centres, fold the dough around them and close. Press the seams well, shape the dough into balls and place, spaced apart, on a lightly floured dish cloth. Make sure the work counter isn't too cold – if necessary, put the cloth on a pastry board. Cover the dumplings with a dish cloth and leave to rise, about 5 minutes.

Put the dumplings into the simmering, salted water, cover with a lid and cook for 8 minutes. Don't lift the lid in this time and don't turn the dumplings over.

Use a slotted spoon to take the dumplings out of the water, drain, arrange on warm plates and drizzle with the hot butter. Mix the poppy seeds with the icing (confectioners') sugar and sprinkle over the dumplings. Dust with more icing (confectioners') sugar if desired.

Baked Apples

Preparation time:		20 minutes
Cooking time:		35 minutes
Serves:		4

4 tsp	orange liqueur	4 tsp
2 tbsp	raisins	2 tbsp
4	large, fragrant apples	4
½ cup/1¼ oz	almond paste	30 g
1 tbsp	orange marmalade	1 tbsp
¼ cup/1¼ oz	candied orange peel	30 g
½ cup/2 oz	coarsely chopped hazelnuts	50 g
*	ground cinnamon	*
½ cup/4 fl oz	semi-dry white wine	125 ml
¼ cup/1½ oz	butter	40 g
*	Vanilla Sauce (p. 359), to serve or vanilla ice cream, to serve	*

Add the orange liqueur to the raisins and soak for at least 15 minutes. Wash and core the apples. Preheat the oven to 200°C/400°F/Gas Mark 6.

Mix the almond paste with the marmalade, chop the orange peel then add it to the mix with the hazelnuts, raisins and their soaking liquid. Season with a little cinnamon.

Arrange the apples side by side in an ovenproof dish, fill the cavities with the almond mixture and pour over the wine. Cut the butter into small pieces and place over the apples. Put the dish on the middle shelf of the oven and bake for 30–35 minutes. Serve hot with Vanilla Sauce or vanilla ice cream.

Chocolate Sauce

Preparation time:		5 minutes
Cooking time:		5 minutes
Makes:		about 500 g/1 lb 2 oz

9oz	dark couverture chocolate	250 g
¼ cup/2 oz	honey	50 g
1 cup/8 fl oz	milk	250ml
*	ground cinnamon	*
¼ tsp	vanilla seeds	¼ tsp
*	whipped cream (optional)	*
*	liqueur (optional)	*

Finely chop the chocolate and mix with the honey in a bowl.

Combine the milk with a little cinnamon and the vanilla seeds in a pan and bring to a boil. Add the chocolate and stir to a smooth sauce. Use as an accompaniment for ice cream, creams and mousses, crepes and fruit.

This sauce is served cold, so let cool well. If desired, mix in a little cream whipped to soft peaks. A dash of rum, orange liqueur or coffee liqueur will round off the flavour.

Vanilla Sauce

All regions

Preparation time:		5 minutes
Cooking time:		15 minutes
Makes:		about 500 ml (2 cups/17 fl oz)

2	vanilla beans	2
scant 1 cup/7 fl oz	milk	200 ml
scant 1 cup/7 fl oz	double (heavy) cream	200 ml
scant ¼ cup/1½ oz	caster (superfine) sugar	40 g
3	egg yolks	3
2	eggs	2

Split the vanilla bean lengthwise and scrape out the seeds. Combine the milk, cream, half of the sugar and the vanilla seeds and beans in a pan and bring to a boil, then keep warm.

In a metal mixing bowl, whisk the egg yolks with the eggs and remaining sugar until thick and pale. Stir the hot vanilla-infused milk into the egg mixture.

Place the bowl over a bain-marie and stir constantly and gently with a spatula, avoiding the sides of the bowl. For optimum binding and thickening, the temperature of the liquid should be about 80°C/175°F. Then strain through a sieve. Return the vanilla beans to the sauce and let cool a little.

Fruit Salad

All regions

| Preparation time: | | 20 minutes |
| Serves: | | 4 |

1	lemon	1
scant ¼ cup/1½ oz	caster (superfine) sugar	40 g
½	bunch mint	½
3	peaches	3
3	nectarines	3
¾ cup/3½ oz	raspberries	100 g
1¼ cups/5 oz	blackberries	150 g
1¼ cups/5 oz	red currants	150 g
*	toasted sliced almonds	*

Squeeze the lemon. Combine 100 ml (½ cup/3½ fl oz) water with the lemon juice and sugar in a pan and bring to a boil. Pick, wash and pat dry the mint leaves and coarsely chop 8 leaves. Add to the syrup and let cool.

Wash, halve, stone (pit) and cut the peaches and nectarines into slices. Sort the raspberries. Wash the blackberries and red currants and let dry. Remove any stems from the red currants.

Put the berries into a deep plates or glasses. Arrange the peaches and nectarines over them. Pour over the syrup and garnish with the whole mint leaves.

This fruit salad can of course be made with other seasonal fruits, such as apples, pears, oranges and strawberries. As a topping, toast sliced almonds in a frying pan or skillet and scatter over the fruit before serving.

Elderberry Soup

Northern Germany

Preparation time:		30 minutes
Cooking time:		15 minutes
Serves:		4

For the elderberry soup:

2½ cups/11 oz	elderberries	300 g
1	pear	1
4	pickled plums	4
*	salt	*
⅓ cup/2¾ oz	caster (superfine) sugar	70 g
1 tbsp	unwaxed lemon zest	1 tbsp
½ cup/4 fl oz	red wine	125 ml
2 tbsp	cornflour (cornstarch)	2 tbsp

For the egg white dumplings:

2	egg whites	2
2 tbsp	caster (superfine) sugar	2 tbsp

For the elderberry soup: Remove the stems from the elderberries, wash and let drain. Peel the pear and cut into small pieces. Combine the chopped pear with the berries and plums in a pan. Add 1 litre (4½ cups/34 fl oz) water, a pinch of salt, the sugar and lemon zest. Cook over a medium heat for 10 minutes.

Press the stewed fruit through a sieve or purée in a food mill, return to the pan and bring back to a boil. Mix the wine with the cornflour (cornstarch) and add the mixture to the soup. Bring to a boil briefly, remove from the heat, and adjust the seasoning.

For the egg white dumplings: Beat the egg whites to stiff peaks, gradually adding the sugar. Continue to beat until firm and glossy. Use a teaspoon to form dumplings and poach in gently simmering water, about 5 minutes. Use a slotted spoon to take the dumplings out of the water and serve in the hot soup. The soup can also be served cold.

Chilled Fruit Soup

All regions

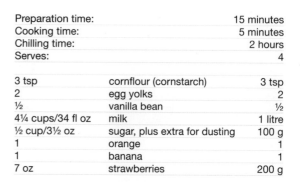

Preparation time:		15 minutes
Cooking time:		5 minutes
Chilling time:		2 hours
Serves:		4

3 tsp	cornflour (cornstarch)	3 tsp
2	egg yolks	2
½	vanilla bean	½
4¼ cups/34 fl oz	milk	1 litre
½ cup/3½ oz	sugar, plus extra for dusting	100 g
1	orange	1
1	banana	1
7 oz	strawberries	200 g

Dissolve the cornflour (cornstarch) completely with a little cold water and the egg yolks. Split the vanilla bean. Combine the milk with the sugar and vanilla bean in a pan and bring to a boil. Whisk in the cornflour (cornstarch) mixture, let simmer briefly, remove from the heat and let cool, stirring often. Then remove the vanilla bean and stir the soup very well. Chill for 2 hours in the refrigerator.

Peel the orange, divide into segments, and cut into small pieces. Peel and slice the banana. Wash, trim, and pat dry the strawberries. Cut into quarters. Mix the fruit and add a little sugar. Fill soup plates with the soup and spoon over the fruit.

Rum-Soaked Raisins

All regions

Preparation time:		10 minutes
Resting time:		2 hours
Serves:		4

½ tbsp	black tea leaves	½ tbsp
3 tbsp	rum	3 tbsp
⅓ cup/2 oz	raisins	50 g

Bring 100 ml (scant ½ cup/3½ fl oz) of water to a boil in a pan. Remove the pan from the heat and add the tea leaves. Cover with a lid and steep for 5 minutes.

Strain the hot tea through a sieve into a bowl and add the rum. Add the raisins and let steep for at least 2 hours. Let drain before use.

Apple Purée

All regions

Preparation time:		10 minutes
Cooking time:		15 minutes
Serves:		4

2¼ lbs	cooking apples (e.g. Bramley)	1 kg
1	lemon, juiced	3 tbsp
scant ½ cup/3 oz	caster (superfine) sugar	80 g
½	cinnamon stick	½

Peel, quarter, core, and cut the apples into pieces. Squeeze the lemon. Combine the apples with 5 tablespoons of water, the lemon juice, sugar and cinnamon in a pan and bring to a boil. Cover with a lid and braise over a low heat for 10–15 minutes until tender.

Discard the cinnamon and purée the apples. Adjust the seasoning with sugar.

Apple Compote

All regions

Preparation time:		5 minutes
Cooking time:		10 minutes
Serves:		4

1 lb 9 oz	apples	750 g
scant ½ cup/3 oz	caster (superfine) sugar	80 g
1	lemon, juiced	1
2 strips	unwaxed orange zest	2
½	cinnamon stick	½

Peel, quarter, core and cut the apples, as desired, either into wedges or 2 cm (1 inch) chunks.

Combine the apples, 500 ml (2 cups/17 fl oz) water, the sugar, lemon juice and orange zest and cinnamon in a pan and simmer for 5–10 minutes, depending on the degree of ripeness, until soft. Before serving, remove and discard the cinnamon and orange zest.

Pear Compote

All regions

Preparation time:		10 minutes
Cooking time:		10 minutes
Serves:		4

1 lb 9 oz	firm pears	750 g
scant ½ cup/3 oz	caster (superfine) sugar	80 g
1	lemon, juiced	1
2 strips	unwaxed orange zest	2
½	cinnamon stick	½

Peel, quarter, core and cut the pears, as desired, either into wedges or 2 cm (1 inch) chunks.

Combine the pears, 500 ml (2 cups/17 fl oz) water, the sugar, lemon juice, orange zest and cinnamon in a pan and simmer for 5–10 minutes, depending on the degree of ripeness, until soft. Before serving, remove and discard the cinnamon and zest.

Elderberry and Pear Compote

All regions

Preparation time:		10 minutes
Cooking time:		15 minutes
Serves:		4

¾ cup/7 oz	elderberries	200 g
1 tbsp	cornflour (cornstarch)	1 tbsp
1¼ cups/10 fl oz	heavy red wine	300 ml
⅓ cup/2¼ oz	caster (superfine) sugar	60 g
½	vanilla bean	½
1 strip	unwaxed lemon zest	1
1 strip	unwaxed orange zest	1
¾ inch	cinnamon stick	2 cm
2 x 1¼ oz	pears	2 x 30 g
1 tbsp	lemon juice	1 tbsp

Sort and wash the elderberries. Dissolve the cornflour (cornstarch) in 2 tablespoons wine. Caramelise half of the sugar in a pan. Deglaze the pan with the remaining wine and simmer until reduced by a third.

Stir the cornflour (cornstarch) into the liquid in the pan and simmer for 2–3 minutes. Split the vanilla bean, add to the pan with the lemon and orange zests, cinnamon and berries and simmer gently for 5 minutes.

Peel, quarter, core and cut the pears into thin wedges. Add the pears to the pan and simmer for 3 more minutes.

Remove the pan from the heat, adjust the seasoning with lemon juice and let cool slightly. Remove and discard the whole spices.

Rhubarb Compote

All regions

Preparation time:		20 minutes
Cooking time:		25 minutes
Serves:		4

1lb 5 oz	young rhubarb	600 g
2 tbsp	raspberries	2 tbsp
5	strawberries	5
1 cup/7 oz	caster (superfine) sugar	200 g
2 strips	unwaxed lemon zest	2
2 strips	unwaxed orange zest	2
2 shards	cinnamon stick	2 shards
1	vanilla bean, split	1
1	star anise	1
1–2 tbsp	cornflour (corn starch)	1–2 tbsp
*	icing (confectioners') sugar	*
*	lemon juice	

Trim and wash the rhubarb. Cut the stems crosswise into about 1 cm (½ inch) lengths and spread out inside a casserole dish. Sort and wash the raspberries. Wash, trim, and halve the strawberries. Spread the berries out over the rhubarb. Preheat the oven to 180°C/350°F/Gas Mark 4.

Combine the sugar in a pan with 75 ml (⅓ cup/2½ fl oz) water, the lemon and orange zests, cinnamon, the split vanilla bean and star anise, then boil for a few minutes to a syrup. Pour the syrup over the rhubarb mixture, cover with a lid or aluminium foil, and put the dish on the middle shelf of the oven for about 25 minutes.

Take the rhubarb out of the oven, remove the lid and let cool slightly. Carefully strain the sauce through a sieve into a pan. Take the raspberries and strawberries out of the dish and press through the sieve into the pan. Remove the spices from the rhubarb.

Dissolve the cornflour (cornstarch) completely in a little cold water. Reduce the syrup, stir in the cornflour (cornstarch) and simmer for 2 minutes. Pour the thickened syrup over the rhubarb and adjust the seasoning with the icing (confectioners') sugar and lemon juice.

Plum Compote

All regions

Preparation time:		5 minutes
Cooking time:		5 minutes
Resting time:		3 hours
Serves:		4

1 lb 2 oz	plums	500 g
⅓ cup/2¾ oz	caster (superfine) sugar	70 g
½	lemon, juiced	½
½	cinnamon stick	½
½	vanilla bean	½
3 tbsp	heavy red wine	3 tbsp
2 tbsp	port	2 tbsp
1 tbsp	cornflour (cornstarch)	1 tbsp

Wash, halve, and stone (pit) the plums. Halve again. Mix the plum quarters with the sugar, lemon juice, cinnamon and vanilla bean. Add the red wine and port.

Strain the wine mixture through a sieve into a small pan. Join the plum quarters together to make whole plums.

Dissolve the cornflour (cornstarch) completely in a little cold water. Reduce the wine mixture, stir in the cornflour (cornstarch), and gently simmer for 2 minutes. Pour the sauce over the plums and rest for several hours.

Wine-Poached Plums

All regions

Preparation time:		20 minutes
Serves:		4

14 oz	plums	400 g
2 tbsp	caster (superfine) sugar	2 tbsp
8 tbsp	heavy red wine	8 tbsp
5 tbsp	port	5 tbsp
½	vanilla bean, scraped	½
1 shard	cinnamon stick	1 shard
1 strip	unwaxed orange zest	1 strip
1 tbsp	cold butter	1 tbsp

Wash, quarter and stone (pit) the plums. Lightly caramelise the sugar in a pan. Deglaze the pan with the red wine and port and simmer to reduce by half.

Add the vanilla bean, cinnamon and orange zest. Mix in the butter. Add the plums and cook for 2–5 minutes, depending on their degree of ripeness. Remove and discard the whole spices.

Desserts

Aniseed Cookies

All regions

Preparation time:		25 minutes
Drying time:		12 hours
Cooking time:		30 minutes
Makes:		about 100

1 tsp	aniseeds	1 tsp
*	butter, for greasing	*
*	flour, for dusting	*
4	eggs	4
3 cups/11 oz	icing (confectioners') sugar	300 g
2½ cups/10–11 oz	plain (all-purpose) flour	275–300 g

Finely crush the star aniseeds in a mortar. Grease two baking sheets with butter and dust with flour.

Beat together the eggs and sifted icing (confectioners') sugar for 10 minutes with an electric mixer until thick, pale and fluffy. Then briefly blend in the aniseeds.

Sift the flour, then add it to the beaten egg mixture, first with a whisk, then fold in with a spatula. Adjust the amount of flour according to the size of the eggs. The dough should have a consistency that holds its shape and does not spread when the cookies are shaped, but allows the surface of the cookie to smooth out.

Use a teaspoon to place small mounds of dough on the greased baking sheets, spacing them 3 cm (1¼ inch) apart. Let dry out overnight at a temperature of 15–18°C/59–65°F.

Preheat the oven to 150°C/300°F/Gas Mark 2. Bake the cookies, one baking sheet at a time, on the middle shelf of the oven for about 15 minutes, or until light golden. The cookies should have a frill around the bottom and a small white peak on top. Let cool.

Aachen-Style Gingerbread (Aachener Printen)

Aachen and North Rhine-Westphalia

Preparation time:		45 minutes
Resting time:		12 hours 30 minutes
Cooking time:		16 minutes
Makes:		about 50

¼ cup/ 1¼ oz	brown sugar	35 g
¾ cup/5½ oz	honey	165 g
1¾ cups/7 oz	plain (all-purpose) flour	200 g
5 tsp	cornflour (corn starch)	5 tsp
scant ¼ cup/¾ oz	candied lemon peel	20 g
scant ⅛ cup/¼ oz	candied orange peel	10 g
½ tsp	baking powder	½ tsp
1 tbsp	whole milk	1 tbsp
⅛ tsp	baking soda	⅛ tsp
¾ cup/3 oz	rock sugar (rock candy)	80 g
2 tbsp	coarsely chopped walnuts	2 tbsp
1–2 tsp	gingerbread spice mix	1–2 tsp
*	butter, for greasing	*
*	flour, for dusting	*

Mix the brown sugar with 50 ml (scant ¼ cup/1⅔ fl oz) cold water and combine in a pan with the honey. Heat slowly to 80°C/176°F. Let cool to about 37°C/99°F, then gradually work in the flour. Cover and let rest overnight at room temperature.

Preheat the oven to 180°C/350°F/Gas Mark 4. Sprinkle the cornflour (corn starch) over a baking sheet and toast in the oven for about 15 minutes or until medium brown, stirring a little from time to time. Mix with 125 ml (½ cup/ 4¼ fl oz) cold water in a pan and bring to the boil for a few minutes, until the liquid thickens a little and runs off the spoon as a thread. Let the starch glaze cool slightly.

Finely chop the candied peels. Dissolve the baking powder with the milk in a cup and dissolve the baking soda with 1 tsp water in another cup. Finely crush the rock sugar (rock candy). Knead all these ingredients together with the candied orange and lemon peels, walnuts and gingerbread spice mix into the dough.

Raise the oven temperature to 220°C/425°F/Gas Mark 7. Grease two baking sheets with butter and dust with flour.

Roll out the dough to a 5-mm (¼-inch) thick rectangle and cut into 10 × 2.5-cm (1-inch) strips. Lay the strips on the baking sheets, spaced a few centimeters (about an inch) apart, and let dry for 15 minutes at room temperature.

One at a time, place the baking sheets on the middle shelf of the oven and bake the gingerbread for about 8 minutes. Brush with the starch glaze and bake again for a few more minutes, until the gingerbread turns medium brown and glossy. Let cool and store in tin containers.

Apricot-Filled Cookies

All regions

Preparation time:	30 minutes
Cooling time:	30 minutes
Cooking time:	10 minutes
Makes:	about 30

2 cups/8 oz	plain (all-purpose) flour	220 g
*	salt	*
½	unwaxed lemon, zested	½
½	vanilla bean, seeds removed	½
½ cups/6¼ oz	ground almonds	180 g
1½ cups/5 oz	icing (confectioners') sugar	150 g
1	egg	1
scant 1 cup/7 oz	cold butter	200 g

For finishing:		
½ cup/2 oz	icing (confectioners') sugar	50 g
2 tbsp	vanilla sugar	2 tbsp
scant 1 cup/9 oz	apricot preserve	250 g

Make a shortcrust pastry dough by mixing the flour with a pinch of salt, the lemon zest, vanilla bean seeds, ground almonds, icing (confectioners') sugar, egg and butter, then kneading until smooth. Shape into a ball, cover with clingfilm (plastic wrap) and rest in the refrigerator for 30 minutes.

Preheat the oven to 180°C/350°F/Gas Mark 4. Roll out the dough until about 2 mm(¹⁄₁₆ inch) thick, then cut out 6-cm/2¼-inch discs using a cookie cutter. Lay the discs on baking sheets lined with parchment paper, then use a smaller diameter cookie cutter to cut out the centre of half of the discs to create rings. Bake all the cookies in batches for 8–10 minutes, or until light golden, then let cool on a rack.

Mix the icing (confectioners') sugar with the vanilla sugar. Lay the cookie rings side by side and dust with a thick coating of the sugar mixture.

Spread a thin layer of apricot preserve over the remaining cookies and then cover with the rings. Put the remaining apricot preserve into a piping (pastry) bag and pipe a little in the hole in the centre of the cookie ring.

Layered Gingerbread Cubes (Dominosteine)

Dresden

Preparation time:	1 hour 30 minutes
Resting time:	24 hours
Cooking time:	15 minutes
Makes:	about 150

For the gingerbread:		
scant ¼ cup/1¼ oz	brown sugar	35 g
¾ cup/5½ oz	honey	165 g
1¾ cup/7 oz	plain (all-purpose) flour	200 g
½ tsp	baking powder	½ tsp
1 tbsp	whole milk	1 tbsp
⅛ tsp	baking soda	⅛ tsp
scant ½ cup/3 oz	rock sugar (rock candy)	80 g
4 tsp	minced candied lemon peel	4 tsp
2 tsp	minced candied orange peel	2 tsp
2 tbsp	chopped walnuts	2 tbsp
1–2 tsp	gingerbread spice mix	1–2 tsp
*	butter, for greasing	*
*	flour, for dusting	*
¾ cup/7 oz	apricot preserve	200 g
1 lb 5 oz	dark couverture chocolate	600 g
¼ cup/2 oz	cocoa butter or solid coconut oil	50 g

For the jelly:		
7	sheets gelatine	7
2½ cups/1 lb 8½ oz	quince jelly	700 g
1	lemon, juiced	1

For the marzipan:		
½ cup/6 oz	marzipan (almond paste)	175 g
1¾ cups/6 oz	icing (confectioners') sugar	175 g

For the gingerbread: Mix the sugar and honey with 50 ml (scant ¼ cup/2 fl oz) water in a pan, then gently heat to 80°C/176°F. Let it cool to about 37°C/99°F, then gradually work in the flour. Rest overnight at room temperature.

Dissolve the baking powder with the milk in a cup and dissolve the baking soda with 1 tsp water in another. Knead into the dough with the sugar, peel, nuts and spice.

Preheat the oven to 180°C/350°F/Gas Mark 4. Grease a baking sheet and dust with flour. Roll out the dough to a 3-mm (⅛-inch) thick rectangle (about 25 × 40 cm/ 10 × 15¾ inches), transfer to the greased baking sheet with an adjustable baking frame. Bake for 10–15 minutes.

Heat the preserve in a pan. Let it simmer briefly, then blitz with a stick (immersion) blender until smooth. Take the gingerbread out of the oven, spread with the preserve.

For the jelly: Soften the gelatine in cold water. Melt the jelly with the lemon juice in a pan. Squeeze the gelatine, then stir into the warm jelly. Let it cool and start to set, then pour over the gingerbread evenly. Chill until set.

For the marzipan: Mix the marzipan (almond paste) with the sugar and work it into a dough. On a work surface dusted with sugar, roll out to a rectangle the same size as the gingerbread. Remove the baking frame. Using a rolling pin, lay the marzipan over the jelly. Cover, rest overnight, then cut into 2.5-cm (1-inch) cubes.

Chop the chocolate and combine it with the cocoa butter. Melt in a heatproof bowl set over simmering water. Dip the cubes into the chocolate, letting the excess drain away. Allow to set, then store in an airtight container.

Gingerbread Wafer Cookies

All regions

Preparation time:	35 minutes
Resting time:	6 hours
Cooking time:	30 minutes
Makes:	about 20

For the gingerbread:		
½ tsp	baking powder	½ tsp
3 tsp	rum	3 tsp
½ cup/ 1¼ oz	candied lemon peel	30 g
½ cup/1½ oz	candied orange peel	40 g
scant ⅔ cup/7 oz	ground almonds	200 g
scant ½ cup/ 2 oz	ground hazelnuts	50 g
⅓ cup/1½ oz	plain (all-purpose) flour	40 g
*	salt	*
1 tsp	gingerbread spice mix	1 tsp
4	egg whites	4
2 cups/ 6¾ oz	sugar	190 g
⅔ cup/4½ oz	marzipan (almond paste)	130 g
20	round wafers	20
1 cup/5 oz	blanched almonds	150 g

For the glaze:		
1	egg white	1
1 cup/3½ oz	icing (confectioners') sugar	100 g
1 tbsp	lemon juice	1 tbsp

For the gingerbread: Dissolve the baking powder in 2 tsp rum in a small bowl. Dice the lemon and orange peel and mix with the rest of the rum, then mince. Mix with the almonds, hazelnuts, flour, a pinch of salt and the gingerbread spices.

Beat the egg whites with a third of the sugar until creamy, then gradually add the remaining sugar and beat to stiff peaks.

Mix the marzipan (almond paste) with a little beaten egg white until smooth. Stir in the dissolved baking powder, then gradually fold in the gingerbread and nut mixture, alternating with the beaten egg whites.

Spread the mixture in domes over the wafers. Top with blanched almonds or other nuts, then lay on baking sheets lined with parchment paper. Rest the gingerbread cookies in a dry place for 6 hours.

Preheat the oven to 170°C/340°F/Gas Mark 3½. Bake the gingerbread cookies on the middle shelf of the oven for about 30 minutes. Remove them from the oven and let cool until lukewarm.

For the glaze: Mix the egg white with the sifted icing (confectioners') sugar and lemon juice until smooth. Spread over the lukewarm cookies. Allow to set, then store in an airtight container.

Shortbread Cookies

Lower Saxony

Preparation time:	30 minutes
Cooling time:	30 minutes
Cooking time:	15 minutes
Makes:	about 50

¾ cup/5½ oz	butter, at room temperature	160 g
1¼ cups/ 4 oz	icing (confectioners') sugar	120 g
*	salt	*
1	pinch vanilla bean seeds	1
2¼ cups/9 oz	plain (all-purpose) flour	250 g
1	egg white	1
½ cup/3½ oz	coarse or decorating sugar	100 g
2	unwaxed limes	2
2 tbsp	apricot preserve	2 tbsp

Use an electric mixer with a dough hook to mix the butter, icing (confectioners') sugar, a pinch of salt and the vanilla bean seeds in a bowl and knead until smooth. Sift the flour over the mixture and rub in with your fingers until crumbly. Quickly knead to a firm shortbread dough. Shape the dough into one or two logs about 2 cm (¾ inch) in diameter, cover with clingfilm (plastic wrap) and rest in the refrigerator for 30 minutes.

Preheat the oven to 170°C/340°F/Gas Mark 3½. Beat the egg white with a fork. Brush the dough logs on all sides with the beaten egg white and roll them in the coarse or decorating sugar, pressing lightly. Cut the logs into about 5-mm (¼-inch) thick slices. Arrange spaced about 2 cm (¾ inch) apart on baking sheets lined with parchment paper.

Bake the cookies on the middle shelf of the oven for about 15 minutes or until light golden, then let them cool.

If desired, use a zester to make thin strings of zest from 2 unwaxed limes. Simmer the lime zest in a little water for 3–5 minutes, then strain into a sieve, refresh in iced water and drain well.

Squeeze the juice from 1 lime. Combine 2 tbsp apricot preserve with 1 tbsp lime juice in a pan. Simmer for 2–3 minutes, then stir in the lime zest. Decorate each cookie with 2–3 strings of lime zest. Glaze with the apricot mixture. Allow to set, then store in an airtight container.

Deep-Fried Almond Pastries (Mutzenmandeln)

Rhineland

Preparation time:	30 minutes
Cooling time:	3 hours
Cooking time:	5 minutes
Makes:	about 40

2	eggs	2
4 tsp	marzipan (almond paste)	4 tsp
½ cup/3½ oz	caster (superfine) sugar	100 g
1¾ cups/7 oz	plain (all-purpose) flour	200 g
2½ tbsp	cornflour (corn starch)	2½ tbsp
½ tsp	baking powder	½ tsp
1 tbsp	chopped sliced almonds	1 tbsp
1 tsp	rum	1 tsp
1 tsp	rose water	1 tsp
2 tbsp	melted butter	2 tbsp
1 tbsp	double (heavy) cream	1 tbsp
*	salt	*
1	pinch grated unwaxed lemon zest	1
*	flour, for dusting	*
*	oil, for deep-frying	*

Separate 1 egg into two bowls. Grate the marzipan (almond paste) into the bowl with the egg yolk and knead together. Add the egg white, the remaining egg and half of the sugar, then beat with an electric mixer for a few minutes until fluffy.

Mix together the flour, cornflour (corn starch), and baking powder. Add to the almond mixture with the almonds, rum, rose water, melted butter, double (heavy) cream, a pinch of salt and lemon zest, then knead to a smooth dough. Shape the dough into a block, cover with clingfilm (plastic wrap) and rest in the refrigerator for about 3 hours.

Roll out the dough on a floured work surface to a thickness of about 1 cm (½ inch), then use an oval-shaped cookie cutter to cut out about 40 pastries. Put plenty of oil in a pan and heat to 160–170°C/325–340°F. Deep-fry the pastries for about 5 minutes or until golden brown, turning once. Drain on paper towels. Coat with the remaining sugar.

Frankfurt-Style Pastries (Frankfurter Bethmännchen)

Frankfurt am Main and Hesse

Preparation time:	30 minutes
Cooking time:	30 minutes
Makes:	about 35

¾ cup/2½-3 oz	unblanched whole almonds	65-80g
scant 2 cups/9 oz	marzipan (almond paste)	250 g
1 cup/3½ oz	icing (confectioners') sugar	100 g
¾ cup/3½ oz	ground almonds	100 g
4–5 tbsp	rose water	4–5 tbsp
1	egg, separated	1
5 tbsp	whole milk	5 tbsp

Bring a small pan of water to the boil. Add the whole almonds and blanch in the boiling water for about 5 minutes. Strain in a sieve, refresh in iced water, then squeeze the almonds out of their skins. Halve the blanched almonds.

Make a dough by crumbling the marzipan (almond paste) and kneading it together with the icing (confectioners') sugar and ground almonds. Add 3 tbsp rose water, then knead in the egg white. Add a little more rose water, if needed.

Preheat the oven to 180°C/350°F/Gas Mark 4. Line two baking sheets with parchment paper.

Shape the marzipan dough into about 2.5 cm (1 inch) balls and arrange them spaced apart on the baking sheets. Press 3 almond halves vertically and evenly spaced into each ball, pointed end up, to make a roughly pyramidal shape.

Mix the egg yolk with the milk and 1 tbsp rose water, then brush the pastries with the glaze. Bake the pastries on the second shelf from the bottom of the oven for about 15 minutes, or until light golden. Let them cool, then store in airtight containers.

Almond Crescent Cookies

All regions

Preparation time:		20 minutes
Cooling time:		30 minutes
Cooking time:		15 minutes
Makes:		12

2⅓ cups/10½ oz	marzipan (almond paste)	300 g
scant 1 cup	icing (confectioners') sugar	90 g
1	egg white	1
1 cup/2¾ oz	sliced almonds	80 g
3½ oz/½ cup	dark chocolate frosting	100 g

Coarsely grate the marzipan (almond paste) into a mixing beaker. Add the sugar and egg white and, using an electric mixer with whisk attachment, mix on the lowest speed until smooth.

Preheat the oven to 180°C/350°F/Gas Mark 4. Line a baking sheet with parchment paper. Use a tablespoon to scoop out 12 equal portions of the almond mixture. Roll in the sliced almonds and shape into rolls 5 cm (2 inches) long. Bend the rolls into crescent shapes, place on the baking sheet and lightly flatten.

Position the baking sheet on the middle shelf inside the oven and bake until golden, about 15 minutes. Take the cookies out of the oven, let cool and carefully detach from the parchment paper.

Melt the chocolate frosting in a heatproof bowl set over simmering water or in a microwave. Dip each end of the crescents in the melted frosting, then arrange on parchment paper to set. Enjoy freshly made or store for up to 2 weeks in an airtight container.

Vanilla Crescent Shortbread Cookies

Southern Germany

Preparation time:		30 minutes
Cooling time:		30 minutes
Cooking time:		30 minutes
Makes:		about 80

1 cup/9 oz	soft butter	250 g
1 cup/3½ oz	icing (confectioners') sugar	100 g
*	salt	*
1	vanilla bean, seeds removed	1
1	egg	1
2⅔ cups/11 oz	plain (all-purpose) flour	300 g
1⅓ cups/5 oz	ground almonds	150 g
¼ cup/2 oz	caster (superfine) sugar	50 g
2 tbsp	vanilla sugar	2 tbsp

Use an electric mixer with a dough hook or a dough scraper to mix the butter with the icing (confectioners') sugar, a pinch of salt and the vanilla bean seeds until smooth. Incorporate the egg with a dough scraper or rubber spatula.

Sift the flour over the butter mixture, sprinkle with the almonds and rub into the mixture until crumbly. Quickly knead to a smooth shortbread dough. Shape the dough into a log about 1.5 cm (¾ inch) in diameter, cover with clingfilm (plastic wrap) and rest in the refrigerator for 30 minutes.

Preheat the oven to 175°C/345°F/Gas Mark 3¾. Line two baking sheets with parchment paper.

Cut the logs into discs, then use your hands to shape the pieces into small crescent shapes. Arrange the cookies on the baking sheets. Bake the cookies on the middle shelf of the oven for 12–15 minutes, or until golden.

Mix the sugar with the vanilla sugar on a flat plate. Take the cookies out of the oven. While still as hot as possible, coat the cookies in the sugar mixture, then let them cool completely. Store the cookies in an airtight container (preferably a tin container) in a cool and dry place. They will stay fresh for several weeks.

Nut Triangles

All regions

Preparation time:		30 minutes
Cooling time:		40 minutes
Cooking time:		30 minutes
Makes:		40

For the pastry:

2 cups/7¾ oz	plain (all-purpose) flour	220 g
1 level tsp	baking powder	1 level tsp
½ cup/3½ oz	sugar	100 g
1 tbsp	vanilla sugar	1 tbsp
1	egg	1
½ cup/3½ oz	soft butter	100 g
*	salt	*
*	butter, for greasing	*

For the topping:

⅔ cup/5 oz	butter	150 g
¾ cup/5 oz	caster (superfine) sugar	150 g
2 tbsp	vanilla sugar	2 tbsp
1 cup/ 3½ oz	ground hazelnuts (flour)	100 g
1¾ cups/ 7 oz	hazelnuts, chopped	200 g
3 tbsp	apricot preserve	3 tbsp

For the chocolate frosting:

3½ oz	dark chocolate	100 g
4 tsp	cocoa butter	4 tsp

Preheat the oven to 180°C/350°F/Gas Mark 4. Grease a 32 × 40-cm (12½ × 15¾-inch) baking pan with butter.

For the pastry: Sift the flour and baking powder into a mixing bowl. Add the other ingredients and use an electric mixer with a dough hook to work everything into a smooth dough. Transfer to the greased baking pan, then use a rolling pin to roll out the dough to an even thickness, about 3 mm (⅛ inch) thick.

For the topping: Melt the butter in a pan and stir in the sugar, vanilla sugar and 3 tbsp cold water. Remove from the heat. Incorporate the ground hazelnuts (flour) and chopped hazelnuts, then let it cool for about 10 minutes.

Spread apricot preserve over the pastry in the baking pan, then cover with the topping and bake on the middle shelf of the oven for 25–30 minutes. Take the cookies out of the oven, set aside to cool, then cut into 8-cm (3¼-inch) squares, then halve on the diagonal to make triangles.

For the chocolate frosting: Coarsely chop the chocolate and melt along with the cocoa butter in a heatproof bowl set over simmering water or in a microwave. Dip two corners of the triangles in a little chocolate, then arrange on parchment paper to set. Store in airtight containers.

Black and White Cookies

All regions

Preparation time:		40 minutes
Cooling time:		5 hours
Cooking time:		12 minutes
Makes:		about 50

4 cups/1 lb	plain (all-purpose) flour	450 g
1½ cups/5 oz	icing (confectioners') sugar	150 g
1	pinch grated unwaxed lemon zest	1
1	pinch vanilla bean seeds	1
*	salt	*
2	egg yolks	2
1⅓ cups/11 oz	soft butter	300 g
3 tbsp	cocoa powder	3 tbsp
*	flour, for dusting	*

Sift the flour onto a clean work surface or pastry board and make a well in the centre. Put the icing (confectioners') sugar, lemon zest, vanilla bean seeds, a pinch of salt and the egg yolks into the well. Cut the butter into cubes and scatter around the edges. Use your hands to knead everything into a smooth dough. Shape into a rectangular block, cover with clingfilm (plastic wrap) and rest in the refrigerator for 2-3 hours.

Halve the dough and knead the cocoa powder into one half to make the black dough. Cover both doughs with clingfilm and rest in the refrigerator for a further 1-2 hours.

Preheat the oven to 190°C/375°F/Gas Mark 5. Cut off one-third of each type of dough and set aside in the refrigerator for encasing. Knead the doughs again, separately, then roll out each one on a floured work surface to 8-mm (¼-inch) thick rectangles, and cut into 8-mm (¼-inch) wide strips. Brush the dough strips with a little water and arrange groups of 9 black and white strips to form blocks in a chequerboard pattern (3 layers of 3 strips). Refrigerate again.

Take the set-aside doughs and roll each one out until 3 mm (⅛ inch). Brush with a little water, then encase each chequerboard bar in either the black or white dough. Refrigerate again.

Cut the bars crosswise into 5-mm (¼-inch) thick slices. Lay the square cookie slices on a baking sheet lined with parchment paper and bake on the middle shelf of the oven for 10–12 minutes. Take the cookies out of the oven and set aside to cool. Store in airtight containers.

Coconut Macaroons

All regions

Preparation time:	30 minutes
Cooling time:	30 minutes
Cooking time:	10 minutes
Makes:	about 25

1 cup/3½ oz	desiccated coconut	100 g
1¾ cups/5 oz	caster (superfine) sugar	150 g
3	egg whites	3
3 tsp	candied orange peel	3 tsp
*	salt	*
¾ cup/5 oz	dark chocolate frosting	150 g

Mix the desiccated coconut, sugar, egg whites, orange peel and a pinch of salt in a metal bowl. Put the bowl over simmering water and heat while stirring to 60°C/140°F. The mixture will turn into a runny liquid first, before solidifying. Take the bowl off the heat and let the mixture cool completely.

Preheat the oven to 190°C/375°F/Gas Mark 5. Line two baking sheets with parchment paper. Transfer the coconut mixture to a pastry bag with a medium star tip and pipe small mounds of the mixture onto the baking sheets.

Bake the macaroons on the lowest shelf of the oven for about 8 minutes, or until their bottoms start to turn brown. Take the macaroons out of the oven and set aside to cool on a rack.

Break up the frosting into pieces in a metal bowl, set over simmering water and stir until it melts. Dip the macaroon bottoms into the frosting to a depth of 5 mm (¼ inch), then arrange on parchment paper to set.

Embossed Cookies (Springerle)

Southern Germany

Preparation time:	1 hour
Resting time:	1 hour
Drying time:	24 hours
Cooking time:	20 minutes
Makes:	about 10

2½ cups/1 lb 2 oz	caster (superfine) sugar	500 g
4	eggs, separated	4
*	salt	*
1	lemon, zested	1
2	pinches baking soda	2
1-2 tsp	kirsch	1-2 tsp
4½ cups/1 lb 2 oz	plain (all-purpose) flour	500 g
*	cornflour (corn starch)	*

Mix the sugar and egg yolks together well. Beat the egg whites to stiff peaks with a pinch of salt, then immediately stir into the egg yolk mixture. Incorporate the lemon zest and whisk with an electric mixer until the mixture is creamy and relatively firm.

Dissolve the baking soda in the kirsch. Sift the flour over the egg mixture, work in a little, add the dissolved baking soda and knead to a smooth dough. Cover the dough and set aside to rest for 1 hour.

Divide the dough into 10 equal portions and roll out over a clean work surface (or a large pastry board) to 1-cm (½-inch) thick sheets. Do not use flour. Dust the dough sheets on both sides with a little cornflour (corn starch) and rub with your hands until smooth. Press the wooden springerle molds into the dough (the size of the mold will determine the number of cookies) and remove. Trim off the excess dough from the edges or use a pastry wheel. Alternatively, use a springerle rolling pin, applying an even pressure as you roll and working in one continous slow movement. After rolling, cut the cookies apart along the marked lines. Lay the cookies on trays or baking sheets lined with parchment paper, cover with clean dish towels, then set aside to dry for 24 hours at room temperature.

The next day, preheat the oven to 140°C/275°F/Gas Mark 1. As a test, lay 1 springerle cookie on a baking sheet greased with butter (only at this point) and bake on the second shelf from the bottom of the oven for about 30 minutes. Open the oven door a little from time to time to allow any steam to escape. The surface of the cookies should turn white and the frill forming around their base should turn a light golden color. If the baked underside is too dry, brush the underside of the unbaked cookies with a little water before placing on the greased baking sheets.

Take the freshly baked cookies out of the oven, cover with a cloth and set aside to cool. Store for up to 4 weeks in an airtight tin container.

Cinnamon Stars

Baden-Württemberg

Preparation time:		40 minutes
Resting time:		12 hours
Cooking time:		30 minutes
Makes:		about 50

For the marzipan:		
⅔ cup/5 oz	marzipan (almond paste)	150 g
4	egg whites	2
2 tbsp	candied orange peel	2 tbsp
4 tsp	candied lemon peel	4 tsp
1⅓ cups/5 oz	ground almonds (flour)	150 g
scant 1 cup/3½ oz	ground hazelnuts (flour)	100 g
1 tsp	ground cinnamon	1 tsp
4 cups/14 oz	icing (confectioners') sugar	400 g

For the glaze:		
2	egg whites	2
2⅔ cups/9¼ oz	icing (confectioners') sugar	260 g

For the marzipan: Mix the marzipan (almond paste) with 2 egg whites until smooth. Mince the orange and lemon peel and mix with the almond mixture, ground almonds and hazelnuts, cinnamon, icing (confectioners') sugar, and the remaining egg whites. Set aside to rest for at least 30 minutes, but preferably overnight.

Dust a work surface with ground almonds and roll out the marzipan to a 1 cm (½ inch) thickness.

For the glaze: Beat the egg whites with the icing (confectioners') sugar until thick and fluffy, then spread over the marzipan.

Preheat the oven to 170°C/340°F/Gas Mark 3½. Line two baking sheets with parchment paper. Use a star-shaped cookie cutter, about 5 cm/2 inch diameter, to cut out the cookies, dipping the cutter in water between each cut. Lay the cookies on the baking sheets and bake for 12–15 minutes, or until light golden. Take the cookies out of the oven and set aside to cool completely. Store in airtight tin containers.

Cinnamon Rolls (Franzbrötchen)

Hamburg

Preparation time:		1 hour
Rising time:		1 hour
Cooking time:		20 minutes
Makes:		about 10

4 cups/1 lb	plain (all-purpose) flour	450 g
2 tbsp	fresh yeast	2 tbsp
¾ cup/6 fl oz	whole milk	170 ml
2	egg yolks	2
¾ cup/5 oz	caster (superfine) sugar	145 g
*	salt	*
1	pinch vanilla bean seeds	1
1	pinch grated unwaxed lemon zest	1
3 tbsp	soft butter	3 tbsp
1⅓ cups/11 oz	cold butter	300 g
*	flour, for dusting	*
½ tsp	ground cinnamon	½ tsp

Sift 375 g (3⅓ cups/13 oz) flour into a bowl and make a well in the centre. Crumble the yeast and dissolve completely in a little milk. Combine the yeast with the remaining milk, egg yolks, 45 g (¼ cup/1¾ oz) sugar, a pinch of salt, the vanilla bean seeds and lemon zest in the well. Cut the soft butter into cubes and scatter around the edges. Work the ingredients from the inside out to create a dough. Knead for another 5–10 minutes, or until it becomes elastic. Cover with clingfilm (plastic wrap) and refrigerate for 30 minutes.

Cut the cold butter into small pieces and combine with 30 g (¼ cup/1¼ oz) flour in an electric mixer and knead until firm and smooth. Set aside in the refrigerator.

Roll out the leavened dough into a 1.5-cm (⅝-inch) thick rectangle. Roll out the beurre manié (butter and flour mixture) over a floured work surface to a rectangle just under half the size of the dough. Lay the beurre manié over one side of the dough leaving an uncovered space around the three edges. Fold over the other half of the dough and press the edges together to encase completely. Roll out into a 2-cm (¾-inch) thick rectangle.

Fold the dough into thirds like a letter. Transfer the dough to a large, floured plate, cover with clingfilm (plastic wrap), and rest in the refrigerator for 10 minutes.

Again, roll out the dough to a 2-cm (¾-inch) thick rectangle, rolling along the length of the folded dough. Fold in the two shorter edges to meet at the centre and then fold in half, like a book. Cover the dough again with clingfilm and rest for at least 10 minutes. Repeat the process one more time and cool before shaping.

Roll out the dough to a large rectangle about 20 cm (8 inches) wide. Mix the remaining sugar with the cinnamon and sprinkle in an even layer over the dough. Starting from the longer side, roll up tightly. Refrigerate for 10 minutes.

Preheat the oven to 180°C/ 350°F/Gas Mark 4. Cut the roll crosswise into 3-cm (1¼-inch) thick slices. Use a thick wooden spoon handle to make a deep groove lengthwise into the top surface of each slice. Space the pastries apart on two baking sheets lined with parchment paper and rest for 15 minutes at room temperature.

Bake for about 20 minutes, or until golden brown. Take the rolls out of the oven and set aside to cool.

Cakes, Cookies & Sweet Breads

Waffles

Preparation time:		20 minutes
Cooking time:		15 minutes
Makes:		about 8

2½ cups/10 oz	plain (all-purpose) flour	280 g
1½ tsp	baking powder	1½ tsp
¼ cup/2 oz	brown sugar	50 g
3½ oz	butter	100 g
3	eggs	3
*	salt	*
2 cups/16 fl oz	buttermilk	475 ml
1	bean vanilla seeds	1
½ tsp	ground cinnamon	½ tsp
1	pinch grated unwaxed lemon zest	1
*	butter, for greasing	*
*	icing (confectioners') sugar	*
*	fruit compote, to serve	*

You will need a waffle maker or waffle iron to make this recipe.
Preheat the oven to 80°C/175°F. Sift the flour with the baking powder into a bowl and mix with the sugar. Melt the butter in a small pan over low heat.

Separate the eggs. Beat the egg whites with a pinch of salt to stiff peaks. Mix the egg yolks with the buttermilk, melted butter, vanilla bean seeds, cinnamon, lemon zest and a pinch of salt until smooth, then pour over the flour and sugar mixture and quickly mix to a thick batter. Fold in the beaten egg whites.

Heat the waffle maker and grease with butter. Make about 8 waffles with the batter in batches, keeping them warm in the preheated oven while you make the rest. Dust with a little icing (confectioners') sugar and serve with a fruit compote if desired.

Flaky Apple Turnovers

Preparation time:		45 minutes
Resting time:		12 hours
Cooking time:		20 minutes
Makes:		12

For the pastry:		
3 cups/12 oz	plain (all-purpose) flour	350 g
1 tbsp	baking powder	1 tbsp
*	salt	*
1¾ cups/12 oz	low-fat Quark	350 g
1½ cups/12 oz	cold butter	350 g
*	flour, for dusting	*
1	egg white	1
1	egg yolk	1
3 tbsp	double (heavy) cream	3 tbsp
⅓ cup/3½ oz	apricot preserve	100 g
1 tbsp	apricot brandy	1 tbsp

For the filling:		
2¼ lb	tart cooking apples	1 kg
	(e.g. Boskoop or Granny Smith)	
¼ cup/ 1½ oz	butter	40 g
¼ cup/2 oz	caster (superfine) sugar	50 g
1	pinch vanilla bean seeds	1
1	pinch ground cinnamon	1
½	unwaxed lemon	½

For the pastry: Sift the flour with the baking powder and a pinch of salt onto a clean work surface or pastry board. Make a well in the middle and put in the Quark. Cut the cold butter into cubes and scatter around the edges. Use a large knife to chop up everything, then quickly knead into a smooth dough.

Roll out the dough over a floured work surface to a 1-cm (¼-inch) thick rectangle. Fold over the shorter side into the middle, then fold over again, like a letter. Roll out again, then repeat the folding action. Cover the dough with aluminum foil and rest in the refrigerator overnight.

For the filling: Peel, quarter, core and dice the apples. Melt the butter until frothy in a pan, then add the diced apples, sugar, vanilla bean seeds, cinnamon and the lemon juice and zest. Cook the apple until tender but firm to the bite. Strain in a sieve and let cool. Preheat the oven to 200°C/400°F/Gas Mark 6.

Roll out the dough on a floured work surface to about 3 mm (⅛ inch) thick and cut out 10–12-cm (4–5-inch) discs. Brush the edges of the pastry discs with egg white, put the apple filling on to one half of the disc, then fold the other side over the filling. Press down well on the edges. Beat the egg yolk with the double (heavy) cream and brush over the turnovers.

Lay on a greased baking sheet and bake the turnovers for about 20 minutes, or until golden brown. Remove from the oven. Heat the apricot preserve with 2 tbsp water and the apricot brandy, then glaze the turnovers while still hot.

Deep-Fried Pastries (Auszogne)

Bavaria

Preparation time:		1 hour
Rising time:		65 minutes
Cooking time:		15 minutes
Makes:		12

½ cup/4½ fl oz	whole milk	130 ml
4 tsp	yeast	4 tsp
3⅓ cups/13 oz	plain (all-purpose) flour	375 g
scant ¼ cup/1½ oz	caster (superfine) sugar	40 g
3	eggs	3
2	egg yolks	2
½	vanilla bean, seeds removed	½
½ tsp	grated unwaxed lemon zest	½ tsp
*	salt	*
3 tbsp	soft butter	3 tbsp
*	flour, for dusting	*
*	oil, for deep frying	*
*	icing (confectioners') sugar	*

Heat the milk until lukewarm. Crumble the yeast into the milk and stir until dissolved. Mix the yeast and milk mixture in a bowl with about 150 g (1⅓ cup/5 oz) flour. Cover with clingfilm (plastic wrap) and let rise in a warm place for 20 minutes.

Mix the yeast starter with the remaining flour, the sugar, eggs, egg yolks, vanilla bean seeds, lemon zest, and a pinch of salt in a bowl, then knead using an electric mixer with a dough hook. Gradually knead in the butter. Continue to knead for a further 5–10 minutes or until the dough becomes smooth and comes away from the sides of the bowl. Cover the dough with clingfilm (plastic wrap) and let rise at room temperature for about 25 minutes.

Divide and shape the dough into 12 smooth balls of equal size. Put onto an oiled baking sheet and brush with a little oil. Cover with clingfilm (plastic wrap) and let rise in a warm place for 15–20 minutes, or until they double in size.

Heat the oil in a large, shallow pan or deep-fryer to 160°C/325°F. Lightly oil your hands, then carefully stretch the dough balls to flatten them, leaving a wide and thick edge and a thin centre. Put into the hot oil and fry until golden brown. Take out of the pan with a slotted spoon or skimmer and drain on paper towels. Dust with icing (confectioners') sugar before serving.

German Jelly-Filled Doughnuts (Gefüllte Krapfen)

All regions

Preparation time:		1 hour
Rising time:		1 hour 45 minutes
Cooking time:		15 minutes
Makes:		15–18

½ cup/4½ fl oz	whole milk	130 ml
4 tsp	yeast	4 tsp
scant ½ cup/1¾ oz	caster (superfine) sugar	45 g
3⅓ cups/13 oz	plain (all-purpose) flour	375 g
2	eggs	2
2	egg yolks	2
½	vanilla bean, seeds removed	½
½ tsp	grated unwaxed lemon zest	½ tsp
*	salt	*
1 tsp	rum	1 tsp
4½ tbsp	soft butter	4½ tbsp
*	flour, for dusting	*
*	oil, for deep-frying	*
*	apricot or redcurrant preserve	*
*	icing (confectioners') sugar	*

Heat the milk until lukewarm (40°C/104°F at most). Crumble the yeast into the milk and stir until dissolved. Add a pinch of sugar. Mix the yeast and milk mixture in a bowl with about 150 g (1⅓ cup/5 oz) flour. Cover with clingfilm (plastic wrap) and let rise in a warm place for 20 minutes.

Mix the yeast starter with the remaining flour and sugar, the eggs, egg yolks, vanilla bean seeds, lemon zest, a pinch of salt and the rum in a bowl, then knead using an electric mixer with a dough hook. Gradually knead in the butter. Continue to knead for a further 5–10 minutes or until the dough becomes smooth and comes away from the sides of the bowl. Cover the dough with clingfilm (plastic wrap) and let rise at room temperature for 25 minutes.

Knead the dough again and let it rise for a further 15 minutes. Divide the dough into 15–18 equal portions (about 40 g/1½ oz), transfer to a lightly floured work surface and shape into smooth balls. Stand the balls, seam-side down, spaced 5 cm (2 inches) apart on a floured cloth. Lightly flatten them and dust with flour. Cover with a clean dish towel and set aside to rise for 1 hour, or until they have almost doubled in size.

Heat the oil in a large, shallow pan or deep-fryer to 160°C/325°F. Put the dough balls, smooth-side down, into the hot oil, cover and fry for 2 minutes. Use two wooden spoon handles to turn the doughnuts over. Fry the underside until light, turn over again and fry both sides a little longer. Briefly immerse the doughnuts, then take out of the pan with a slotted spoon or skimmer and drain on paper towels. Set aside to cool for 5–10 minutes.

Make a hole in the base of each doughnut with the handle of a wooden spoon. Use a piping (pastry) bag fitted with a filler tip (a long and narrow round pastry tip) to fill the doughnuts with apricot or redcurrant preserve. Dust the tops with icing (confectioners') sugar before serving.

Deep-Fried Raisin Buns (Kirchweihnudeln)

Bavaria

Preparation time:		20 minutes
Rising time:		1 hour
Cooking time:		45 minutes
Makes:		15

⅔ cup/5 fl oz	whole milk	150 ml
4 tsp	yeast	4 tsp
4½ cups/1 lb 2 oz	plain (all-purpose) flour	500 g
¾ cup/3½ oz	raisins	100 g
½ cup/3½ fl oz	sour cream	100 ml
2 oz	caster (superfine) sugar	50 g
2	eggs	2
1 tsp	grated unwaxed lemon zest	1 tsp
*	salt	*
¼ cup/2¼ oz	soft butter	60 g
*	flour, for dusting	*
3¼ cups/1 lb 10 oz	clarified butter	750 g
*	icing (confectioners') sugar	*

Heat the milk until lukewarm (40°C/104°F at most). Crumble the yeast into the milk and stir until dissolved. Mix the yeast and milk mixture in a bowl with about 150 g (1⅓ cup/5 oz) flour. cover with clingfilm (plastic wrap) and let rise in a warm place for 20 minutes. Lightly dust the raisins with flour and set aside.

Mix the yeast starter with the remaining flour, the sour cream, sugar, eggs, lemon zest and a pinch of salt in a bowl, then knead using an electric mixer with a dough hook. Gradually knead in the butter. Once it has become well combined, continue to knead for a further 5–10 minutes or until the dough has become smooth and comes away from the sides of the bowl. Mix the raisins into the dough, cover with clingfilm (plastic wrap) and let rise at room temperature for about 25 minutes.

Cover a work surface or large pastry board with clean dish towels, dust with flour and lightly rub the flour into the towels. Use a spoon to divide the dough into 15 equal portions, dust with a little flour and shape into smooth balls. Stand the balls, seam-side down, spaced apart on the floured dish towels. Cover with more dish towels and set aside to rise for another 15–20 minutes, or until they have doubled in size.

Heat the clarified butter in a large, shallow pan or deep-fryer to 160°C/325°F. Cut a cross into the tops of the dough balls with scissors, then use a slotted spoon or skimmer to put the buns in batches into the hot oil. Fry for 8–10 minutes on both sides, or until golden or medium brown.

Take out of the pan with a slotted spoon or skimmer and drain on paper towels. Dust with icing (confectioners') sugar before serving. Best served lukewarm and enjoyed with coffee.

Sugar-Coated Doughnuts (Prilleken)

Saxony-Anhalt and Lower Saxony

Preparation time:		30 minutes
Rising time:		1 hour
Cooking time:		30 minutes
Makes:		about 20

scant 1 cup/7 fl oz	whole milk	200 ml
2 tbsp	fresh yeast	2 tbsp
4½ cups/1 lb 2 oz	plain (all-purpose) flour	500 g
⅓ cup/2¼ oz	caster (superfine) sugar	60 g
2	egg yolks	2
1 tsp	salt	1 tsp
scant ¼ cup/1½ oz	soft butter	40 g
*	flour, for dusting	*
3¼ cups/1 lb 10 oz	clarified butter, for deep-frying	750 g
¾ cup/5 oz	sugar, for dredging	150 g

Heat the milk until lukewarm (40°C/104°F at most). Crumble the yeast into the milk and stir until dissolved. Mix the yeast and milk mixture in a bowl with about 150 g (1⅓ cup/5 oz) flour. Cover with clingfilm (plastic wrap) and let rise in a warm place for 20 minutes.

Mix the yeast starter with the remaining flour, the sugar, egg yolks and a pinch of salt, then knead using an electric mixer with a dough hook. Gradually knead in the butter. Continue to knead for a further 5–10 minutes or until the dough becomes smooth and comes away from the sides of the bowl. Cover the dough with clingfilm (plastic wrap) and let rise at room temperature for about 25 minutes.

Cover a work surface or large pastry board with clean dish towels, dust with flour and lightly rub the flour into the towels. Use a spoon to divide the dough into 18–20 equal portions, dust with a little flour and shape into smooth balls. Stand the balls seam-side down, spaced apart on the floured dish towels. Cover with more dish towels and set aside to rise for a further 15–20 minutes or until they have doubled in size.

Heat the clarified butter in a large, shallow pan or deep-fryer to 180°C/350°F. Carefully hold a dough ball in both hands, make a hole in the middle without removing any dough, and quickly shape into rings.

Working in batches, put the doughnuts into the hot oil, cover with a lid and fry for 2 minutes. Turn the doughnuts over and fry for a further 2–3 minutes, or until golden to medium brown. Take out of the pan with a slotted spoon or skimmer and drain on paper towels. Dust with sugar while still hot.

German Butter Cookies (Spritzgebäck)

All regions

Preparation time:		20 minutes
Cooking time:		15 minutes
Makes:		about 12

1 cup/7¾ oz	butter	220 g
scant 1 cup/3¼ oz	icing (confectioners') sugar	90 g
*	salt	*
1	pinch grated unwaxed lemon zest	1
1	vanilla bean, seeds removed	1
1	egg	1
2⅔ cups/11 oz	plain (all-purpose) flour	300 g
7 oz	dark couverture chocolate	200 g

Cream the butter with the icing (confectioners') sugar, a pinch each of salt, lemon zest and vanilla bean seeds. Incorporate the egg. Gradually stir in the flour to make a smooth and creamy batter.

Fill a piping (pastry) bag fitted with a wide star tip. Preheat the oven to 190°C/375°F/Gas Mark 5. Pipe into shapes on a baking sheet lined with parchment paper. Bake for 10–15 minutes, or until golden brown.

Coarsely chop the couverture chocolate and melt in a heatproof bowl set over simmering water. Dip half of each cookie in the chocolate and set aside on baking parchment to cool.

Frisian-Style Plum and Cream Pastry

Friesland

Preparation time:		30 minutes
Cooking time:		30 minutes
Makes:		8 portions

1 lb	frozen puff pastry	450 g
*	flour, for dusting	*
scant ¼ cup/1½ oz	caster (superfine) sugar	40 g
scant 1 cup/9 oz	plum butter (puree)	250 g
1	pinch ground cinnamon	1
2 cups/17 fl oz	double (heavy) cream	500 ml
2 tbsp	icing (confectioners') sugar	2 tbsp

Lay the two individual puff pastry sheets side by side and let thaw. Preheat the oven to 210°C/415°F/Gas Mark 6½.

Halve the pastry sheets. Lay one half sheet over the other, brush with water, then roll out over a lightly floured work surface to make two 30-cm (11¾-inch) squares. Cut out two 28–30-cm (11–11¾-inch) discs and lay each on a baking sheet lined with parchment paper. Prick each disc several times with a fork. Brush one sheet with water and sprinkle evenly with 20 g (¾ oz) sugar. Bake for 12–15 minutes, or until golden brown.

Shortly before baking the other disc, brush it with water, sprinkle with the remaining sugar, and cut into 8 equal sections. Separate the sections slightly, leaving a small space between them. Bake the same way as the first disc. Let both discs cool.

Shortly before serving, mix the plum butter (purée) with the cinnamon and spread an even layer over the first whole pastry disc. Whip the double (heavy) cream with the sugar to stiff peaks, put into a pastry bag with a star-shaped nozzle and pipe a thick even layer of the whipped cream over the plum butter. Cover the cream with the second pastry disc cut into sections. Slice into individual portions and serve immediately.

Funnel Cakes

Preparation time:		25 minutes
Cooking time:		20 minutes
Makes:		about 20

½ cup/4¼ fl oz	whole milk	125 ml
½ cup/ 3½ oz	butter	100 g
1 tbsp	caster (superfine) sugar	1 tbsp
*	salt	*
1⅓ cups/5 oz	plain (all-purpose) flour	150 g
5	eggs	5
*	clarified butter, for frying	*
*	icing (confectioners') sugar	*

Combine the milk, butter, sugar and a pinch of salt in a pan with 125 ml (½ cup/4 fl oz) water and bring to a boil while stirring constantly. Add all of the sifted flour and quickly beat with a wooden spoon to form a smooth, round clump, leaving a white coating on the bottom of the pan.

Transfer to a bowl and immediately incorporate an egg. Add the next egg only once the pastry has become smooth and elastic. Repeat until all the eggs have been incorporated.

Heat the clarified butter in a large pan or deep-fryer to 180°C/350°F. Transfer the choux pastry to a piping (pastry) bag fitted with a star tip. Cut parchment paper into a 10-cm (4-inch) square, then pipe thick rings of choux pastry onto the paper.

Lift the parchment paper and carefully slide the piped pastry ring into the hot fat. Fry the cakes one at a time until golden brown. The choux pastry can also be baked until golden brown in an oven at 200°C/400°F/Gas Mark 6 for about 15 minutes.

Take the cakes out of the pan with a slotted spoon or skimmer and drain on paper towels. Dust with icing (confectioners') sugar before serving.

German-Style Sticky Buns

Preparation time:		35 minutes
Rising time:		45 minutes
Cooking time:		20 minutes
Makes:		about 20

For the dough:		
1½ cups/1 lb 2 oz	plain (all-purpose) flour	500 g
8 tsp	yeast	8 tsp
1 cup/8 fl oz	whole milk	250 ml
⅓ cup/2¼ oz	caster (superfine) sugar	60 g
*	salt	*
1 tsp	grated unwaxed lemon zest	1 tsp
½ cup/2¼ oz	butter	60 g
*	flour, for dusting	*
1	egg yolk	1
3 tbsp	whole milk	3 tbsp
scant 1 cup/5 oz	raisins	150 g
¾ cup/7 oz	apricot preserve	200 g
1 tbsp	lemon juice	1 tbsp
2 tbsp	apricot brandy	2 tbsp

For the filling:		
1¼ cups/10 oz	marzipan (almond paste)	280 g
¼ cup/2 oz	double (heavy) cream	50 ml
2 tbsp	rum	2 tbsp
1	egg	1
¾ cup/3 oz	ground almonds (flour)	80 g
1	vanilla bean	1
1	pinch ground cinnamon	1

For the dough: Sift the flour into a bowl and make a well in the centre. Heat the milk until lukewarm (40°C/104°F at most). Crumble the yeast into the milk and stir until dissolved, then pour into the well. Sprinkle with the sugar, whisk with a little of the flour, cover with clingfilm (plastic wrap) and let rise in a warm place for about 15 minutes.

Add a pinch of salt, the lemon zest and butter to the bowl, then use an electric mixer with a dough hook to knead to a smooth dough. Cover and let rise for a further 30 minutes. Briefly knead the dough again, then roll out over a floured work surface to a 30 × 40-cm (11¾ × 15¾-) inch rectangle.

For the filling: Mix the marzipan (almond paste) with the other ingredients until smooth, then spread out in an even layer over the dough. Leave a 2.5-cm (1-inch) space uncovered along the length of the dough edge. Beat the egg yolk with the milk and brush along the uncovered edge. Preheat the oven to 180°C/350°F/Gas Mark 4.

Spread the raisins over the almond mixture and roll up the dough, finishing at the edge brushed with the egg and milk mixture. Use a sharp knife to cut the roll into about 20 thick slices, and lay on two baking sheets lined with parchment paper. Brush with the remaining egg and milk mixture, then bake for about 20 minutes, or until golden brown.

Combine the apricot preserve and lemon juice with 2 tbsp water in a pan. Bring to a boil, blend with a stick (immersion) blender, then add the apricot brandy. Use the mixture to glaze the hot buns.

Choux Puffs with Vanilla Cream

All regions

Preparation time:	45 minutes
Cooling time:	2 hours
Cooking time:	30 minutes
Makes:	12

For the vanilla cream:

⅓ cup/1¼ oz	cornflour (corn starch)	35 g
1 cup/8 fl oz	whole milk	250 ml
1	vanilla bean	1
*	salt	*
⅓ cup/2½ oz	caster (superfine) sugar	75 g
1 sheet	gelatine	1 sheet
1 tbsp	orange liqueur	1 tbsp
1⅔ cups/14 fl oz	double (heavy) cream	400 ml

For the choux puffs:

*	melted butter, for greasing	*
*	flour, for dusting	*
½ cup/3½ fl oz	whole milk	100 ml
¼ cup/1¾ oz	butter	45 g
¾ cup/4¾ oz	plain (all-purpose) flour	140 g
4	eggs	4
*	icing (confectioners') sugar, for dusting	*

For the strawberries:

2¼ cups/9 oz	strawberries	250 g
2 tbsp	icing (confectioners') sugar	2 tbsp
1	dash lemon juice	1

For the vanilla cream: Dissolve the cornflour (corn starch) completely in a little milk. Split the vanilla bean. Combine the remaining milk with a pinch of salt, the sugar and vanilla bean in a pan and bring to a boil. Stir in the cornflour, simmer for 2 minutes, then remove the vanilla.

Soften the gelatine in a bowl of cold water. Heat the orange liqueur in a small pan without letting it boil. Squeeze the gelatine well, dissolve in the liqueur and incorporate into the vanilla mixture. Set aside to cool. Whip the double (heavy) cream into stiff peaks, stir a third into the cooled vanilla mixture, then fold in the remainder. Cover the vanilla cream and refrigerate for 2 hours.

For the choux puffs: Preheat the oven to 210°C/415°F/ Gas Mark 6½. Grease a baking pan with melted butter and dust with flour. Combine the milk with 100 ml (scant ½ cup/3½ fl oz) water and the butter in a pan and bring to a boil. Add all the flour and stir with a wooden spoon until a layer forms on the bottom of the pan. Transfer to a bowl and cool.

Whisk in the eggs, one at a time, using an electric mixer. Transfer the pastry to a piping (pastry) bag fitted with a large star tip. Pipe 12 puffs, about 5 cm (2 inches) in diameter over the baking sheet. Spray the oven with water, then bake for 25–30 minutes, or until golden. Allow to cool.

For the strawberries: Wash, trim and quarter the strawberries and put into a bowl. Sift over the icing (confectioners') sugar, add the lemon juice and mix. Cut off the top third of the puffs. Fill a piping (pastry) bag with the cream and pipe over the bottom of the puffs. Cover the cream with the strawberries, pipe over with the remaining cream and replace the caps. Dust with sugar before serving.

Tree Cake (Baumkuchen)

Saxony (Saxony-Anhalt) and Brandenburg

Preparation time:	20 minutes
Cooking time:	25 minutes
Makes:	about 60 portions

¼ cup/3¼ oz	plain (all-purpose) flour	90 g
¼ cup/3¼ oz	cornflour (corn starch)	90 g
½ tsp	baking powder	½ tsp
1	egg	1
½ cup/4 oz	marzipan (almond paste)	120 g
1 cup/8 oz	butter	230 g
7	egg yolks	1
1 cup/7 oz	caster (superfine) sugar	200 g
1	pinch ground cinnamon	1
1	pinch vanilla bean seeds	1
7	egg whites	7
*	salt	*
*	butter, for greasing	*

Sift the flour, cornflour (corn starch), and baking powder together into a bowl.

Work the egg into the marzipan (almond paste). Use an electric mixer to whisk the butter with the egg yolks, a third of the sugar, the cinnamon, vanilla bean seeds and marzipan (almond paste) in a bowl until light and fluffy.

Beat the egg whites with the remaining sugar and a pinch of salt to stiff peaks. Fold the flour mixture into the butter mixture, alternating with the beaten egg whites.

Grease a baking sheet and line with aluminum foil. Place a baking frame half its size on top of the baking sheet. Grease the frame and foil with butter. Pour the batter into the frame to a depth of 2 mm and smooth. Turn on the oven grill (broiler), position the baking sheet on the middle shelf inside the oven and grill (broil) until the cake layer turns light golden. Pour another layer of batter into the frame and grill (broil) again. Repeat until all of the batter is used up.

Remove the baking frame, turn the cake over onto a rack and let cool. Cut into 3-cm (1¼-inch) squares and serve.

Strawberry Cream Roll

All regions

Preparation time: 30 minutes
Cooking time: 12 minutes
Serves: 8-10

For the sponge cake:		
4	eggs	4
½ cup/3½ oz	granulated sugar	100 g
1 tbsp	vanilla sugar	1 tbsp
*	salt	*
½ tsp	grated unwaxed lemon zest	½ tsp
⅔ cup/2½ oz	plain (all-purpose) flour	65 g
⅔ cup/2½ oz	cornflour (corn starch)	65 g
2 oz	melted butter	50 g
¼ cup/2 tbsp	sugar, for sprinkling	2 tbsp

For the filling:		
3½ cups/14 oz	strawberries	400 g
2	sheets gelatine	2
1⅔ cups/14 fl oz	double (heavy) cream	400 ml
¼ cup/2 oz	caster (superfine) sugar	50 g
1 tsp	vanilla sugar	1 tsp

Preheat the oven to 210°C/415°F/Gas Mark 6½. Line a baking pan with parchment paper.

For the sponge cake: Use an electric mixer to whisk the eggs with the sugar, vanilla sugar, salt, and lemon zest in a bowl until the mixture is very smooth and no longer increases in volume (this should take about 5 minutes).

Mix the flour with the cornflour (corn starch), sift over the egg mixture and loosely fold. Quickly fold in the melted butter. Spread an even thickness of batter over the parchment paper, put the baking pan on the middle shelf inside the oven and bake for about 12 minutes, or until golden brown.

Lay a clean dish towel on a work surface, sprinkle with the sugar and turn the sponge cake out on to the towel. Remove the parchment paper and roll up the cake in the towel. Let it cool.

For the filling: Wash, trim and quarter the strawberries. Soften the gelatine in a bowl of cold water. Whip the double (heavy) cream to stiff peaks with the sugar and vanilla sugar. Put the softened gelatine into a small pan over a low heat and dissolve. Remove the pan from the heat, stir 2–3 tbsp double (heavy) cream into the warm gelatine, then quickly stir into the rest of the whipped cream until smooth.

Unroll the sponge and spread an even layer of the whipped cream over the top, leaving a 2-cm (1¾-inch) band of uncovered sponge at the top edge. Distribute the strawberries evenly over the sponge and roll up loosely, from the bottom to the top. Position on a plate with the seam side under the roll and refrigerate for 1–2 hours.

Transfer to a cake plate, dust with icing (confectioners') sugar, cut into about 2-cm (1¾-inch) thick slices and garnish with any remaining whipped cream.

Apple Pie

All regions

Preparation time: 40 minutes
Resting time: 2 hours
Cooking time: 1 hour
Serves: 10–12

For the pie crust:		
1½ cups/6 oz	soft butter	175 g
¾ cup/2½ oz	icing (confectioners') sugar	75 g
½	vanilla bean, seeds removed	½
½	unwaxed lemon, zested	½
*	salt	*
2	egg yolks	2
2¼ cups/8½ oz	plain (all-purpose) flour	240 g
*	flour, for dusting	*
*	butter, for greasing	*
4 tbsp	sponge cake crumbs	4 tbsp
1	small egg	1
2 tbsp	double (heavy) cream	2 tbsp

For the filling:		
2¼ lb	apples	1 kg
2 tbsp	butter	2 tbsp
3 tbsp	caster (superfine) sugar	3 tbsp
1 tbsp	vanilla sugar	1 tbsp
½ tsp	ground cinnamon	½ tsp
½ tsp	grated unwaxed lemon zest	½ tsp
1 tbsp	lemon juice	1 tbsp
scant ½ cup/2 oz	slivered almonds	50 g
⅓ cup/2 oz	raisins	50 g

For the pie crust: Use an electric mixer with a dough hook or a dough scraper to mix the butter with the icing (confectioners') sugar, the vanilla bean seeds, lemon zest and a pinch of salt in a bowl and work until smooth. Mix in the egg yolks one at a time, but do not beat. Finally, add the flour and knead only for the time it takes for the pastry to become smooth. Shape into a flat rectangle, cover with clingfilm (plastic wrap) and rest for 2 hours in the refrigerator.

For the filling: Peel, quarter, core and cut the apples into 1–1.5-cm (½–¾-inch) dice. Sweat the diced apple in a deep frying pan or skillet with the butter, sugar, vanilla sugar, cinnamon and lemon zest for about 10 minutes. Add the lemon juice, almonds and raisins, then drain and let cool.

Preheat the oven to 180°C/350°F/Gas Mark 4. Briefly knead the pastry dough again. Take about a third of the pastry and roll out over a floured work surface to a 3-mm (⅛-inch) thickness, and cut out a disc the size of the springform pan you are going to use (26 cm/10¼ inch diameter is ideal). Lay the disc on parchment paper, prick with a fork and set aside in the freezer. Grease the springform pan with butter. Roll out the remaining pastry to a 3-mm (⅛-inch) thickness and line the base and sides of the pan. Sprinkle the bottom with the sponge cake crumbs.

Whisk the egg with the double (heavy) cream. Spread the apple filling over the crumbs, fold the overhanging pastry over the filling and brush with the whisked egg. Take the pastry disc out of the freezer and use the parchment paper to slide it over the filling, pressing lightly around the edges. Brush with the rest of the whisked egg and bake for about 1 hour, or until golden brown.

Sunken Apple Cake

Southern Germany

Preparation time:		20 minutes
Cooking time:		50 minutes
Serves:		10–12

¾ cup/6¼ oz	soft butter	180 g
1¾ cups/6¼ oz	icing (confectioners') sugar	180 g
3	eggs, at room temperature	3
*	salt	*
½ tsp	grated unwaxed lemon zest	½ tsp
1	pinch vanilla bean seeds	1
1 tbsp	dark rum	1 tbsp
1 cup/4 oz	plain (all-purpose) flour	120 g
½ cup/2¼ oz	cornflour (corn starch)	60 g
1 tsp	baking powder	1 tsp
¼ cup/2 fl oz	whole milk	50 ml
2 tbsp	melted butter, for greasing	2 tbsp
1–2 tbsp	flour, for dusting	1–2 tbsp
5	apples	5
*	icing (confectioners') sugar	*

Beat the butter with an electric mixer in a bowl until creamy. Incorporate the icing (confectioners') sugar and eggs, then stir for a few minutes until a very loose and light mixture. Incorporate a pinch of salt, the lemon zest, vanilla bean seeds and rum. Mix the flour, cornflour (corn starch) and baking powder, then sift over the butter mixture and incorporate with the milk to make a smooth batter.

Preheat the oven to 180°C/350°F/Gas Mark 4. Brush a 26-cm (10¼-inch) diameter springform pan with melted butter and dust with flour. Pour the batter into the pan and smooth.

Peel, halve and core the apples. Cut several parallel incisions into the curved side of the apple halves. Lay the apple halves on the batter, spaced evenly, curved side up, and place the pan inside the lowest third of the oven. Bake for about 50 minutes, or until golden brown. Take the cake out of the oven and let cool. Dust with icing (confectioners') sugar before serving.

Pear Tart

All regions

Preparation time:		45 minutes
Cooling time:		2 hours
Cooking time:		1 hour 10 minutes
Serves:		12–14

For the tart case:		
¾ cup/6 oz	soft butter	175 g
¾ cup/2½ oz	icing (confectioners') sugar	75 g
½	vanilla bean, seeds removed	½
½	unwaxed lemon, zested	½
*	salt	*
2	egg yolks	2
2¼ cups/8½ oz	plain (all-purpose) flour	240 g
*	flour, for dusting	*
*	butter, for greasing	*
*	dried legumes, for blind baking	*

For the filling:		
5 tbsp	apricot preserve	5 tbsp
1¾ cups/14 oz	canned pear halves	400 g
2½ oz	dark couverture chocolate	75 g
3	eggs	3
½ cup/4½ oz	marzipan (almond paste)	125 g
1 cup/4½ oz	soft butter	125 g
⅔ cup/4½ oz	caster (superfine) sugar	125 g
1	vanilla bean, seeds removed	1
*	salt	*
⅔ cup/ 2½ oz	plain (all-purpose) flour	75 g
1 tsp	baking powder	1 tsp
1 tbsp	slivered almonds	1 tbsp

For the tart case: Use an electric mixer with a dough hook or a dough scraper to mix the butter with the icing (confectioners') sugar, vanilla bean seeds, lemon zest and a pinch of salt in a bowl and work until smooth. Mix in the egg yolks one at a time. Add the flour and knead the pastry until smooth. Shape into a flat block, cover with clingfilm (plastic wrap) and chill in the refrigerator for 2 hours.

Preheat the oven to 200°C/400°F/Gas Mark 6. Briefly knead the pastry, then roll out over a floured work surface to a 3-mm (⅛-inch) thickness. Grease a 28-cm (11-inch) springform pan and line with the pastry to halfway up the sides. Prick the pastry with a fork, cover with parchment paper and fill to the top with dried legumes.

Blind-bake the tart case on the middle shelf inside the oven for about 20 minutes. Take the tart case out of the oven, then remove the parchment paper and legumes. Lower the oven temperature to 180°C/350°F/Gas Mark 4.

For the filling: Purée the apricot preserve with a stick (immersion) blender. Warm half in a pan, then brush over the case. Drain the pears. Chop the chocolate. Separate 1 egg. Mix the egg white with the marzipan (almond paste) in a bowl until smooth. Mix the butter with the sugar, vanilla bean seeds and a pinch of salt in a bowl. Add the egg yolk and beat until pale and fluffy. Add the almond mixture and incorporate the last eggs. Sift the flour and baking powder over the mixture, then fold in the chocolate. Pour the filling over the tart case and smooth. Arrange the pears curved side up. Bake for 50 minutes.

Toast the almonds in a dry pan until golden. Glaze the tart with the rest of the preserve and scatter over the nuts.

Egg Liqueur Cake

All regions

Preparation time:	30 minutes
Cooking time:	40 minutes
Serves:	8–10

For the batter:		
1¾ cups/7 oz	ground almonds	200 g
5	eggs	5
⅓ cup/3 oz	soft butter	80 g
⅓ cup/3 oz	caster (superfine) sugar	80 g
½	vanilla bean, seeds removed	½
1 tsp	baking powder	1 tsp
½ cup/3½ oz	grated dark chocolate	100 g
*	salt	*
2 tbsp	rum	2 tbsp
*	butter, for greasing	*

For the frosting:		
scant 1 cup/11 fl oz	double (heavy) cream	300 ml
2 tbsp	caster (superfine) sugar	2 tbsp
½ cup/4¼ fl oz	egg liqueur (e.g. Advocaat)	125 ml

For the batter: Toast the ground almonds in a dry frying pan or skillet and let cool. Separate the eggs.

Cream the butter with 2 tbsp sugar and the the vanilla bean seeds. Add the egg yolks one at a time, and beat until thick and fluffy. Preheat the oven to 170°C/340°F/Gas Mark 3½.

Mix the baking powder with the toasted almonds and chocolate. Beat the egg whites with a pinch of salt and the remaining sugar to stiff peaks and add to the egg and butter mixture. Sprinkle the almond mixture over the top, add the rum, then fold.

Grease a 24-cm (9½-inch) springform pan with butter and fill with the batter. Smooth the surface. Bake on the middle shelf of the oven for about 40 minutes. Unmold the cake and let cool on a rack.

For the frosting: Whip the double (heavy) cream to stiff peaks with the sugar. Spread a third of the whipped cream over the cake in a thick layer. Put the rest into a piping (pastry) bag and pipe tight swirls of cream around the top edge. Carefully pour the egg liqueur over the top of the cake. Refrigerate until ready to serve.

Strawberry Tart

All regions

Preparation time:	25 minutes
Cooking time:	30 minutes
Serves:	10–12

3	eggs	3
*	salt	*
⅓ cup/2½ oz	caster (superfine) sugar	75 g
⅔ cup/2½ oz	plain (all-purpose) flour	75 g
*	butter, for greasing	*
*	flour, for dusting	*
5¼ cups/1 lb 5 oz	strawberries	600 g
1 packet	clear cake glaze	1 packet
2 tbsp	caster (superfine) sugar	2 tbsp
1 cup/8 fl oz	light-coloured fruit juice	250 ml
scant 1 cup/7 fl oz	double (heavy) cream	200 ml

Preheat the oven to 180°C/350°F/Gas Mark 4. Separate the eggs. Beat the egg whites with a pinch of salt and the sugar to soft peaks, gradually adding the sugar. Beat the egg yolks and add to the beaten egg whites. Sift over the flour and fold everything together.

Grease a 26-cm (10¼-inch) tart pan or springform pan with soft butter and dust with flour. Pour the mixture into the pan and bake on the second shelf of the oven for 20–30 minutes, or until golden brown. Let cool for a few minutes, then unmold on to a rack.

Trim, wash and halve the strawberries and starting at the centre, arrange cut-side down and slightly overlapped over the tart case.

Mix the clear cake glaze with the sugar and fruit juice in a small pan, and bring to a boil while stirring. Use a teaspoon to spread the glaze quickly and evenly over the strawberries.

Whip the cream to stiff peaks. Cut the strawberry tart into portions, arrange on dessert plates and accompany with the whipped cream.

Sunken Cherry Cake

All regions

Preparation time:	25 minutes
Cooking time:	45 minutes
Serves:	10–12

⅔ cup/4¾ oz	soft butter	140 g
¾ cup/ 4¾ oz	caster (superfine) sugar	140 g
1	vanilla bean, seeds removed	1
4	eggs	4
*	salt	*
⅓ cup/3 oz	grated dark chocolate	80 g
¾ cup/2 oz	dry breadcrumbs	50 g
1⅓ cup/5 oz	ground hazelnuts	150 g
2¼ cups/1 lb 2 oz	sour cherries	500 g
*	butter, for greasing	*
¼ cup/2 oz	apricot preserve	50 g
¼ cup/1¼ oz	slivered almonds, toasted	30 g

Cream the butter with half of the sugar and the vanilla bean seeds. Separate the eggs. Add the egg yolks one at a time while beating until fluffy.

Preheat the oven to 175°C/345°F/Gas Mark 3¾. Mix together the grated chocolate, breadcrumbs and hazelnuts. Beat the egg whites with a pinch of salt and the remaining sugar and add to the egg and butter mixture. Pour over the breadcrumb mixture and fold everything together to make a smooth batter.

Wash and pit the cherries. Grease a 26-cm (10¼-inch) springform pan with butter and fill with the batter. Smooth the surface, scatter the cherries all over and lightly press into the batter. Position the pan on the middle shelf inside the oven and bake for 40–45 minutes. Set aside to cool on a rack.

Meanwhile, heat the apricot preserve with 2 tbsp water and mix until smooth with a stick (immersion) blender. Brush over the cake with the glaze while still hot and sprinkle over the slivered almonds.

Prince Regent Torte

Bavaria

Preparation time:	45 minutes
Resting time:	24 hours
Cooking time:	1 hour
Serves:	12–16

For the chocolate cream:

2 cups/17 fl oz	double (heavy) cream	500 ml
9 oz	dark chocolate	250 g
2 tbsp	rum	2 tbsp

For the sponge layers:

scant 1¼ cups/9 oz	butter	250 g
1¼ cups/9 oz	caster (superfine) sugar	250 g
4	egg yolks	4
1	pinch grated unwaxed lemon zest	1
½	vanilla bean, seeds removed	½
4	egg whites	4
*	salt	*
1⅔ cups/6¼ oz	plain (all-purpose) flour	180 g
⅔ cup/2¾ oz	cornflour (corn starch)	70 g
1 tsp	baking powder	1 tsp
*	sugar, for sprinkling	*

For the chocolate glaze:

⅓ cup/3½ oz	apricot preserve	100 g
7 oz	dark couverture chocolate	200 g
⅓ cup/3½ fl oz	condensed milk	100 ml
3 tsp	honey	3 tsp

For the chocolate cream: Bring the cream to a boil in a pan and finely chop the chocolate. Take the cream off the heat, drop in the chocolate and stir until dissolved, then add the rum. Blend briefly with a stick (immersion) blender and rest in the refrigerator for 24 hours.

For the sponge layers: Cream the butter with 100 g (½ cup/3½ oz) sugar, then gradually add the egg yolks, lemon zest and vanilla bean seeds. Beat the egg whites with a pinch of salt to stiff peaks while gradually adding the remaining sugar. Sift the flour with the cornflour (corn starch) and baking powder, then fold with the beaten egg whites into the batter.

Preheat the oven to 180°C/350°F/Gas Mark 4. Lay eight sheets of parchment paper side by side. Divide the batter into equal portions on each sheet. Spread out to form 28-cm (11-inch) discs, then bake one at a time for 7 minutes until golden brown. Sprinkle the sponge discs with sugar.

Beat the chocolate cream until fluffy. Lay one sponge disc inside a cake ring and cover with a little chocolate cream. Alternate the other sponge discs with more chocolate cream inside the cake ring, pressing lightly on each disc.

For the chocolate glaze: Warm the apricot preserve in a small pan, strain through a sieve and brush over the torte. Melt the dark couverture chocolate in a heatproof bowl set over simmering water. Stir in the condensed milk and honey, then glaze the cake with the mixture.

Blueberry Cheesecake

All regions

Preparation time:		25 minutes
Cooling time:		1 hour
Serves:		8–10

5¾ oz	almond cookies	170 g
½ cup/4½ oz	butter	125 g
2 sheets	gelatine	2 sheets
1	lemon, juiced	1
⅔ cup/5 fl oz	whole-milk yoghurt	150 m;
2⅔ cups/1 lb 5 oz	cream cheese	600 g
1¼ cups/11 fl oz	double (heavy) cream	300 ml
4 tbsp	white wine	4 tbsp
2 tbsp	caster (superfine) sugar	2 tbsp
1 tsp	cornflour (corn starch)	1 tsp
½	cinnamon stick	½
⅔ cup/3½ oz	blueberries	100 g

Crush the cookies in a food processor or with a rolling pin. Melt the butter and stir into the cookie crumbs.

Line a 22-cm (8½-inch) diameter springform pan with parchment paper. Spread the crumbs evenly across the base of the pan. Press with your fingertips to firm, then chill in the refrigerator.

Soften the gelatine in a bowl of cold water. Heat the lemon juice in a small pan. Squeeze the gelatine well with your hands, then dissolve in the lemon juice. Incorporate 1–2 tbsp yoghurt, then add the remaining yoghurt and cream cheese, and mix until smooth.

Whip the cream to stiff peaks and stir about a third into the cream cheese mixture. Loosely fold in the rest until smooth. Pour the cream cheese mixture into the pan over the cheesecake base, smooth the surface and chill again.

Mix the wine with 4 tbsp water and the sugar, and dissolve the cornflour (corn starch) in a little of the liquid. Combine the remaining liquid with the cinnamon in a pan, bring to a boil, then thicken with the corn starch. Briefly bring to a boil, remove from the heat, then remove and discard the cinnamon stick. Add the blueberries and let cool.

Carefully pour the mixture over the centre of the cheesecake and spread out, leaving a 3-cm (1¼-inch) wide band of white around the edge. Refrigerate again and serve chilled.

Cheesecake Tart

All regions

Preparation time:		30 minutes
Cooling time:		1 hour
Cooking time:		2 hours 10 minutes
Serves:		10–12

For the tart case:

1 cup/3½ oz	icing (confectioners') sugar	100 g
scant 1 cup/7 oz	soft butter	200 g
1	egg	1
2⅔ cups/11 oz	plain (all-purpose) flour	300 g
*	flour, for dusting	*
*	butter, for greasing	*
*	dried legumes, for blind baking	*

For the filling:

2 cups/14 oz	low-fat Quark	400 g
1⅔ cups/14 fl oz	sour cream	400 g
2	egg yolks	2
¾ cup/5¼ oz	caster (superfine) sugar	160 g
3 tbsp	plain (all-purpose) flour	3 tbsp
½	unwaxed lemon, zested	½
4	egg whites	4
*	salt	*

For the tart case: Use an electric mixer with a dough hook to briefly work the icing (confectioners') sugar with the butter. Add the egg and continue to knead. Finally, add the flour and knead only for the time it takes for the pastry to become smooth. Shape the pastry into a flat block, cover with clingfilm (plastic wrap) and chill in the refrigerator for 1 hour.

Preheat the oven to 200°C/400°F/Gas Mark 6. Roll out the pastry over a floured work surface to a thickness of 3 mm (⅛ inch). Grease a 26-cm (10¼-inch) springform pan and line with the pastry. Prick the pastry with a fork, cover with parchment paper and fill with dried legumes.

Blind-bake the tart case on the middle shelf inside the oven for about 20 minutes. Take the tart case out of the oven, then remove the parchment paper and legumes and bake the crust for a further 7 minutes, until the bottom begins to turn brown. Lower the oven temperature to 160°C/325°F/Gas Mark 3.

For the filling: Mix the Quark with the sour cream, egg yolks, 40 g (scant ¼ cup/1½ oz) sugar, the flour and lemon zest. Beat the egg whites with a pinch of salt to stiff peaks, gradually adding the remaining sugar. Fold the beaten egg whites into the cream cheese mixture and then pour the filling into the tart case.

Bake the tart on the lowest shelf inside the oven for 15 minutes. Run an oiled knife around the tart, between the filling and case, to a depth of 2 cm (¾ inch). Bake the tart for a further 75 minutes, taking the pan out of the oven for 10 minutes every 15–20 minutes. Let cool until lukewarm, cut into slices and serve.

Cakes, Cookies & Sweet Breads

Rhubarb Cheesecake Tart

All regions

Preparation time:	35 minutes
Cooling time:	1 hour
Cooking time:	45 minutes
Serves:	10–12

For the tart case:

2 tsp	marzipan (almond paste)	2 tsp
½ cup/4 oz	soft butter	120 g
1	egg yolk	1
⅔ cup/2¼ oz	icing (confectioners') sugar	60 g
*	salt	*
1⅔ cups/6¾ oz	plain (all-purpose) flour	190 g
*	flour, for dusting	*
*	butter, for greasing	*
2 oz	dark or white couverture chocolate	50 g

For the filling:

14 oz	rhubarb	400 g
¾ cup/5 oz	caster (superfine) sugar	150 g
2 tsp	instant vanilla pudding powder	2 tsp
*	pinch ground cinnamon	*
*	pinch salt	*
1¼ cups/9 oz	low-fat Quark	250 g
2	eggs	2
½	unwaxed lemon, zested	½
½ tsp	grated unwaxed orange zest	½ tsp
⅔ cup/5 fl oz	double (heavy) cream	150 ml

For the tart case: Use an electric mixer with a dough hook to work all of the ingredients into a smooth dough. Shape the pastry into a flat block, cover with clingfilm (plastic wrap), and chill in the refrigerator for at least 30 minutes.

For the filling: Trim, wash and cut the rhubarb into 5-mm (¼-inch) dice. Mix with 100 g (½ cup/3½ oz) sugar and let stand for 10 minutes. Briefly mix again, then transfer to a sieve and let drain.

Mix the remaining sugar in a bowl with the instant vanilla pudding powder and a pinch of cinnamon and salt. Mix the Quark, eggs and orange and lemon zests with the sugar mixture until smooth. Whip the cream to soft peaks and fold in.

Preheat the oven to 180°C/350°F/Gas Mark 4. Roll out the pastry to a thickness of 3 mm (⅛ inch). Grease a 26-cm (10¼-inch) springform pan and line with the pastry, then chill in the refrigerator for 30 minutes.

Blind-bake the tart case for 15–20 minutes, or until golden brown. Raise the oven temperature to 200°C/400°F/Gas Mark 6.

Coarsely chop the couverture chocolate and melt in a heatproof bowl set over simmering water or in the microwave. Spread over the tart case. Evenly distribute the rhubarb over the case, spread the cream cheese mixture over the top and smooth. Lightly bake for 20–25 minutes, until the cream cheese filling begins to puff up. Let cool until lukewarm, cut into slices and serve.

Redcurrant Tart (Träubleskuchen)

Baden-Württemberg and Bavaria

Preparation time:	30 minutes
Cooling time:	1 hour
Cooking time:	50 minutes
Serves:	10–12

2⅔ cups/11 oz	plain (all-purpose) flour	300 g
½ cup/3½ oz	caster (superfine) sugar	100 g
scant 1 cup/7 oz	butter, diced	200 g
1	egg	1
*	butter, for greasing	*
4	egg whites	4
¾ cup/5 oz	caster (superfine) sugar	150 g
½ cup/2 oz	ground almonds, toasted	50 g
¼cup/1 oz	cornflour (corn starch)	25 g
2 tbsp	semolina	2 tbsp
3⅓ cups/1 lb 2 oz	redcurrants	500 g

Use an electric mixer with a dough hook to work the flour, sugar, butter and egg into a sweet pastry dough. Cover with clingfilm (plastic wrap) and chill in the refrigerator for 1 hour.

For the filling: Beat the egg whites to stiff peaks, gradually adding the sugar. Continue to beat until firm and glossy. Loosely fold in the ground almonds, cornflour (corn starch), and semolina until smooth. Strip the redcurrants from their stems and wash. Incorporate into the batter.

Preheat the oven to 180°C/350°F/Gas Mark 4. Roll out the pastry over a floured work surface to a thickness of 3 mm (⅛ inch). Grease a 26-cm (10¼-inch) springform pan and line with the pastry. Prick the pastry several times with a fork. Pour the batter into the tart case, smooth the surface and bake for 45–50 minutes.

Chocolate Layer Cake

All regions ⬭ 🥕

Preparation time:	40 minutes
Cooling time:	24 hours
Cooking time:	1 hour
Serves:	10–12

For the chocolate cream:

2½ cups/20 fl oz	double (heavy) cream	600 ml
5 oz	dark chocolate	150 g
1⅓ cups/5 oz	chopped nut brittle or	150 g
	chopped roasted nuts	

For the sponge layers:

3½ oz	dark couverture chocolate	100 g
5	eggs	5
scant ½ cup/3½ oz	soft butter	100 g
⅓ cup/1¼ oz	icing (confectioners') sugar	30 g
⅔ cup/4½ oz	caster (superfine) sugar	125 g
1 tsp	baking powder	1 tsp
scant 1 cup/3½ oz	plain (all-purpose) flour	100 g
6 tbsp	lingonberry preserve	6 tbsp
8 tsp	raspberry brandy	8 tsp
*	chocolate shavings, to decorate	*

For the chocolate cream: Bring the cream to a boil in a pan and finely chop the chocolate. Melt the chocolate in the cream. Blend briefly with a stick (immersion) blender, cover and chill in the refrigerator for 24 hours.

For the sponge layers: Melt the couverture chocolate in a heatproof bowl set over simmering water and then let cool to 30°C/86°F. Separate the eggs. Cream the butter with the icing (confectioners') sugar and gradually incorporate the egg yolks and the melted chocolate. Preheat the oven to 180°C/350°F/Gas Mark 4.

Beat the egg whites with the sugar and add to the egg and butter mixture. Sift the baking powder and flour together over the mixture. Fold in until smooth. Line a 26-cm (10¼-inch) springform pan with parchment paper. Pour the batter into the pan and smooth the surface. Position the pan on the middle shelf of the oven and bake for 50–60 minutes. Unmold and let cool on a rack.

Use an electric mixer to whip the chocolate cream to soft peaks, then incorporate the chopped nut brittle or roasted nuts.

Use a sharp knife to cut the sponge cake crosswise into three equal discs. Mix the lingonberry preserve with the raspberry brandy and soak the bottom sponge layer with half. Spread a third of the chocolate cream over the bottom sponge and cover with the second sponge layer. Spread the sponge with the lingonberry mixture, then with the chocolate cream, and cover with the last sponge layer. Spread a thick layer of chocolate cream all over the cake, put the remaining cream in a pastry (piping) bag and decorate the top with more piped cream. Sprinkle with chocolate shavings.

Black Forest Cake

Baden-Württemberg 🥕

Preparation time:	45 minutes
Cooking time:	50 minutes
Cooling time:	3 hours
Serves:	16

For the sponge layers:

*	butter, for greasing	*
*	flour, for dusting	*
6	eggs	6
1½ cups/5 oz	sugar	150 g
*	salt	*
1 cup/4 oz	plain (all-purpose) flour	120 g
⅓ cup/1½ oz	cocoa powder	40 g

For the cherries:

3 cups/1 lb 2 oz	sour cherries (from a jar)	500 g
1 tsp	icing (confectioners') sugar	1 tsp
¾ cup/6 fl oz	red wine	180 ml
⅓ cup/2½ fl oz	port	70 ml
1 tbsp	cornflour (corn starch)	1 tbsp
3 tbsp	caster (superfine) sugar	3 tbsp
1	pinch ground cinnamon	1
1	pinch ground cloves	1
½ tsp	grated unwaxed orange zest	½ tsp
1 tsp	honey	1 tsp

For the cream:

3 sheets	gelatine	3 sheets
3⅓ cups/27 fl oz	double (heavy) cream	800 ml
scant ½ cup/3 oz	sugar	80 g
8 tbsp	kirsch	8 tbsp
4 tbsp	chocolate shavings	4 tbsp

Grease a 26-cm (10¼-inch) springform pan and dust with flour. Preheat the oven to 175°C/345°F/Gas Mark 3¾.

For the sponge layers: Separate the eggs into two bowls. Beat the egg yolks with 1–2 tbsp sugar until thick and pale. Beat the egg whites with a pinch of salt and the remaining sugar to soft peaks. Sift the flour and cocoa and fold in, alternating with the egg whites and yolks. Pour into the pan and bake for 50 minutes. Allow to cool completely.

For the cherries: Drain the cherries and reserve 250 ml (1 cup/8 fl oz) of liquid. Caramelise the icing (confectioners') sugar in a pan, then deglaze with the wine and port and reduce by half. Dissolve the cornflour in a little cherry liquid. Add the sugar, spices and zest, then bring to a boil. Reduce the heat, stir in the cornflour and simmer for 2 minutes. Add the cherries and adjust the sweetness with honey. Let cool, then set aside 16 cherries. Cut the cake crosswise into three equal layers. Soak the bottom layer with 2 tbsp kirsch. Top with half the cherries.

For the cream: Soften the gelatine in water. Whip the cream with the sugar to stiff peaks. Heat 4 tbsp of kirsch in a pan. Squeeze the gelatine well, dissolve in the kirsch, then incorporate into the cream.

Spread a quarter of the cream over the cherries. Top with the second sponge, soak with kirsch, add the cherries and spread with cream. Cover with the last layer of sponge. Put the cream in a piping bag with a star tip. Cover with cream and mark out 16 sections. Decorate each section with cream, topped with a cherry and chocolate shavings in the middle. Chill for 1 hour.

Yeasted Bundt Cake (Hefegugelhupf)

All regions

Preparation time:		30 minutes
Rising time:		1 hour 15 minutes
Cooking time:		50 minutes
Serves:		16–18

2–3 tbsp	raisins	2-3 tbsp
2 tbsp	rum	2 tbsp
2⅔ cups/11 oz	plain (all-purpose) flour	300 g
½ cup/4¼ fl oz	whole milk	125 ml
1 tbsp	yeast	1 tbsp
¼ cup/2 oz	caster (superfine) sugar	50 g
½ cup/4 oz	soft butter	120 g
1 level tsp	salt	1 level tsp
1	pinch vanilla bean seeds	1
1 tsp	grated unwaxed lemon zest	1 tsp
3	egg yolks	3
⅓ cup/1½ oz	slivered almonds	40 g
½ cup/4 oz	melted butter	120 g
⅔ cup/2¾ oz	flaked almonds	70 g
*	flour, for dusting	*
*	icing (confectioners') sugar, for dusting	*

Mix the raisins with the rum. Sift the flour into a bowl and make a well in the centre. Heat the milk until lukewarm. Crumble the yeast into the milk and stir in a small pan until dissolved. Pour the yeast and milk mixture into the well, sprinkle with 1 tsp sugar, then mix with a little of the flour. Cover the yeast starter with clingfilm (plastic wrap) and let rise in a warm place for 15 minutes.

Cream the butter with the remaining sugar, salt, vanilla bean seeds and lemon zest. Add the egg yolks and continue to beat until the mixture is pale and fluffy. Add the butter mixture to the starter dough. Put the dough into a stand mixer or use an electric mixer with a dough hook to knead until it becomes shiny and elastic and comes away from the sides of the bowl. Drain the raisins, knead into the dough together with the slivered almonds, cover and let rise in a warm place for 20 minutes.

Brush the inside of a 2-litre (10-cup) bundt pan with 2 tbsp melted butter and sprinkle with the flaked almonds. Briefly knead the dough, dust with a little flour and shape into a ball. Make a hole in the middle of the dough and put into the bundt pan. Cover and let rise again in a warm place for 30-40 minutes. Preheat the oven to 175°C/345°F/Gas Mark 3¾.

Bake the cake on the lowest shelf of the oven for about 50 minutes. Take the cake out of the oven, let cool a little, then carefully unmold. Brush the cake with the remaining melted butter, transfer to a rack and let cool completely. Dust with icing (confectioners') sugar before serving.

Frankfurt-Style Crown Cake (Frankfurter Kranz)

Frankfurt am Main and Hesse

Preparation time:		45 minutes
Baking time:		1 hour 15 minutes
Cooling time:		1 hour
Serves:		16–18

For the sponge:		
1 cup/9 oz	soft butter	250 g
*	salt	*
1 tbsp	vanilla sugar	1 tbsp
1 tsp	grated unwaxed lemon zest	1 tsp
1¼ cups/9 oz	caster (superfine) sugar	250 g
5	eggs	5
2 tbsp	rum	2 tbsp
3½ cups/14 oz	plain (all-purpose) flour	400 g
scant 1 cup/3½ oz	cornflour (corn starch)	100 g
1 tsp	baking powder	1 tsp
*	butter, for greasing	*
*	flour, for dusting	*

For the buttercream:		
scant ½ cup/2 oz	cornflour (corn starch)	50 g
2 cups/18 fl oz	whole milk	500ml
3	egg yolks	3
*	salt	*
¼ cup/2 oz	caster (superfine) sugar	50 g
1 cup/9 oz	soft butter	250 g
1½ cups/4½ oz	icing (confectioners') sugar	125 g

For the almond brittle:		
scant 1 cup/3½ oz	flaked almonds	100 g
1½ tbsp	butter	1½ tbsp
¼ cup/2¼ oz	sugar	60 g

Preheat the oven to 180°C/350°F/Gas Mark 4.

For the sponge: Beat the butter with a pinch of salt, the vanilla sugar and zest until fluffy. Gradually incorporate the sugar, alternating with 1 egg, then beat until pale and creamy. Add the rum. Sift the flour with the cornflour (corn starch) and baking powder, and fold into the batter.

Grease a 26-cm (10¼-inch) ring cake mold with butter and dust with flour. Fill with the batter, tap to level, then bake for 60–75 minutes. Let cool a little, turn out on to a rack, then let cool completely.

For the buttercream: Dissolve the cornflour (corn starch) in a little milk and mix in the egg yolks. Combine the remaining milk with a pinch of salt and the sugar in a pan and bring to a boil. Whisk the cornflour and egg yolks in and simmer for 2 minutes. Transfer to a bowl, cover with clingfilm (plastic wrap) in direct contact with the surface of the custard and let cool to room temperature. Beat the butter with the sugar until pale and fluffy. Add the custard a spoonful at a time, beating to a velvety cream.

For the almond brittle: Combine the almonds with the butter and sugar in a pan over medium heat and caramelise while stirring to make a pale brittle. Spread out over parchment paper and let cool.

Cut the sponge crosswise into three equal rings. Spread two rings with a third of the buttercream each, and place one on top of the other to make two layers. Put the third ring on top and cover with the remaining buttercream. Chop up the brittle and sprinkle over the cake. Decorate the top with buttercream swirls, each topped with a cherry.

Marble Cake

All regions

Preparation time:		25 minutes
Cooking time:		1 hour 10 minutes
Serves:		16–18

scant 1 cup/7 oz	soft butter	200 g
1½ cups/5 oz	icing (confectioners') sugar	150 g
1 tbsp	vanilla sugar	1 tbsp
½ tsp	grated unwaxed lemon zest	½ tsp
6	eggs	6
2 tbsp	rum	2 tbsp
1¾ cups/7 oz	plain (all-purpose) flour	200 g
1 tsp	baking powder	1 tsp
scant 1 cup/ 3½ oz	blanched almond meal (flour)	100 g
1½ tbsp	cocoa powder	1½ tbsp
2¾ oz	dark couverture chocolate	70 g
1	pinch salt	1
¾ cup/5 oz	caster (superfine) sugar	150 g
*	soft butter, for greasing	*
*	flour, for dusting	*
*	icing (confectioners') sugar, for dusting	*

Preheat the oven to 175°C/345°F/Gas Mark 3¾. Grease a 2-litre (10-cup) bundt pan with butter and dust with flour. Beat the butter with the icing (confectioners') sugar, vanilla sugar and lemon zest in a bowl until fluffy. Separate the eggs. Gradually stir the egg yolks into the butter mixture. Add the rum, then beat until pale and fluffy.

Sift the flour with the baking powder into a bowl. Incorporate the almond meal. Sift the cocoa powder into another bowl. Finely grate the couverture chocolate into the bowl with the cocoa.

Beat the egg whites with a pinch of salt and a third of the sugar until creamy, then gradually add the remaining sugar and beat to stiff peaks. Fold in the beaten egg whites, alternating with spoonfuls of flour mixture, into the butter mixture.

Fill the bundt pan with a little more than half of the batter. Mix the cocoa and chocolate mixture with the remaining batter and pour this darker batter over the light batter in the pan. Swirl a fork through both layers of batter to create a marbling effect.

Bake the cake on the lowest shelf of the oven for about 1 hour 10 minutes. Take the cake out of the oven and let cool for 10 minutes in the pan. Carefully unmold and let cool completely. Dust with icing (confectioners') sugar and cut into slices before serving.

Red Wine Cake

All regions

Preparation time:		25 minutes
Cooking time:		55 minutes
Serves:		16–18

*	butter, for greasing	*
*	flour, for dusting	*
1⅓ cups/10 oz	soft butter	280 g
1¼ cups/8½ oz	caster (superfine) sugar	240 g
1 tbsp	vanilla sugar	1 tbsp
6	eggs	6
2½ cups/10 oz	plain (all-purpose) flour	280 g
1 tsp	baking powder	1 tsp
1 level tsp	ground cardamom	1 level tsp
1 level tsp	ground cinnamon	1 level tsp
½ tsp	ground allspice	½ tsp
½ tsp	freshly grated nutmeg	½ tsp
½ tsp	ground cloves	½ tsp
3½ oz	dark chocolate	100 g
1	pinch salt	1
⅔ cup/5 fl oz	red wine	150 ml
*	icing (confectioners') sugar, for dusting	*

Preheat the oven to 175°C/345°F/Gas Mark 3¾. Grease a 2-litre (10-cup) bundt pan with butter and dust with flour.

Use an electric mixer to cream the butter with half of the sugar and the vanilla sugar in a bowl. Separate the eggs. Gradually add the egg yolks to the creamed butter, then beat until pale and fluffy.

Sift the flour with the baking powder into a bowl. Add the cardamom, cinnamon, allspice, nutmeg and cloves, then stir to combine. Coarsely chop the chocolate and add to the flour mixture.

Beat the egg whites with a pinch of salt to soft peaks, gradually adding the remaining sugar. Fold the flour mixture a little at a time into the butter mixture, alternating with the wine and beaten egg whites.

Fill the bundt pan with the batter, smooth to level, then bake on the lowest shelf of the oven for 50–55 minutes. Take the cake out of the oven and let cool for a few minutes in the pan. Carefully unmold and let cool completely. Dust with icing (confectioners') sugar and cut into slices before serving.

Bremen-Style Yeasted Cake with a Hazelnut Filling

Bremen

Preparation time:	25 minutes
Rising time:	1 hour 45 minutes
Cooking time:	35 minutes
Serves:	15

For the dough:		
½ cup/3½ fl oz	whole milk	100 ml
4 tsp	fresh yeast	4 tsp
2⅔ cups/11 oz	plain (all-purpose) flour	300 g
scant ½ cup/1½ oz	caster (superfine) sugar	40 g
1	egg	1
½ tsp	salt	½ tsp
½ tsp	unwaxed lemon zest	½ tsp
¼ cup/2¼ oz	butter	60 g

For the filling:		
scant ¼ cup/2 oz	marzipan (almond paste)	50 g
scant ¼ cup/2 oz	apple purée (from a jar)	50 g
1⅓ cup/5 oz	roasted hazelnuts, chopped	150 g
scant ½ cup/1½ oz	caster (superfine) sugar	40 g
½ tsp	ground cinnamon	½ tsp
1 tbsp	lemon juice	1 tbsp
1 tsp	grated unwaxed lemon zest	1 tsp
1 tsp	grated unwaxed orange zest	1 tsp
½	vanilla bean, seeds removed	½
1 tbsp	rum	1 tbsp
*	butter, for greasing	*
scant ⅓ cup/3 oz	apricot preserve	80 g
*	icing (confectioners') sugar, for dusting	*

For the dough: Heat the milk in a small pan until lukewarm. Crumble the yeast into the milk and stir until dissolved. Combine the flour with the yeast and milk mixture, sugar, egg, salt and lemon zest and knead slowly. Gradually add the butter and knead everything into a smooth dough. Cover and let rise in a warm place for 60–90 minutes.

For the filling: Coarsely grate the marzipan (almond paste) and work together with the apple purée until smooth. Mix the hazelnuts with the marzipan (almond paste) and apple mixture, sugar, cinnamon, lemon juice, orange and lemon zests, vanilla bean seeds and rum.

Preheat the oven to 190°/375°F/Gas Mark 5. Grease a 30-cm (11¾-inch) loaf pan with butter. Gently warm the apricot preserve and purée with a stick (immersion) blender.

Roll out the dough into a 30 × 40-cm (12 × 16-inch) rectangle. Brush with the apricot preserve and spread with an even layer of filling. Roll the shorter sides inwards from left and right until they meet in the middle, then place with the opening facing upward in the loaf pan. Cover the dough and let rise for a further 15 minutes.

Bake the cake on the middle shelf inside the oven until golden brown, about 35 minutes. If the top browns very quickly, cover the pan with parchment paper. Take the cake out of the oven and let cool. Dust with icing (confectioners') sugar and cut into slices before serving.

No-Bake Chocolate Cookie Cake (Kalter Hund)

All regions

Preparation time:	20 minutes
Cooling time:	12 hours
Serves:	15

1¼ cups/9 oz	coconut oil	250 g
4	eggs	4
2½ cups/9 oz	icing (confectioners') sugar	250 g
1 cup/4½ oz	cocoa powder	125 g
11 oz	butter cookies	300 g
*	oil, for greasing	*

Melt the coconut oil in a heatproof bowl set over simmering water or in the microwave, heating only as much as necessary.

Use an electric mixer to beat together the eggs, icing (confectioners') sugar and cocoa powder until frothy, then incorporate the warm coconut oil one spoonful at a time.

Grease a 30-cm (11¾-inch) loaf pan with oil and line with parchment paper. Make alternating layers of the chocolate mixture and butter cookies in the pan, starting with the chocolate so that when the cake is unmolded, it is encased in chocolate. Transfer to a cool place to set. When set, carefully unmould the cake from the pan and cut into slices.

Gingerbread Loaf

All regions

Preparation time:		30 minutes
Rising time:		12 hours
Cooking time:		50 minutes
Serves:		15

scant ¼ cup/1¼ oz	brown sugar	35 g
¾ cup/5¾ oz	honey	165 g
1 ¾ cup/7 oz	plain (all-purpose) flour	200 g
scant ¼ cup/1 oz	cornflour (corn starch)	25 g
1 tsp	baking powder	1 tsp
1 tbsp	milk	1 tbsp
1 level tsp	baking soda	1 level tsp
1	egg yolk	1
4 tsp	chopped candied lemon peel	4 tsp
4 tsp	chopped candied orange peel	4 tsp
1–2 tsp	gingerbread spice mix	1–2 tsp
*	butter, for greasing	*
*	flour, for dusting	*

Mix the brown sugar and honey with 50 ml (scant ¼ cup/ 2 fl oz) water in a pan and heat slowly to 80°C/176°F. Let cool to about 37°C/99°F, then gradually work in the flour. Cover and let rest overnight at room temperature.

Preheat the oven to 180°C/350°F/Gas Mark 4. Sprinkle the cornflour (corn starch) over a baking sheet and toast in the oven for about 15 minutes, or until medium brown, stirring a little from time to time. Mix the toasted cornflour with 125 ml (½ cup/4¼ fl oz) hot water in a pan, bring to a boil for a few minutes until the liquid thickens a little, running off the spoon as a thread. Let the starch glaze cool slightly.

Dissolve the baking powder with the milk in a cup and dissolve the baking soda with the egg yolk in another cup. Knead both ingredients into the starter together with the candied orange and lemon peels and gingerbread spices.

Preheat the oven to 200°C/400°F/Gas Mark 6. Grease a 30-cm (11¾-inch) loaf pan with butter and dust with flour. Pour the batter into the pan. Bake on the second shelf from the bottom of the oven for about 50 minutes. Shortly before the end of the cooking time, brush the top of the cake with the starch glaze.

As soon as the loaf turns medium brown and glossy, take the pan out of the oven, let cool a little and unmold. Let cool completely and cover with aluminum foil to keep the loaf fresh.

Bremen-Style Christmas Fruit Bread

Bremen

Preparation time:		30 minutes
Soaking time:		12 hours
Rising time:		2 hours
Cooking time:		1 hour
Serves:		15

For the fruit mixture:		
¾ cup/3½ oz	almonds	100 g
scant ⅓ cup/2 oz	candied lemon peel	50 g
scant ⅓ cup/2 oz	candied orange peel	50 g
3½ cups/1 lb 2 oz	raisins	500 g
½ cup/3½ fl oz	dark rum	100 ml

For the dough:		
⅔ cup/5 fl oz	whole milk	150 ml
3½ tbsp	fresh yeast	3½ tbsp
scant ½ cup/1½ oz	caster (superfine) sugar	40 g
3½ cups/14 oz	plain (all-purpose) flour	400 g
1	pinch salt	1
1 tsp	grated unwaxed lemon zest	1 tsp
1 tsp	vanilla sugar	1 tsp
1	pinch ground cardamom	1
1 cup/9 oz	soft butter	250 g
*	flour, for dusting	*
*	butter, for greasing	*

For the fruit mixture: Coarsely chop and toast the almonds. Very finely chop the orange and lemon peels. Mix the almonds with the raisins, orange and lemon peels and rum in a bowl, then cover and let steep overnight.

For the dough: Heat the milk in a small pan until lukewarm. Crumble the yeast into the milk and stir until dissolved. Mix the yeast and milk with a pinch of sugar and 200 g (1¾ cups/7 oz) flour, then knead to make a thick dough. Cover and let rise in a warm place for about 20 minutes.

Add the remaining flour and sugar, a pinch of salt, the lemon zest, vanilla sugar and cardamom to the yeast starter. Use an electric mixer with a dough hook or a stand mixer to knead. After about 1 minute, gradually add the butter and knead into the dough.

Knead the dough until it becomes elastic, about 10 minutes. Dust the dough with flour and cover with clingfilm (plastic wrap). Let rise at room temperature for about 1 hour, or until it doubles in size.

Grease a 30-cm (11¾-inch) loaf pan with a thick coat of butter. Briefly knead the rum-soaked fruit into the dough. Transfer the dough to a lightly floured work surface and press lightly to spread. Fold over the sides so that they meet at the centre, creating an elongated shape. Roll up the dough to fit the pan, then put into the pan, seam-side down, and let rise for 30 more minutes.

Preheat the oven to 190°C/375°F/Gas Mark 5. Cut out a piece of parchment paper and lay directly on the dough. Cover the pan with a lid or aluminum foil, position inside the lowest third of the oven and bake for 1 hour. Lower the oven temperature to 175°C/345°F/Gas Mark 3¾ after 45 minutes.

Take the pan out of the oven, remove the lid or foil and let cool slightly. Unmold onto a rack. Let the bread cool until lukewarm and cover with aluminum foil. Ideally, let rest for 1–2 weeks in a cool place.

Fruit-Filled Pound Cake (Königskuchen)

All regions

Preparation time:		20 minutes
Cooking time:		1 hour
Serves:		15

1 cup/9 oz	butter	250 g
2 cups/7 oz	icing (confectioners') sugar	200 g
1	unwaxed lemon zest	1
4 tsp	orange liqueur	4 tsp
6	eggs	6
1¾ cups/7 oz	plain (all-purpose) flour	200 g
scant 1 cup/3½ oz	cornflour (corn starch)	100 g
1 tsp	baking powder	1 tsp
¼ cup/2 oz	caster (superfine) sugar	50 g
1 cup/5 oz	golden raisins	150 g
⅓ cup/2 oz	candied orange peel, chopped	50 g
scant 1 cup/3½ oz	coarsely chopped almonds	100 g
*	butter, for greasing	*
	sugar, for coating	*

Preheat the oven to 180°C/350°F/Gas Mark 4. Mix the butter with the icing (confectioners') sugar, lemon zest and orange liqueur. Separate the eggs. Gradually incorporate the egg yolks into the butter mixture.

Mix the flour, cornflour (corn starch) and baking powder, and incorporate into the egg and butter mixture. Beat the egg whites to stiff peaks, gradually adding the sugar. Fold the beaten egg whites into the batter. Sprinkle the raisins, candied orange peel and almonds over the top, then loosely mix until evenly distributed.

Grease a 30-cm (11¾-inch) loaf pan with butter and sprinkle with sugar. Pour the batter into the pan and smooth the surface to level. Bake on the middle shelf inside the oven for 1 hour until golden brown. After about 15 minutes of the cooking time, score lengthwise along the centre of the cake with a knife to a depth of 1 cm (½ inch), which will allow the cake to rise better. Take the cake out of the oven, let it cool a little, then unmold.

Chocolate Pound Cake

All regions

Preparation time:		25 minutes
Cooking time:		45 minutes
Serves:		15

For the batter:		
1½ cups/6¼ oz	ground hazelnuts	180 g
⅔ cups/5 oz	chopped dark chocolate	150 g
⅔ cups/5 oz	soft butter	150 g
¾ cup/2¾ oz	icing (confectioners') sugar	70 g
1 tbsp	vanilla sugar	1 tbsp
8	egg yolks	8
2 cups/3½ oz	sponge cake crumbs	100 g
1 tsp	baking powder	1 tsp
8	egg whites	8
1	pinch salt	1
*	butter, for greasing	*

For the glaze:		
⅔ cups/5 oz	chopped dark chocolate	150 g
⅓ cup/2¾ fl oz	condensed milk	80 ml
1 tbsp	honey	1 tbsp

For the batter: Preheat the oven to 175°C/345°F/Gas Mark 3¾. Spread the ground hazelnuts over a baking sheet, roast on the middle shelf of the oven for 5–10 minutes until golden brown, stirring often. Let cool.

Warm the dark chocolate in a metal bowl set over simmering water, stirring until it has melted.

Use an electric mixer to cream the butter with 2 tbsp icing (confectioners') sugar and the vanilla sugar in a bowl. Gradually incorporate the egg yolks and beat until pale and fluffy. Stir in the melted chocolate.

Mix in the roasted hazelnuts, sponge cake crumbs, and baking powder. Beat the egg whites with a pinch of salt until creamy, then gradually add the remaining icing (confectioners') sugar and beat to stiff peaks. Fold the beaten egg whites a little at a time into the chocolate batter, alternating with the nut mixture.

Grease a 30-cm (11¾-inch) loaf pan with butter and line with parchment paper. Pour the batter into the pan, position the pan on the lowest shelf inside the oven and bake for 40–45 minutes. Take the pan out of the oven and let the cake cool in the pan for 10 minutes, then carefully unmold onto a rack and let cool completely.

For the glaze: Warm the dark chocolate with the condensed milk and honey in a metal bowl set over simmering water, stirring constantly until it has melted. Brush the glaze over the cake and let harden. Cut the cake into slices, regularly wetting the knife with water.

Yeasted Butter and Sugar Cake

All regions ◔ ✑

Preparation time:	15 minutes
Rising time:	50 minutes
Cooking time:	20 minutes
Serves:	12–16

For the dough:

⅔ cup/5 fl oz	whole milk	150 ml
2 tbsp	fresh yeast	2 tbsp
3½ cups/14 oz	plain (all-purpose) flour	400 g
¼ cup/2 oz	caster (superfine) sugar	50 g
1	egg	1
*	salt	*
⅓ cup/2¾ oz	soft butter	70 g
*	melted butter, for greasing	*
*	flour, for dusting	*

For the topping:

⅔ cup/5 oz	cold butter	150 g
scant ½ cup/2 oz	slivered almonds	50 g
½ cup/3½ oz	sugar	100 g

For the dough: Heat the milk in a small pan until lukewarm. Crumble the yeast into the milk and stir until dissolved. Mix the yeast and milk mixture with the flour, sugar, egg and a pinch of salt, then knead using an electric mixer with a dough hook. Add the butter and knead for a few more minutes, until the dough becomes elastic.

Shape the dough into a ball, put into a bowl and cover with clingfilm (plastic wrap). Let rise in a warm place for about 30 minutes.

Grease a 30 × 40-cm (12 × 16-inch) tray bake (sheet cake) pan with melted butter and dust with flour. Roll out the dough thinly over a floured work surface and line the pan. Cover with a dish towel and let rise for a further 20 minutes.

For the topping: Preheat the oven to 220°C/425F/Gas Mark 7. Use your finger or the handle of a wooden spoon to make dimples all over the dough, spaced about 2 cm (¾ inch) apart. Cut the cold butter into 1-cm (½-inch) cubes and put one cube in each dimple, spreading out the rest of the cubes between them. Scatter with slivered almonds and sprinkle with the sugar.

Bake the cake on the middle shelf of the oven for about 5 minutes, then lower the oven temperature to 200°C/400°F/Gas Mark 6 and bake for a further 12–15 minutes. Take the pan out of the oven and let the cake cool on a rack. Cut into portions. Best served freshly baked and lukewarm, accompanied with coffee.

Apricot and Cream Cheese Cake

All regions ◔ ✑

Preparation time:	40 minutes
Cooling time:	2 hours
Cooking time:	50 minutes
Serves:	12–16

For the pastry:

¾ cup/6 oz	soft butter	175 g
¾ cup/2½ oz	icing (confectioners') sugar	75 g
½	vanilla bean, seeds removed	½
½	unwaxed lemon, zested	½
1	pinch salt	1
2	egg yolks	2
2¼ cup/8½ oz	plain (all-purpose) flour	240 g

For the topping:

5 cups/2¼ lb	Quark	1 kg
1 cup/7 oz	caster (superfine) sugar	200 g
½ tsp	grated unwaxed lemon zest	½ tsp
1	pinch salt	1
1 tbsp	vanilla sugar	1 tbsp
3	eggs	3
⅔ cup/5⅔ fl oz	double (heavy) cream	160 ml
¼ cup/1¼ oz	cornflour (corn starch)	30 g
scant 1 cup/3½ oz	slivered almonds	100 g
2¼ lb	apricots	1 kg
*	butter, for greasing	*
scant 1 cup/9 oz	apricot preserve	250 g

For the pastry: Use an electric mixer with a dough hook or a dough scraper to mix the butter with the icing (confectioners') sugar, the vanilla bean seeds, lemon zest and a pinch of salt in a bowl and work until smooth. Mix in the egg yolks one at a time, but do not beat. Finally, add the flour and knead only for the time it takes for the pastry to become smooth. Shape into a flat block, cover with clingfilm (plastic wrap), and chill in the refrigerator for 2 hours.

For the topping: Mix the Quark with half of the sugar, the lemon zest, a pinch of salt and the vanilla sugar. Add the eggs and cream, then incorporate with the remaining sugar mixed with the cornflour (corn starch) followed by the slivered almonds.

Peel, halve, pit and cut the apricots into wedges. Preheat the oven to 200°C/400°F/Gas Mark 6.

Roll out the pastry over a lightly floured work surface into a rectangle a little larger than a 30 × 40-cm (11¾ × 15¾-inch) tray bake (sheet cake) pan. Grease pan and line with the pastry. Prick several times with a fork. Spread the topping in an even layer over the pastry and cover with the apricots.

Bake on the lowest shelf inside the oven until golden brown, about 50 minutes. Heat the apricot preserve, purée with a stick (immersion) blender, then brush over the cake.

Each season you can find these moist sheet cakes also topped with fresh cherries, peaches or plums. The almonds acquire a particular nutty flavour when toasted until golden brown in a dry frying pan or skillet over medium heat.

Vanilla Cream Cake with Almonds (Bienenstich)

All regions

Rising time:		65 minutes
Rising time:		1 hour
Cooking time:		25 minutes
Serves:		12-16

For the dough:		
⅔ cup/5½ fl oz	milk	160 ml
4 tsp	fresh yeast	4 tsp
3¼ cups/13 oz	plain (all-purpose) flour	370 g
¼ cup/1¾ oz	sugar	45 g
1 tsp	vanilla sugar	1 tsp
½-1 tsp	salt	½-1 tsp
1	egg	1
1	egg yolk	1
½	unwaxed lemon, zested	½
scant ¼ cup/2 oz	butter	50 g
*	butter, for greasing	*

For the topping:		
½ cup/4½ oz	butter	125 g
⅔ cup/4½ oz	sugar	125 g
scant ¼ cup/1½ oz	honey	40 g
⅓ cup/2¾ fl oz	glucose syrup	75 ml
⅓ cup/2¾ fl oz	double (heavy) cream	75 ml
2¼ cups/9 oz	sliced almonds	250 g

For the vanilla custard cream:		
2 cups/17 fl oz	milk	500 ml
scant ⅔ cup/4 oz	sugar	120 g
1	vanilla bean	1
⅔ cup/ 2¾ oz	instant vanilla pudding (custard) powder	75g
6 sheets	gelatine	6 sheets
3 cups/25 fl oz	double (heavy) cream	750 ml

For the dough: Heat the milk in a pan until lukewarm. Dissolve the yeast in the milk then mix with 90 g (¾ cup/ 3¼ oz) flour to a smooth dough. Cover and rise in a warm place for 15 minutes.

Knead the starter with the remaining flour, the sugar, vanilla sugar, salt, egg, egg yolk, and zest. Gradually add the butter and knead until the dough becomes elastic. Put into a bowl, cover with clingfilm (plastic wrap), and let rise in a warm place for 30 minutes. Grease a 30 × 40cm (11¾ × 15¾ inch) cake pan. Knead the dough, then roll out and line the pan. Prick with a fork, then chill for 20 minutes.

For the topping: Combine the butter with the sugar, honey and syrup in a pan and bring to a boil. Deglaze with the cream and stir in the almonds. Bring to a boil, transfer to a bowl, and cool. Spread the topping over the dough. Let rise in a warm place for 15 minutes. Bake at 200°C/400°F/Gas Mark 6 for 20-25 minutes, until golden.

For the vanilla cream: Combine ⅞ of the milk with the sugar, vanilla and a pinch of salt in a pan and bring to a boil. Dissolve the pudding with the remaining milk, stir into the hot milk and bring to a boil. Transfer to a dish. Cover with clingfilm (plastic wrap) touching the surface and cool. Soften the gelatine in cold water and squeeze. Mix with 2 tbsp pudding in a pan, heat and dissolve. Mix with the rest of the pudding. Whip the cream to stiff peaks and fold in.

Halve the cake and fill with the custard. Mark out 12-16 portions, then chill until firm.

Apple Streusel Cake

All regions

Preparation time:		30 minutes
Cooking time:		45 minutes
Serves:		12-16

For the topping:		
4½ lb	fragrant apples (e.g. Boskoop)	2 kg
1	lemon, juiced	1
¼ cup/2 oz	sugar	50 g
½ tsp	ground cinnamon	½ tsp

For the streusel:		
1⅓ cup/5 oz	plain (all-purpose) flour	150 g
⅔ cup/4 oz	sugar	120 g
½ tsp	grated unwaxed lemon zest	½ tsp
1	pinch ground cinnamon	1
½ cup/4 oz	melted butter	120 g
⅔ cup/3 oz	slivered almonds	80 g

For the batter:		
1 cup/9 oz	butter, softened	250 g
1¼ cups/9 oz	sugar	250 g
*	salt	*
1	pinch vanilla bean seeds	1
5	eggs	5
3 cups/12 oz	plain (all-purpose) flour	350 g
5 tsp	baking powder	5 tsp
*	butter, for greasing	*
*	icing (confectioners') sugar, for dusting	*

For the topping: Peel, quarter, core, and cut the apples into slices. Drizzle with lemon juice. Mix the sugar with the cinnamon.

For the streusel: Mix the flour with the sugar, lemon zest, and cinnamon. Add the melted butter and rub in with your fingers until crumbly. Loosely incorporate the slivered almonds. Set aside in the refrigerator.

Preheat the oven to 180°C/350°F/Gas Mark 4.

For the batter: Cream the butter with the sugar, a pinch of salt, and the vanilla bean seeds. Gradually add the eggs, and whisk with an electric mixer until thick and fluffy. Sift the flour and baking powder over the mixture and mix.

Grease a 30 × 40cm (11¾ × 15¾ inch) sheet cake pan with butter and fill with the batter. Smooth, then spread the apple slices evenly over the surface. Finally, cover with the streusel, dust with the sugar and cinnamon mix. Bake on the middle shelf of the oven for 40-45 minutes, until golden brown and crispy. Dust with icing (confectioners') sugar and cut into portions.

Dresden-Style Yeasted Cake

Saxony, Dresden and Thuringia

Preparation time:	40 minutes
Rising time:	40 minutes
Cooking time:	1 hour
Serves:	12-16

For the dough:

4 tsp	fresh yeast	4 tsp
½ cup/4¼ fl oz	lukewarm milk	125 ml
2⅔ cups/11 oz	plain (all-purpose) flour	300 g
¼ cup/2 oz	sugar	50 g
2	egg yolks	2
1 tbsp	almond liqueur	1 tbsp
*	salt	*
1	pinch vanilla bean seeds	1
1	pinch grated unwaxed lemon zest	1
scant ¼ cup/2 oz	soft butter	50 g
*	melted butter, for greasing	*
*	flour, for dusting	*

For the Quark:

scant ½ cup/3½ oz	butter	100 g
1 cup/7 oz	sugar	200 g
2	eggs	2
5 cups/2¼ lb	Quark	1 kg
⅔ cup/2¾ oz	instant vanilla pudding (custard) powder	75 g
2 cups/17 fl oz	milk	500 ml
*	salt	*
¾ cup/3½ oz	Rum-Soaked Raisins (p. 362)	100 g

For the custard:

2 cups/17 fl oz	milk	500 ml
⅔ cup/2¾ oz	instant vanilla pudding (custard) powder	75 g
¾ cup/5 oz	sugar	150 g
scant 1 cup/7 oz	butter	200 g
6	eggs	6

For the dough: Dissolve the yeast in the milk. Combine with the flour, sugar, egg yolks, liqueur, a pinch of salt, the vanilla and zest, and knead together. Add the butter and knead for a few more minutes until the dough becomes elastic. Cover rise in a warm place for about 30 minutes.

Grease a 30 × 40cm/11¾ × 15¾ inch cake pan with butter and dust with flour. Roll out the dough thinly over a floured work surface. Line the pan. Prick the dough several times with a fork, then briefly let rise again.

For the Quark: Cream the butter with half of the sugar. Gradually incorporate the eggs and Quark. Dissolve the pudding (custard) powder in a little milk. Combine the remaining milk and sugar with a little salt in a pan and bring to a boil. Stir the powder into the hot milk and bring back to a boil. Stir the custard into the Quark. Spread the over the dough in the pan and scatter over with the Raisins (p. 362). Preheat the oven to 175°C/345°F/Gas Mark 3¾.

For the custard: Prepare a custard as described previously (p. 362) with the pudding powder, milk, and half of the sugar. Beat the butter until fluffy. Separate the eggs and stir the yolks into the butter. Beat the whites to stiff peaks with the remaining sugar. Mix with the custard and fold into the butter and egg. Spread the custard over the Quark. Bake 1 hour. Rest for a few hours before serving.

Danube Waves Cake (Donauwelle)

All regions

Preparation time:	40 minutes
Cooking time:	30 minutes
Cooling time:	30 minutes
Serves:	12-16

For the batter:

scant 1¼ cups/9 oz	butter	250 g
1¼ cups/9 oz	sugar	250 g
1 tsp	unwaxed lemon lemon zest	1 tsp
6	egg yolks	6
3 cups/12 oz	plain (all-purpose) flour	350 g
5 tsp	baking powder	5 tsp
2 tbsp	cocoa powder	2 tbsp
3 tbsp	milk	3 tbsp
6	egg whites	6
1½ cups/9 oz	sour cherries, pitted	250 g
*	butter, for greasing	*

For the topping:

⅔ cup/2¾ oz	cornflour (corn starch)	70 g
3	egg yolks	3
1 cup/8 fl oz	milk	250 ml
1	vanilla bean	1
*	salt	*
scant ½ cup/3 oz	sugar	80 g
scant ½ cup/3½ oz	butter, softened	100 g
8 tsp	orange liqueur	8 tsp
1 cup/9 oz	couverture chocolate	250 g

For the batter: Cream the butter with 100 g (½ cup/3½ oz) sugar and the lemon zest. Add the egg yolks one at a time, and beat until thick and fluffy. Mix the flour with the baking powder. Mix the cocoa powder with the milk and beat the egg whites to stiff peaks with the remaining sugar. Fold the beaten egg whites and flour mixture into the batter.

Preheat the oven to 180°C/350°F/Gas Mark 4. Grease a 30 × 40cm (11¾ × 15¾ inch) sheet cake pan with butter and fill with half of the batter. Mix the other half with the cocoa mixture and pour over the light batter. Smooth the surface. Distribute the cherries over the batter and bake the cake on the middle shelf of the oven for about 30 minutes.

For the topping: Mix the cornflour (corn starch) with the egg yolks and a little milk. Split the vanilla bean. Combine the remaining milk with the vanilla bean, a pinch of salt, and the sugar, and bring to a boil in a small pan. Stir in the corn starch mixture. Let boil briefly, then transfer to a bowl, cover with parchment paper, and let cool. Press the custard through a strainer, then stir until it thickens.

Gradually incorporate the butter, add the liqueur, and spread evenly over the cake. Set aside in the refrigerator.

Chop then melt the couverture chocolate in a heatproof bowl set over simmering water. Let cool a little, then pour over the cake and spread evenly with an offset frosting spatula. As soon as the frosting sets, use a serrated spatula to create a wave pattern over the surface. Cut into portions and serve.

Braided Sweet Yeast Bread (Hefezopf)

All regions

Preparation time:	25 minutes
Rising time:	1 hour 20 minutes
Cooking time:	30 minutes
Makes:	1 loaf

For the dough:

⅔ cup/5 fl oz	milk	150 ml
4 tsp	yeast	4 tsp
2⅔ cups/11 oz	plain (all-purpose) flour	300 g
¼ cup/2 oz	sugar	50 g
2	egg yolks	2
1 tsp	almond liqueur (e.g. amaretto)	1 tsp
*	salt	*
1	pinch vanilla bean seeds	1
1	pinch unwaxed lemon zest	1
scant ¼ cup/2 oz	butter, softened	50 g
2 tbsp	raisins	2 tbsp
1 tbsp	rum	1 tbsp
*	melted butter, for greasing	*
*	flour, for dusting	*
1	egg	1

For the glaze:

½ cup/2 oz	icing (confectioners') sugar	50 g
1 tsp	rum	1 tsp
1 tbsp	sliced almonds	1 tbsp

For the dough: Heat the milk until lukewarm and put into a bowl. Crumble the yeast with your fingers and dissolve in the milk. Add the flour, sugar, egg yolk, almond liqueur, a pinch of salt, the vanilla bean seeds, and lemon zest. Use an electric mixer or stand mixer with a dough hook to knead everything into a dough. Add the butter and knead the dough until it becomes shiny and elastic, and comes away from the sides of the bowl.

Cover and let rise in a warm place for just under 30 minutes, until it doubles in volume. Mix the raisins with the rum in a small bowl. Briefly knead the dough again and let rise for 30 more minutes.

Preheat the oven to 180°C/350°F/Gas Mark 4. Grease a baking sheet with melted butter and dust with flour.

Drain the raisins and add to the dough. Briefly knead the dough again, divide into three portions and shape each one into a rope-like strand. Braid the three strands into a loaf. Lay the loaf on the baking sheet, cover, and let rise again in a warm place for 20 more minutes

Beat the egg, brush the loaf, and bake on the middle shelf inside the oven for 25-30 minutes. Let cool completely.

For the glaze: Mix the icing (confectioners') sugar with 1 tbsp of water and the rum. Toast the sliced almonds in a dry skillet (frying pan) until golden brown. Glaze the loaf and sprinkle with the toasted sliced almonds.

Poppy Seed Strudel

All regions

Preparation time:	40 minutes
Rising time:	30 minutes
Cooking time:	25 minutes
Serves:	8-10

For the dough:

½ cup/4¼ fl oz	milk	125 ml
4 tsp	fresh yeast	4 tsp
2⅔ cups/11 oz	plain (all-purpose) flour	300 g
¼ cup/2 oz	sugar	50 g
2	egg yolks	2
1 tsp	almond liqueur (e.g. amaretto)	1 tsp
*	salt	*
1	pinch vanilla bean seeds	1
1	pinch unwaxed lemon zest	1
¼ cup/2 oz	butter, softened	50 g
*	melted butter, for greasing	*
*	flour, for dusting	*
1	egg	1
1 tbsp	double (heavy) cream	1 tbsp
*	icing (confectioners') sugar, for dusting	*

For the filling:

4	apples (e.g. Braeburn)	4
1⅔ cups/7 oz	poppy seeds	200 g
scant 1 cup/7 fl oz	milk	200 ml
⅓ cup/2¾ fl oz	brewed coffee	80 ml
½	vanilla bean	½
1	cinnamon shard	1
2	eggs	2
*	salt	*
scant ¼ cup/1½ oz	sugar	40 g
2 tbsp	icing (confectioners') sugar	2 tbsp
1 tsp	unwaxed lemon zest	1 tsp

For the dough: Heat the milk until lukewarm. Crumble the yeast and dissolve in the milk. Mix with the flour, sugar, yolks, liqueur, a pinch of salt, vanilla and zest. Knead to a dough by hand or using a mixer. Add the butter and knead until elastic. Shape into a ball, put into a bowl and cover. Rise in a warm place for 30 minutes.

For the filling: Cut the apples into 5-10 mm (¼-½ inch) dice. Finely grind the poppy seeds. Combine with the milk and coffee in a pan. Simmer for 10 minutes. Add the apples, vanilla and cinnamon, remove from the heat. Cool for 10 minutes. Discard the vanilla and cinnamon.

Separate the eggs. Beat the whites with a pinch of salt and the sugar to firm peaks. Beat the egg yolks with the sugars and lemon zest until fluffy. Mix the poppy seed mixture with the yolks and fold in the beaten egg whites.

Preheat the oven to 180°C/350°F/Gas Mark 4. Grease a baking sheet. Roll out the dough thinly over a floured surface into a 40 cm (15¾ inch) square, then halve into rectangles. Lay one rectangle on a dish cloth. Make a thick band of filling along one side. Leave a 5 cm (2 inch) wide space free of filling at the shorter ends and fold inward. Use the cloth to roll up the strudel. Lay seam-side down, on the baking sheet. Repeat to make a second.

Whisk the egg with the cream. Brush the strudels with butter and bake until golden, about 25 minutes. Allow to cool for 30 minutes. Cut into portions and dust with sugar.

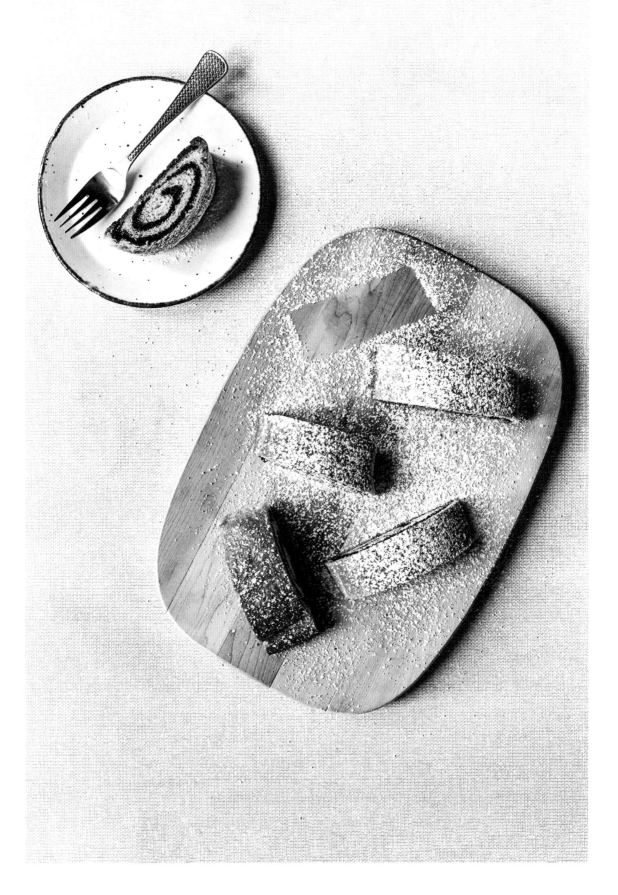

Twisted Hazelnut Loaf (Nusszopf)

All regions

Preparation time:	30 minutes
Rising time:	1 hour 30 minutes
Cooking time:	30 minutes
Makes:	1 loaf

For the dough:		
⅔ cup/5 fl oz	milk	150 ml
4 tsp	fresh yeast	4 tsp
2⅔ cups/11 oz	plain (all-purpose) flour	300 g
¼ cup/2 oz	sugar	50 g
2	egg yolks	2
1 tsp	almond liqueur (e.g. amaretto)	1 tsp
*	salt	*
1	pinch vanilla bean seeds	1
1	pinch unwaxed lemon zest	1
scant ¼ cup/2 oz	butter, softened	50 g
*	flour, for dusting	*
scant ¼ cup/2 oz	melted butter	50 g
⅓ cup/3½ oz	apricot preserve	100 g

For the filling:		
1¾ cup/7 oz	ground hazelnuts (flour)	200 g
¾ cup/5 oz	sugar	150 g
1 tsp	vanilla sugar	1 tsp
½	unwaxed lemon, zested	½
1	lemon, juiced	1
5 tbsp	double (heavy) cream	5 tbsp
1	egg white	1
*	salt	*

For the dough: Heat the milk until lukewarm and put into a bowl. Crumble the yeast and dissolve in the milk. Add the flour, sugar, egg yolks, almond liqueur, a pinch of salt, the vanilla seeds, and lemon zest. Use an electric mixer with a dough hook to knead everything into a dough. Add the butter and knead the dough until it becomes shiny and elastic, and comes away from the sides of the bowl.

Cover and let rise in a warm place, about 30 minutes, until it doubles in volume. Briefly knead the dough again and let rise for 30 more minutes.

For the filling: Mix the ground hazelnuts (flour) with 100 g/3½ oz sugar, the vanilla sugar, lemon zest and juice and cream. Beat the egg whites with a pinch of salt and the remaining sugar to firm peaks and fold into the hazelnut mixture.

Preheat the oven to 190°C/375°F/Gas Mark 5. Roll out the dough over a floured work surface into a 30 × 40 cm (11¾-15¾ inch) rectangle. Brush with the melted butter and spread the filling evenly, leaving a 1-2 cm (½-¾ inch) wide edge without filling.

Roll up the dough, starting from the longer side, then lay the roll on its seam and cut in half lengthwise. With the cut side of both halves facing outward, carefully twist like a rope, then press the ends to join. Transfer the loaf to a baking sheet lined with parchment paper and let rise in a warm place for 20-30 more minutes.

Bake the loaf on the second shelf from the bottom of the oven for 30–35 minutes, until medium brown. In the meantime, bring the apricot preserve to a boil in a pan and puree with an stick (immersion) blender. Take the loaf out of the oven, glaze with the apricot preserve, and let cool.

Sunken Gooseberry Cake

All regions

Preparation time:	30 minutes
Cooking time:	30 minutes
Serves:	12-16

6⅔ cups/2¼ lb	gooseberries	1 kg
⅔ cup/5 oz	butter, softened	150 g
*	salt	*
1 tsp	vanilla sugar	1 tsp
½	unwaxed lemon, zested	½
¾ cup/5 oz	sugar	150 g
3	eggs	3
3⅓ cups/13 oz	plain (all-purpose) flour	375 g
2½ tsp	baking powder	2½ tsp
3 tbsp	milk	3 tbsp
*	butter, for greasing	*
*	flour, for dusting	*
scant ¼ cup/1½ oz	melted butter	40 g
2-3 tbsp	sugar, for sprinkling	2-3 tbsp

Trim and wash the gooseberries, then drain thoroughly. Preheat the oven to 200°C/400°F/Gas Mark 6.

Using an electric mixer, beat the butter with a pinch of salt, the vanilla sugar, and lemon zest until pale and fluffy. Incorporate the sugar and eggs a little at a time, alternating between them. The result should be a glossy cream. Should the butter not bind with the egg, warm the mixing bowl a little by dipping in warm water and beat again. Beat everything until fine, pale, and fluffy.

Sift the flour with the baking powder and use a spatula to gradually fold into the butter mixture, adding the milk if necessary.

Grease a 30 × 40cm (11¾ × 15¾ inch) sheet cake pan with butter and dust with flour. Spread the batter in the pan and smooth, using a rolling pin if necessary. Brush with melted butter and distribute the gooseberries over the surface.

Bake the cake on the second shelf from the bottom of the oven for about 30 minutes, until golden brown. Take out of the oven, sprinkle with sugar, and let cool.

Yeasted Plum Cake with Streusel (Zwetschgendatschi)

Southern Germany

Preparation time: 30 minutes
Rising time: 50 minutes
Cooking time: 40 minutes
Serves: 12-16

For the dough:

½ cup/4¼ fl oz	milk	125 ml
4 tsp	yeast	4 tsp
2⅔ cups/11 oz	plain (all-purpose) flour	300 g
¼ cup/2 oz	sugar	50 g
2	egg yolks	2
1 tsp	almond liqueur (e.g. amaretto)	1 tsp
*	salt	*
1	pinch vanilla seeds	1
1	pinch grated lemon zest	1
scant ¼ cup/2 oz	soft butter	50 g
*	melted butter, for greasing	*
*	flour, for dusting	*

For the topping:

4½ lb	plums	2 kg
2 oz	sponge cake crumbs	50 g
2 oz	sugar	50 g
½ tsp	ground cinnamon	½ tsp

For the streusel:

4½ oz	plain (all-purpose) flour	125 g
scant ½ cup/6¾ oz	sugar	90 g
1 tbsp	vanilla sugar	1 tbsp
scant ½ cup/3½ oz	melted butter	100 g
*	salt	*
1	pinch ground cinnamon	1
⅔ cups/2½ oz	flaked almonds	75 g

For the dough: Heat the milk until lukewarm. Crumble the yeast into the milk and stir to dissolve. Mix the yeast and milk mixture with the flour, sugar, egg yolks, liqueur, a pinch of salt, the vanilla and lemon zest. Knead into a dough by hand or using an electric mixer with a dough hook. Add the butter and knead for a few more minutes until the dough becomes elastic. Shape the dough into a ball, put into a bowl, and cover with clingfilm (plastic wrap). Let rise in a warm place, 30 minutes.

Grease a 30 × 40cm (11¾ × 15¾ inch) sheet cake pan with melted butter and dust with flour. Roll out the dough thinly over a floured work surface and line the pan. Prick several times with a fork.

For the topping: Wash, halve, and pit the plums. Score each plum half lengthwise to about halfway. Sprinkle the dough with the sponge crumbs and cover with the plum halves, packed tightly together. Mix the sugar and cinnamon in a small bowl and sprinkle over the plums.

For the streusel: Mix the flour with the sugar, vanilla sugar, melted butter, and a pinch of salt and cinnamon, and rub together with your fingers until crumbly. Loosely mix in the flaked almonds, then spread an even layer of streusel over the cake. Let rise again for 20 minutes.

Preheat the oven to 175°C/345°F/Gas Mark 3¾. Bake the cake for 30-40 minutes, until golden brown. Take out of the oven, let cool, then cut into portions. The cake can be served with a little whipped cream.

Sweet Yeast Bun (Stutenkerl)

Westphalia and Münster

Preparation time: 20 minutes
Rising time: 1 hour 20 minutes
Cooking time: 20 minutes
Makes: 4

For the dough:

⅔ cups/5 fl oz	milk	150 ml
scant ½ cup/3½ oz	butter, softened	100 g
4½ cups/1 lb 2 oz	plain (all-purpose) flour	500 g
2 tsp	dried yeast	2 tsp
1/3 cup/2½ oz	sugar	75 g
1 level tsp	salt	1 level tsp
1 tsp	unwaxed lemon zest	1 tsp
1	egg	1
1	egg white	1

For the figures:

*	flour, for dusting	*
1	egg yolk	1
2 tbsp	milk	2 tbsp
20	raisins	20
4	plaster or clay pipes	4
	(from a craft store)	

For the dough: Heat the milk in a pan and add the butter to melt. Mix the flour and yeast well in a mixing bowl. Add the remaining ingredients. Use a stand mixer or hand mixer with a dough hook to knead to a smooth dough, starting on the lowest speed for about 5 minutes and then at high speed. Cover with clingfilm (plastic wrap) and let rise in a warm place, about 30 minutes.

For the figures: Briefly knead the dough over a floured work surface, then divide into four portions and shape into 20 cm (7¾ inch) long cylinders. Roll out a little over a lightly floured work surface to a flat oval with a thickness of about 1 cm (½ inch). Trim the dough from the sides and use the scraps to make arms and legs. Make a round head. You can also use a stutenkerl cutter to create the figures.

Lay the figures on a baking sheet lined with parchment paper. Mix the egg yolk with the milk, brush the figures, and make eyes and a few buttons from raisins. Position the pipe at mouth height and press lightly into the body. Let rise again for 20 minutes.

Preheat the oven to 180°C/350°F/Gas Mark 4. Bake the figures until golden brown, about 20 minutes. Let cool.

Christmas Fruit Loaf (Kletzenbrot)

Southern Germany

Marinating time:	24 hours
Preparation time:	25 minutes
Cooking time:	70-90 minutes
Makes:	2-3 loaves

1½ cups/11 oz	dried pears	300 g
⅔ cups/3½ oz	dried figs	100 g
2½ cups/11 oz	prunes, pitted	300 g
1¼ cup/5 oz	dried dates, pitted	150 g
1¼ cup/5 oz	dried apricots, pitted	150 g
1¾ cups/9 oz	raisins	250 g
⅓ cup/2 oz	candied orange peel	50 g
4 tsp	candied lemon peel	4 tsp
1 tsp	ground cinnamon	1 tsp
1	pinch ground star anise	1
½ tsp	ground cloves	½ tsp
⅓ cup/2¾ fl oz	rum	80 ml
⅓ cup/2¾ fl oz	plum brandy	80 ml
1⅓ cups/7 oz	hazelnuts	200 g
2¼ lb	bread dough	1 kg
*	flour, for dusting	*

The previous day, soak the pears in cold water overnight.

On the actual day, transfer the pears and their soaking water to a pan and simmer gently, about 10 minutes. Pour into a strainer, let drain, and cut into large dice. Dice the figs, prunes, dates, and apricots. Combine in a bowl with the pears, raisins, orange and lemon peel, cinnamon, a pinch of star anise, the cloves, rum, and plum brandy and mix well. Cover and leave to steep for 12 hours.

Finely chop the hazelnuts. Knead the fruit and spice mixture, together with the hazelnuts, into the bread dough. Dust with flour and shape into 2 or 3 oval loaves. Lay the loaves on a baking sheet lined with parchment paper and let rise for 30 minutes in a warm place. Preheat the oven to 180°C/350°F/Gas Mark 4.

Bake the loaves on the middle shelf inside the oven, for 70-90 minutes, depending on the size, brushing with water every 10 minutes to allow the bread to develop an attractive crust. Tap on the underside of the loaves. The bread is done when you hear a hollow sound.

Take out and let cool on the baking sheet. Wrap with aluminum foil and rest for several days. Accompany with cheese or simply spread with butter.

Poppy Seed Cake (Schmand-Mohn-Kuchen)

Thuringia, Hesse and Lower Saxony

Preparation time:	35 minutes
Rising time:	40 minutes
Cooking time:	50 minutes
Serves:	12-16

For the dough:		
½ cup/4¼ fl oz	milk	125 ml
4 tsp	fresh yeast	4 tsp
2⅔ cups/11 oz	plain (all-purpose) flour	300 g
¼ cups/2 oz	sugar	50 g
2	egg yolks	2
1 tbsp	almond liqueur	1 tbsp
*	salt	*
1	pinch vanilla seeds	1
1	pinch unwaxed lemon zest	1
¼ cup/2 oz	butter, softened	50 g
*	melted butter, for greasing	*

For the poppy seed paste:		
2¾ cups/22¾ fl oz	milk	675 ml
¾ cups/5 oz	sugar	150 g
⅓ cup/3¼ oz	butter	90 g
*	salt	*
½	vanilla bean	½
1⅔ cups/7 oz	poppy seeds	200 g
⅓ cup/2 oz	semolina	50 g
scant ¼ cup/1¼ oz	raisins	30 g
1	egg	1
1 tsp	unwaxed lemon zest	1 tsp

For the sour cream:		
⅔ cup/2¾ oz	instant vanilla pudding (custard) powder	75g
1½ cups/5 oz	sugar	150 g
*	salt	*
6 cups/3 lb	smetana (sour cream)	1.4 kg
2	eggs	2
2	egg yolks	2
1 tsp	unwaxed orange zest	1 tsp
1 lb	canned apricot halves	450 g

For the dough: Heat the milk in a pan until lukewarm. Crumble the yeast and dissolve in the milk. Combine the yeast and milk with the flour, sugar, egg yolks, liqueur, a pinch of salt, the vanilla, and zest then knead. Add the butter and knead until elastic. Put into a bowl, cover, and let rise in a warm place, about 30 minutes.

Grease a 30 × 40cm (11¾ × 15¾ inch) cake tin with butter. Roll out the dough thinly on a and line the bottom of the pan. Prick with a fork, then briefly let rise again.

For the poppy seed paste: Mix the milk with the sugar, butter, and salt in a pan and bring to a boil. Scrape the vanilla seeds into the milk. Whisk in the poppy seeds and semolina, then simmer for 4 minutes. Let cool. Add the raisins, egg and zest and discard the vanilla.

For the sour cream: Mix the pudding powder with the sugar and a pinch of salt in a bowl, then add the sour cream, eggs, and yolks and mix until smooth. Add the orange zest. Drain the apricots well in a strainer.

Preheat the oven to 175°C/345°F/Gas Mark 3¾. Spread the paste over the dough. Top with sour cream and apricots. Bake for 50 minutes.

Easter Lamb Cake

All regions   ⚘

½ cup/3½ oz	butter, softened	100 g
1 cup/3½ oz	icing (confectioners') sugar	100 g
1	pinch vanilla seeds	1
1	pinch unwaxed lemon zest	1
2	egg yolks	2
scant 1 cup/3½ oz	plain (all-purpose) flour	100 g
1 tsp	baking powder	1 tsp
2	egg whites	2
*	salt	*
*	soft butter, for greasing	*
*	flour, for dusting	*
*	icing (confectioners') sugar, for dusting	*

Preparation time: 20 minutes
Cooking time: 45 minutes
Serves: 8-10

Preheat the oven to 180°C/350°F/Gas Mark 4. Cream the butter with half of the sugar, the vanilla seeds, and lemon zest with an electric mixer, until the sugar has dissolved completely. Gradually stir the egg yolks.

Sift the flour with the baking powder. Beat the egg whites with the rest of the sugar and a pinch of salt to soft peaks. Fold the flour a little at a time into the butter mixture, alternating with the beaten egg whites.

Grease an Easter lamb mold with butter and dust with flour. Pour in the batter through the opening and carefully tap the mold against the work surface to spread the batter evenly inside the mold. Bake in the oven for about 45 minutes.

Take out of the oven and let the lamb cake steam for a few minutes inside the mold. Carefully unmold. Let cool completely and dust liberally with icing (confectioners') sugar.

Dresden-Style Christmas Stollen

Saxony   ◐ ⚘

Soaking time: 12 hours
Preparation time: 30 minutes
Rising time: 1 hour 30 minutes
Cooking time: 1 hour
Makes: 2 loaves

For the fruit mixture:

scant 1 cup/3½ oz	chopped almonds	100 g
1¾ cup/9 oz	zante currants	250 g
1¾ cup/9 oz	raisins	250 g
⅓ cup/2 oz	candied lemon peel, minced	50 g
⅔ cup/3½ oz	candied orange peel, minced	100 g
½ cup/4 fl oz	rum	120 ml
2	drops bitter almond extract	2
1	vanilla bean	1
½	unwaxed lemon, zested	½
½	unwaxed orange, zested	½

For the dough:

⅔ cup/5 fl oz	milk	150 ml
⅔ cup/6¾ oz	yeast	90 g
⅓ cup/3 oz	honey	80 g
4½ cups/1 lb 2¾ oz	cake flour	520 g
2⅔ cups/11 oz	plain (all-purpose) flour	300 g
2	eggs	2
2	egg yolks	2
1¾ cups/14 oz	butter, softened	400 g
*	flour, for dusting	*
1½ tsp	salt	1½ tsp
*	butter, for greasing	*
*	flour, for dusting	*
1 cup/9 oz	clarified butter, melted	250 g
1 cup/7 oz	vanilla sugar	200 g

For the fruit mixture: The previous day, mix the almonds, currants, raisins, peels, rum, extract, seeds from the vanilla, and grated zests in a bowl. Cover with clingfilm (plastic wrap), soften overnight at room temperature.

For the dough: Heat the milk until lukewarm. Crumble the yeast into the milk and stir to dissolve. Mix the yeast and milk with the honey and 200 g (1¾ cups/7 oz) cake flour to a thick dough. Cover and rise in a warm place for 15 minutes. Add the remaining flour, the eggs, egg yolks, and 100 g (scant ½ cup/3½ oz) butter to the starter. Knead into a dough with an electric mixer or a stand mixer with a dough hook. Gradually knead the butter into the dough, until it becomes elastic. Dust with flour and cover with clingfilm (plastic wrap). Let rise at room temperature for 1 hour, until doubled. Knead in the fruit, nuts and salt.

Grease two stollen molds with butter and dust with flour. Preheat the oven to 220°C/425F/Gas Mark 7. Divide the dough in half and shape into thick ovals. Use a rolling pin to flatten a little, starting from the middle, then fold the thinner edges in to the centre. Lay the loaves seam-side up in the molds then close. Let rise for 15 more minutes.

Lower the oven to 175°C/345°F/Gas Mark 3¾, and bake for 50-60 minutes. Take the stollen out of their molds, let cool a little, and brush all over with butter while still warm. Dust with sugar and let cool completely. Wrap with aluminum foil and rest for 1 week in the refrigerator.

Yeasted Raisin Pancakes (Struwen)

Westphalia and Münster

Preparation time:		20 minutes
Rising time:		50 minutes
Cooking time:		20 minutes
Makes:		about 20

scant 1½ cups/7 oz	raisins	200 g
1⅔ cups/13 fl oz	milk	375 ml
1½ oz	fresh yeast	42 g
4½ cups/1 lb 2 oz	plain (all-purpose) flour	500 g
⅓ cup/2¼ oz	sugar	60 g
1	egg	1
1 level tsp	salt	1 level tsp
*	clarified butter, for frying	*
*	icing (confectioners') sugar, for dusting	*
¾ cup/7 oz	lingonberry compote, to serve	200 g

Put the raisins into a bowl, cover with warm water, and soak for 15 minutes. Drain well in a strainer and pat dry.

Heat the milk in a pan until lukewarm. Crumble the yeast and dissolve in 200 ml (scant 1 cup/7 fl oz) lukewarm milk. Mix the yeast and milk mixture in a bowl with about 150 g (1⅓ cups/5 oz flour), cover with clingfilm (plastic wrap), and let rise in a warm place for 20 minutes.

Mix the starter with the remaining flour and lukewarm milk, the sugar, egg, and salt. Knead for a few minutes using an electric mixer with a dough hook until bubbles appear and the dough is thick and soft.

Finally, mix the raisins into the dough, cover with plastic wrap and let rise at room temperature for 30 more minutes.

Heat a large skillet (frying pan) over medium heat and melt 1 tbsp of clarified butter, covering the bottom of the skillet well. Using two spoons, put 1 heaped tbsp of dough into the skillet and flatten slightly to a diameter of 1-1.5 cm (½-⅝ inch). Make more pancakes, slightly spaced apart. Fry for 2-3 minutes on each side until golden brown. Drain on paper towels.

Arrange the pancakes on heated plates, dust with icing (confectioners') sugar, and accompany with the lingonberry compote. Serve as fresh as possible.

Easter Bread

All regions

Preparation time:		30 minutes
Rising time:		65 minutes
Cooking time:		30-40 minutes
Makes:		1 loaf

scant ¼ cup/1¼ oz	candied orange peel	30 g
3 tbsp	rum	3 tbsp
½ cup/3 oz	raisins	80 g
2¼ cup/9 oz	plain (all-purpose) flour	250 g
⅓ cup/2½ fl oz	milk	75 ml
4 tsp	yeast	4 tsp
3	egg yolks	3
2 tbsp	sugar	2 tbsp
½	vanilla bean	½
*	salt	*
1	pinch unwaxed lemon zest	1
⅓ cup/2½ oz	butter, softened	75 g
*	flour, for dusting	*
*	melted butter, for basting	*
⅓ cup/3 oz	apricot preserve	80 g
½ cup/2 oz	icing (confectioners') sugar	50 g
1 tbsp	lemon juice	1 tbsp

Mix the orange peel with 1 tsp of rum, then mince. Mix the raisins with the remaining rum in a small bowl.

Put the flour into a bowl and make a well in the centre. Heat the milk in a pan until lukewarm. Crumble the yeast into the milk and stir to dissolve. Pour the yeast and milk mixture into the well, mix with some of the flour to a thick paste, and dust with a little flour. Cover the starter and let rise in a warm place, about 15 minutes, until slight cracks appear on the surface.

In the meantime, beat the egg yolks with the sugar, seeds from the vanilla bean, a pinch of salt, and the lemon zest in a bowl until pale and fluffy. Beat the butter until fluffy in a second bowl.

Add the beaten egg yolks to the bowl with the starter and briefly mix. Add the butter, then use an electric mixer or stand mixer with a dough hook to knead to a smooth and elastic dough. Drain the raisins, then quickly knead together with the orange peel into the dough. Cover and let rise, about 20 more minutes.

Dust the dough with a little flour, then knead into a rounded loaf and place seam-side down on a baking sheet lined with parchment paper. Brush the dough with butter, score with a criss-cross pattern, cover with a cloth, and let rise in a warm place for 20-30 minutes.

Preheat the oven to 170°C/340°F/Gas Mark 3½. Bake the loaf on the middle shelf inside the oven for 30-40 minutes, until golden. Take out of the oven and let cool.

Combine the apricot preserve with 2 tbsp of water in a pan, bring to a boil, and blend with an stick (immersion) blender, then brush over the loaf. Sift the icing (confectioners') sugar into a small bowl and dissolve completely with the lemon juice and 1-2 tbsp of water. Glaze the loaf.

Glossary

Glossary

Glossary

Arme Ritter (French Toast)
A simple dessert using slices of white bread or rusks soaked in sweetened egg and milk, then fried. Served sprinkled with cinnamon and sugar, vanilla sauce or sabayon – the name is thought to have come from poor knights, known as *Arme Ritter*, who could not afford meat, so improved their stale bread with milk and eggs.

Auszogne (Deep-Fried Pastries)
Traditional Bavarian yeast pastries, deep-fried in clarified butter and dusted with icing (confectioners') sugar. Before baking, the dough should be stretched so you can almost see through it.

Backerbsen (Soup Pearls)
Pea-sized choux pastry dumplings, served in soups.

Baumkuchen (Tree Cake)
Very fine sponge cake baked in layers on a long, rotating roller over an open fire. The name is attributed to the pattern of rings that is visible as soon as the cake is cut – it looks like a tree stump. It is served either fresh, in slices or divided into little squares, which are then covered with chocolate coating or a glaze.

Berliner Luft (Berlin Air)
Frothy dessert made with eggs, sugar, lemon and gelatine, served with raspberry sauce. The dessert is red and white, reflecting the colours traditionally associated with Berlin.

Bismarckhering (Pickled Herring)
Herring fillets marinated in vinegar and spices. Named after Imperial Chancellor Otto von Bismarck, who enjoyed them so much that he gave his fishmonger permission to sell them as *Bismarckhering.*

Bockwurst
A boiled sausage of well-seasoned beef and pork, sometimes flavoured with garlic. Usually eaten hot with mustard and potato salad or bread rolls. Traditionally served with Bock lager.

Brathering (Fried Herring)
Herring that are fried then marinated in vinegar, onions and spices.

Bratwurstbrät (Bratwurst Sausage Meat)
Coarse or fine raw meat used to make traditional sausages.

Bremer Klaben (Bremen-Style Christmas Fruit Bread)
Popular at Christmas, this is a sweet white yeasted bread with almonds, raisins and currants.

Bries (Sweetbreads)
The thymus glands of calves or lambs, they consist of white, soft tissue that can be grilled, braised or stewed, but are most commonly eaten fried.

Bubespitzle (Potato Fingers)
Swabian name for a dish known as *Schupfnudeln* elsewhere in Germany: a dough of mashed potatoes, flour and eggs is made into pointed little rolls, then fried in oil until crisp.

Deie (Bacon and Cheese Flatbreads)
A Swabian speciality, this rustic flatbread is served with either sweet or savoury toppings; traditionally sour cream, onions and bacon, but also leek, potato and cheese or with apples and cinnamon.

Dicke Bohnen (Fava Beans)
Known in German as *Dicke Bohnen*, *Acker Bohnen*, *Sau Bohnen* or *Puffbohnen*, this bean is part of the fabaceae family. The large beans have a sweet and delicate taste.

Dippehas (Hare in a Pot)
A home kitchen classic from the Rhein-Hesse region. Jointed rabbit and pork are layered in a pan, sprinkled with onion, garlic and juniper berries and wine is poured over the top. The name in the local dialect means 'jugged hare'.

Döbbekuchen (Potato Casserole with Smoked Pork and Bacon)
Potato recipe from the Rhineland-Palatinate. This dish of potatoes, onions, dried meat and simple spices is baked in a pot in the oven. The literal translation is 'pot cake'.

Donauwelle (Danube Waves Cake)
Fruity tray cake with cherries, buttercream and chocolate. The wave pattern in the dark and light dough, and on the chocolate glaze, represents the waves on the Danube river.

Eierstich (Royale)
Egg whisked with milk or stock. This savoury custard is solidified in a bain marie and diced into small pieces. It is a popular addition to soups.

Eisbein (Boiled Ham Hock)
Also known as *Schweinshaxe*, this salted and boiled ham can be prepared in various ways, for example, roasted and served with sauerkraut.

Errötendes Mädchen (Raspberry and Buttermilk Mousse)
Traditional northern German dessert cream made of buttermilk, gelatine and cranberries or lingonberries. Originally from Schleswig-Holstein, its red colour gives the dish its name, which translates as 'blushing maiden'.

Essiggurken (Picked Cucumber)
Small cucumbers, pickled in vinegar with herbs and spices.

Falscher Hase (Meatloaf)
Minced meat in a loaf filled with hard boiled eggs, 'false rabbit', as it is known in German, was originally a cheap alternative to a real roast rabbit.

Franzbrötchen (Cinnamon Rolls)
A baked speciality of Hamburg. Sweet, baked yeasted rolls filled with cinnamon and sugar, similar to the version known as *Zimtschnecken*, or 'cinnamon snails'.

Gaisburger Marsch (Beef Stew)
A Swabian speciality stew named after an area of Stuttgart. It is made with vegetables, potato wedges, Swabian *Spätzle*, which are noodle-like dumplings, and beef.

Gänseweißsauer (Goose Legs in Aspic)
A dish from northern Germany, the goose is cooked in water with a cow trotter, diced vegetables, bouquet garni and spices. The stock is seasoned with vinegar and poured over the tender meat, which has by that point fallen off the bone, and chilled to allow the jelly to firm up.

Gefillde Klees (Meat-Stuffed Potato Dumplings with a Cream Sauce)
A speciality of Saarland, these potato dumplings are stuffed with minced meat or coarse liver sausage. Served with sauerkraut, cream and bacon sauce.

Götterspeise (Flavoured Gelatine Desserts)
A traditional dessert also known as *Wackelpudding*, which means 'wobble pudding', they consist of gelatine, sugar and flavourings, and are usually served with whipped cream or vanilla sauce. The German name translates as 'food of the gods'.

Grüner Speck (Fresh Back Bacon)
Fresh, uncured back bacon.

Mettbrötchen (Seasoned Raw Minced Pork Sandwich)
A sandwich of coarsely minced pork, seasoned with spice. Another name for this is *Hackpeter*, which literally means chopped meat, *Hacke*, with parsley, *Petersilie*.

Hackus und Knieste (Potatoes with Pork Patties)
This dish's name comes from the words used in the Harz region for minced pork with small potatoes, and is often accompanied with cucumber and onions.

Halve Hahn (Cheese and Mustard Sandwich)
A small dish from the Rhineland consisting of half a slice of wheat-and-rye bread, *Graubrot,* or dark rye bread, *Schwarzbrot.* Served with a soft curd cheese called Harzer, also known as *Weisslacker* or *Bierkäse* cheese.

Handkäse (Sour Curd Cheese)
A sour-milk cheese originally shaped by hand. Unripe, the inside has a white crumbly consistency. It is sometimes made with caraway.

Hasenpfeffer (Braised Hare)
A dish dating from the Middle Ages that uses hare or rabbit meat on the bone, along with the animal's innards, blood and red wine. The addition of *Pfeffer*, meaning pepper, indicates that it is hot or spicy.

Hering (Herring)
Atlantic fish that is popular both fried and marinated. *Grüner* herring is fresh, *Brathering* is fried, *Bückling* is smoked, *Salzhering* is salted. It is also available canned.

Himmel un Ääd (Black Pudding with Onions, Bacon and Apple Mashed Potatoes)
Traditional Westphalian dish – meaning 'heaven and earth' – made of potatoes, being the fruit of the earth, and apples, the fruit of heaven. It is served with fried onion rings and black pudding.

Kalter Hund (No-Bake Chocolate Cookie Cake)
A quick-to-make cake; cookies are placed in a loaf pan in layers with melted coconut oil, cacao, eggs and sugar then chilled, turned out and sliced. The name means 'cold dog', and refers to its being 'as cold as a dog's muzzle' when served.

Kastenpickert (Potato Loaf)
A speciality of Lippe in the east of North Rhine-Westphalia, this yeasted, loaf-style potato cake sometimes includes raisins. Before serving, it is sliced and fried in butter until golden. Served with turnip sauce and liver sausage.

Katenschinken (Cottage Ham)
A northern German ham speciality of Schleswig-Holstein. Dry cured then stored for a few weeks under a cloth to 'burn through' allowing the tenderness, aroma and colour to develop. It is then cold-smoked for four weeks. Its name comes from it originally being smoked in the rafters above the hearths of small farm cottages, or *Katen.*

Kletzenbrot (Christmas Fruit Loaf)
Christmas bread from Bavaria and Swabia. with dried fruit, mainly pears, nuts, cinnamon, aniseed and fennel.

Knödel (Dumplings)
A side dish made of either potato, wheat flour or semolina usually shaped into balls. The dumplings are either boiled in salted water or steamed.

Köthener Schusterpfanne (Köthen-Style Roast Pork Neck)
A speciality of Saxony-Anhalt; pork neck roasted with pears and potatoes.

Kratzede (Pancake Scrapings)
A recipe from Baden-Württemberg of pancakes that are cooked in the traditional manner and then shredded in the pan. Usually served with asparagus and ham on the side.

Kroketten (Potato Croquettes)
Rolls or patties of potato mixture, breaded and fried in plenty of oil.

Labskaus (Corned Beef and Potato Hash)
A northern German sailor's dish. Potatoes, boiled beetroot (beets) and corned meat are mashed with a dash of beef bouillon and cucumber pickling liquid. The dish is served with a fried egg, pickled herring and pickled cucumbers.

Lye Bread
Yeasted dough pastries soaked in lye, usually sprinkled with pretzel salt, then baked. Often eaten just with butter. Popular in southern Germany, where they are shaped as pretzels or sticks.

Lübecker Schwalbennester (Lübeck-Style 'Swallows' Nests')
A northern German speciality in which a veal or turkey escalope is made into a roulade with ham and boiled egg, seared and cooked in a frying pan. The roulade is then cut widthways and served with mashed potato.

Lübscher Plettenpudding (Lübeck-Style Trifle)
Originally known as 'diplomat pudding', this dessert took its current name after featuring in Thomas Mann's hugely popular novel set in Lübeck, *Buddenbrooks,* published in 1901. It is made of sponge cake, raspberries, raspberry jam, macaroons, custard, gelatine and sherry or raspberry brandy.

Martinsgans (Saint Martin's Goose)
A traditional dish served on Saint Martin's Day (11 November), comprising crispy, roast goose served with red cabbage, apples and potato dumplings. Publicity-shy Saint Martin, upon hearing of his election to the rank of bishop, hid himself in a goose shed – the geese betrayed him with their cackling, and are still paying for it to this day.

Matje Hering (Matjes Herring)
Young, salted herring that haven't yet spawned. The *Matjes* are soaked in a preserving brine and eaten raw, after the bones and skin are removed. The name comes from the Dutch *meisjes*, meaning girl or *maagdelijk*, which translates as maidenly.

Mettenden Würstchen (Mettenden Sausages)
Smoked pork sausages. Most popular in the north west of Germany, Mettenden sausages can be eaten cold or added to a soup or stew.

Millirahmstrudel (Quark and Sour Cream Strudel)
A Viennese pastry filled with small pieces of bread, moistened with milk. It also contains egg yolk, icing (confectioners') sugar, butter, vanilla, grated lemon peel, sour cream, Quark and raisins. The pastry is glazed with milk, sugar and egg.

Münsterländer Töttchen (Münsterland-Style Veal Stew)
A traditional dish from the Münsterland region, with various meats boiled down with vinegar and onions to make a spicy ragout. Today veal tongue is more commonly used, but in the past offal (variety meats) was more prevalent. It is usually served with dark rye bread and parsley potatoes.

Nordseekrabben (North Sea Prawns [Shrimp])
Finger-length shrimp that are usually cooked on fishing boats before coming to shore.

Obatzda (Bavarian Cheese Dip)
A traditional Bavarian cheese dip comprising aged soft cheese, usually camembert, mixed with pepper, paprika, caraway, onions and butter.

Panhas (Scrapple)
A typical Westphalian dish, also known as *Blutkuchen,* meaning 'blood cake'. It is in essence a fried slice of sausage, paired with sugar beet syrup, sauerkraut and vegetables.

Pfefferpotthast (Peppered Beef Stew)
A traditional Westphalian dish. Large cubes of beef ribs are cooked in a broth with plenty of diced onions, root vegetables and a bay leaf in a pan. Peppered, bound with breadcrumbs and served with gherkins (dill pickles), cranberry compote and potato dumplings.

Pfitzauf (Popovers)
Traditional, delicate egg-batter pastry with a crispy crust, baked in a special mould, popovers are left to rise, and subsequently spill over, in the oven, hence their name. This Swabian pastry is usually served with vanilla sauce or fruit compote.

Pichelsteiner Eintof (Pichelsteiner Stew)
A hotpot in which the pan is filled with layers of sliced beef, veal, pork and mutton, beef marrow, onion, carrot, celery and potato and strips of white cabbage.

Pinkelwurst (Pinkel Sausage)
A speciality of Bremen in northern Germany. The sausage is made with pork, bacon, oats or barley groats, onions and other spices. Historically, the sausage mixture was encased in the edible small intestines of pigs, known as *Pinkel*.

Pluckte Finken (Bean, Apple and Bacon Stew)
A popular hotpot from Bremen, consisting of haricot beans, bacon, carrots, potatoes and apples. Pieces of whale blubber, known as *Vinken*, were originally used in the dish. The name, meaning 'plucked whale blubber', was kept even though blubber is no longer used.

Plumm un Tüffel (Meat, Potato and Prune Stew)
This dish, literally 'plums and potatoes' in the local Mecklenburg-West Pomerania dialect, consists of prunes and potatoes cooked with smoked pork and onions.

Pottasche (Potash)
Potash is a leavening agent that helps particularly heavy types of dough, particularly gingerbread, to rise.

Potthucke (Potato Loaf with Smoked Pork Sausage)
Traditional potato dish from the Sauerland region, made with *Mettwurst*, bacon and onions. Its name translates as 'that which sits in the pan'.

Prilleken (German Doughnuts)
Known elsewhere as *Krapfen,* this is a carnival speciality from Brunswick. Yeasted dough is baked in a ball or ring shape and sprinkled with sugar. The name comes from the method of making the doughnuts – *Prilleken* means 'roll with your hands'.

Pumpernickel
A very dark, coarse-grained rye bread without crusts, baked in steam in closed tins for 16 to 24 hours.

Rinderschmorbraten (Pot Roast)
Braised beef marinated in red or white wine.

Sauerkraut
Grated, salted white cabbage. The fermentation process encourages lactic acid to develop, giving the cabbage a distinctive taste and making it easy to digest. Sauerkraut is full of vitamins. It can be eaten raw, in salads, steamed or braised to serve as an accompaniment to savoury dishes.

Saumagen (Stuffed Pork Stomach)
Bratwurst sausage meat, with cubes of pork belly, shoulder ham, potatoes, day-old rolls and spices, stuffed into a pork stomach and boiled in salted water, served with sauerkraut.

Saure Zipfel (Bratwurst Cooked in Vinegar)
Also known as *Blaue Zipfel,* this dish is from the Upper Palatinate. Raw *Bratwurst* are cooked in simmering water with onions and spices until firm and blueish. It is served with *Schwarzbrot,* meaning dark rye bread, and wine or beer.

Schaufelbug (Top Blade Roast)
A popular beef cut that is deal for roasting or using in a hearty soup.

Schäufele (Roasted Pork Shoulder)
The name of this dish means 'scapula', in reference to the part of the animal it uses.

Scheiterhaufen (Bread Pudding)
A baked Bavarian dessert made of a mixture of bread rolls and egg with raisins, almonds and slices of cinnamon-spiced apple. Served with vanilla sauce.

Schnüsch (Bean, Vegetable and Ham Stew)
The name means something akin to 'all over the place': a traditional soup from Schleswig-Holstein consisting of young vegetables cooked in milk, butter or cream.

Schwäbische Kalbsvögerl (Swabian-Style Veal Roulade)
Flattened veal escalopes coated with mustard, bacon and roast veal made into roulades then braised in white wine and meat stock. The escalopes are cut from the shank, which is the size of a small bird, known as *Vogel* – hence the dish name 'veal birds'.

Schweinepfeffer (Peppered Pork Stew)
A ragout of pork braised in red wine. Its accompanying sauce is made of stock, roux and blood. Traditionally, it is served with potato dumplings and sauerkraut.

Soljanka (Spicy and Sour Soup)
A traditional sausage soup, originally from Ukraine, made with paprika, pickles and onions. It can also be made with fish or mushrooms.

Spundekäs (Cream Cheese Dip)
From Hesse, this is a mixture of cream cheese and Quark seasoned with paprika. It is usually served with pretzels or wheat-and-rye bread.

Steckerlfisch (Fish Grilled on a Stick)
Whole gutted white fish, put on a wooden stick or skewer and grilled, traditionally, by carefully holding the stick over the embers of a fire.

Spätzle Maker
A tool for making *Spätzle* dumplings that is held over boiling water, pressing the *Spätzle* into shape as they drop into the water.

Spice Mix
An equal mix of peppercorns: black, long, cubeb green, pink and Szechuan, as well as allspice, which is then ground to a powder.

Strammer Max (Open-Faced Ham and Fried Egg Sandwich)
A slice of bread and butter with ham and a fried egg. Originally part of the cuisine of Saxony and now popular throughout Germany.

Struwen (Yeasted Raisins Pancakes)
Yeasted pancakes with raisins from the region around Münster, usually eaten on Good Friday. The name comes from the old-Saxon word *Struva,* which means 'a bit crinkly'.

Stutenkerl (Sweet Yeast Bun)
A traditional Advent pastry, *Stutenkerl*, also known as *Weckmann*, refers to the shape of the bun and *Kerl* means 'fellow': a little man made of flour, sugar, fat and yeast.

Teltower Rübchen (Teltow Turnips)
Small, tasty cultivated species of white turnip, originally grown near Berlin in light soil. They are peeled, then steamed and glazed.

Quark
Also known as *Topfen*, this unripened cream cheese is made from pasteurised milk, cream or skimmed milk. Quark is very versatile and is used in many savoury and sweet dishes.

Tuert (Meat and Spinach Pie)
Meat pie from the region near Münster, consisting of pork and puff pastry.

Verschleiertes Bauernmädchen (Veiled Peasant Girls)
A dessert from Holstein made of caramelised dark rye breadcrumbs, stewed apple and cinnamon, layered in glasses and topped with whipped cream and fruit.

Versoffene Jungfern (Drunken Maidens)
A classic dessert from Upper Franconia, it is a lightly whipped egg-white mixture formed into small dumplings, then fried in hot oil. Once the spiced red wine sauce has been poured over, they are reminiscent of a young maiden's cheeks reddened by alcohol, hence the name.

Weinbergschnecke (Burgundy Snail)
A land snail that can be found in all temperate regions of Europe. It used to be a popular ingredient and is considered a delicacy today, cultivated mostly in special snail gardens.

Weißwurst (White Sausages)
A speciality of Munich. Boiled sausage made of veal, beef, pork, bacon and connective tissue seasoned with cooking salt, which is where it gets its light white-grey colour from. It is served boiled and 'peeled hot' – in other words, you suck the sausage meat from the skin.

Welfenspeise (Guelph Pudding)
A dessert from Lower Saxony, comprising a vanilla cream with a layer of white wine custard. The dish is named after the noble family, the Guelphs.

Westfälisches Blindhuhn (Westphalian Vegetable, Fruit and Bacon Stew)
A traditional hotpot made of white and green beans, carrots, potatoes, apples, pears and streaky bacon. The name *Blindhuhn* is taken from the country saying, 'even a blind chicken sometimes finds a grain,' suggesting that everyone will find something they like in this stew.

Wiener Wurst (Frankfurter)
Long, thin little sausages made of finely chopped and seasoned beef, veal and pork, which are then boiled and smoked.

Index

Recipe Notes

Butter should always be unsalted.

Eggs, fruit and vegetables are assumed to be medium size, unless otherwise specified.

All sugar is white caster (superfine) sugar and all brown sugar is cane or Demerara, unless otherwise specified.

Milk is always whole, unless otherwise specified.

Herbs are always fresh, unless otherwise specified.

Mustard means prepared mild mustard, such as Dijon, unless otherwise specified.

Meat, fish and vegetable stocks are assumed to be homemade or gluten free.

When no quantity is specified, for example of oils, salts and herbs, quantities are discretionary.

When using lye, take extra precaution as it is highly corrosive; do not allow to come into contact with the skin.

Exercise caution when foraging for ingredients; any foraged ingredients should only be eaten if an expert has deemed them safe to eat.

All herbs, shoots, flowers, and leaves should be picked fresh from a clean source.

Some recipes include raw or very lightly cooked eggs, meat or fish and fermented products. These should be avoided by the elderly, infants, pregnant women, convalescents, and anyone with an impaired immune system.

Exercise caution when making fermented products.

Exercise a high level of caution when following recipes involving any potentially hazardous activity, including the use of high temperatures, open flames, using a blowtorch and when deep-frying. In particular, when deep-frying, add food carefully to avoid splashing, wear long sleeves, and never leave the pan unattended.

Cooking and preparation times are for guidance only, as individual ovens vary. If using a convection (fan) oven, follow the manufacturer's instructions concerning oven temperatures.

Measurement Notes

Cup, metric and imperial measurements are given throughout. Follow one set of measurements, not a mixture, as they are not interchangeable.

All spoon measurements are level.
1 teaspoon = 5 ml; 1 tablespoon = 15 ml.

Australian standard tablespoons are 20 ml, so Australian readers are advised to use 3 teaspoons in place of 1 tablespoon when measuring small quantities.

About the Author

Alfons Schuhbeck hails from Bavaria, and is regarded as an authority on German cuisine. In addition to his work as a chef and broadcaster, Schuhbeck is a restaurateur and businessman, with an online food business, wine bistro, spice shop, ice-cream parlour, two restaurants and a cooking school.

Picture Credits

Phaidon Press Limited
Regent's Wharf
All Saints Street
London N1 9PA

Phaidon Press Inc.
65 Bleecker Street
New York NY 10012

phaidon.com

First published in English 2018
© 2018 Phaidon Press Limited

ISBN: 978 0 7148 7732 7

Concept and text developed and published by ZS Verlag
GmbH as *Deutschland – das Kochbuch*
© ZS Verlag GmbH 2017

A CIP catalogue record for this book
is available from the British Library and
the Library of Congress.

Commissioning Editor: Emily Takoudes
Project Editor: Eve O'Sullivan
Production Controller: Lisa Fiske
Photography: Danielle Acken
Design: Julia Hasting
Typesetting: Michael Wallace

The publisher would like to thank
Vanessa Bird, David Devonport, Jane Ellis,
Lesley Malkin, Gregor Shepherd and
Kate Slate for their contributions to the book.

Printed in China

Icon Credits
The Noun Project: Dairy free, sumhi_icon; Gluten free,
Briand Rabideau; One pot, Adnen Kadri; Vegetarian,
Guillaume Beaulieu; Less than 30 minutes, AlfredoCreates.
com/icons & Flaticonde; Less than 5 ingredients, Alfsonso
Juan Dillera; Beef, Road Signs; Chicken, Hernan D
Schlosman; Pork, Ealancheliyan; Lamb, Evgeni Moryakov;
Fish, Vladimir Belochkin.